THE HOLISTIC
GARDENER

THE HOLISTIC
GARDENER

Margaret Elphinstone
Julia Langley

Series editor: John Button

THORSONS PUBLISHING GROUP
Wellingborough, Northamptonshire
·
Rochester, Vermont

First published 1987

The authors and publishers would like to thank
the following for permission to reproduce copyright material:
Allen and Unwin (Publishing) Ltd., for Kathleen Raine's 'Heirloom'
Wallace and Sheil Agency, for Marge Piercy's 'The Seven of Pentacles'
David Higham Associates Ltd., for Elizabeth Jennings' 'In a Garden'
The Women's Press, for Susan Griffin's 'Forest'

British Library Cataloguing in Publication Data

Elphinstone, Margaret
The holistic gardener.
1. Gardening — Great Britain
I. Title   II. Langley, Julia
635'.0941   SB453.3.G7

ISBN 0-7225-1267-8

Printed in Great Britain by
Hazell Watson & Viney Limited,
Member of the BPCC Group,
Aylesbury, Bucks

We would like to thank all the people who have taught us about gardening, and in particular the people who lent us books and helped us with this project, especially June Nelson, Jack Porteous, Patrick Upton and Marijke Wilhelmus. We would particularly like to thank Margaret's stepfather who read all the proofs (twice). Julia would like to thank her new husband, Arthur Abbie, for his loving support. We are also grateful to the gardens at The Findhorn Foundation and Laurieston Hall, and to our editor, John Button, for helping to guide the book into print. Most of all we would like to thank our families who made the gardens we grew up with, and our children who have grown up with the gardens we have made.

Contents

How To Use This Book

She gave me childhood's flowers,
Heather and wild thyme,
Eyebright and tormentil,
Lichen's mealy cup
Dry on wind-scored stone,
The corbies on the rock,
The rowan by the burn.

Sea-marvels a child beheld
Out in the fisherman's boat,
Fringed pulsing violet
Medusa, sea-gooseberries,
Starfish on the sea floor,
Cowries and rainbow-shells
From pools on a rocky shore.

Gave me her memories,
But kept her last treasure:
'When I was a lass', she said,
'Sitting among the heather,
'Suddenly I saw
'That all the moor was alive!
'I have told no one before'.

That was my mother's tale.
Seventy years had gone
Since she saw the living skein
Of which the world is woven,
And having seen, knew all;
Through long indifferent years
Treasuring the priceless pearl.

Kathleen Raine
Heirloom

How To Use This Book

If you don't need a gardening book, you are lucky. Gardening is a practical affair, and there is no better way to pass on a skill than for one person to show another what to do. People showed each other how to garden for centuries before they thought of learning how to do it out of books; but now we live in a world where our domestic lives, including looking after our own piece of land, are lived in comparative isolation. Many people don't get involved with a garden until they have one of their own, and even if their families ever knew about gardening, it's often too late to ask. And so we turn to books.

The problem with writing or using a general gardening book is that the subject is exhaustive. It could be expanded to include every possible kind of garden, every known variety of every plant we can think of, everything that ever did or possibly might happen to each plant, and every detail of the autobiography of both the authors. Faced with the restrictions of one volume, we have had to be selective. The autobiographies, you will be relieved to hear, have hardly crept in at all. The lists may not include all your favourites, but they include most of ours, and a few others besides. Lines have to be drawn somewhere, and we have tried to draw them consistently if sometimes arbitrarily. Having said that, we have tried to cover the whole field—or plot if you're lucky—within this volume. We see it as a catalyst rather than as an encyclopedia. If you want to know everything about plant breeding, rock gardens or prize gooseberries, you will have to look further, but we have tried to indicate the avenues that are there to be explored.

Thematically, the book moves from the general to the more specific, falling roughly into four sections. The function of the first four chapters is to provide the ecological and human context within which we work: they are the 'why' of gardening rather than the 'how'. The first two chapters are introductory, giving a broad framework for the detail which is to follow. Chapters three and four look more closely at the background to gardening: the plants that are the living material with which we work, the long tradition of gardens and gardening which have shaped our attitudes to the plants, and the way gardeners have developed those plants.

Chapters five to nine are for practical use in the garden. They supply the 'how'—how to look at the land that we have, how to decide what to do with it, how to encourage the land and the plants to do well. Whereas the early chapters are about attitudes, this section is about turning those attitudes into practice.

In the third section of the book, each chapter is devoted to a particular group of plants, divided according to their function in the garden. These are followed by lists of individual plants—vegetables, fruit, flowers, and shrubs and trees. The reader should bear in mind that any classifications in nature are beset by exceptions; that all divisions, including ours, tend to be arbitrary; and that any lists are bound to be incomplete. Lists are finite and nature isn't.

HOW TO USE THIS BOOK

The fourth section makes everything else available. We have said that this book is intended as a catalyst, and the bibliography is there to help you follow up the ideas that we have brought together. This is not a work of detailed scholarship; it is an attempt to make connections. We are indebted to the many other authors who have researched particular aspects of the subject, and made original material available to us in their own books. You will therefore find the bibliography diverse. As it helped us to bring so much material together, so it should help you to take it apart and choose the bits you want to pursue.

The index is as essential a tool as a spade if you want to make full use of this book. It can lead you to the particular plant, technique or idea that you want, as and when you want it. It also serves as easy access to the plant lists, some of which are given (as chapter four will explain) in botanical Latin. Do not despair. If you want to sow forget-me-nots and have never heard of *myosotis*, look up forget-me-nots in the index, and it will tell you the Latin name and where to find it.

We hope you enjoy using this book. At least it should be fat enough to press flowers in, and just the right size to keep the light off a small seed tray.

The Holistic Approach

Under a sky the color of pea soup
she is looking at her work growing away there
actively, thickly like grapevines or pole beans
as things grow in the real world, slowly enough.
If you tend them properly, if you mulch, if you water,
if you provide birds that eat insects a home and winter food,
if the sun shines and you pick off caterpillars,
if the praying mantis comes and the ladybugs and the bees,
then the plants flourish, but at their own internal clock.

Connections are made slowly, sometimes they grow underground.
You cannot tell always by looking what is happening.
More than half a tree is spread out in the soil under your feet.
Penetrate quietly as the earthworm that blows no trumpet.
Fight persistently as the creeper that brings down the tree.
Spread like the squash plant that overruns the garden.
Gnaw in the dark and use the sun to make sugar.

Weave real connections, create real nodes, build real houses.
Live a life you can endure: make love that is loving.
Keep tangling and interweaving and taking more in,
a thicket and bramble wilderness to the outside but to us
interconnected with rabbit runs and burrows and lairs.

Live as if you liked yourself, and it may happen:
reach out, keep reaching out, keep bringing in.
This is how we are going to live for a long time: not always,
for every gardener knows that after the digging, after the planting,
after the long season of tending and growth, the harvest comes.

Marge Piercy
The Seven of Pentacles

The Holistic Approach

Holistic means being part of the whole, and acting within the whole system. To be a gardener is to interact with the land, and thus to be involved with the planet in one of the most fundamental ways possible. Such interactions can of course be unaware or unconscious, often downright disastrous, but for better or worse they alter the whole. This is true of every human activity, but it is difficult to forget the truth of it in the garden. If we smother the land with poisons nothing will grow. If we give nothing back to the land we will watch it grow weaker year by year. If we add compost to the soil and nurture our plants with care, we hope to have abundant yield and a healthy garden.

This book presents a certain attitude to gardening as one of many human activities. It is not intended to set hard and fast rules about exactly what methods and practices are good or bad. It will not make decisions for you. The solutions offered are all organic, but it is not intended to deal out guilt or blame if you sometimes choose otherwise. We suggest ways of discovering the best solutions, but we have not written a book of rules.

Perhaps the most important thing to remember is that the implications of any involvement with the land are endless. It may not be obvious as we spray aphids with an aerosol spray that we are destroying the ozone layer around the earth, and drastically altering the micro-ecology of our cabbage patch. It may not appear that the careful tending of three saplings in our back garden is helping in the reafforestation of the planet. But holistic living means living in right relation to our own small whole, and then expanding outwards into a concern for the whole planet of which we know ourselves to be a part.

Individual effort may appear infinitesimal, but we are part of the system, and when we pluck one thread the whole web vibrates.

The gardener's vision

In order to work our gardens we have to get to know them: the vagaries and characteristics of the land; the type of soil; the aspect; the microclimate. We must look at what is already growing there, see what thrives and what the land seems designed to support. We need to observe the local wildlife, the birds, insects and animals that may be friendly or not so friendly.

People see gardens in different lights. Children have a particular vision, which does not always coincide with the gardener's: they know the best climbing trees, how to get to the back of the herbaceous border without being seen, when the first strawberries are ready, or what the view is like from under the rhubarb leaves. In the same way only you, the gardener in that garden, will know exactly where the sand turns to loam, or where the builder's rubble is buried. No one but the pruner knows where the birds' nests are, or where the leaf curl was last summer. Only you will know that a particular rose bush is doing so well because that's where you buried your cat.

But the gardener does not only accept things as they are, and this is where the vision begins. The gardener is always thinking about variations,

15

healing, and change.

To realize such a vision, it is essential to have some idea about the possibilities. You need to know what plants are available, and which will grow well together. You need to know about growing and propagating plants, and their special needs. It always helps to know what other gardeners have done. A tour of a garden can be used as a seedbed for ideas. All gardens have something to yield in the way of wisdom, whether it be a National Trust showpiece or the garden next door. Your garden does not exist in isolation, and you can constantly explore the possibilities, which are endless.

Here we reach the fundamental difference between gardening and other forms of creative work, for the material of gardening is alive, constantly changing from season to season and year to year. A garden is never finished, because garden time has no end. The gardener retains the vision, chooses plants, imposes changes on the land, but the plants have a life of their own. Without the growth and cyclical change of the living plants and soil the garden could not begin to exist.

So the gardener holds the vision and works with nature to bring the garden in line with the vision. The vision, of course, changes all the time. The garden will impose its own tendencies. Weeding out endless lupin seedlings, you may one day decide that this part of the garden is destined to be a lupin paradise and leave some of them to flourish. The vision is adapted, but the broad outlines remain. Eventually you will know your garden so well that the vision is constantly at the back of your mind. When you are looking at other people's gardens you will suddenly see a solution to your own problem or the right plant for the right place in your garden.

Both garden and vision exist in a continuum of space and time. The garden is a specific place, but it never remains the same, changing—in this country at least—from season to season and year to year. The gardener is constantly visualizing the garden as it will be in spring, in summer, in autumn and in winter. Plants will grow and flower and die, trees and shrubs will grow tall and alter the nature of the space they occupy. A border of impenetrable greenery and colour in summer will give way in winter to open ground with a view of distances beyond. You can never sit back and say 'this is it'. Gardening is an exercise in letting go; the flowers of today will be gone tomorrow. Unless you can live in the present, the effort of creating a garden is pointless. There is nothing to wait for but the unfolding of the vision, and that is already happening all the time.

The spirit of the garden

Everyone has heard about gardeners talking to their plants. Most gardeners are aware of working with intuition as well as with knowledge, and we know that there are many people who have what we call 'green fingers'. The relationship of the gardener to plants and the soil is a relationship between entities which are alive. An element of unpredictability arises, or—perhaps more accurately—of individuality. We may decide that some people are just better able to grow things, while other people's gardens are just not so harmonious. We can call it intuition, a 'knack', but what we really seem to be noticing is how far a person has absorbed the quality of the materials they are dealing with.

Few gardeners need to put their relationship with their garden into words. They are more inclined to talk about the plants themselves, or the state of the soil or the weather. But you only have to watch an expert gardener at work, pruning a difficult tree for example—how they look at it, consider it, become totally absorbed in it so that the tree and the gardener seem to be part of one process—to be aware that there is more happening than a mere enactment of rules laid down in a book. And the result will be more than a tree pruned according to the rules, it will be in one sense a work of art; in another, it will now express the essence of the tree itself, as if that were exactly what the tree was meant to be like all the time. Japanese zen gardeners have always had the conscious intention of enhancing nature, so that you might stand in a garden and be quite unaware that anyone had intervened or interfered, were it not that the arrangement of plants and rocks and water was more exquisite than in the wild, because each element had been understood and considered, placed just so, to express the unique quality that it held.

Plants have neither nerves nor brains in the sense that we have. They do not 'think' or 'feel' like humans. But they are alive, and respond to intervention as living things. They do not express our will. They express themselves. There are gardeners who are in touch with what the garden wants. Some reach this

rapport by conscious meditation or questioning. Others know they are able to work in this way because that's just the way you do things. Whatever language you use, the communication is two-way. The gardener holds the vision for the garden, but the vision itself comes from 'listening' to the garden.

Again we touch on the indefinable. It is common knowledge that wild places have their own atmosphere. A wood can be a place of peace and repose, or of daunting wildness. Water is healing, both restful and invigorating. Weather dominates us, and our spirits alter in response to it. Places and seasons have their own effect on us. It is impossible to assess how far these perceptions are subjective. No one has ever been in a garden with nobody in it.

A garden is an entity. To co-create with nature will result in a garden which embodies the vision of the gardener fused with the essence of the place. As an entity the garden takes on a life of its own. Its character is particular to itself, distinct from its surroundings without ceasing to be part of them. While remaining an embodiment of nature, it is as objective as any work of art. It is unique as the fused substance of a person and a place.

Garden Plants

Perdita   Sir, the year growing ancient,
Not yet on summer's death nor on the birth
Of trembling winter, the fairest flowers o' th' season
Are our carnations and streak'd gillyvors,
Which some call nature's bastards: of that kind
Our rustic garden's barren; and I care not
To get slips of them.

Polixenes   Wherefore, gentle maiden,
Do you neglect them?

Perdita   For I have heard it said
There is an art which, in their piedness, shares
With great creating nature.

Polixenes   Say there be;
Yet nature is made better by no mean
But nature makes that mean: so, over that art,
Which you say adds to nature, is an art
That nature makes. You see, sweet maid, we marry
A gentler scion to the wildest stock,
And make conceive a bark of baser kind
By bud of nobler race. This is an art
Which does mend nature—change it rather—but
The art itself is nature.

Perdita   So it is.

Polixenes Then make your garden rich in gillyvors,
And do not call them bastards.

Perdita   I'll not put
The dibble in earth to set one slip of them;
Nor more than, were I painted, I would wish
This youth should say 'twere well, and only therefore
Desire to breed by me. Here's flowers for you:
Hot lavender, mints, savoury, marjoram,
The marigold, that goes to bed wi' th' sun
And with him rises, weeping: these are flowers
Of middle summer, and I think they are given
To men of middle age. Y'are very welcome.

William Shakespeare
A Winter's Tale, Act IV, Scene IV

Garden Plants

Wild plants establish themselves wherever they can get a roothold, and their forms and diversity have remained beyond computation. Without wilderness our gardens would have no meaning, since they are merely the point where human activity and the abundance of the plant world combine to form new patterns. In order to understand our garden plants, we need to have some idea of the environments from which they came, where their wild relations still live. We must turn to the wilderness itself.

We now know very well that we depend upon wilderness for our survival. We need the trees of the equatorial rain forests to maintain the balance of oxygen in the atmosphere. We need the scrub that covers vast areas of marginal land to hold down the thin soil beneath it. We need our hedgerows and coppices to preserve our topsoil and our shrinking heritage of wildlife. The destruction of the last remnants of the wilderness would be our destruction too. As growers of plants, we are also aware of another connection. Without the huge pool of wild plant resources, we cannot grow edible crops which will remain permanently hardy and disease-resistant. If there are no wild places, then ultimately there will be no gardens, and no food.

Every garden exists within an environment. Rural gardeners in Scotland may grow redcurrants, strawberries and rhubarb, but they are unlikely to bother with bilberries, hazelnuts or mushrooms if these are provided gratis in the woods and hills around them. If you live in a place where blackberries abound in the autumn hedgerows, it seems a fairly obvious plan to invest in a few trees of cooking apples. We are constantly relating our gardens to our own particular supply of wilderness, whether by bringing home a bucketful of peat from the moors or fetching a load of seaweed from the nearest beach for the compost. If our own wilderness has been polluted or destroyed, we perceive at once that we are proportionally poorer. Gardeners living on the shores of the Irish Sea around the Sellafield nuclear plant, for example, may decide not to use seaweed as fertilizer any more. If we look out on to waste land and paved streets, our gardens have to be designed to shut out what is outside instead of embracing it. Instead of looking out on woods and hills we must feast our eyes on a trellis of laburnum or clematis which may hide the traffic from sight but not from hearing. We have often come to perceive our gardens not as a point of connection with what is around us, but our place of escape from it. But we still open our hearts and minds to the glory of green variety and richness. The fabulous and infinite abundance of plants can help to soothe our fears, and support us in a belief that life is good, with a rightness and order about it.

The cultivated plants which we now take for granted are the results of thousands of years of cultivation. They are the bequest both of the infinite variety of the natural world, and of the ingenuity of generations of plant breeders.

The 'natural garden', in the sense of being unpolluted by human touch, is a contradiction in terms. The plants are as artificial as their environment. They are the result of centuries of interaction between people and plant.

The plant breeders

Plant breeding began when people first collected seeds and grew them together under special conditions. They thus caused the fixation and improvement of the qualities for which they had chosen those plants in the first place. They took only the plants best adapted to their purpose, and then ensured cross-pollination of those plants by growing them all together. They must also soon have discovered the possibilities of vegetative reproduction, so that certain strains could be reproduced identically over many generations. Before long the cultivated plants would have become noticeably different from their wild ancestors. For example, we know that European cabbages became distinct from their wild ancestors under cultivation by the pre-Celtic peoples of Europe. Garden celery is mentioned in *The Odyssey*, which takes it back nearly three thousand years. Onions were probably developed as a food crop simultaneously in Ancient Egypt and Sumeria. Grapes had already been cultivated for centuries when they arrived in Egypt about five thousand years ago. We tend to think that the American vegetables were first 'discovered' in the sixteenth century. In fact the tomato had been bred as a garden plant throughout Aztec times. Leeks originated in Chinese gardens in the millenium before Christ. We inherit from the whole Earth.

Our traditional cottage garden flowers developed through human intervention in the same way. Some, such as foxgloves and flag irises, are our own natives, selected and cultivated in British gardeners since the Middle Ages. We may buy named varieties of foxglove out of a catalogue, or we may go into the woods and dig some up. The local woodland ones may be wild species, or they may be escapes from somebody's garden. It doesn't matter; our indigenous plants connect our gardens to the local environment in an obvious and satisfying manner. Some of our garden plants were imported so long ago that they are often thought to be natives: as long as travellers have been coming to Britain, they have been bringing plants with them, either deliberately or accidentally. The earliest deliberate introductions tended to be practical—saffron crocuses were imported by the Romans for the cultivation of the spice. Wild daffodils are also thought to be a Roman introduction, but as Wordsworth noted, they have not hesitated to naturalize themselves. The garden varieties now familiar to us were, however, only bred in the second half of the nineteenth century.

Tulips were first selected in ancient Persian gardens, developed in the gardens of the Ottoman Empire, and finally brought into the form we now know by the Dutch market gardeners of the sixteenth century, who imported them from Turkey. The Dutch also bequeathed us our hyacinths, through a long and exciting process of selection that spanned the sixteenth and seventeenth centuries.

Many of the 'new' flowers brought from the Americas in the same years were not new to gardeners at all. The Aztec and Inca of Central and South America had made flower gardens before the first daffodils were planted in Britain. The three species of dahlia which arrived in Spain from Mexico in 1789, and were brought to Kew in 1798, appear to have been garden varieties, not botanical species.

Most gardeners are aware of the huge

debt to China and Japan. Chinese gardeners were among the first breeders of roses, lilies, peonies, chrysanthemums, hollyhocks, water lilies, narcissi and oriental poppies, as well as many of our familiar shrubs. Fruit trees were selected for the beauty of their blossom as well as for their harvest.

Plant breeding gained a new impetus in Europe in the seventeenth century. The increasing influx of plants from newly discovered continents, and the revival and growth of scientific enquiry, were responsible. Botanists were beginning to examine and exchange plants out of botanical curiosity. A new understanding of basic botany dramatically changed the possibilities open to plant breeders.

In 1692, the appropriately-named Nehemiah Grew discovered that plants, as well as animals, are sexually differentiated, and botanists were quick to exploit the discovery that deliberate variation by cross-breeding was possible. It was soon discovered that closely-related species can hybridize, and that hybrids are often larger and hardier than their parents—what we call 'hybrid vigour'. There was no looking back.

At the same time, gardening in Britain was receiving a new impetus from the French and Flemish immigrants of the seventeeth and eighteenth centuries. Coming from a long tradition of market gardening, refugees from France and Holland brought with them their own strains of seed, bulbs and corms. Equally important, they brought their skills as gardeners in selection and plant breeding. On the continent, florists' flowers were already an established commercial proposition. The early British florists or flower breeders (nothing to do with modern flower sellers) aimed to produce specimen blooms of large size and

perfect shape. They exploited the recent discoveries in botany to the full, and used them to create new varieties and hybrids on a scale which has never been repeated.

The fashion for flower breeding spread rapidly, helped by the changing society of the industrial revolution. For the new florists were not the landowners who had dominated gardening tradition throughout the centuries; in the eighteenth century the owners of large estates were turning their estates into landscaped parkland which reached to the very doors of the house. Flowers, among the aristocracy, were out. The passionately-committed florists of the eighteenth century were the new employed of the industrial revolution. Artisans, particularly weavers, often still worked at home. They had little space to make gardens, yet did have the benefit of being constantly on the premises to give the attention required to nurse new plants along. The early florists' flowers were often referred to as 'mechanics' flowers', and their breeders were often disparaged both by the botanists in their universities and the gentry in their newly-designed parks. Nevertheless, some of the florists and plant collectors, working under conditions of poverty and with minimal resources, produced flowers without whose descendants our gardens would be much poorer, as well as a multitude of varieties which may never be seen again.

However, the industrial revolution is not primarily remembered by most as being the fruitful soil of new plants. The florists' flowers were among its victims. The mechanics and weavers who tended them ceased to work at home, with leisure to minister to their plants, but were swallowed up by the factories and mills. Mass housing and paved streets replaced the cottages and small gardens, and finally excessive air pollution poisoned the tender varieties. The pinks of Paisley were among the first to suffer for lack of clean air. By 1850 they were gone.

The second half of the nineteenth century brought a radical change in plant breeding due to the new science of genetics. Most gardeners are aware that their gardens would not be quite the same without Mendel (1822-1884). Some knowledge of genetics is essential to have any idea how modern plant breeders work. Perhaps all that most gardeners care to know is that when Mendel crossed tall peas with dwarf peas he didn't get medium peas, but more tall peas. In the next generation, however, the tall peas produced both more tall peas and dwarf peas in due proportion. It was not until after his death that the implications sank in, but as gardeners we have inherited the results.

It is useful for the gardener to know how plant breeding is done, and quite possible to try it. The basic qualification has not changed over the centuries —the ability to recognize and select desirable characteristics where they occur. Once perceived, plants with suitable characteristics are made to self-pollinate—the seeds can subsequently be registered as a separate variety. Characteristics can also be encouraged by the equivalent of natural selection— for example, deliberately exposing seeds to tough conditions so that over a period only the hardiest plants will set seed.

Most cultivated varieties are produced by variation through sexual reproduction. Basically, the plants selected as parents are emasculated by removing their stamens and anthers to prevent self-pollination. Usually they are cross-pollinated from the second parent by hand, and then the flowers are covered with bags to protect them from other pollinating agents. This is usually done in the controlled environment of a greenhouse, though this is sometimes impractical, as for example with trees. The seeds are collected and nursed to maturity in controlled conditions. The plant breeder has certain characteristics in mind for which the average gardener will be looking out when examining the seed catalogues. In relation to ornamental plants, these can be summed up fairly simply:

1) Vigour
2) Disease and pest resistance (often done by breeding in a strain from a wild species)
3) Frost resistance
4) Longevity (difficult to achieve because it takes a long time to select!)
5) Habit (compact and dwarf plants are increasingly popular in small gardens, especially if staking is rendered unnecessary, though they may lose some of the vigour of the taller originals)
6) Flower characteristics (a controversial issue, being largely a matter of taste. This includes size, form, appearance of petals, pattern, colour and fragrance. The demand for sheer size is decreasing in favour of number and neatness of blooms)
7) Adaptability to soil and climate

Most gardeners have come across F_1 hybrids, and know that they are both reliable and expensive. They have been bred through a long process to produce a guaranteed uniform crop, being genetically identical. This is done by making the parents genetically 'pure' by repeated self-pollination, taking from eight to twelve generations. Cross-pollination between the two lines is then ensured as described above, and the resulting seeds are sown that year. This complicated and lengthy method explains the expense.

However, the gardener should be aware of the drawback to these hybrids, which has far-reaching implications for the relationship between gardeners and the firms that sell the seeds. It is not possible to collect seeds from F_1 hybrids, because they will not breed true. After producing one completely reliable and uniform crop, subsequent generations will show a wild diversity. The desired characteristics can be produced with a high degree of reliability, just once. But most gardeners will be thinking about more than one harvest.

Plant breeding, like the human population, has expanded exponentially. The varieties of ornamental garden plants are vast and bewildering. In 1964 the Plant Varieties and Seeds Act stated that new varieties of plant have to be registered, and that to be registered it must be proved that they are sufficiently different from any existing type. To the gardener wading through possible choices for next year's chrysanthemums this piece of legislation may sound like a welcome relief, but the implications are rather more complex, as we shall see.

Food crops are another matter.

Food producers, on however small a scale, affect the entire web of life upon this planet. As you survey your humble rows of radishes, you may not feel that the future of the Earth is in your hands, but by buying the seeds you bought, sowing them and feeding them the way you did, you have already contributed your atom to one side of the balance or the other. If we turn for the moment from your vegetable plot to the world situation, the relationship of your food crops to the crisis on the planet will become more obvious.

The interdependence of the world's resources of seed for food crops is frightening in its implications. The seed potatoes you buy in your local shop depend for their existence on a chain of circumstances extending from Scotland, through the EEC, and on to the USA and ultimately to the Andes. In buying them, you are as far from being self-sufficient as any human being has ever been. In considering our sources of seed supply, we see at once that we do not garden as Robinson Crusoes, but always as part of a political, economic and social process.

Before the neolithic revolution it is estimated that, world-wide, about 1,500 species of wild plants were used for food. Over the planet as a whole, early farmers probably grew around five hundred different kinds of vegetable. Today about two hundred vegetable species are grown by gardeners worldwide, only eight of which are grown by market gardeners on a large scale. About twenty species are grown commercially for field cultivation.

The major food crops of the world are even more limited: three crops—wheat, rice and maize—account for over 75% of the world's cereal consumption. More and more people are being fed by fewer and fewer plant species.

History provides many warnings of the dangers of crop uniformity. In the sixteenth century English explorers returned from the 'New World' with *one* variety of potato, which was planted throughout northern Europe, rapidly becoming a staple crop in many areas. John Evelyn promoted its extensive use in England as a garden crop for the poor, encouraging the Royal Society to investigate its potential as a staple food crop. Only the Irish accepted it eagerly, with disastrous results when, in the mid-nineteenth century, extensive potato blight decimated crops. Two million people died of starvation, and another two million emigrated to the continent whence their failed crop had originated.

In 1970 disease affected half of the US corn harvest, leading to a widespread realization that we have put ourselves in a situation of acute danger. In many parts of the world, including Europe, wheat is our staple cereal crop. All wheats are notoriously susceptible to rust; since more wheat is grown each year and the varieties become fewer, it could only be a matter of time before crop failure overtakes us.

The economic world is shrinking, and the fact is that the origins of nearly all the most important world food crops are plants native to Third World countries. In all pre-industrial societies there have always been numerous varieties of the basic crops, all subsistence farmers being to some extent plant-breeders with expert knowledge of their own plants and their environment. And all subsistence farmers know that the only realistic insurance policy is one of diversity. The more different crops you grow, the more likely you are to have some survive even in the most disastrous years. Diversity allows stability. But seed stocks, the basic building blocks of human survival, are notoriously susceptible to changing economic conditions. Food aid to Afghanistan, for example, has meant increased dependence on imported food. Widespread hunger and the availability of food without needing to grow it has meant that farmers have in many cases eaten their stocks of seed, and irreplaceable varieties have thus been lost for ever. The enforced growing of cash crops has also affected local economies and ecological balances. More ironically, in South America commercial imports of potato are replacing the traditional indigenous varieties with the uniform and genetically-impoverished stock of the USA. Not only is this unnecessary and dangerous to crop survival, but the protein content of the US potato is less than half that of the indigenous varieties—a vital difference for people for whom the potato is a staple food. It is the same story all over the world.

In Western industrial societies, we tend to assume that our food supplies are secure because seeds are safely preserved in common genetic pools or seed banks, mostly in the USA. However, we still need the resources of wild plants and long-cultivated varieties in the Third World to ensure that genetic variations that we may need are still evolving. Of all US food crops, of which there are over a thousand, only Jerusalem artichokes, sunflowers and cranberries come from native North American plants. The loss of the wild species which are the close relatives of our cultivated species is the greatest single threat to future food supplies, because there will be no further resistant genetic stock to draw from. We all know how rapidly the world's wilderness is being annihilated, and it is estimated that for every plant species that disappears, between ten and thirty other interdependent plant and animal species are also doomed.

Not only are the wild plant species at risk. The cultivated varieties which have been bred over many generations are also threatened. Both wild plants and cultivated varieties have to be imported continually into Western industrialized countries, as the very limited seed stock in these countries acquires diseases to which it has no resistance. There has to be a living stock of new genetic material if the resistance to constantly-mutating pests and viruses is to be maintained.

Much of the stored genetic plant

material is in the hands of large corporations. An FAO report of 1978 pointed out that one company had two-thirds of the world's banana seed in storage. These companies do not habitually divulge information about the seed strains they hold, but clearly they wield a vast amount of political and economic power through having private control over the world's genetic resources of food crops. Large-scale corporate interest was further stimulated in 1961, when the International Convention for New Varieties of Plants made it mandatory to patent plant varieties and collect royalties. This was followed in Britain by the Plant Varieties and Seeds Act of 1964. Private enterprise wasted no time in exploiting the offered market.

We have now reached a situation where the diversity necessary for secure food supplies is no longer tolerated by the market. We have been compelled to eliminate the seed variety that is required for our survival. Between 1965 and 1974, open-pollinated varieties of Brussels sprout dropped from 49 to 30, while hybrid varieties rose from one to 41. The significance of these changes will be readily grasped by gardeners. Hybrids may produce a reliable and vigorous crop, but they cannot be bred true from seed. The promotion of hybrids militates against individual seed storing and collection. By selling hybrids, the corporations have created an instant permanent market (and a new source of finance from royalties) among the subsistence farmers who used to collect and preserve their own seed. The financial benefits ensure that wherever possible seed companies develop uniform hybrids rather than self-pollinating varieties. It makes holistic gardening a difficult series of choices.

In Europe, gardeners are also affected by EEC policies on seed stocks. Originally intended to standardize the licensing of new varieties, since 1981 the *Common Catalogue* has been operative in all EEC countries. It lists the few varieties of each vegetable which are 'legal' in terms of being valid for commercial use—these are now the only varieties which can be bought and sold in member countries. The effects on gardeners have been instant and frighteningly far-reaching. The first and immediate effect was a drastic limitation in the selections offered by seed companies in their catalogues; those who specialized in old or unusual varieties were either knocked out of the market or forced to streamline their stock in line with the new regulations. The old-established firms can now no longer be relied upon to conserve the traditional varieties. This means that the varieties upon which our future may depend can only be preserved by amateur gardeners, or by establishments which are able to disseminate seeds with no expectation of financial reward. Not only is it illegal to sell unlisted varieties—it is also illegal to grow them, if they are a cross-pollinating species, anywhere near a commercial 'legal' variety. In the UK the fine for growing other varieties in close proximity to commercial crops can be up to £400. The only EEC government which has shown any concern about the new regulations is that of West Germany, where gardeners have been invited to add seed samples to a national storage scheme.

It must also be borne in mind that the listed varieties have been developed with commercial interests in mind. The gardener wants hardy crops which can be grown in sucession, whereas the commercial grower wants more—a crop which will grow predictably and uniformly, and will be ready for harvesting and processing all at the same time. The gardener wants tasty, nutritional food which will sustain a healthy household; the commercial grower wants more—eye-catching, attractive-looking products which will appeal to the eye of the consumer. Thus the water content of tomatoes has been carefully increased through genetics to create a bigger, shinier vegetable. Recollections of the delicious fruits and vegetables of childhood are not just a trick of our nostalgic memory, they are an alarming reality. As gardeners and as eaters, the seeds we are being offered as 'legal' are not what we want.

There are, however, rays of light on the bleak horizon. They are in the nature of individual flames and flickerings, as one would expect from a (literally) grass-roots movement. There are many farmers in Third World countries who have returned, disillusioned, to their old crop varieties. There is also an international network, centred in Rome, at the International Board for Plant Genetic Resources, which extends into most industrialized countries. The USSR probably has the world's most representative seed collection.

Nearer home, and of vital import to every holistic gardener in this country, we have the Henry Doubleday Research Association, and few gardeners looking for an alternative to commercial pressures upon their land will not have encountered the writings of their president, Lawrence Hills. Hills has been quite clear about the effects of the EEC regulations: 'We are losing perhaps four hundred varieties a year, but many more will go all over Europe [in] the mad scramble to produce more and more F_1 hybrids. *This works to the detriment of the gardener*, for plant breeders concentrate almost exclusively on producing varieties for food processors. . . If you are looking for varieties with real taste, resistance to bolting, long harvesting periods, tender skins in the case of tomatoes, for instance, the choice is ever receding.'

Among its services to organic gardeners, the HDRA provides information and supplies of fruit and vegetable varieties which are otherwise difficult or impossible to obtain. The new centre of the HDRA, at Ryton near Coventry, will incorporate a seed-saving circle, which will display the types of plant which can best be grown for seed, and give information on how to conserve seed successfully. It will also be possible to see the old vegetable varieties under cultivation. This new venture is only an extension of the years of campaigning for the survival of the old plant species, and their preservation at the Centre's previous home at Braintree. The HDRA produces an annual catalogue of 'Heritage Seeds', as Hills in his introduction says: 'In an attempt to stem further losses (of traditional vegetable varieties) and to bring the delights of the past to a generation reared on F_1 hybrids'. The list contains new as well as traditional varieties, but they have all been chosen by the same criteria, those of the organic gardener who wishes to produce a tasty and nutritious food crop.

Another HDRA publication, *Save Your Own Seed*, explains clearly why seed saving is an important part of a gardener's activities, and gives detailed practical advice about collecting and preserving seed from the basic vegetable crops. It also gives sound advice about which varieties to start with.

Ultimately, the work of bodies such as the HDRA depends upon the support and interest of the network of amateur gardeners who look after so many acres of this country in spite of the pressures of agribusiness. Some members of this network are involved in local organizations such as the Soil Association and HDRA groups, others simply know one another. But the conservation and future development of our stocks of garden plants finally depend on us, the gardeners. Pat Roy Mooney, whose book *Seeds of the Earth* provided much useful information for this chapter, sums up his analysis with a direct appeal to the holistic gardener: 'You can make a direct contribution to genetic conservation by planting your own garden with non-hybrid varieties, and by saving your seeds for future gardens. You can also share your seeds with other gardeners, and set aside some space for the growing of traditional endangered seeds.'

The plant stock of the future is what we make it. We have inherited it from the gardeners and plant breeders of the past, and it is our job to pass it on, ever-changing, but basically intact.

The explorers

Our gardens draw their material from the wilderness, and in more ways than one remain our point of connection with it. The stocks of garden plants that have developed through the centuries have continually been enriched and extended by donations from the wild areas of the world. The explorers who discovered them have ranged everywhere, from the rubbish tips of Bolton where Roy Lancaster found his first Middle Eastern exotic sprouting from seeds brought in with rags used to make wallpaper, to the furthest reaches of the Himalayas and the Andes.

We can differentiate between the plants which had long been cultivated in one part of the world before being transported to and 'discovered' in another, and the wild plants which had remained undisturbed by human beings in remote areas of wilderness until a Victorian gentleman emerged through the undergrowth with a microscope and glass case at the ready. Having made the distinction we need not let it trouble us too much. Some rhododendrons were found in uninhabited valleys, others in monastery gardens. We may owe both to the efforts of J.D. Hooker, without whom most Scottish estates and many English ones would be unrecognizable. On the whole the later explorers gave us our ornamental plants, and while our vegetables are often the result of centuries of cultivation, many of our ornamental garden plants have only recently been developed from the wild species. They may even be vegetative successors of one wild plant.

The earliest explorers and travellers remain undocumented. No doubt traders carried plants with them along the major trade routes of the world. It would be interesting to know how the leek reached medieval Europe from ancient China, but we are unlikely to discover the details. It seems probable that deliberate introductions were made by traders, who took plants along with their other goods from one locality to another; and by the ubiquitous accidental dispersal of seeds which is as common to human beings as to birds and shaggy dogs. However, it was the Renaissance that inspired a new type of plant hunter—the explorer. The earliest plant hunters were not necessarily botanists. They may have been looking for the gold of El Dorado, but they came home with potatoes, tomatoes, pineapples and runner beans, which have stood us in better stead in the long run. It is interesting to note, by the way, that the runner bean was first introduced for its ornamental red flowers, only later to be valued as a vegetable.

The plant explorers were both collectors with gardens in mind, and botanists. The seventeenth century, which saw the explorations of the Tradescants, also marked the flowering of botanical science in a series of treatises and plant lists, then known collectively as 'herbals'. William Turner was the first Englishman to study plants in this manner, and in 1551 he produced his *New Herball*. This was followed in 1578 by Henry Lyte's *Niewe Herbal* or *History of Plants*, which was a translation of an earlier Dutch work. In 1597, Gerard's *Herball* gives notes on the whereabouts of rare plants in Britain, and also gives a catalogue, fascinating to all students of garden plants, of the plants in his garden at Holborn. These early herbals provided a context into which the explorers' discoveries could be incorporated. However, the problem for us is that before Linnaeus, there was no standard system of plant classification, so we are often frustrated by being unable to identify exactly what was being referred to under which name. The problems of naming plants are discussed later in this chapter.

The first explorer who set out specifically to collect plants was John Tradescant (1608-1662). He started his career as gardener to Lord Salisbury, and later became gardener to Charles I. His first plant-collecting expedition was sponsored by Salisbury, who sent him to Europe to buy 'roots, flowers, seeds, trees and plants.' He followed this with trips to Algeria and Russia. As gardener to the king, he sent a collector to Virginia, and later followed this up by going in person. His personal museum of plants and related natural history was housed at Tradescant's Ark in Lambeth. His Lambeth garden was enriched with new trees from America: among them red maple and American plane. His son, also John Tradescant, followed in his footsteps, and also collected widely in Virginia, coming home with a collection which included the red columbine, scarlet cardinal flower, phlox, lupin and aster, and also the perennial *Tradescantia virginia*.

The work of the Tradescants was followed up by other explorers during the next two centuries. Other imports from the New World included golden rod, evening primrose, yucca, and French and African marigolds (the misnomer 'African' was applied later, when new varieties of this Mexican flower reached Britain via Africa in the 1890s, whence they had been shipped in American fodder exported for the use of the mules and horses used in the Boer War).

In 1768-71, Cook made his first voyage round the world. He took with him as botanist Joseph Banks, who subsequently became director of Kew Gardens. Thereafter Banks made no more voyages himself, but he sent plant hunters all over the world, and the living proof of their industry has thrived at Kew and in gardens all over Britain ever since. Francis Masson was one of them: he spent ten years in South Africa, sending home, among much else, pelargoniums and many species of *Erica*. William Kerr was sent to China, where he was shown many new plants in the nursery gardens of Canton, including the tiger lily and new species of rose and water lily. The combination of explorers in the field and the developing botanic gardens back at Kew was a gift to gardeners: the rare seeds and tender plants returned by long hazardous voyages were studied and nurtured in optimum conditions, and new varieties bred which were suitable for native gardens. Heated greenhouses were only invented in the later eighteenth century, but they were not slow to be used. No one who has visited Kew will readily forget the oldest plants living in the world, the cycads of Africa, South-East Asia, Australia and the Americas. One of these cycads was brought to Kew in 1775 by Francis Masson, and since then has attained its full height of thirteen feet.Kew Gardens themselves were finally opened to the public in 1840, and the new plants from distant parts of the Empire were the greatest attractions. In 1848 the Great Palm House was opened, designed by Hooker, and has drawn the crowds ever since. In Edinburgh, the outstanding collections in the glasshouses have recently been augmented by an excellent exhibition about the explorers themselves.

By the 1820s the new greenhouses had become commonplace. Nurserymen were becoming accustomed to handling tender plants such as orchids, and the possibilities of using semi-hardy plants in gardens were starting to be explored. Large houses were beginning to vaunt conservatories of exotic design, and orchid collecting was rapidly becoming a mania. In these favourable circumstances the dahlia, originally from Central America, entered its heyday. In 1818 the first ball dahlia was bred at Lee's nursery in Hammersmith, and during the 1830s dahlias became a craze in France and England. By 1835, the interest in wild mountain scenery and exploration was echoed by a new fanaticism for Alpine plants, and rockeries and cool houses became the latest cult.

The explorers remained active. Another Victorian invention greatly facilitated the job of transporting new species home, as well as tending them when they got there. This was the Wardian case, accidentally discovered by Ward in 1830. A keen naturalist, he had put a chrysalis in a jar with some earth and replaced the stopper. After a time a fern and a grass appeared, and lived happily in their closed environment for four years, until the whole jar was destroyed by accident. In 1833 Ward tried planting ferns and grasses in two sealed plant cases. No water was ever added. The same jar, complete with living contents, went on show eighteen years later at the Great Exhibition of 1851. Two other plant cases, equipped with plants, were sent on a voyage to Sydney, and when the contents arrived alive and unharmed, the way forward for collectors was open. Previously, transporting plants and seeds had been a risky undertaking, often doomed to failure.

The Tradescants' initial explorations in North America were followed up in later centuries, not only by travelling Europeans, but also by American citizens such as John Bartram (1699-1777). The most prolific collector in North America was a Scot, David Douglas, who brought many conifers to Europe, including the Douglas fir, and many herbaceous and annual plants which are now common in almost every garden border.

The best-known collector in Asia was J.D. Hooker (1817-1911), who gave rhododendrons their place in British gardens. During his first plant-collecting expeditions in Sikkim he sent home thirty-six new species of rhododendron. The seeds he sent had started producing plants at Kew before Hooker himself reached home, and formed the beginning of Kew's famous rhododendron dell. Twenty-eight of the species he collected proved to be new to science. Hooker's descriptions of the Himalayan landscape also acted as an inspiration, and rhododendrons rapidly became an integral part of British gardening, particularly in Scotland, where the climate and soil were generally well-suited to them. Just one of these species, *R. griffithianum*, became one of the parents of 128 hardy hybrids grown in Britain. By 1900, a hundred separate species of rhododendron were being cultivated in Britain.

Other collectors, such as Kingdon-Ward, Ludlow, Sherrif and Taylor carried on where Hooker left off. In 1842 the Treaty of Nanking made it possible for foreigners to visit China. The Royal Horticultural Society, (founded in 1804) was quick to send out Robert Fortune, who in nearly twenty years sent home 126 new species, including a new species of honeysuckle, winter jasmine, and weigela. George Forrest followed him in southern China, and discovered 120 more species of rhododendron, ranging from prostrate plants to forest trees. Nielsen, in the 1890s, discovered another forty species while collecting for the firm of Veitch. Ernest Wilson, William Purdom and Reginald Farrer also brought back a wealth of plant treasures.

Then in the 1860s Japan was opened up to Western collectors for the first time. The Japanese lily, once back in London, created such a sensation that gentlemen visitors took off their hats to it. Japan proved a particularly suitable collecting ground for the British, having a similar maritime climate, so that many plants made the transition to their new home very easily. Among the plants brought from Japan in the nineteenth century came Japanese anemones, mahonia, flowering currant, flowering cherry and forsythia. Japanese azaleas also arrived, via the Continent, to harmonize with Hooker's rhododendrons.

The naming of plants

At some point, the gardener who grows flowers, trees and shrubs is going to have to come to grips with their names. Some plants only have Latin names, though most of those common to our gardens also have English names, sometimes several of them. The usual objection to these common names is that they can't be understood internationally. You may wonder how often it will be necessary to converse about gardening in a foreign tongue, but even at home there can be confusion, and has been for centuries. The old-fashioned gillyflower, as in Shakespeare's 'carnations and streak'd gillvors', comes from the French *giroflier*—a clove tree. In English it came to be applied to any flower that could be said to smell of cloves, and much research has gone into identifying early references less haphazardly. Similarly, 'sops-in-wine' have been identified as wallflowers, honesty, stocks and marigolds. We have not grown more accurate. Different gardeners will refer to buttercups, daisies or cornflowers by the name of 'bachelor's buttons'. The old names are delightful, but it is helpful to know that 'love in idleness' or 'heart's ease' is also *Viola tricolor* if you want to order the right plant from the nursery.

Understanding the Latin names will help you to understand your plants. They are not arbitrary labels—they refer to the whole system, laid down by Linnaeus and enormously expanded since, for the classification of plants and animals. Where plants were concerned, the original system involved counting first the male parts of the flower, the stamens, then the female parts, the carpels or stigmas. These numbers fitted the plants into a filing system, which could be added to by further subdivision. This simple system was adapted and often superceded as botany advanced, but Linnaeus' contribution of a system of classification in itself paved the way for the more detailed study and analysis of plants.

Botanical Latin is now a system of its own, developed over the last 250 years for its own specific purpose, and now established world-wide. In 1978 the International Code of Botanical Nomenclature laid down the rules for the first universally-accepted system, and in 1980 the International Code for Cultivated Plants provided an extended supplement for the naming of cultivated plants. The task is immense, and complete rationalization is still a mirage on the horizon, and not an issue for the average gardener to lose sleep over. We have been supplied by the botanists with a system that works, and once you allow your mind to encompass the basic rules, they can be used by gardeners who are interested in what they grow.

The naming of a plant begins with its genus. A genus is a group of plants which are physically similar or closely related. Some genus names are familar, such as 'chrysanthemum' and 'dahlia'; others are less familiar—we are more used to using 'horse chestnut', for example, than 'aesculus'. Related genera make up a family.

A genus consists of a number of species, a species being defined as a group of plants which can cross-fertilize one another, though there are exceptions—some different species within a genus will cross-fertilize and produce fertile offspring. Some genera have only a few species—*Althaea* (hollyhock) has only twelve—and others have a multitude: there are over two hundred species of chrysanthemum and over five hundred of erica. A plant is described first by its genus, which can be written as an initial if it is clear which genus is being used, and then by its species; thus bell heather is *E. (Erica) cinerea*.

The subdivisions of species are less clear-cut. It is important to remember that the word 'variety' is used in two distinct senses. 'Varietas' is a subdivision of species of wild plants, referring to the different groupings within a species which occur naturally. A cultivated variety, with which the term 'variety' is often used synonymously, is a plant selected or hybridized from its natural ancestor. Some cultivated varieties have been given Latin names, which makes it difficult to distinguish them from the natural botanical varieties: for example, *E. cinerea* 'Carnea' is a cultivated variety of bell heather, not a variety that evolved in the wild. Whether the cultivated variety name is in Latin or English, the classifiers say that it should now be written in ordinary type and put in inverted commas, while the botanic varieties should be in italics like the genus and the species. More often, and invariably since 1959, cultivated varieties have been given 'fancy names', so that *E. cinerea* 'C.G. Best' is clearly a cultivated variety, in this case named after the plant breeder who produced it.

We have already seen that a hybrid is a plant produced by crossing two different species or varieties. Such a plant is given its own genus name, followed by the species name preceded by a multiplication sign; thus *Prunus x yedoensis* is a hybrid ornamental cherry.

A basic grasp of this nomenclature will be a great help, as most nurseries use it in their catalogues, and most gardening reference books will list plants under their Latin names. In becoming familiar with it, the gardener will be rewarded by noticing connections and relationships between plants, and by becoming aware of their origins in a fairly painless manner.

The History of
Our Gardens

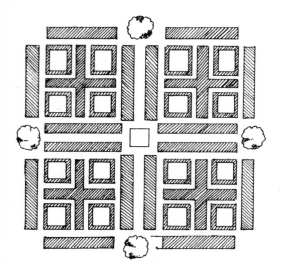 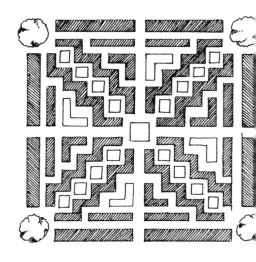

God Almighty first planted a garden. And indeed it is the purest of human pleasures. It is the greatest refreshment to the spirits of man; without which, buildings and palaces are but gross handyworks: and a man shall ever see that when ages grow to civility and elegancy, men come to build stately sooner than to garden finely; as if gardening were the greater perfection.

Francis Bacon
Of Gardens

 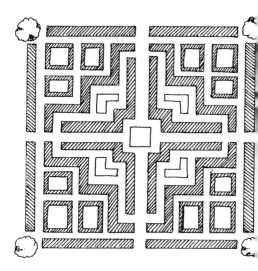

The History of Our Gardens

Each garden is unique, and every gardener has an individual idea of what a garden should be. However, gardens are as much a product of society as any other human creation. Throughout history they have reflected the time to which they belong, and gardens everywhere are the expression of the place in which they are made. Early gardens in the Middle East were designed as restful oases of shade and water in cities where stone streets and buildings must have pitilessly reflected back the glare of the sun. Conversely, a garden in the Scottish islands may be a place of repose from salt-laden winds, where plants of unaccustomed luxuriance can flourish within walls and windbreaks. Very often we design our gardens with the intention of hiding what is around us, whereas the eighteenth century landscape architect had exactly the opposite aim in mind: to open up the surrounding parkland, and create long vistas that finally merged into the countryside. A very pleasant prospect for the person who owned the lot.

Gardens tend to relate closely to contemporary architecture, our houses and gardens together being the expression of the way we live. So the designs of sixteenth century knot gardens may echo the patterns on the ceilings at Hampton Court, and the Victorian kitchen garden may be as separated from the ornamental garden as the kitchens and sculleries are from the drawing-room within the house. The lurid carpet bedding beloved by the Victorians coincides interestingly with the introduction of bright analine dyes. Trends were also dictated by the limitations of land tenure, and we have already seen how the intensive gardening of the early florists was a reflection of their circumstances within a society, just as the great parklands of Capability Brown were only made possible by the years of enclosure.

Garden historians have tended to concentrate on the ornamental gardens created by the owning classes of a society, just as histories of clothes have applied themselves to aristocratic fashions. It is less easy to find a history of British vegetable gardens than of landscaped ornamental gardens around stately homes. It is, of course, a fact that ideas are begun and developed by those who have the resources to do so, so that to look at the knot garden at Hampton Court is to go to the source of sixteenth century gardening tradition. Also, it is usually around the great houses that the past has been conserved most effectively, in gardens as well as in architecture and interior design. In recent years, however, perspectives on the past have altered, in gardening as much as in any other aspect of history, so that there are now excellent accounts of the British cottage garden tradition, and descriptions of how gardens fitted into most peoples' everyday life.

Traditions which we may accept as facts of life grew up in response to particular circumstances, which may or may not be appropriate to us. Perhaps you keep your vegetables tucked away at the very bottom of the garden, miles from the kitchen door, and hidden behind a paling fence adorned wth a clematis and a climbing rose, because an image lurked at the back of your mind of the Victorian villa, which had a lawn flanked by herbaceous borders, a drive bordered by pink rhododendrons, a shrubbery at the back, and the vegetables beyond that, out of sight of all the upstairs windows. The Victorian owner was in turn thinking of the landscaped gardens of the nineteenth century stately home, and used the same tradition, but scaled down. It was not inconvenient for somebody who had a cook and a gardener. You probably have neither, and a good deal less land too. It might be helpful to consider what people without servants were doing with their gardens a hundred years ago.

In Britain, our gardens are the obvious result of our system of land tenure. An aerial view of Britain makes this very clear. Most people live in large cities, and in some areas of them have no access to garden land at all. In the suburbs there is a familiar and distinctive pattern of rectangular enclosures around each square house. These are used in a variety of ways according to the tastes of their owner, but particular traditions are clearly discernible. In the country, the same pattern occurs in villages and around isolated houses, and here and there a large house will have grounds around it, a formal garden merging into woodland or parkland. Most of the land is used for farming, but the overall acreage of British land that belongs to individual gardeners must be very high indeed.

Our attitudes to land ownership and tenure, which have created the gardens we think of as normal, might seem quite extraordinary to societies that regard land in a different way. The limitations are obvious; the imposition of the suburban rectangle makes it difficult to design a garden without the straight lines which we are told are never found in nature. Perhaps even more importantly, we cannot choose our living space according to the lie of the land. We cannot look for the best soil, establish the boundaries that seem appropriate, avoid frost hollows or windswept hilltops, or even the wrong ley lines if that matters to us. We may only have access to public land, and many people would find cities quite uninhabitable without the parks and gardens that relieve the buildings. We may have an allotment. Allotment gardens tend to have established features of their own, and are usually designed for production rather than ornament.

The way we use our gardens is a direct result of the way we own our land. Some people have no land, some have a great deal. Many of the great gardens that have influenced British garden traditions are accessible to everyone, and are kept up by the National Trust, the Department of the Environment, and local authorities. Collectively, we might be said to own several botanic gardens in our major cities, and many local parks and gardens. But to be a gardener for most of us means having access to a piece of private land, and what we can do as gardeners is dictated by the extent of that.

It is possible to look at gardening as an activity finely poised between art and agriculture. Gardening as art, which we would tend to classify as ornamental gardening, leads us back to a tradition of painting, interior design and architecture, the product of city life and what we might call the finer points of civilization. Gardening as small-scale agriculture leads us back along a different path, and a longer one, to the earliest growers of food. We can see the first gardens either as our first attempts to control the produce of the land on which we live, or as the first burgeoning of a creative instinct.

The usual response to this dichotomy is to divide gardening activity down the middle with a firm line, with vegetables and fruit on one side, and ornamentals on the other. Like all artificial divisions, this has its disadvantages. A rigid division carried into the layout of the garden is neither the most practical nor the most ornamental way to use our land. The plants themselves resist categorizing. After all, they are living beings like us, and few of us would like to be categorized as solely useful or beautiful.

Perhaps the most useful tradition for many gardeners to follow is that of the cottage garden, with aromatic herbs lining the path to the door, the rows of vegetables behind them, and the fruit trees beyond that, and borders round the house filled with flowers that were attractive, aromatic or useful—sometimes all three. A further dimension is added to this attractive mixture by the importance of companion planting. If we edge our vegetable beds with tagetes and grow garlic with the roses, the conventional divisons are lost, but we are still left with something beautiful, if unusual by certain traditional standards.

However, although we may wish to blur the boundaries, we do grow our flowers and vegetables in different ways, and often in different places. Some needs are different; vegetables require heavier feeding as we are aiming at crop production, and the same species tend to be grown together, which means that more attention must be paid to eliminating pests. With flowers we are thinking about other needs, such as colour and design. The emphasis in different parts of the garden varies, but we don't have to be totally rigid about it.

If we know what the background to our gardening is, it becomes possible to select thoughtfully what we want from it, and not to be bound unconsciously by conventions that may not be appropriate for us. The rest of this chapter gives a brief survey of the traditions which have shaped our gardens, both ornamental and kitchen, and points out some of the types of garden in fashion today.

The olive is a symbol of peace, and certainly a tradition of gardening can flourish only if the gardener is left in untroubled possession of a piece of land. We may like to think that the tradition of cottage gardening in Britain goes back to the dawn of history, but the fact is that the gardens we now describe as cottage gardens came into existence only in the fifteenth century, and belonged to the new class of yeoman farmers who for the first time had enough land, leisure, and freedom from civil war to do their own growing.

Until the end of the feudal period the mass of the population did not own their own land. Serfs had no gardens, and no labour of their own to work them. They had to work both the lord's land and the common land. In time of war they sought shelter within the lord's castle and drove the cattle within his gates. Only the rich had gardens; the poor could only be agricultural labourers. The agricultural workers of later centuries worked long hours on the land, and had very few resources with which to maintain gardens of their own. They were more likely to have a yard and keep a pig than to grow rows of flowers and vegetables.

The gardens from which we inherit our traditions come not from the abiding peasantry, but from foreign innovators. We can trace our heritage from Rome, from France, from Italy, and later from Japan, China and the Americas. Just as the plants we grow are brought from all over the world and changed by generations of growers, so the gardens we create are drawn from a wide net of civilizations and cultures. In this respect our gardens, however beautifully they blend in with our landscape, are a product of urban rather than of rural life. It is, and always was, in cities that the need for a living plant environment is most felt. The first attempts at Eden were in Babylon and the cities of Sumeria.

The first urban civilization in southern Britain was the Roman, and it is usually with Roman gardens that the story of British gardening is begun. The Romans transported the conventions of contemporary Italian gardening to their new province, using formal designs of clipped trees and hedges liberally interspersed with statuary. We also know that they grew vegetables in unprecedented variety, but the vegetable garden was situated well away from the house, as one might expect in a slave economy. It seems unlikely that they exploited the peculiar properties of the British climate in the ornamental garden—a climate so congenial to luxuriant green growth and seasonal variety. However, the Romans did introduce many of our herbs, vegetables and nut trees, which are often assumed to be indigenous. Being used to a varied diet, they expected a far more diverse vegetable garden than anything yet known in this country.

The Romans otherwise had little to give in terms of cultivating the land. They did not make colonies in order to develop them, but to exploit them, and so, for example, their demand for grain left the fertile soil of North Africa a desert. Although in Britain Roman goods and ideas percolated from town to country, the people continued to farm the land in the old way. The formal garden was the gift of an urban

civilization to the British countryside, and when the civilization vanished, that concept of gardening vanished too.

The Saxons were a rural people, and they changed the English agricultural landscape far more than the Romans had done, gradually developing it over six centuries in a pattern of open fields, cultivated in strips, surrounding the villages which were the basic unit of society. Within this context of land use some of the Roman plant imports continued to flourish, including vines in the south. Some of our basic words for plants are Anglo-Saxon. 'Wort' and 'wéod' are both words for a small herb or plant, and so an 'ort-geard' is a plant-dwelling—hence orchard.

However, there can have been little wealth or leisure to develop gardens until we find gardens emerging in the medieval convents and monasteries. These gardens had the advantages of security, wealth and intensive labour. They needed to be self-supporting, and they had some of the best land in the country to cultivate. The gardens were divided into separate areas, including orchards, herb gardens—both medicinal and culinary—vegetable plots, and a lawn within the cloisters, with a well or fountain—or sometimes a tree—in the middle. In the larger establishments there might even be a private garden for the prior or prioress.

The emphasis was on the intensive cultivation of herbs and vegetables. The plots were small, but carefully sited and tended. There was a wide variety of fruits, often imported from France. The cultivation of flowers was probably less important, though there are records of flower gardens within monasteries. The only improved garden flowers were roses and lilies, which came to assume a mythological significance, both in the sacred and secular traditions. Flower gardens were more likely to be found around the palaces and castles of the rich. These gardens were still very small, tucked away in the complex of buildings surrounding the castle. In a country torn by civil war no one was likely to think in terms of landscaped gardens extending for acres outside the fortifications. The first description of such a garden dates back to 1250, when the queen had plans made for a garden 'with two good high walls around, so that no one may be able to enter.' Many women since have probably felt just the same! Within the high walls there would probably have been a grass or chamomile lawn. Britain has always had an advantage in this respect over the southern gardens from which so many of our traditions have been imported. We have a climate conducive to stretches of green turf, which are easy on the eye and gentle under the feet. As well as grass, medieval gardens would have had trees, often an arbour, which provided much-needed privacy when indoor life provided none—and flowers. As well as lilies and roses, indigenous wild plants were used profusely, with small blooms and pale subtle colours—a far cry from the conventional idea of a flower garden today.

With the sixteenth century came two changes which totally altered British gardens. The first was lasting internal peace: under the Tudors gardens no longer needed to be designed with one eye to the next civil disruption. Houses were no longer fortified, so the transition from indoors to outdoors could be gentler, and the garden could become more of an extension of the living space of the house. The second change was the influx of new ideas from Italy, often via France, which caused a renaissance in gardening concepts as in everything else. These developments were first seen around the palaces and great houses, but slowly filtered through and altered the appearance of the countryside. Along with new ideas of what a garden should be came new plants, the results of the earliest plant-hunting expeditions. Slowly, over the next two centuries, the emphasis shifted until flowers took a more and more significant part in the making of an ornamental garden. In the vegetable garden, new food crops from the Americas were being grown for the first time.

Tudor gardens were usually large square or rectangular plots. They were divided by symmetrical paths, meeting at the centre at a round flower bed or fountain. The rectangular plots formed between the alleys were planted out in the new fashion, with low hedges of rosemary, lavender, thyme, germander or thrift, clipped low and arranged in intricate patterns of either ribbon or heraldic designs—hence the 'knot' garden. At first the spaces between the hedges were plantless, and covered with coloured pebbles or chalk to give background to the knot itself; as new flowers became available and gardeners became more interested in them, the spaces between the hedges were planted with carpets of flowers.

At the same time as this new burgeoning of formal gardening and the importation of many new ornamental plants, the kitchen and vegetable gardens flourished behind their walls, now well away from the house itself. New vegetables, such as our familiar red carrot, were arriving with the flowers, and garden produce was rapidly becoming less monotonous. Herb and vegetable gardens were planned with the same symmetrical formality as the ornamental gardens. Sometimes the design incorporated both, as in a design by William Lawson of 1618, which divides a garden into six rectangular sections, of which four are for vegetables and fruit, one is a forecourt, and one a knot garden.

Running parallel to the large gardens was a more homely tradition. Life for the poorer classes was never secure, and farmers and labourers continued to suffer times of reversals and terrible poverty right up to the agricultural depression of the 1880s. But in some areas and for some people, times were growing easier after the fifteenth century, particularly in the fertile counties of southern England. The cottage garden as we think of it does not emerge distinctly in many areas until the end of the eighteenth century, but it began to exist in Tudor times, with the beginnings of what would become the middle classes. Better gardens created not only improved surroundings but improved diet. Vegetables became more popular among all classes now that there was more variety than endless peas, beans and onions.

By the end of the eighteenth century there were two basic shapes of cottage garden: the first with the house facing on to the road or street with a small front garden, and the main garden at the side or behind; the second with the house set back from the road with a path leading through the garden up to the front door, with beds on each side. The path might be lined with herbs and flowers, with the vegetables growing behind them, and the fruit trees lining the sides of the garden beyond. In addition to plants, many people used their gardens for bees, or perhaps had a pond. These gardens were the closest sixteenth and seventeenth century forerunners of our own, unless we happen to live in a stately home, and it is to these gardens that we can usefully turn for ideas which are both attractive and labour saving. Centuries of trial and error and common sense are there

to help us to maintain a garden as part of the whole environment. Cottage gardeners have used companion planting for hundreds of years before pesticides were thought of. For example, foxgloves were traditionally dotted about among other plants, as their beneficial effects were known, whereas they were later spurned in formal bedding schemes and well-sprayed market gardens. Plants were planted where they were wanted, so that many houses still have a rosemary bush at the door, useful to scent the house or flavour the mutton, or just to pinch between your fingers on the way past. Fruit trees at the end of the garden still give us early beauty in spring and apples tasting better than anything a shop can offer in the autumn.

The eighteenth century also saw a fundamental change in the formal gardening traditions of the great houses. This time the change constituted a rebellion against excessive formalization. Paralleled by the Gothic style in architecture and literature, there was a demand that gardens should be 'natural'—more wild and romantic, and less symmetrical. This change in taste happened at the same time as a dramatic change in land use—the enclosures. Disastrous for the peasantry, the enclosing of land opened up possibilities of landscaping for the owning classes which had previously been undreamt of. The word 'park', originally used to refer to a game reserve, took on a new meaning as an area around a country house exclusively designed to afford a 'prospect' for the landowners. Not only arable land vanished to make way for these new conceptions; whole villages were demolished and, if the tenants were lucky, built elsewhere. Tenants of the new model villages in fact fared well, since the housing was usually of a higher standard than they had experienced before, and there was often scope for them to have cottage gardens of their own.

William Kent (1685-1748) was the first of the new school of landscape architects. Lancelot (Capability) Brown (1715-83) became even more influential. Kent's gardens followed the romantic tradition, with no straight lines or regularities, 'with sudden changes of scene to ravish and surprise the beholders of temples, cascades, groves, and statues in unexpected corners.' Few modern gardeners could afford to keep a real hermit in a grotto.

Capability Brown's great contribution to the English garden was to remove it entirely. The park was everything, and at Stowe, Blenheim and Burghley the formal gardens were taken out and the landscaped parkland came up to the walls of the house, with only an invisible ha-ha separating the pasture from the lawn.

Although much was lost to the landscape movement, much was gained. Tracts of wilderness were wiped out, but the new groves of trees that replaced them were a valuable contribution to the ever-diminishing tree population of Britain. The garden, foreign in origin and formal in conception, was no longer something quite separate from the British countryside. The eighteenth century landscaping tradition looked out into the country, moving from the house to the horizon in carefully blended stages. The conception of the country was highly stylized and romantic, but it was a conception that was actually put into effect. After the landscapers had created their world, much of England really was like that, and in places still is.

With Humphrey Repton (1752-1818) the landscape movement changed again, and in a way that gardeners probably appreciated, for he brought the garden itself back into the design. With him the 'prospect' was no longer everything, and the garden was once again a place in which to *be*, not merely to look out upon. He reintroduced flower beds, terraces and rose gardens, and created shrubberies and conservatories for the first time. Perhaps this development was the only possible response to the strides made in flower breeding in the eighteenth century, and the new garden flowers that were being imported and improved —not by the owning classes, but by the botanic collectors and florists. With Repton the landowners could begin to exploit these possibilities as well.

With the nineteenth century we find these varying traditions—the cottage gardens, the large parks and the florists' gardens—coming together and influencing a new burgeoning of gardening activity, the gardens that were recognizably the forerunners of our own. We see the beginnings of traditions which still dominate our garden plots: the annual bed, the rock garden, the herbaceous border, the shrubbery, the walled vegetable garden. We may not have all of these in our garden, but we are beginning to be on home ground.

One of the creators of the nineteenth century garden was a Scot, John Loudon (1783-1843). After his death his wife, Jane, continued his work until her own death in 1858. The Loudons inherited Repton's ideas, but worked on a far smaller scale, that of the increasing number of garden owners who were working with anything up to a couple of acres. John Loudon produced the first *Encyclopedia of Gardening* in 1822, and edited *The Gardener's Magazine*, which had a profound influence on gardening styles. His work gave rise to the style known as 'the gardenesque', a mixture of design features and plants which looks back to many traditions, and scales them down to the possibilities within a small garden. He advocated terraces and conservatories, and a lawn interspersed with flower beds and perhaps a rockery. He also emphasized the plants themselves more strongly than had been the case before. Trees and shrubs could be grown as single features or in groups, and pruning in the style we see it today became important for the first time. Loudon encouraged the use of imported plants, and an increasing number of improved garden varieties. In the vegetable garden he lists a variety of vegetables which would be unusual in most modern gardens, where we have become accustomed to only a few varieties.

We may recognize the general ambience of all this as familiar enough, but an essential difference is often overlooked. These gardens may have been designed and run by amateur gardeners who owned their own houses, but the gardening itself was almost always done by a gardener, or even gardeners, however small the establishment. Only the cottage gardens were made by the sole labour of their owners, and they have an economy to them which the gardenesque or Victorian style lacks. We still live with gardens that are the results of a tradition where labour was available if you could afford it, and where you had little land of your own if you could not. Too many of us are defeated by large gardens, and still conform to the old designs and methods that demand our constant labour.

In 1832 the lawnmower was invented, which meant that lawns became a possibility for those who could not keep large areas of grass scythed and tended.

Another revolutionary change occured with the development of the greenhouse. Forcing plants under cover, or taking them into shelter at night, is a practice known since Roman times. Growing plants on 'hot beds'— beds where heat was generated by the breakdown of manure or compost, was continued up to the sevententh century. It was not until the eighteenth century that there was a widespread use of glass frames. The first greenhouses were built in the sixteenth and seventeenth centuries, exclusively as orangeries. In 1816, however, the rôle of greenhouses as forcing houses was made possible by the development of hot water heating systems, followed in the 1830s by the first production of sheet glass. Since then, both half-hardy and tender flowers and vegetables have been an integral part of the character of the British garden.

The Victorian garden is still seen to its best advantage in its descendent, the municipal parks and gardens tradition. Here we are most likely to see dazzling carpets of bedding plants, pink tulips and blue forget-me-not followed inexorably by salvias and lobelia, geraniums and white alyssum, pink and white begonias, and ubiquitous marigolds. Many parks still maintain Victorian greenhouses that put out all these stunning annuals like clockwork at the end of May; in the first week in June all is revealed, and there it stays until it is whisked out for chrysanthemum time in September. In winter, of course, we have only the image of mass graves. In the shrubbery there was also a new blaze of colour from the new varieties of azalea and rhododendron. There were also numerous new varieties of evergreens, especially all kinds of conifer. The old perennial flowers were once again relegated to the cottage gardens, and the vegetable garden was prolific but kept discreetly out of sight.

From this we inherit our attitude to

annuals, which is probably the most wasteful use of garden labour that we employ. Before the Victorians, hardy annuals were a part of the cottage garden, being tough and prolific and able to take care of themselves. We may still rely on sowing our calendulas and candytuft, nasturtiums and night scented stock each year. We may also carefully plant out our half hardy annuals in seed trays, prick them out and grow them on, to plant out in June just for the love of them. In moderation this is a pleasure, but it isn't obligatory if our garden has an established system of its own, with plants to fill the beds or reappear through the year, blending with and giving way in due time to one another.

The reaction came in the 1880s. The forerunner of the Surrey School was William Robinson, who was for many years in charge of the herbaceous section of the Royal Botanic Society's gardens in Regents Park. His most influential book, *The English Flower Garden*, was published in 1883. This book went through many editions and is still in print, as is his earlier work, *The Wild Garden*. In both books he forcefully presented a completely different approach to gardening. In his own words, he recommends growing 'plants of other countries, as hardy as our hardiest wild plants . . . without further care or cost.' He liked to see plants naturalized in a 'wild' setting— one of his greatest gifts to us has been the notion of planting spring bulbs, especially daffodils, in drifts in a semi-wild setting. He encouraged the return of the old cottage garden perennials and new perennials from abroad. Robinson's emphasis was all on the plants themselves; he had little to say about layout or design, but he brought the plants back into focus.

The trend he had started was carried further by Gertrude Jekyll (1843-1932), who also included a greater emphasis on landscape. She often worked in partnership with Edwin Lutyens, the architect. Gertrude Jekyll came to gardening from a background in painting, and only turned to garden design when her poor eyesight began to fail. She was part of the movement which included Ruskin and William Morris, and was herself expert in various crafts. The combination of this background with an interest in gardening led her to work with William Robinson on his magazine *Gardening* in 1875, which supplied a new stimulus to the wild gardening tradition. This was typified by her own house, designed by Lutyens, with the garden she had created for herself at Munstead Wood. Unfortunately neither exists today, and few gardens of the type designed by Jekyll can still be seen— notable exceptions are Hidcote in Gloucestershire, designed by Major Lawrence Johnston, and Sissinghurst in Kent, designed by Vita Sackville-West. The influence of Gertrude Jekyll can still be detected in our use of naturalized plants in subtle colours, and in the herbaceous border. Her ideas about herbaceous borders have had to be modified in modern contexts because they were extremely labour-intensive to execute—at one time there were seventeen gardeners working at Munstead Wood.

Her herbaceous borders were always planned to the last detail to provide horizontal drifts of very subtle gradations in colour. She made much use of foliage plants, and brought back many cottage garden plants of delicate shades, very different from the carpet beds of annuals in the Victorian garden. Like Robinson, she emphasized the 'wild' garden, naturalizing bulbs and other plants like polyanthus and azalea within woodland. She brought back the concept of a gradual gradation from the garden itself to the surrounding countryside. Anyone who has maintained a 'wild' garden knows that it requires plenty of attention, but the effect was one of increased naturalness as one moved away from the centre.

This quick romp through nearly two thousand years of gardening traditions in Britain may have left us breathless, but it may also serve to put the twentieth century garden into a new perspective. It has indicated some of the sources of what we often assume to be the 'normality' of the gardens we see today.

The purpose of looking at the past is to get a clearer idea of what it is that we are doing today, and why. We may be making a rock garden because the Victorians were fascinated by Alpine landscapes, or a herbaceous border because we have seen Gertrude Jekyll's style carried a stage further at Sissing-hurst. We may edge our front path with lavender like an eighteenth century cottage gardener, or surround our formal beds with attenuated box hedges like the last vestiges of the knot garden. The choice is ours, but it helps to know that there are choices. Garden centres may suggest to us that in late spring we must plant our annual beds, but if our circumstances are closer to those of the eighteenth century cottager in terms of resources and labour, then perhaps we should do better to look at other possibilities. The layout of nearly every suburban garden may tell us that the vegetables, if they are grown at all, should be planted in neat rows at the back, well away from the flowers, but perhaps it is only six hundred years of gardening for the owning classes that has made us think like that. Perhaps not, but at least knowing about the past can make our decisions about our own gardens conscious ones.

Planning Your Garden

But plough not an unknown plain:
First you must learn the winds and changeable ways of its weather,
The land's peculiar cultivation and character,
The different crops that different parts of it yield or yield not.
A corn-crop here, grapes there will come to the happier issue:
On another soil it is fruit trees, and grass of its sweet will
Grows green . . .
Nature imposed these laws, a covenant everlasting,
On different parts of the earth right from the earliest days when
Deucalion cast over a tenantless world the stones
From which arose mankind, that dour race.

Virgil
Georgics
translated by C. Day Lewis

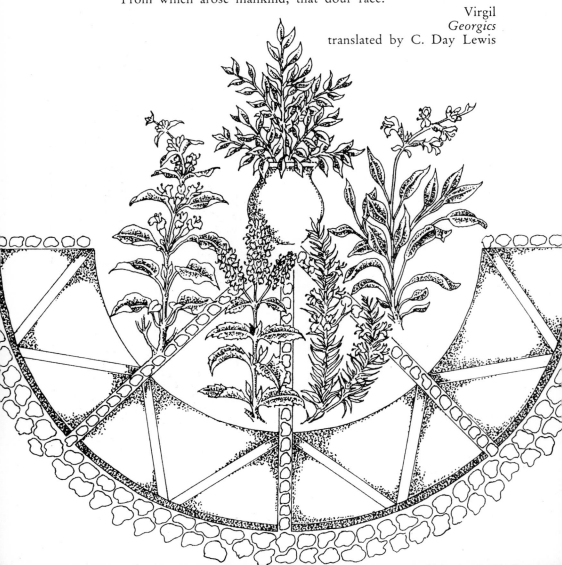

Planning Your Garden

The questions to ask yourself when you are planning a garden are, firstly, 'What is your garden like?', and secondly, 'What do you want from your garden?'. The answers to the first question will determine the possibilities for the second.

Some things are just not possible. A north-facing terrace will never be much fun to lounge on; azaleas will never grow well on an alkaline soil; it will be next to impossible to construct a football pitch on a 45° slope. You will have to live with your garden as it is or can reasonably become with your loving attention, and set your sights accordingly. There is always something that will flourish in any part of any garden, but you must take into account the prevailing conditions—climate, aspect, soil, minerals, humus, micro-organisms, water, air, and the plants already growing there—and work creatively with them. It is worth looking for plants that are going to be happy, rather than watching them sulk while you force your will on them. Many of your dreams will materialise with time, and the more closely you work with what your garden has to offer, the easier the task will be.

Climate

Every part of the Earth has a particular and unique climate, and to be a successful gardener it would help to learn about the detailed rainfall, sunshine, wind and temperature patterns in and around your garden.

On the large scale, useful generalizations can be made. In the northern hemisphere, northern areas tend to be colder than southern ones. The east of Britain is often colder in winter though sunnier than the Gulf-Stream-warmed west, delaying the first appearance of spring flowers. The west of Britain receives up to 70"/175cm of rainfall a year from the prevalent westerly air-stream, while the east can receive as little as 25"/62cm a year. Hilly and mountainous areas, and south and west facing coasts, receive the most rain,

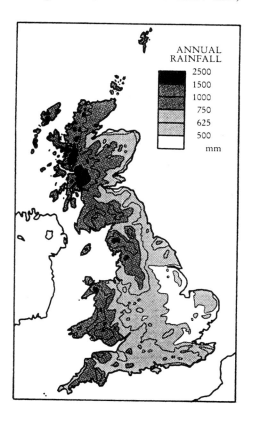

ANNUAL RAINFALL

	2500
	1500
	1000
	750
	625
	500
	mm

Great Britain—annual rainfall

although detailed rainfall patterns are complex, especially in the summer months.

The prevailing winds in Britain are the south-westerlies, though for long periods, especially during high pressure spells (anticyclones), winds can come from almost any direction. Long periods of light north and east winds can bring severe winter frosts. Wind force and direction will vary according to the lie of the land around you, so take full account of local conditions.

Climate maps will give you a general idea of the climate of your area, though remember that they will not give precise details about your exact location. Altitude will affect your local climate—a seaside location can delay the first autumn frost by several weeks compared with a garden only a few miles inland, due to the warming effect of the sea itself. Cities will retain warmth, but be more likely to experience heavy storms. In general there is a two-day time lag in spring and autumn frost dates for every 100'/30m rise above sea level. Spring is said to have arrived when the daily mean temperature (the average of the maximum and the minimum) is above 45°F/7°C.

In spring, be aware that the microclimate of your garden will affect sowing times. Monitor the mean daily temperature (or even better, the soil temperature, which is less subject to day-to-day fluctuations), or watch when the weed seeds start to germinate.

Even with a detailed knowledge of your garden's microclimate, planting out delicate half-hardy annuals like French marigolds and marrows is always risky. In many parts of Britain a night frost can grab young plants even in June, so be prepared to cover them with straw or a light sheet if you have any suspicion of a night frost.

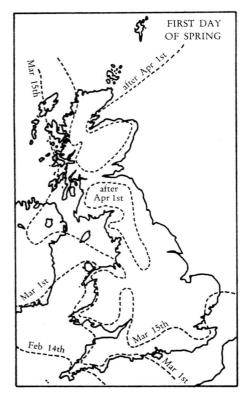

The first day of spring

If you have weather-watching neighbours, their statistics and diagnoses can be very useful.

Aspect

The way your garden faces provides you with both opportunities and limitations. A south-facing slope or a garden open to the south provides the most sunshine and warmth, which some plants love and demand. These plants will also do well with a south-westerly aspect. A south-easterly aspect has the danger of bright sun in early spring mornings, which can damage plants that have been frozen during the night. Bright sunshine can be particularly harmful to newly-opening buds and tender new shoots and leaves.

Northerly aspects are not as difficult as they may seem, and tough plants will be very happy there—for example *Chaenomeles* (*cydonia*, known as *japonica*), winter jasmine, cotoneaster, rambler rose 'Gloire de Dijon', clematis 'Nelly Moser', morello cherry and blackcurrant bushes. In a north-facing border, shrubs can include mahonia and forsythia, brightened with perennials such as peonies, lupins, columbines and primroses. Always check the variety of the species of plant you want to grow. Local wind exposure must also be taken into account. Primroses will be happy with a north-facing aspect, but not if they have a cold north-east wind ripping across them. Provide shelter as quickly as possible. Invest in cloches, extra strong plants, and late-sown vegetables.

The slope of the garden is also important, affecting the run-off of cold winds, and perhaps creating frost pockets. A garden in a valley bottom collects cold night air, causing localized frost patches. Look carefully at the surrounding trees and other shelter—the shelter and shade they provide can make a big difference to what you can grow.

Soil

Whatever plans you have for your garden, it is essential to know your soil. 'Soil,' says Edward Hyams in his *Soil and Civilization*, is 'a biological, an organic, a living entity.' Topsoil is made up of mineral particles, humus, micro-organisms, water and air. It is the interrelationships between these parts which make up the living, breathing organism.

To find out about this 'living entity' in your garden, the first thing to do is expose the soil profile by digging out a hole 3'/1m deep. The sides of the hole will reveal two distinct layers, the lower layer—harder and lighter—is the subsoil, the upper—darker and more crumbly—is the topsoil. There are alluvial topsoils in China 25'/8m deep, but you will be lucky if you have 9-12"/22-30cm, and you can manage with just 4"/100mm. If you are gardening on a slope, you might not find your subsoil until you have dug down 24"/60cm at the bottom of the slope, while it may stop your spade at 2"/50mm at the top of the slope. It is important to know when you are going to meet subsoil, and to know what sort of subsoil it is. The subsoil will not necessarily be the same type as the topsoil—a gravel subsoil beneath a clay topsoil would ensure good drainage, whereas clay under anything will obstruct drainage, making the topsoil cold and acid. Subsoil, because of the lack of organic matter, lacks fertility, and should not be mixed with topsoil or placed over it.

Mineral particles

The mineral particles of soil may include clay, silt, sand, gravel and stones, with phosphorus, potassium, calcium, iron, magnesium, manganese, boron, copper, zinc, sulphur, fluorine, silicon, iodine, cobalt, chlorine, molybdenum, bromine, lithium, nickel, platinum, ruthenium, silver, sodium, strontium, tungsten and vanadium.

Soil texture depends on the size of the mineral particles. Sandy soils have 35% of their particles 0.1-0.5mm in diameter, silt soils 35% 0.002-0.05mm, and clay soils 30% 0.002mm or less. A loam—the ideal garden soil—is a mixture of ⅓ clay, ⅓ silt and ⅓ sand.

A sandy soil will be easy to work, warm quickly in spring, and drain easily. It is poor in plant foods, because rapid water movement washes out nutrients, and large air spaces mean that organic matter breaks down quickly, either into the air or into the water running through the soil. It tends to be acid, and it dries out easily in summer.

A silt soil is easy to work and rich in nutrients. It is rather a fragile soil, and tends to form an impermeable layer called a 'hard pan' 9-18″/22-45cm below the soil surface. This impedes drainage and aeration. Silt soils also 'cap' easily at the soil surface.

Clay soils are very rich in nutrients. They are late to warm in spring, heavy to work, and have poor drainage. They are sticky when wet, and tend to bake hard in summer.

Loam combines the best attributes of clay, sand and silt. All types of soil can become very good garden soils if well worked with organic materials.

It is important to find out the type of soil you have, so you can work it in the best way in order to improve it. Ask the neighbours, though remember that the soil can change over distances of only a few yards. To check for yourself, mix together three or four samples of soil from the garden, and add one tablespoonful to a glass of water. After giving it a good stir, wait until the mixture has settled and the water is clear again. Sand will settle first, then silt, then fine clay, and lastly a dark layer of humus, and you may have some undecayed organic matter floating on the water. Judge the proportions of your soil and work it accordingly.

Even in our own garden we can see that minute differences in soil type can influence certain plants. Roses and cauliflowers will dislike sands and gravels: they demand the best loam. The alkaline/acid balance is also crucial to what kinds of plants can grow in the soil. Rhododendrons and azaleas love an acid soil, for example, and will never be happy in an alkaline one.

Trace elements in the soil—iron, manganese, molybdenum, copper, zinc and boron—make a big difference to a plant's ability to thrive. Some plants cannot stand too much or too little of some of these elements. Cauliflowers will have brown rotting curds if they do not get enough boron, and their growing points will die if they get insufficient molybdenum. Yet one plant's 'too much' is another plant's 'just right'; there are strains of thrift and vernal sandwort which will live on tips containing excessive amounts of copper, and some grasses are extremely adaptable.

Humus

An important aspect of a soil is the presence or absence of decayed matter, which is host to soil bacteria, fungi, microscopic soil animals, and larger animals like worms. Humus is decayed animal and vegetable matter, and without humus in the soil, mineral particles are barren. 'Humus' can either be taken widely to describe any organic matter in the soil, including compost or well-rotted manure, or we can save the word for the real stuff, a neutral brown jelly-like substance. Plants and animals excrete and die, and are broken down by fungi, earthworms, ants, and other insects and micro-organisms. This is then broken down by more micro-organisms into simple foodstuffs for plants, and the sponge-like texture retains these simple foods as mineral salts in solution.

Micro-organisms

Micro-organisms—fungi and bacteria—break down organic material into humus, then into the ammonia compounds, nitrites, and the nitrates needed by growing plants. Other bacteria—the azobactors—convert atmospheric nitrogen into nitrates, which is the only form in which plants can absorb nitrogen. There are also bacteria which release phosphoric acid from the mineral element of the soil.

Anything that disturbs the micro-organisms in the soil or changes their balance also disturbs the life of the soil and the plants that grow in it. As well as harming earthworms and other soil-dwelling creatures, chemical fertilizers and pesticides can destroy the micro-organic world too, turning the soil to an inert mineral substance, infertile and subject to erosion, only supporting life if spread with more expensive and energy-wasting fertilizers.

Mycorrhizal associations

Beneficial fungi grow on the roots of many plants. These fungi include members of the genus *Boletus*, and the poisonous Fly Agaric (*Amanita muscaria*). A mat of mycelium grows through and around the roots, isolating them from the surrounding soil, providing nutrients and moisture. Plants in this association grow better than those without a fungal partnership.

Water

Water in soil is not pure—it is a solution of soluble mineral salts. In a mineral soil, water will tend either to sink or evaporate. Decaying matter and humus will hold water in the soil where plants can use it. Plants need water for photosynthesis, and minerals for nutrition. If there is too much water in the soil, the roots of the plant will drown through lack of oxygen.

Air

After heavy rainfall, all the air spaces in the soil will be full of water. If this does not drain away within about three days, damage can be done to the roots of plants. This is one reason why plants tend to do badly during a wet summer when it rains a little every day rather than the occasional heavy cloudburst. Plants and plant roots need air, and so do the micro-organisms in the soil. Both can be poisoned by a build-up of carbon dioxide in the soil. Good drainage also means good aeration.

Pollution

We cannot escape pollution in our gardens, but we can take steps to alleviate its effects. Some problems are increasing despite pressure from people concerned about the environment. Gardeners should check the pH of their soil every year to gauge the effects of acid rain. Radioactivity in our soil and vegetation is more insidious. On the other hand, certain sorts of pollution can sometimes help gardeners—sulphur pollution in city air has kept the fungal rose disease, black spot, at bay for many years.

In residential areas, a common pollutant of soil and air is lead from vehicles exhausts, or lead-based paint peeling off old houses. Plant ornamentals between the road and your edible crops, and do not plant edible crops too near the walls of a house where you suspect old paint may be lead-based. If you think your soil may be poisoned, have it tested, and if necessary build raised beds using soil from another area. Wash any suspect food in 2pts/1l water mixed with 2-3 tablespoonsful of vinegar, then rinse in clean water.

If you buy treated sewage sludge, there is a risk of heavy metal pollution. Sludge is best used for ornamentals rather than edible plants.

Nitrates and phosphates in synthetic fertilizers are water-soluble, and can get into lakes and rivers, causing lush growth of plants and algae, which die and are broken down by bacteria, demanding large amounts of oxygen from the water. This can kill fish and other water-dwelling organisms by suffocation. Excessive nitrates in our water supply are not good for human beings either, and synthetic nitrate fertilizers should be consistently shunned. Even if the use of synthetic nitrate fertilizers were completely halted, it would take 10-100 years for most ground water in the country to return to natural nitrate levels.

Chemical pesticides can cause contamination of our soil, ground water and air, damaging fish, birds and friendly insects, as well as ourselves.

Herbicides can damage soil for a very long time, although recovery can be speeded up by repeated hosing with water, plus heavy doses of compost. If you are buying straw, check that it has not been sprayed with a hormone herbicide such as 2-4-5T—this can distort or kill your tomatoes and other plants.

Specific chemicals which can have a harmful effect in your garden include:
Gamma HCH Lindane: Persistent, dangerous to all animals, and restricted in twenty countries; an active ingredient of Secto 'Garden and Greenhouse Insect Killer', Boots' 'Ant Destroyer', and others.
Permethrin: Evidence from the USA indicates that it is a carcinogen; used in Boots' 'Caterpillar and Whitefly Killer', Secto 'System Insect Killer', and many others.
Metaldehyde: Poisonous to all animals; sold as slug pellets by ICI, Fisons, Boots etc.
Mercorous chloride (Calomel): A fungicide WHO has listed as 'extremely hazardous'; used in ICI 'Club Root Control', PBI 'Calomel Dust', and many others.
Benomyl: Systemic fungicide, causes contact allergies, and possible genetic defects; used in ICI 'Benlate Plus Activex' among others.
Glyphosphate: A herbicide irritating to eyes, skin and respiratory system; used in Murphy's 'Tumbleweed' among others.

Plant cover

Without a blanket of plants over and within the soil, the surface is exposed to sun, wind, frost and rain. The soil will eventually die, and be washed or blown away.

It is good gardening practice to keep as much of the soil area as possible under plant cover. Where this is not possible, mulch as much of the bare soil as you can unless there is a particular reason for leaving it uncovered. Mulches and green manures are looked at in chapter six, and mulches as weed suppressants are covered in chapter seven.

What do you want from your garden?

We have many different expectations of our gardens, which we need to think about carefully in order to plan. The main thing that most people need from their garden is food. Growing food is very rewarding, but also very demanding in terms of time and energy. To feed a family of four predominantly from your garden you will need about $300yd^2/260m^2$ of land—the size of a small allotment. With limited labour resources you need to be very clear about how you use your land, and how much time and loving energy you can give to it.

If you have a small garden, and space is the limiting factor, you might consider growing fruit in and around the ornamental garden, or in tubs around the paved garden. Raspberries, gooseberries, blackcurrants and strawberries do not take up too much room, and give much more than they take in every way. Apples and pears can be grown as cordons, fans and espaliers if you have little space but plenty of time to keep them properly pruned, but if you are not able to look after them trained fruit trees can be a disaster.

In a small garden it is often tempting to put too much in it, especially when you are trying hard to feed yourself. Remember some of the basic rules of gardening—trees and shrubs can easily fill a small garden, which is unfair to the trees and to anything else sharing the space. Your vegetables will not appreciate having to fight for sunlight.

Herbs mix well with ornamentals and with vegetables, where they provide good companion plants and help to repel pests. Plant a herb bed near the house to encourage yourself to use the herbs, and they in turn will enjoy the shelter.

Your primary reason for having a garden may be to rest and relax in it: a space for a deck chair or a hammock surrounded by pleasant greenery and varied shapes upon which to rest your eyes. Plenty of terrace and minimum-work shrubberies might be the best idea. Don't be fooled into thinking that a lawn is an easy option; it is not. It demands much more time, energy, machinery and petrol than a beautiful shrubbery. Unless you want a football pitch for the children or somewhere to put up a tent, your life does not have to be controlled by a green monster: you may prefer to fill your garden with riotous shrub roses, or long grass and wild flowers, shaking and shimmering in the summer breeze.

Is your main reason for a garden to have a beautiful and harmonious place where you can express your creativity? You may want to give your heart to your garden as a painter gives to a canvas, bringing beauty into your own and other people's lives. You may want

your garden to be an oasis, away from the aggravations and ugliness of the outside world, or you may want to take advantage of views of rolling green hills or glorious vistas of misty mountains. You may want to create a wildlife refuge. This does not mean total neglect (unless you want it to): it means informed neglect, and the creation of a garden that is right for you and the other life that inhabits it.

A washing line must figure in almost every garden, even the most beautiful and harmonious. If your garden is very small, the drying green may dominate, but it can still be made beautiful with plants. The use of the garden as a playground can be very disheartening for the gardener, but this is the way the cookie crumbles if you have a small garden and small and growing children. Playgrounds are inimical to fragile plants. When I was learning to ride a bicycle I was constantly falling into my mother's herbaceous border. While you have such activities in your garden it is best to put tender plants in pots in the house, and grow tough grass, trees and shrubs. If you have room, vegetable, fruit and flowers can be grown a safe distance from the playground. This only happens for a few years in our lives. Children are as beautiful as flowers and even more interesting to be with. Afterwards, dug-in turf makes lovely soil for fruit, vegetables and flowers when the time comes.

The ground plan

When you have investigated and thought about all these factors in relation to your garden, you are ready to draw a plan. It helps if the plan you draw is accurate and to scale, and the larger you can draw it the more detail you will be able to show. A good way of trying alternatives is to draw a base plan in ink, showing the permanent structures—house, outbuildings, roads, hedges and large trees—and then use tracing paper overlays to try out different possibilities.

A pivotal point of the garden is the compost heap, and while you may not choose to display your compost, it should not be banished to an inconvenient spot at the bottom of the garden. It needs to be near the lawn for grass mowings, near the house for household waste, and near the flower and vegetable beds to save carrying it long distances when it is ready. A quarter to a third of the way down the garden would do nicely.

It can be useful to have all your garden 'utilities' in the same area—compost heap, greenhouse, potting shed, tools, incinerator, water supply —though be careful they do not get in each other's way. The toolshed should not shade the greenhouse, and the incinerator should not be in danger of burning down the toolshed, though it is useful to have the incinerator near the compost heap—unsuitable compost material can be burned, and the useful ash transferred to the compost heap. A leafmould heap and a manure heap would fit well into this area, and a cold frame if there is space. You might like to pave this area, though not of course under the compost bins.

If you choose to screen the utility area with hedging, consider making it productive by using fruit trees and bushes, though rambling roses, clematis or honeysuckle are attractive. The extensive use of edible plants in a decorative garden is discussed in a fascinating book by Rosalind Creasy called *Edible Landscaping*—this incorporates many ideas for combining the functions of the garden, though she (in California) has pecans and grapefruits as well as apples and currants.

Lawns, paths, terraces and ponds

Lawns, paths, terraces and ponds bring form to our garden, linking the garden and our human activities closely together. We may think that the concrete path leading to the garage just takes us to the car and the lawnmower, but it also has an influence on the pattern of our garden. The terrace brings the house into the open, and connects the garden with the house. Our lawn may be a bowling-green carpet, a sinuous and wandering sea of grass, or a children's playground. Whatever the function of the grass in our garden, it is still the perfect foil for the varied colours of flowers, shrubs and trees.

Lawns

Don't have too much lawn—it is a waste of productive soil, time, energy, and petrol for the mower. Grass and wild flowers are very beautiful left wild. To help maintain a meadow effect, mow the wild patch after it has seeded in summer. Otherwise just mow the bits of the lawn where it is important to have short grass—around the flower and vegetable beds, where you want to relax, where the baby is going to play, and where you want the badminton net.

If you are going to make a new lawn, the cheapest method is to sow seed. Choose seed according to the type of lawn you want. For a fine decorative lawn buy fescues and bents. A lawn in shade, under trees for instance, needs a mixture based on *Poa nemoralis*. For hard-working grass patches use a mixture including tough perennial ryegrass. The sowing rate is about $1\frac{1}{2}oz/yd^2$ ($50g/m^2$).

When preparing the ground for a new lawn, make sure you remove all the perennial weeds and stones. Check the drainage. If you have a lot of moss or rushes, or water shows in a 24"/60cm hole in winter, you may have to drain. If you have good garden soil you will not need to add anything. If your soil is very sandy or is newly thrown up barren subsoil, you will need to add dried sludge at 1-2lb/yd^2 (0.5-1k/m^2), or a 2"/50mm thickness of peat with 8oz/yd^2 (250g/m^2) of mixed bonemeal and fishmeal. If you have a clay soil, it will be helped by 8oz/yd^2 (250g/m^2) of gypsum mixed with half a bucket of sand. Fork it into the top 3-4"/75-100mm, then rake flat. Roll or tread it, then rake and remove stones again. Sow your lawn either March-May or August-September.

Turves can be used at any time of year as long as it is not too dry or too frosty. They are expensive, but give a solid and usable lawn very quickly. During their first year, mow both new seed and new turf lawns on the highest mower setting.

You don't have to dose your lawn with weedkillers and other poisons. Speedwell and daisies are very pretty. If your weeds are prickly or unsightly, dig them out. Mowings are very useful in the compost heap, and it is a waste to pollute them with weedkillers and mosskillers. If the lawn is hungry, top dress it with ½ bucket/yd^2 (m^2) of well-rotted compost, manure or sewage sludge. Watch out for heavy metal pollution in the sewage sludge. A spray of seaweed solution twice a year will cheer the lawn, as will a raking in spring and autumn.

Mow at least once a week from May to August. Do not cut the grass below ½"/12mm or above 1½"/37mm. If it is dry, do not cut it very short, and leave the collecting box off. Worms help drainage, and their casts spread fertility on the surface of the lawn. Brush them to spread them over the grass when they are dry.

Paths
Decide why and where you want your paths. Watch where people go and design your paths accordingly. A curved path will not enhance your garden if people have made a short cut straight across the lawn. The path should also be built with its purpose in mind. For the weight of a car going into the garage you will need concrete, concrete slabs or stone slabs. Cobbles, bricks or gravel are prettier, but more expensive and harder to lay. The edges of a concrete driveway can be softened with aubretia and other cushion-forming plants.

In the garden, the least heavily used paths can be made of grass. Harder-used paths can be of stone or concrete stepping stones in the grass. For the hardest use, you are back to gravel, stone, concrete or bricks. To take a barrow, a path needs to be at least 24"/60cm wide.

Spreading perennials and shrubs along the paths and around steps soften the outline. Cushion and mat-forming plants can be grown between paving and bricks as long as the plants don't object to being walked on. Aromatic plants, such as creeping thyme, add scent as well as beauty.

Terraces and paved gardens
These are lovely in the sun, but tend to become slimy in the wet. Use bleach and water, and scrape away the moss and algae, though little plants in the cracks and joints will not like it. A terrace should be large enough for a table and chairs, and for containers for flowers and shrubs. If you decide to have a pool, it can often look its best in a paved part of the garden.

Ponds
Ponds can provide great delight both for you and for the frogs, toads, birds and bees in your garden. Ideally,

circulate the water with a fountain or waterfall—this will need a small electric pump, and will keep the water fresh.

A pond can be the central feature in a small garden, or provide a mysterious corner. It is best to have stones or paving immediately round it, and trees some way away. Shade represses flowering, especially of water lilies, and the pool will soon fill with rotting leaves, harming fish and plants and making a lot of work for the gardener.

Pools go well with rock gardens, and with bog or water gardens. There is a useful chapter on pool and waterside plants in Frances Perry's *Garden Plants for Everyone*, which gives details about how and where to build a pool, as well as many possible plants to use in or near the water.

Where to get your plants

There are various ways of stocking a garden. People who have grown attached to their gardens will always have them at the back of their minds, so that when they see the right plants they recognize them at once. The question is, where best to look? Stocking a garden can cost a fortune or nothing at all, although the latter requires time and ingenuity.

The first choice is: at what stage do you want to collect the plant? You can buy a young oak tree in a container and pay pounds; you can plant an acorn and pay nothing. Seeds are available from most plants for the taking, but to raise them you will need patience, and the right conditions, which may include a greenhouse and a propagator. Remember that seeds of cultivated varieties may not breed true. You will be safer propagating the plants you want vegetatively. Most other gardeners won't object to giving away cuttings, but creeping round public gardens with a pair of secateurs is unlikely to be met

with approval. You can always ask.

All gardens produce surplus plants, whether they be seedlings, runners, bulbs, or perennials that need lifting and dividing. Many plants that are destined for the compost heap turn out to be exactly what somebody else wants. There is an element of serendipity in all but the most rigidly planned gardens.

Wild plants need to be considered carefully. It is not a good idea to collect plants from the wild; it is probably illegal, and certainly not good ecological practice. You can always collect seeds, and wild flower seeds can now be bought very easily. Remember that wild flowers will seem out of place in a formal border of cultivated varieties, and are best naturalized in less formal parts of the garden. It has become fashionable to sow wild flower seeds in rough grass, and flowers from woods and hedgerows will be most at home on similar sites. Some plants which have become increasingly rare in the wild are now correspondingly popular in gardens. You seldom see meadows full of cowslips any more, and rarely come across a bank of wild primroses, but it may help a little to know that both these plants are flourishing and increasing in people's gardens. This is not to say that the few left in the wild should be taken away from where they belong.

Nearly all gardeners are prepared to spend money on their gardens. The more immediate the results desired, the greater the cost. You can buy container-grown shrubs and trees and have an instant structure to your garden. You can buy annuals in May at your local garden centre and have an annual border as easily as opening a tin. If you have money and no time, this is a sensible way to do it, but if you can find the time, you can enjoy watching your plants develop, and you will have a wider choice.

You can buy most plants as seeds. If you send off for seed catalogues they usually arrive by January. The advantage of growing from seed is that plant diseases are rarely transmitted at the seed stage, and seeds sown at home only need to be moved at the necessary growth stages. Many plants hate being moved. It is sensible to grow annuals from seed whenever possible as they come to maturity in a few months, their whole cycle being completed within a year: this includes most vegetables. In the peak months from March to June there will be pressure on your greenhouse space or windowsills until the seedlings are ready to be planted out, but this timescale will be acceptable to most gardeners. Biennials are well worth growing from seed, and most herbaceous perennials can be grown from seed within a couple of seasons.

Growing trees and shrubs from seed as opposed to buying young plants is a matter of balancing time and trouble against cash saving. Think carefully before being tempted by the descriptions in the seed catalogues. They offer the best choice of varieties you are likely to get, but you may not see the results for years. Growing trees from seed can mean a lot to a gardener. If you burn wood or peat in your house it may feel like just recompense; if trees are being felled all around you it may be a positive contribution to your environment.

Seed catalogues are good informative literature in their own right. Some firms specialize in the old strains of seeds, ensuring that the older varieties do not die out in the face of overriding commercial pressures. The catalogue produced by the Henry Doubleday Research Association lists many rare fruit and vegetable varieties. Seed catalogues offer the gardener the widest choices and the greatest challenges. Think before you order, but do order.

Seeds can, of course, be bought in your local shops. Probably one or two suppliers will be available to you in this way, though the choices will be more limited. Keep an eye on the shops through the year—they can do some of your planning for you by drawing your attention to what everyone is planting at a particular time. Remember, though, that suppliers will try to get in early, and may have plants for sale before the safest planting time.

Most gardeners will buy shrubs and trees as young plants. The recent boom in garden centres has made pot-grown and container-grown plants available everywhere at most times of year. It is worth seeking out your local nurseries and looking round them from time to time. Ideally, they will be specifically geared to supply your area, and this is important. There is no point ordering rhododendrons if your garden is mostly chalk: your local nurseries should have something more appropriate. Check the plants in garden centres and nurseries carefully. If they are dried out, rootbound, or showing any sign of pests or diseases, don't buy. Look for healthy plants which fit their containers comfortably, and show no signs of deprivation of light, water or nutrients. Beware of plants in containers that are not container-grown— sometimes plants are stuck in pots just to sell them.

The widest choices are available by mail order. If you intend to buy only plants which have been grown organically, you may well have to resort to mail-order unless you are lucky enough to have a local organic nursery. Local sources of organic plants might be discovered by enquiring from the local branch of the Soil Association.

The nursery from which you order

your plants should give you detailed instructions for unpacking, acclimatizing and planting. The plants will arrive at the appropriate time of year—usually autumn or spring. Choose carefully, especially if you are buying something like fruit trees, where you have to work out flowering times to correspond for cross-fertilization, early or late crops, suitable hardiness for your area, and your personal tastes. Make sure the plant you choose will adapt to its environment and your needs. Take note of its ultimate size. Over-enthusiastic ordering leads to overcrowding, and difficult decisions later when something has to go. Plants cost more than seeds, and you can quickly run up an alarming total. The catalogues are often excellent, helpful and informative, but they are also advertizing. Try not to be seduced by glossy pictures, and read the details about each plant. 'Choice' used as an adjective in catalogues is usually a euphemism for 'difficult'.

Continuous planning

Plan from season to season and day to day. Try to keep your records in a diary or card index, and on your overlay ground plans. When planning, or planting new plants, it is useful to know, and ideally to record, where each plant is growing, from tall trees to tiny vegetable plants. Note the variety of each plant or row of plants, the date you sow or plant it, the density of planting, and the plant's progress. If it is a productive crop, note too when you harvest it, the yield, any problems with pests and diseases, and plant and animal friends you have noticed. It is a good idea to wander round the garden every morning and evening during the growing season, checking the health of your plants. The most important learning in gardening comes from observation.

Do not despair, however, if you do not have the time or inclination to do all these things—the plants will still grow.

Helping Your Garden Along

When rosy May comes in wi' flowers
To deck her gay, green-spreading bowers,
Then busy, busy are his hours
 The gard'ner wi' his paidle.

The crystal waters gently fa'
The merry birds are lovers a'
The scented breezes round him blaw,
 The gard'ner wi' his paidle.

When purple morning starts the hare
To steal upon her early fare,
Then thro' the dew he maun repair—
 The gard'ner wi' his paidle.

When day, expiring in the West,
The curtain draws o' Nature's rest,
He flies to her arms he lo'es best,
 The gard'ner wi' his paidle.

Robert Burns

Helping Your Garden Along

'You cannot grow plants, you can only encourage or discourage them' says Gerard Smith in his book *Organic Surface Cultivation*. This involves us in learning where our plants grow best, what they grow in, how they multiply, how we can encourage the growth we desire, how we can collect seeds, and how to look after the physical framework of the garden.

Shelter

In general, wind is a friend. It keeps the soil and the gardener cool in summer, brings rainclouds to water our garden, and helps to pollinate some of our crops. In exposed positions, however, the wind will make the soil too cool in spring, and will cut up the delicate leaves of tender shrubs, flowers and vegetables.

The simplest form of shelter is a windbreak. A hedge or fence, tall plants, or even tall grass will protect plants from wind and the salt it may carry, stop the soil being blown about, conserve moisture, raise the temperature near the ground surface and of the soil, and create a stillness which will attract beneficial insects and relaxed human beings. Solid walls and fences tend to cause air turbulence, so it is better to use hedges and leave spaces in fences and walls in order to filter and slow down the air flow. Flowering currant hedges are very good around orchards and the flower garden; they come into leaf early, before the fruit trees flower.

Greenhouses

The biggest, best and most expensive shelter for our plants is a greenhouse.

This will make the most of the sun, raise the average temperature, keep out the wind, and conserve moisture in the soil and around the plants. Your greenhouse should be as big as the site and your pocket will allow, because you want it to hold as many plants as possible, and because there is less temperature fluctuation within a larger volume of air.

The largest area of glass in the greenhouse should face south, to get maximum sunlight. This means that plants might have to be shaded in

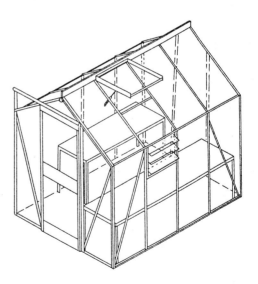

A typical greenhouse

summer, but it will make the most of the limited sunshine during the other seasons. Keep the greenhouse away from the shade of trees or buildings, but a very exposed site is not a good idea. It will get cold in spring, and winter gales may blow the glass out. Choose a span roof or lean-to to suit your site, and wood or aluminium to fit your fancy. Wood is warmer and simpler to fix supports to; aluminium is lighter (in both senses), cheaper, and easier to maintain.

Ventilation is very important in a greenhouse, and ideally you should be able to raise one-third of the roof area. If your greenhouse comes without sufficient ventilation, and most of them do, it is a good idea to fit a louvre window in a side wall. Automatic vents are useful, particularly in a small greenhouse where the temperature fluctuations can be violent.

A watering can or barrel of water should be kept in the greenhouse, so that the water temperature when you water your greenhouse plants is much the same as the soil temperature—cold water can give plants a shock in hot weather.

There is a problem with greenhouses: glass, polythene and plastic filter out essential sectors of the sun's light spectrum, leading to a reduction of the plants' vitamins A and C, an inferior protein quality, and trace element deficiencies.

Propagation boxes

The speediest, cheapest and best-lit method of propagation is an electrically-heated box in the greenhouse. I have made these out of wood, plastic bags, sand and a special heating wire, and they have been neither difficult to construct nor expensive, giving plenty of effective propagation space.

Seeds can also be germinated either in a seed tray or a propagator on the mantelpiece or a window sill. There are good small propagators (heated and unheated) that you can buy in shops and garden centres—some have built-in thermostats.

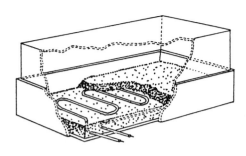

A heated propagator

Cold frames

Cold frames are very useful for early crops, and for hardening off crops between greenhouse and garden. They are also good places in which to strike cuttings and overwinter seedlings.

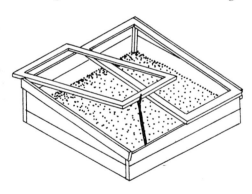

A cold frame

They can either be used over good soil, in which you plant directly, or to contain pots or boxes of plants, which has the advantage of being able to move the plants easily. Anything grown in a greenhouse or cold frame must be hardened off before planting outside.

Polythene tunnels and cloches

One of the most important functions of shelter is the extension of the growing season. This is most obvious in the use of polythene tunnels and cloches. Polythene tunnels may be large walk-in structures used like cheap greenhouses, or small tunnels, about 30"/75cm high, placed over early salad crops, beans, peas, potatoes and early brassicas. It is important to start ventilation when the weather begins to warm up, and to remove the small tunnels before the weather gets too hot.

You have a choice of glass or corrugated plastic for cloches. Glass is more expensive, but less likely to break or

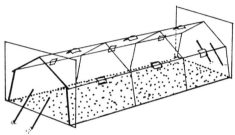

Glass cloches

blow around, though when glass does break you are more likely to hurt yourself than you are with plastic. Cloches are more versatile for a small area, but polythene tunnels are cheaper and easier to use over a larger area.

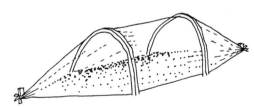

A polythene tunnel

Polythene tunnels and cloches can be placed over crops in August, such as early carrots sown in July for a November crop, thus extending the season into early winter as well as into early spring. Cloches can also be very useful for keeping excessive water off plants in very wet springs and summers.

Drainage and irrigation

Drainage

Before you decide what to do about drainage you will need to look carefully at the existing drainage in your garden, and at what you want to do with the garden. You could leave a soggy garden as it is and grow only primulas and other damp-loving plants, or you could create lazy-beds built up and surrounded by boards or bricks. If, on the other hand, your garden is really wet and you don't just want a water garden, the soil must be drained properly.

First dig a hole 24"/60cm deep, feeling and looking to see whether a pan of hard earth is causing your drainage problem. This is a layer of minerals and compacted soil 9-18"/ 22-45cm below the soil surface, which must be broken up to allow for good drainage and root growth. If the hole fills up rapidly with water, then drastic action is necessary in the form of field drains and a soakaway. Find the lowest

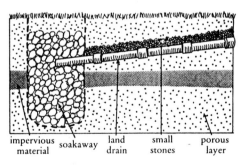

imympervious material   soakaway   land drain   small stones   porous layer

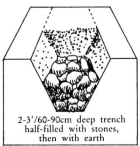

2-3'/60-90cm deep trench
half-filled with stones,
then with earth

point in the garden—the place where the rushes and moss grow—and dig a soakaway 4'/1.2m deep and 4'/1.2m square. In some cases you may need to go a lot deeper than this to get through a layer of impermeable rock or clay.

Dig trenches to the soakaway with a slope of between 1:20 and 1:40 (absolute minimum slope 1:100), and use clay or plastic drainage pipes. Fork the bottom of the soakaway and fill it with coarse rubble when you have brought your drains into it. Both the soakaway and the drains can be covered with topsoil and be grown over.

Bad drainage causes soil to warm up late in spring, stunts root growth, causes bad soil aeration and acid conditions, which can all lead to fungal root diseases. Worms and soil bacteria will not live in waterlogged soil. Sedges and rushes will grow well under these conditions, and further damage the drainage with their mat of roots.

Irrigation

The best water for our plants is that which occurs naturally. It has plenty of minerals and vitamin-producing bacteria, and a minimum of chemical pollution. Beneficial micro-organisms are killed by the chlorine in tapwater. Washing up and bath water are not good for the soil or our plants, as the soap, detergents and phosphates destroy useful organisms in the soil.

If you are to use the maximum energy of the sun, obtain the maximum food crops from your plants, or just prevent them from being scorched, you will almost certainly have to water them. The best preparation is plenty of organic material in the soil and a good mulch on top of it.

Every plant needs moisture at all stages of its growth, but seeds, seedlings and transplants are particularly vulnerable to very dry conditions, and may need watering every day. The other vulnerable period is during flowering and fruit development. At this time roots stop extending to find new available water, and if there is a shortage of water then is the time to really soak your plants.

Different plants have different needs for water. Potatoes benefit most from watering when the tubers are about the size of marbles, while peas are best watered once at flowering time and again when the pods have formed. A very rough guide to watering is that if you dig down 9"/22cm and find the soil is dry at that depth, water at 4 galls/yd² (20l/m²) per week. Water the plants gently; do not allow run-off or flooding, or you will harm the soil structure, causing minor erosion aand capping of the soil surface. If you are using spray equipment, you can check the watering rate by placing tin cans at soil level in the watering area—at the correct weekly watering rate there will be about 1"/25mm of water in the tins.

Plan your watering system before a drought starts. Every garden needs a watering can. Get one with a detachable fine rose, then you can use the

same can for sprinkling seedlings and large volume watering jobs. A barrel collecting rainwater from the gutters of your house or greenhouse will probably give you enough water for your watering can.

To have any effect, dry soil will need a prolonged soaking, and for this you will need some sort of sprinkler or spray. The water should be evenly distributed, and the spray should be fine

Soil and plant nutrition

Our garden plants are usually foreigners to the environment we have provided for them, and we have to make sure they are getting suitable nutrients, and are not being starved or poisoned.

We have to feed our soil, so that it can make the necessary nutrients available to plants through the action of bacteria, fungi, plant root secretions and mycorrhizal associations. It is safer, cheaper and easier to let nature select the chemicals our plants need, rather than the chemical manufacturers and ourselves interfering.

Compost

For the organic grower, the basis of soil and plant nutrition is compost. Compost recycles waste vegetation, provides for the nutritional needs of soil and plants, and ensures a good crumb structure in the soil, leading to good aeration and moisture retention. You can never have enough compost and often need other sources of soil and plant nutrition, but compost is the best and most important source.

There are many different ways of making compost, and many different structures in which to make it. There are good discussions about composting and compost in Dick Kitto's book *Composting* and in Ben Easy's *Organic Gardening*; here I will just give a tried and tested standard method.

The best and most fine compost is achieved by providing lots of air for the hard-working bacteria, so if you can put energy into turning a heap two or three times you will get your reward in muscles and good compost.

For heat retention and neatness, it is a good idea to make wooden compost bins, and most economical to build two or three next to each other, each forming a cube with a side of about 3½'/ 1m. You can also use special plastic bins or make free-standing heaps,

enough not to damage your plants or cap the soil. Choose the type of equipment which will fit your beds, and suit you and your purse. A rose can be fitted to the end of your hose and held up by your garden fork, though this will tend to give uneven spraying. A static circular spray is cheap, effective and simple, though rather uneven in distribution. Rotary sprays are more complex and expensive, have a tendency to malfunction, and have the same disadvantages as static circular sprays. The best—and most expensive—spray is an adjustable swaying square or rectangular spray. A long thin bed will do very well with a long flat hose with holes in it, which send up a gentle spray

along its whole length. A very good system is trickle irrigation with lay-flat perforated polythene tubing. It can be used at any time of day or night, and will not endanger the soil or the plants. Always get the proper fitting to attach your hose to the tap; shoving the end straight on to the tap just won't work.

At a smaller scale you will need a handspray for syringing boxes of seedlings on windowsills or in the greenhouse. It is best to have two handsprays—one for poisons and the other for water.

A well-planned watering system will save hours of work.

covering them with an old carpet to keep the heat in. Wire mesh bins are only useful if they are insulated with cardboard or many layers of newspaper. Straw bale structures make good bins for a farming family, but are expensive and perhaps difficult to obtain.

To make the heap, start by scavenging. Collect organic waste from your own garden and anybody else's if they threaten to burn it or put it in the dustbin. Visit your greengrocer for rotten vegetables or fruit. Collect seaweed from the seashore if it is free from pollution, and grass mowings that are free from weedkillers. Wood ash has an anti-acid effect and contains potash, especially the ash of hedge prunings and trimmings.

Keep all this lovely material either in a heap with your kitchen waste, or in separate plastic bags near your compost heap. If non-garden waste is kept in airtight bags and added later, the compost heap has a better chance of heating up properly. The garden waste can be put straight on to the compost without any problems. Dick Kitto suggests cutting down the face of the

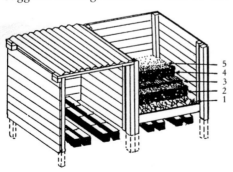

1. 6"/15cm woody materials
2. 8"/20cm organic material
3. ½"/12mm manure
4. 8"/20cm organic material
5. ¼"/6mm wood or peat ash (or whiten with slaked lime)

garden waste heap with a sharp spade and mixing it with the other materials.

Some people build mixed compost heaps; I find it easier to build mine in layers. First make aeration and drainage channels out of wood or bricks, then put 6"/15cm of woody material like nettle stems or bean or pea stalks over them to prevent the channels from being clogged by finer vegetation. Now fork on an 8"/20cm layer of mixed garden refuse and other organic materials, and cover that with a ½"/12mm layer of manure, which can be from any animal from a horse to a guinea-pig—chicken manure is nice and hot. Put on another 8"/20cm layer of organic refuse and whiten the layer with slaked lime, or add a sprinkling of wood or peat ash (do not use coal, coke or anthracite ash—they are too alkaline and contain many impurities which will harm the bacteria needed in the compost heap). Make sure there is not too much soil on the weeds, as this slows down the bacteria. Add water to each layer if the material is too dry. 'Vegan' compost works well too: use kitchen waste or seaweed instead of manure.

If there are a lot of mowings in the heap, add extra lime or ash to counteract the acid. Because lawn mowings become so compact, drive two or three stakes down through the heap to provide extra oxygen, and remove them again when the heap is built. Keep repeating the layers until you have used up all your material. Try to fill the bin, or build the heap as high as possible, within a day or two, and cover it for insulation. Use something warm like an old carpet or paper sacks. Polythene tends to make the heap too wet and cold. Corrugated iron is good if it can be secured over the heap like a little shed roof. You do not want condensation dripping back into the heap; this cools it too quickly.

Things to leave out of your compost heap include prunings and hedge clippings, and clubroot-infested brassica roots. Unless you are a really superior compost maker it is also best to avoid couch grass, ground elder, dock and convolvulus, but if you do use them, knock all the soil off their roots, leave them to dry out in the sun for four months, then add them to the centre of a good hot compost heap. You can add your vacuum cleaner dust if it is relatively free from synthetics. Smash up thick brassica stems and roots with a blunt instrument before putting them on the heap, or keep them for the runner bean trench, where they break down well. Blighted potato haulms will compost if put into the centre of the heap, but I feel safer using manure on my potatoes the next season rather than the compost incorporating the diseased haulms.

Within a fortnight the heap should have heated to above 180°F/82°C, and then the temperature will start to go down. You must then decide what to do with the heap. Either cut the sides off to make a new heap and use the centre, or remix and reheap the lot, or leave it alone. If the heap is dry, add urine; if it is wet, mix in dry materials like hay or straw. If you keep turning the heap it will rot quickly, and will hopefully remain weed-free. If you do not turn the heap, it will contain viable weed seeds, and will take anything up to six months or more to rot down.

When you have made your delicious compost, you can start to spread it around. It can be used at any time of the year in the soil, on the soil surface, or as a mulch for pot plants. It does not smell, and the nutrients in it are easily taken up by the plants. Coarse compost is useful in sandy soils, in pea and bean trenches, and as a mulch (covered by another weed-free mulch).

Manure

Manure is the usual term for the faeces, urine and bedding material from animals. The solids are high in nitrogen (N) and phosphorus (P), and the liquid is high in potash (K). The proportions of these nutrients in the manure of different animals is given in the following table:

	N %	P %	K %
Horse	0.7	0.3	0.6
Cow	0.6	0.2	0.5
Goat	1.4	0.2	1.0
Sheep	0.7	0.3	0.9
Pig	0.5	0.3	0.5
Hen	1.5	1.0	0.5
Duck	0.6	1.4	0.5
Turkey	1.3	0.7	0.5
Rabbit	2.4	1.4	—
Pigeon	5.0	2.4	2.3

(John Bond, Good Food Growing Guide)

In the analysis the proportions may not look very high, but when you are putting it in or on the soil at 10-20lb/yd² (5-10k/m²) or as much as a couple of barrowloads per 12yd² (10m²), it quickly adds up. Dung also provides useful proteins, sugars, hormones, vitamins and bacteria, as well as humus to create a good soil structure.

Keep the dung heap covered to stop the leaching out of nutrients by rainwater, to prevent the loss of nitrogen in the form of gas, and to shut in strong smells. Cat and dog waste is a health hazard if not properly composted. It is better in the middle of the compost heap than on the dung heap.

To get good manure it should be stored for three months to a year. Farmers usually have manure available in spring, which rots down nicely for the autumn or the following spring. Never use fresh dung in the soil or near plants—it will take up nitrogen to help it break down, causing nitrogen starvation. Roots and stems of plants can be scorched by fresh manure, and it can help weeds and fungi to spread in the soil.

It is important not to put too much manure in the soil, since plants are likely to suffer from an overdose of nitrogen, causing excessive leaf growth. Manure is rather acid, so it is good to use it with, for example, potatoes or roses, keeping your compost for less tolerant crops like brassicas. It is best to keep the application of manure and lime six months apart, though you may get away with less: if they are used together nitrogen is lost into the air in the form of ammonia.

Human waste

For a year I composted the material from bucket lavatories with hay. Most of the buckets just had leaf mould added in layers to keep them fresh; they were cleaned out with Elsan fluid. I used the compost around fruit trees, as I did not feel confident about its freedom from virus diseases, and I wouldn't have felt happy about using it with salad vegetables.

Urine is high in potash, and has enough nitrogen in it to make it a useful activator in the compost heap, though care should be taken not to make the compost heap too wet.

A compost heap using human waste should be turned three times during its first three months, and then every three months for a year. It should be used in the autumn.

Mulches

Sometimes the purpose of a mulch is to feed the soil and the plants; sometimes it is purely for weed suppression and moisture retention. Here I am only dealing with feeding mulches; mulches as weed suppressors are dealt with in the chapter on 'Weeding'.

The best feeding mulch is compost if you can make enough of it. No-dig methods of growing are sometimes criticized for needing vast amounts of compost, but compost used as a mulch does not break down and disappear as quickly as when it is in the soil. The excessive aeration in newly-dug soil will cause humus to burn up quite quickly, while compost on the surface will last longer if a further mulch of hay or a similar material is put over it. In the no-dig system a compost mulch 3-4″/75-100mm deep can be applied in autumn, which I then cover with black plastic for the winter. In June a further 1-2″/25-50mm layer of compost can be added and covered with hay, bracken, paper sacks, or anything else you can obtain. After a winter of compost mulch and black plastic covering, the soil is in perfect condition for spring sowing, with a fine moist tilth.

A mulch of old sawdust is very useful around gooseberries and currant bushes, though blackcurrants enjoy a little manure under the sawdust mulch. Peat is the mulch to use around azaleas and rhododendrons, manure is good around roses and for no-dig potatoes, and leaf mould is lovely anywhere. Straw is useful around soft fruit, though it encourages slugs more than hay does, which is a nuisance on strawberries.

Leafmould

Make a chicken-wire enclosure and stack leaves in it. They rot slowly by fungal action, and will upset and cool down the compost bacteria. Water the leaves in layers if they are dry when you stack them, and give them a good stamping down. If the heap dries out during the summer, give it another good watering. Most leafmould is ready to use between one and two years after stacking, but chestnut and plane leaves will take three years. 5yd^3/4m^3 of leaves will give you 2yd^3/1.6m^3 of leafmould.

Leafmould is very useful on sandy soil, where, although it cannot replace the nutritional value of compost, it will provide humus to help retain the nutrients from the compost, and will help to retain moisture. When you use leafmould on an acid soil, extra liming is necessary to counteract the additional acidity. Leafmould makes a good and slightly more nutritious substitute for peat in seed and potting composts. It is a clean mulch for strawberries and other soft fruit, and is very attractive at the same time as helping to retain moisture and keep the weeds under control.

Organic fertilizers

Sometimes our plants take out more food from the ground than we can put back in the form of compost or manure. In these circumstances organic fertilizers are very useful.

Dig all organic fertilizers well into the top few inches of soil—seaweed products go sticky and some other fertilizers go mouldy if they are left on the surface of the soil.

When buying fertilizers, either chemical or organic, there will be an 'analysis' on the side of the bag, and it is useful to know a little about the symbols used, so you can compare one fertilizer with another. The most common constituents are:

Element	Symbol	Typical compound
Nitrogen	N	—
Phosphorus	P	P_2O_5
Potassium	K	K_2O
Calcium	Ca	CaO
Magnesium	Mg	MgO

Seaweed

Seaweed has an advantage over the other fertilizers in that you can get it free if you live within driving distance of the coast. It contains many valuable trace elements and is high in potash. The disadvantages are that it is wet and heavy to transport, rots down to very little, and is frequently polluted by oil products, radioactivity (particularly on the west coast of Britain), or seaborne debris.

If you use seaweed in the compost heap do not put in too much, as it could make the heap too wet. Compost with seaweed in it is particularly enjoyed by potatoes and tomatoes (it is high in potash). If using it in the soil or as a mulch, either dig it in or spread it in autumn, so that it has a chance to rot down before the plants want to use its nutrients.

Seaweed meal

This is very expensive, because it is given to farm animals to supplement their diets. It contains about 2% N, 0.3% P and 2% K. It is recommended by Lawrence Hills as the feed *before* the root crops in the rotation, forked into the soil in the autumn at $4oz/yd^2$ ($120g/m^2$).

Calcified seaweed

This is a lot cheaper than seaweed meal, but not as cheap as liquid seaweed. It will control the pH, bringing it up to 6 but no higher, so reducing the need for lime. It has a high magnesium content as well as all the other seaweed nutrients. Its advantage over seaweed solution is that it improves soil structure and creates a better environment for soil bacteria. The recommended application rates are:

Fruit trees: $10oz/yd^2$ ($300g/m^2$)
Soft fruit: $6oz/yd^2$ ($180g/m^2$)
Vegetables: $6oz/yd^2$ ($180g/m^2$)
Flowers: $4oz/yd^2$ ($120g/m^2$)
Lawns: $2oz/yd^2$ ($60g/m^2$)

Bone meal

Bone meal is very good as a slow-acting source of phosphates, particularly good under trees and shrubs when they are being planted. There is 20-30% phosphate in bone meal, and the usual rate of application is $8oz/yd^2$ ($240g/m^2$)

in autumn. It contains a little nitrogen and is alkaline, so it will sweeten the soil a little. Steamed bone flour gives the quickest release of phosphates, and coarse bone meal the slowest. If left on the surface of the soil cats and dogs will eat it or it will go mouldy. It is expensive.

Dried blood

Dried blood gives a quick-acting nitrogen boost in spring and summer. It contains 12% nitrogen and is used at $1oz/yd^2$ ($30g/m^2$). If you have no compost or liquid manure available, it is a good boost for cabbage in summer or spinach after it has been cut. Dried blood should be mixed into the top 2"/50mm of soil with a hoe, and watered in if the soil is dry. It is water-soluble, so can be used as a liquid feed around plant roots to make it even more quick-acting. It is expensive.

Fishmeal

Fishmeal contains 9% N, 7.7% P and 17% Ca, and is used at $2-4oz/yd^2$ ($60-120g/m^2$). It should be forked or hoed into the surface of the soil in spring; if left on the surface it will go mouldy or animals will eat it, though it works well under a mulch. When buying fishmeal try to avoid products which have chemical potash added—fishmeal has no potash. It is expensive.

Hoof and horn

A very slow and very expensive source of nitrogen; the nitrogen content is 13%. It is better to add compost from the heap to the potting compost, and to mulch trees with manure. If compost and manure are not available, however, use hoof and horn at 1oz/30g to a 2gall/9l bucket of potting compost mixed in autumn, or 4oz/115g per tree when planting fruit trees, or fork out to the drip line of the tree at $4oz/yd^2$ ($120g/m^2$).

Sewage sludge

Useful for a lawn which is hungry after years of providing compost and mulch material. It contains approximately 3% N and 5% P, which is released very slowly, and it has a texture like grey peat. Apply about $8oz/yd^2$ ($240g/m^2$) in March, and on sandy soils the same again in June/July.

Rock phosphate

Useful on soils which are seriously depleted in phosphates. This can happen when the soil is very acid, in areas of high rainfall and where the soil bacteria have been harmed by chemical fertilizers, so they are unable to break down insoluble phosphates. Rock phosphate should be applied in the autumn at $8oz/yd^2$ ($240g/m^2$). It contains 13% P.

Rock potash

Rock potash will release 10% K over two or three years. It should be applied in autumn at $8oz/yd^2$ ($240g/m^2$). In areas of high rainfall, soil which is left bare in the autumn tends to lose its potash, and may become seriously depleted.

Wood ash

Wood ash can have a high proportion of potash if it is from young wood like hedge-clippings and prunings. Keep it in a covered bin, and use it in spring as it is water-soluble, and is easily washed out of the soil. Like a chemical fertilizer, its goodness is used up in six weeks. It is best used in the compost heap as a substitute for slaked lime, but potash-hungry broad beans, raspberries and gooseberries will enjoy a spring dressing. Fork or hoe ash into the soil surface or use it under a mulch. If ash is left on the soil surface it will cake and spoil the tilth. Be careful not to over-apply—$4oz/yd^2$ ($120g/m^2$) is enough.

Soot

Soot contains a small percentage of nitrogen, and is useful for darkening and so warming up the soil between onion sets in early spring. It is acid, so should only be used on neutral or alkaline soils.

Bag compost

Alluring bags of crumbly delicious instant compost are on sale in garden centres and other shops. They are very useful when we have no compost of our own and lots of money. I made two lovely shrub beds with bag compost, bone meal and wood ash spread on the turf and rotavated many times, then covered while still damp with black polythene. The shrubs were planted through the polythene after a few weeks, and did very well despite a subsequent very hot summer. The black polythene came off after about a year.

Bag composts can be dangerously high in heavy metals and pesticide residues used on animals reared on factory farms, so should only be used as an emergency measure.

Liquid feeding

Liquid feeds are given to plants to provide nutrients on infertile soil, to correct deficiencies rapidly—at transplanting, fertilization or fruiting time for example, and to build up the strength of the plant when it is suffering from the effects of pests and diseases. These liquid fertilizers are taken up quickly, and can be used to boost growth when roots are restricted, damaged, are in waterlogged soil, or when top growth is being checked by cold and wind.

All sorts of weird and wonderful liquid feeds can be concocted—usually very smelly. All of these feeds are diluted and used on growing plants in the summer. They should not be allowed to come into contact with leaves or stems, but should be poured on to the soil around the plants. They will feed the soil and the plants very quickly, and should be used once a week or once a fortnight.

Liquid comfrey
(high potash liquid feed)

Comfrey liquid is rich in potash, and is a very good feed for tomatoes, applied once a week after the first truss is set. There are two methods of making comfrey liquid—soaking or pressing.

To soak comfrey, place 15lb/7kg of comfrey in a 20gall/90l water butt and cover with water and a lid. After 3-4 weeks the liquid is ready for use, diluted 1:1 with water. It is rather smelly.

A comfrey press can be made in a big plastic barrel sitting on bricks. A hole is made in the bottom or side of the barrel with a tube leading into a gallon can. Comfrey is piled into the press and weighted with a stone slab. It starts to run in 2-3 weeks, and can be used diluted 30:1 with water. It should be used once a week on tomatoes and potatoes.

Liquid manure

This liquid will be high in nitrates, and is useful, for instance, for cabbages during the summer or for hungry delphiniums. Try to use a manure which you are not using in or on the soil. I collect sheep dung for my liquid manure, and use compost and cow manure in the soil. It is a good idea to give both soil and plants a range of nutritional treats.

To make liquid manure, fill a small woven sack with manure and cover it with water in a barrel. Do not use a steel barrel as it will rust and provide too much iron oxide for the soil. Soak the bag and squeeze it periodically; the liquid should be ready for use after about three weeks. Dilute it to about the colour of weak tea, and use it once a fortnight. At the end of the season mix the soggy manure into the compost heap.

Garden tea

This is a vegetarian liquid feed using nettles, bracken, herbs, and anything else you have around to soak in a bag. Find the concoction which suits you best, and dilute in the same way as liquid manure.

Seaweed solution

It is very easy and not very expensive to buy a seaweed solution liquid feed. This is used as a foliar feed every two weeks during the summer, when plants can absorb nutrients rapidly through their leaves. It can be used to water in transplants, and for watering seedlings and houseplants with good results. Fruit trees and soft fruit appreciate a foliar feed, and seaweed solution around their roots in spring when their leaves are just out, and in the late summer when the fruit is set. I have also sprayed it on the soil before wrapping it up in a winter mulch in the autumn. Seaweed helps plants resist frost and pests.

Lime and pH

The acidity or alkalinity of garden soil can be controlled by using lime, peat or manure. Acidity and alkalinity is measured by a pH level from 1 to 14. Pure water measures 7—higher than 7 is alkaline; lower than 7 is acid. Most garden plants do best in a slightly acid soil—about 6.5 on loam and 5.8 on peat soil. Soil is easily tested with a pH kit, which can be bought from any garden shop, is not too expensive, and is easy to use.

You may inherit a garden which is very acid from the application of chemical fertilizers and manuring every year with no liming. On the other hand your soil may be naturally alkaline, or the previous gardener may have consistently over-limed, which is easily done when using slaked lime. In either case you could have difficulties with the availability of nutrients and trace elements. These minerals are at their most easily available only within particular pH ranges, as shown in the following diagram:

Effects of pH value on nutrient uptake

	pH	4	5	6	7	8
Nitrogen						
Phosphorus						
Potash						
Calcium						
Magnesium						
Iron						
Manganese						
Boron						

(*J.A. Bowers, The Soil Test Kit*)

Humus in the soil feeds the bacteria that make the nutrients and trace elements available. If the soil is thin and lacking in humus, shortages will show up more quickly than in a soil rich in humus, even though the pH may be the same.

Lime will supply calcium which plants need, and will correct an over-acid soil, but a lot of compost makers use no lime on their soil. Manure and acid rain tend to make soils acid, but if you use wood ash or lime in your compost there should be no need to lime the soil. It is best to check the pH of your garden each year in the plot where the potatoes have just been in the rotation, and add lime then if necessary. Do not mix any of the limes with manure. This will cause a release of ammonia gas, and nitrogen will be lost from the manure.

Ground limestone

This is calcium carbonate, and is safe to use for our plants, soil organisms and hands. The speed of its action depends on whether it is coarse or fine. Even if it is fine it should be applied in the autumn, and its maximum liming effect occurs 18 months later. If you want your soil at its highest pH for brassicas in your rotation, limestone should be applied between the potatoes and the legumes, which will then be followed by the brassicas.

Chalk

This is also calcium carbonate, and works in the same way as ground limestone.

Magnesium limestone (Dolomite)

Magnesium limestone is approximately 60% calcium carbonate and 40% magnesium carbonate, and can be very useful where chemical gardening, high rainfall and acid soil have created a shortage of magnesium. It lasts for three to five years, and you can use the same quantities as advised for ground limestone in a soil testing kit.

Slaked (hydrated) lime

This lime is quite dangerous, and unpleasant to use. It is water-soluble and can take the pH higher than 7 if an unwitting overdose is given—the other limes cannot do this. It is easily obtainable in shops, and is useful in the compost heap when there is no wood ash available, in potting composts, or as an emergency measure if your soil is too acid in spring.

Gypsum (calcium sulphate)

This is neutral rather than alkaline, and is used for improving soil structure on clay soils. It causes flocculation—the sticking together of clay particles into crumbs, improving aeration and manageability. Used with magnesium limestone, gypsum is more active. Use $8oz/yd^2$ ($240g/m^2$) of a 9:1 mix of gypsum and magnesium limestone, and hoe into the top 2"/50mm of soil on a still day between autumn and spring.

Seed, cutting and potting compost

It is important to give our seeds the best possible start in life. In the house, cold frame or greenhouse this means using a compost. Garden soil for seeds and pot plants does not usually work well.

There are two types of compost, one is soil-based and the other is soil-less. The soil-based compost is usually mixed to the John Innes Institute formula with loam, peat and sand, and is heavy. The soil-less compost is peat and sand or perlite, is light, and cheaper.

John Innes (1829-1904) left money in his will to found a school for training gardeners. His trustees ignored this, and founded a research institute instead. In 1930 the Institute developed the John Innes seed and potting composts, to standardized formulae. Before that every big garden had its own formulae for compost. While the John Innes Institute provided standards for compost mixtures, many people have their own mixtures which are different.

You too can make your own seed and potting composts at home. It is a good idea to sterilize your soil or loam at 180°F/85°C in the oven or a soil sterilizer, but sterilization is not vital. Do not sterilize garden compost or you will kill useful bacteria and lose nutrients.

Here are some sample recipes for seed, potting and cutting compost from different authors. All figures are in parts by volume. The easiest measure is a 2gall/9l bucket, though some people do it by the shovelful. All should be passed through a ½"/12mm sieve.

Dick Kitto's seed and potting compost

Sifted compost from heap	2
Irish sphagnum peat	2
Horticultural grit/coarse sand	1
Sifted soil (optional)	2

Ben Easy's seed compost No. 1

Sifted compost	1-2
Loam from turf heap	3-4
Peat or leaf mould	3
Horticultural grit	2

Ben Easy's seed compost No. 2

Sifted compost	2
Good soil	2
Horticultural grit	1

plus 2 handfuls fine bonemeal
to every 10lb/4.5kg of compost

John Bond's seed compost

Compost	1
Horticultural grit	1
Loam	2

Cutting compost

Peat	1
Horticultural grit	1

Potting compost

At the moment you cannot buy organic potting composts, and non-organic composts are very expensive, so ideally use an organic recipe, adapting it to your own needs. There is a very good section about seed and potting composts in Ben Easy's book *Practical Organic Gardening*.

John Innes mixtures come in numbers 1, 2 and 3: you use 1 when pricking out seedlings, 2 when potting on or growing on fuchsias and geraniums, and 3 for the growing on of plants like tomatoes and chrysanthemums. The higher the number the larger the amount of fertilizer. Soil-less composts are cheaper but less nutritious, and bigger plants will need feeding sooner. When you have used a potting or seed compost, sprinkle it on the garden where it will be appreciated. You can also recycle and remix your compost.

First, here is a recipe to make 8 gall/36l (4 buckets) of soil-less potting compost:

6 gall/26l moss peat
1½ gall/7l horticultural grit
3oz/85g fine calcified seaweed,
    ground limestone or dolomite
3oz/85g seaweed meal or wood ash
4½oz/135g hoof and horn
4½oz/135g fine bonemeal

The last two ingredients can be replaced by 9oz/270g of blood, fish and bone if it is intended for short-term use. Sift it through a ½"/12mm sieve. Make this compost in the autumn and store it in a bin or bag, watering it if it becomes dry. If making it in spring, add 2oz/50g hydrated lime.

Here now are some different recipes for soil-based potting composts (all figures are in parts by volume):

Ben Easy's potting compost No. 1

Compost	7
Loam	3
Horticultural grit	2
Peat or leaf mould	1

Ben Easy's potting compost No. 2

Compost	1
Loam	1
Peat	1
Horticultural grit	1

G.O. Liss's potting compost No. 1
(for young tomato plants)

Compost	1
Loam	1

plus a 5"/12.5cm pot of bonemeal, a pot of ground limestone, and half a pot of hoof and horn/barrowload.

(for lettuce seedlings leave out
the hoof and horn)

The general principle of the use of seed and potting composts is to move the plants on from a less rich medium to a richer one as they grow bigger and demand more nutrients. You can overfeed plants, and the purest and best garden compost will choke young plants.

Propagation from seed

Most plants can be grown from seed, but some are very slow, some germinate with difficulty, and some do not resemble their parents very closely. There are many alternatives to seeds—suckers, layers, bulbs, grafts, cuttings and root division, which collectively are called vegetative propagation. Most annuals and biennials, however, including nearly all vegetables, are raised from seed.

Raising plants from seed

There are three methods of sowing seeds:

—Outdoors, directly into the plant's permanent position. This is used for flowers which are hardy annuals, and for most vegetables.

—Outdoors in a seed bed. Use this method for brassicas, hardy perennials like lupins and delphiniums, and hardy biennials like Sweet William.

—Indoors on a windowsill, or in a cold frame or greenhouse, in boxes or pots. This applies to half-hardy annuals and early or heat-loving vegetables such as green peppers and tomatoes.

The important rules for seed sowing are to sow shallowly and thinly. Try very hard to follow the instructions for depth of sowing. If seeds are sown too deep, seedlings will die or be weakened before they reach the surface.

Outdoor seed sowing

Make a fine tilth on the surface of the soil. Most seeds and seedlings are very small; they cannot manage in a cloddy environment, and their roots need a medium with good aeration and good moisture retention.

Do not sow until the soil is warm enough—this is when your average daily soil temperature has reached 45°F/7°C, or when the weeds in your garden start to germinate.

To prepare a seed bed after digging, fork the ground over a few weeks before the seeds are to be sown.

Remove any large stones, then rake the ground flat and tread the bed down. Rake again, tread again, then add 1"/25mm of fine compost to the last raking, mixing it into the top 2-3"/50-75mm of soil. The surface of the soil should be dry, and the undersoil damp.

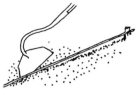

Use string or a garden line to mark out the row. For small seeds use the side of the hoe to draw out a V-shaped drill to the recommended depth. For large seeds like peas and beans, a broad drill or shallow trench can be made using a draw hoe or spade. If the soil is sandy or clay, a little well-rotted compost at the bottom of the drill will help germination. If the soil or compost is dry, soak the drill well before sowing the seeds.

If you are using a no-dig method, carefully draw back the mulch about 2"/50mm each side of the planting line. This should expose a perfect tilth, fine and moist for seed sowing. There is no need to fork or tread—just rake. Make the drill as for the digging method.

Sow your seed carefully. Pour the seed into the palm of one hand, take pinches between the thumb and forefinger of the other, and roll the seed out into the drill to obtain a thin and even sowing. A ½-1"/12-25mm spacing is correct for most seeds; more for bigger seeds. Cover the seeds carefully. The depth of soil over the seed should be roughly three times the diameter of the seed. Tamp down the soil with the back of the rake. Rake after tamping to stop the soil from capping. If you are worried that your soil will go hard or if you will have to water your seeds, sprinkle the top of the drill with a little compost or peat. Try not to water until the seedlings are up, but if you have to water, do it early each morning before the sun gets hot.

Pelleted seeds are useful to be certain of sowing distances. You use less seed with pelleted seeds, but they are expensive, you need to have plenty of moisture in the seed drill, and the germination rate is slightly less than with ordinary seed.

Seeds can be soaked for a day before sowing to ensure they have enough moisture and to speed up germination, but they are awkward to handle, and you cannot be sure that there will be sufficient moisture in the drill to continue germination.

Fluid sowing is a new variation on soaking seeds. The seeds are germinated, then mixed with cellulose wallpaper paste (the kind without fungicides), and squeezed into the seed drill like icing. A very good explanation of this technique can be found in Salter and Bleasdale's *Know and Grow Vegetables*. When you have covered the cellulose and seed mixture with soil you can be sure that the germinated seeds have enough moisture to go on growing. Emergence of seedlings can be as much as 21 days earlier than conventional sowing for parsley, and 12 days for spring carrots.

Broadcast sowing

This is sometimes used for annual flowers, cress and salad mixtures. The seed bed is prepared as usual and seed is sprinkled on it at random, and either raked in or soil sieved over it. It is difficult to weed seedlings sown like this, and they can easily dry out. I prefer V drills drawn in irregular patterns for annual flowers.

Station sowing

This is sometimes recommended for sowing annual flowers, and root vegetables like parsnips. Either a V drill is cut or a dibber is used, and two or three seeds are dropped in at regular intervals. When the seedlings appear, all but one are removed, and the best ones left at the correct spacing to grow on.

Thinning

When seedlings have developed their first set of true leaves they must be thinned to stop overcrowding, which produces elongated, hungry, useless plants. Eat, transplant or compost the thinnings: you will not get good results from transplanted root crop thinnings. Sometimes it is useful to thin to half distance and later to the full growing-on distance. You get bigger and better thinnings to eat, but you may end up forgetting to thin your seedlings properly. It is not usually a good idea to leave thinnings on the soil—carrot thinnings will attract carrot root fly and should be removed immediately. After thinning, give the seedlings a watering with seaweed solution in case their roots have been disturbed.

Seed sowing indoors

A higher proportion of seeds will emerge under the controlled conditions of a windowsill or greenhouse than outside. The plants can also be harvested earlier. Growing seeds and plants inside is fun but time-consuming, and can be expensive.

Use clean boxes with good drainage, either bought plastic boxes or small wooden fish boxes. If new clay pots are used, soak them overnight and dry them before use. Half-height 4-5"/ 100-125mm clay or plastic pots are useful for sowing a few seeds.

Fill the receptacle with seed compost, levelling off the top with a stick or board, then press it flat and firm with a pressing board. Soak the seed compost by standing the box or pot in seaweed solution until the compost surface is wet, or by sprinkling with a watering can. Drain before sowing.

Sow thinly and cover with a little seed compost, silver sand, or not at all according to the seeds. Cover the box with glass and newspaper or black polythene. Keep an eye on the seeds, and when they have emerged, take off the paper and allow a little ventilation. Make the air gap bigger each day, and after a few days take the glass off. From now on, see that the seedlings have plenty of light. If you need to water the seedlings, either immerse them in seaweed solution, use a very fine rose on a watering can, or use a handspray.

Pricking out

When the seedlings have developed their first true leaves they need more space and more food. They may be moved into a small pot or into a larger box of potting compost. Much care is needed during this move. The seed compost in which the seedlings are growing should be damp, and the new potting compost should also be damp.

Remove the seedlings carefully from the seed compost. Hold each seedling gently by the leaves, make a hole in the

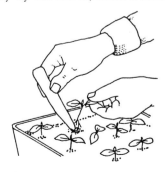

new compost with a pencil or dibber, firm the seedling in, and water in with seaweed solution. Keep the pricked-out seedlings out of the sun for a few days until they start growing. Do not delay pricking out until the seedlings are too large, or the plants will never grow properly.

Transplanting

This is the equivalent of pricking out for bigger plants. They are planted either into larger pots or, having been hardened off, into the garden. It is a good idea to give plants some compost in the bottom of the hole when they are being transplanted: this helps them to get growing again. If you are transplanting during a sunny spell, do it in the evening, and shade the plants with cardbord boxes or paper sacks. In dry weather, water the transplanted plants each morning until they are growing well.

Hardening off

Plants have to adapt slowly to a change in temperature, as well as to wind, sun and rain, especially if they are going to lose some of their roots during transplanting. It is easiest if boxes and pots can be carried to a cold frame. Depending on the weather, the lid of the cold frame can be left open for a few hours each day, and then left open all day for a week. The lid can then be left open a crack at night for a few days, then completely open all night for another week. If you do not have a cold frame, the plants will have to be carried in and out from the windowsill or greenhouse.

Seed storage

In a very good section on the storage of seed in Salter and Bleasdale's *Know and Grow Vegetables*, Dr Gray suggests keeping seed in a sealed glass jar at a temperature of 50°F/10°C with a silica gel to remove moisture, for maximum lifespan. Otherwise, keep your seeds in a dry drawer in a cool room. Do not keep seeds in a shed, in the garage, or in the kitchen. Heat and moisture can kill seeds quite quickly.

Vegetative propagation

With vegetative propagation we can make new plants which have all the characteristics of the parent. Not all plants will grow from cuttings, but many perennials will, and often they root very easily. A cutting forms a callus over the cut stem, leaf or root, and from this the new roots form.

Stem cuttings
Hardwood cuttings are made from mature brown side-shoots from trees and shrubs, taken between July and December. Softwood cuttings are either young shoots from hardwood plants taken in spring, such as fuchsia tips, or from green plants—such as geraniums—in July when nearly-ripened shoots are best. Chrysanthemums, dahlias, delphiniums and lupins can all be cut very young in the spring, when a shoot is taken from below soil level. Never use hollow stems—they will not form roots.

Take cuttings with a sharp knife or razor blade. Cut straight across just below a bud or leaf, or between buds or leaves, or pull a lateral away from a leader with a heel, trimming the frayed edges of skin or bark. Unless taking spring growth, wait until after flowering, and never use flowering stems.

Cuttings should be about 4-12"/10-30cm long (rose cuttings 9"/22cm; medium-sized shrubs 12"/30cm). Tip cuttings of fuchsias should be 2-3"/50-75mm long. Remove the leaves from the part which is to go underground. Hormone rooting compounds are useful for speeding up rooting. Try to find one that is not too poisonous and dangerous to have around.

If hardwood cuttings are strong and hardy they will do fine planted outside in a sandy soil, preferably facing north. They should be ready for transplanting in 9-12 months. Softwoods, heathers and evergreens need to be cosseted. The leaves transpire in the sun and wind, and will die before they can form roots if you are not careful. They will need a box with a plastic or glass lid, or a polythene bag held off the leaves with wire or sticks. To speed things up, and for difficult plants like heathers and resin-producing trees, a mist propagator provides constant warmth and moisture.

Grey-leaved cuttings do not need the same protection, but do need the same shady conditions. All cuttings like crowding—they should be set in the compost nearly touching each other. A good cutting compost can be made with 1 part peat to 1 part horticultural grit. Water the compost thoroughly before the cuttings are put in, then do not water again until the compost is dry 1"/25mm below the surface. Leave them to sweat gently, giving them a little air when you think they are rooting. Give them more air gradually, until you take the cover right off. Transplant them when they are growing well, either into pots, or outside after hardening off.

Leaf cuttings
Leaf cuttings work well for plants like fibrous rooted begonias and African violets. Either the whole leaf and stalk can be used, with the short stalk being pushed into the compost, or the leaf can be cut at several points along the veins, laid flat on the cutting mixture, and weighted down. Keep the cuttings warm and moist.

Root cuttings
When cut into short lengths, the roots of some plants like phlox, anchusa, grape vine and horseradish grow into new specimens. Cut a piece of root

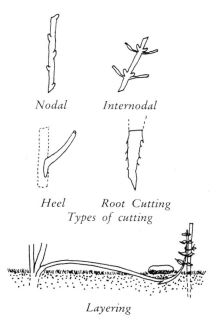

Nodal   Internodal

Heel   Root Cutting
Types of cutting

Layering

1-4"/2.5-10cm long between November and April. For identification, cut the top of the root flat and the bottom sloping. If the root is thick, plant pieces vertically 2"/50mm apart in a cutting mixture, and cover with 1"/25mm of cutting mixture or pure sand. If the root is thin, like phlox, place it horizontally in the cutting compost. Protect from sun, wind and cold. Water when necessary.

Layering

This is a simple method of propagating shrubs and fruit bushes based on the fact that if a branch is wounded and in contact with the soil, it is likely to produce roots.

It is best to do layering in autumn and winter for deciduous trees, in autumn or spring for evergreen trees. Bend a flexible, non-flowering well-grown shoot, and strip off the leaves 9-12"/22-30cm from the tip. Make a small wound on the underside of the branch, bend the branch up at the wound, dig a small hole under the wound, and peg the bent branch into the hole with a piece of wire. Stake the tip upright, and cover the wound with cutting compost. Water the cutting well, and do not allow it to dry out. Check for root growth a year later, and if all is well, sever the branch and transplant it.

Root division

This is a very simple form of propagation. When the plants are dormant, dig them up and divide the root clump. If the plant or shrub is very old, only replant productive parts of the root clump. Divide a large clump with two forks back to back; a small one with your hands and a sharp knife. This method of propagation is very useful for such matted plants as Michaelmas daisy, helenium, phlox and rudbeckias.

Grafting and budding

These techniques are fun, but not often done by most gardeners. If you want to have a go, get a good specialist book from the library.

Planting

Annuals and vegetables are usually grown from seed, but trees, fruit trees and shrubs are most often bought as plants.

Trees and shrubs are supplied by nurseries in three ways: with bare roots, with balled roots, and in containers. No matter which type you buy, the planting hole should be treated according to whether your garden soil is light, medium, or heavy (clay). The infill should not be very different from the surrounding soil, or the roots will have difficulty growing out.

On a light sandy soil, dig a hole 1½-2 times the size of the root ball, and mix the dug-out soil 3 parts soil to 1 part compost or well-rotted manure, plus 1lb/500g hoof and horn, 2lb/1kg coarse bonemeal and 4oz/125g rock potash, before filling in the hole again. For stone fruit, add 3lb/1.5kg of oyster shell chicken grit. On a medium (loam) soil, dig a hole 2-3 times the size of the root ball. Mix the same ingredients into half the soil, then fork this and the unmixed soil into the hole alternately, so there is not a sharp contrast between original and infill soil. On a clay soil, dig a hole twice the size of the root ball, and roughen the sides of the hole to allow the roots to penetrate. Mix the diet supplements with a little soil in the bottom of the hole, and plant the tree or shrub above this in ordinary soil. Put the organic material around the plant, starting 3"/75mm from the trunk, as a mulch. When planting container-grown trees and shrubs you will not need to remove so much soil. Always fork the bottom of the hole to loosen the soil, and after watering give the newly-planted trees and shrubs a mulch of grass mowings or leafmould, again 3"/75mm from the trunk.

Cut off any damaged or diseased wood just above a bud. If a tree needs support, it should be staked when planting to avoid damage to the roots. Stakes 1½"x1½"/32mmx32mm are best for fruit trees. To prevent rotting, they should be treated with creosote or a similar preparation at least three weeks before using, as fresh creosote will damage roots. Drive the stake into the bottom of the planting hole so it gives firm support to the tree. The stake should only reach as far as the first branch, to avoid chafing. Tie the tree loosely to the stake with a nylon stocking or proprietory tie, making sure the tree will not be rubbed by the post. When the tree has settled in the ground, the tie can be tightened. If you have a rabbit or vole problem, protect trunks with plastic covers or wire netting.

Bare root trees and shrubs
These need to be planted between November and March—they are deciduous, and should be dormant when moved. If they arrive when the soil is frozen, snowed over, or too wet, heel them in a 12"/30cm deep trench if you can find some loose soil, otherwise leave them wrapped up in a shed, without heating but protected from frost.

When you are ready for planting, cut any roots that are damaged or withered, and soak the healthy roots overnight in a weak seaweed and water solution. Dig a hole, and make a cone of prepared soil at the bottom. Sit the tree or shrub so that the union between the stock and the scion is at least 4½"/12cm above the soil level, and the old soil line on the trunk is just visible above the new one. Carefully cover the roots with infill mixture or plain soil. When half the hole is filled, tread down and water. Fill in the rest of the hole, treading down firmly and making a basin shape to fill with a final soaking. Mulch well.

Balled root trees and shrubs
These are usually conifers and ever-green ornamentals which have soil around their roots kept in place with sacking. They can be planted between October and late April. The planting hole should be about 6"/15cm deeper than the root ball, and twice as wide. Check that the sacking has not been made rot-resistant—if it has, take it off the root ball very carefully, trying not to disturb the soil. Sit the plant so that the top of the soil ball is 2"/50mm above the soil level, to allow for settling. Fill in and water in stages, untying the top of the sacking when the time comes, and finally filling, firming, and watering in. Mulch well.

Container plants
If you are willing to pay extra, you can buy many trees and shrubs growing in plastic or whalehide pots or bags.

These can be planted at any time of year. The hole should be about 6"/15cm deeper than the container, and twice as wide. Fill the first 6"/15cm with the infill mixture. Cut away or slip off the container, cutting through matted roots round the sides and on the bottom of the root ball with a sharp knife. Fill in the hole in stages, treading and watering each time. Again, mulch well.

Pruning

Pruning is not a mystery: it just needs time and thought. Follow the natural growth habits of the plant, and try to keep it as compact and productive as you want it to be. This means doing a little pruning each year.

Don't grow trees and bushes with a large spreading habit, then try to keep them within bounds by heavy pruning. This is cruel, and a waste of time and effort.

We prune to build up a good-looking strong framework for a plant. With fruit trees, once the framework is established we want to encourage fruiting spurs. On decorative shrubs we want to encourage flowers and leaves, and prevent the plants from becoming straggly. We want to keep hedges dense from bottom to top.

Roughly speaking, the early flowerers need to be pruned before July. For instance, rambler roses, forsythia and winter jasmine should be pruned after they have flowered; raspberries and blackcurrants should be pruned after they have fruited. When plants have their old wood cut out, they put their vigour into new growth for next year.

Later flowerers and fruiters, such as buddleia, hydrangea, apple and pear, should be pruned during their winter dormancy—November in the south of England, February elsewhere.

Prune only if you are sure you are doing the right thing; do not rush in and harm the plant. *The Readers' Digest New Illustrated Guide to Gardening* has a very good section on pruning shrubs as well as clear sections on the pruning of individual fruit trees, and anything else you can think of from heathers and houseplants to rhododendrons. *The Fruit Garden Displayed* from the Royal Horticultural Society has good sections on pruning apple trees and other fruit.

Use sharp secateurs and a sharp saw, making cuts smooth with a sharp knife. When cutting a branch, make sure you cut it underneath first. This prevents tearing of the bark under the branch.

Cut out dead, diseased, feeble and crossing branches. Make sure you cut back into clean healthy wood. Cut above a new bud or flush with the junction of another limb. Never leave a

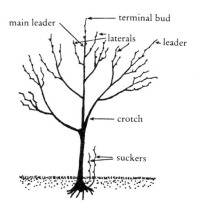

Pruning Terminology (Tree)

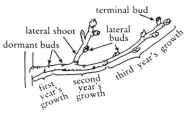

Pruning Terminology (Branch)

snag—fungus will enter and may spread to the rest of the plant. Choose a bud pointing in the direction you want the new growth to go. Make the pruning cut just above, and sloping away from, the bud. If the cut is over ½"/12mm diameter, paint it with Arbrex or the new HDRA *Trichoderma viride*. The former helps callus formation, but the latter also provides an impenetrable barrier against harmful fungi.

Saving seed

It is not difficult to grow plants from your own seed. You will need to grow a few more plants than you can eat, and stop yourself from absentmindedly dead heading all your flowers.

Remove any plants that are not growing true to type before they flower. Isolate the variety from which you want to take seed so that they breed true. Sow early in the year so that the seed can set, ripen and dry before the end of the growing season. Some shrub seeds, such as tree peony and broom, are best sown as soon as you find them; others, like Japanese quinces and camellias, can be stored until the following spring.

Poppies are the easiest seeds to save. They come in their own pepperpot, and if you are not speedy they spread baby plants all around by themselves. Biennial root vegetables are best dug up and stored over winter, then planted out to flower in spring—this includes onions, carrots, parsnip and beetroot. Leeks, salsify and scorzonera can stay in the ground to flower and seed next year. Small seeds are often hard to catch: it is a good idea to tie a plastic bag around the seed head near ripening time.

It is *not* a very good idea to save your own brassica seed, because they all interbreed so easily. Do you want a cross between a cabbage and a cauliflower? Tomatoes are easy to save seed from. Make sure that your variety is true-breeding and not an F_1 hybrid, or you never know what you will end up with. Allow your chosen healthy tomatoes to become fully ripe and just beginning to rot, then wash the seeds out of the mush and dry them on newspaper. If you are going to save seeds from cucumbers, you will have to pollinate the female flowers (the ones with the little cucumbers behind). Find a large male flower, take off the petals, and put it into the female flower. Do this every day for a few days, using a fresh male flower each day, until the female flower starts to wither. Collect these seeds as you would with tomatoes. Marrows, pumpkins, melons, gourds, aubergines and green peppers can all be treated like tomatoes. When saving seed from lettuce, chose the best and biggest and let it bolt, then be quick to catch the seed before it all blows away.

Dry the seeds carefully and store in little labelled packets in a cool airy drawer or sealed jar. Lawrence Hills of the HDRA has written an excellent booklet on this subject called *Save Your Own Seed*.

Weeding

When the gardener has gone this garden
Looks wistful and seems waiting an event.
It is so spruce, a metaphor of Eden
And even more so since the gardener went,

Quietly godlike, but, of course, he had
Not made me promise anything, and I
Had no one tempting me to make the bad
Choice. Yet I still felt lost and wonder why.

Even the beech tree from next door which shares
Its shadow with me, seemed a kind of threat.
Everything was too neat and someone cares

In the wrong way. I need not have stood long
Mocked by the smell of a mown lawn, and yet
I did. Sickness for Eden was so strong.

Elizabeth Jennings
In A Garden

Weeding

Weeding is like housework: it is never finished and it never goes away. From early spring to late autumn the weeds keep springing up, more or less riotously according to the season, the soil and the weather, but always ubiquitous. In winter the gardener can take a rest while the plants are dormant, but at every other time of year there is always some weeding to be done.

Weeds are the most obvious indicator of what kind of treatment a garden is receiving. The first thing any passer-by will notice in a neglected garden is the weeds. If they are not kept under control, they will recolonize the garden at the expense of the plants we have introduced; but if we get too agitated about weeding we will never enjoy being in our garden except when it is snowing.

The word weed comes from the Old English 'wéod', meaning a herb or small plant. The now commonly-accepted definition of a weed is a plant that is growing in what the gardener regards as the wrong place, but it is important to remember that a weed is not a different kind of plant from our cherished garden crops, and it can tell us some very important things about our garden.

To the experienced eye the type and condition of weeds will give away a great deal about the state of the garden. Rose-bay willow-herb, for example, will grow in masses where there is some deficiency in the soil, usually as the result of burning. Poor soil is shown up by the tendency of the weeds to flower and seed as quickly as they can. Groundsel is a particularly good indicator of the state of the soil. In a barren place it will germinate, flower and seed in a matter of weeks. In good soil it will grow several inches tall and produce plenty of green leaf before it flowers. It is not altogether true that the better the soil the worse the weeding problem will be. On better soil they will take longer to seed and be easier to pull up.

A weed is simply a plant that does not fit in with our image of what our garden is to be. So we remove it, but that doesn't mean that it is of no use to us. The amount of weeds we receive as visitors to our gardens is a comforting indication of the health of the land around us. Plenty of weeds suggests plenty of wild flowers outside, plenty of hedgerow and woodland and wild places. Far fewer weeds seed themselves in a city garden than in a garden next to a meadow. If our garden lies adjacent to woods or fields, the price we pay will be nettles and couch grass finding their way under our fences, and clouds of dandelion seedlings coming over the wall with every summer breeze. If we have beautifully weeded gardens all around us our neighbours will have done a lot of work for us, but we will also probably be made aware that there is a standard to be kept up.

We need weeds as the basis of our recycling system: they are a vital source of compost material. No weed is useless, but some are more helpful than others—nettles and chickweed make excellent compost, clovers store valuable nitrogen in their root nodules and enrich the soil wherever they grow. Weeds that have formed seeds have to

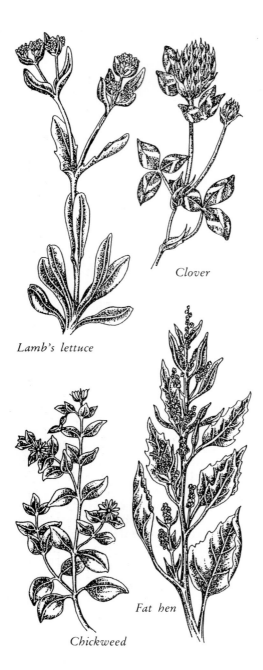

Clover

Lamb's lettuce

Fat hen

Chickweed

rot down at a temperature hot enough to kill the new seeds; in a heap that is too cool the perennial weeds will not rot down, but flourish. Many a heap has been opened to find healthy white shoots of couch grass already rampant. If your compost-making abilities cannot cope, then such weeds must be burned. As an alternative to burning, you can have a noxious weeds pile covered in black polythene, which will rot down and be safe in a few years. Weeding is not just a matter of removing unwanted plants; it is a process of collecting essential nutrients.

So no weed goes to waste. There are, however, different possible destinations for many common weeds. Wild plants provide a varied and relatively unpolluted source of human nutrition, and are most easily gathered from our own piece of land, where we know they are unaffected by exhaust fumes, liver fluke, or other external hazards. Summer salads can be gathered out of the garden without touching our careful rows of lettuce and tomato. Chickweed, young dandelion leaves, sorrel, fat hen seedlings, lamb's lettuce, perhaps with a judicious mix of young hawthorn or beech leaves, can all be used to ring the changes. A wide variety can go into soups or be cooked as vegetables, such as nettles and ground elder. Almost all edible varieties can be made into teas, some of which have medicinal qualities that were once highly prized, such as couch grass for rheumatism and kidney and bladder troubles, and horsetail for skin complaints. Dandelion coffee—made from the roots—is a much cheaper form of caffeine-less drink than anything to be found in a shop (though it does take some work), and almost anything edible can be made into a wine in which to drown the gardener's sorrows.

Any gardener who also keeps live-stock will know that weeds are an excellent source of fresh green food for poultry or rabbits. Some are treats, such as groundsel for hens and dande-lion for rabbits. As a general rule, evergreens tend to be poisonous both for humans and animals.

I would recommend to any gardener wishing to make fuller use of weeds a book by Audrey Wynne Hatfield called *How To Enjoy Your Weeds*, which is full of good information about the most common garden weeds, and contains recipes and eminently practi-cal advice for making the most of every one.

When we weed we are not merely tidying things up; we are recycling plant material. The weeds cannot remain where they are, because they rob the soil of nutrients needed for the plants we have chosen, and being native plants, they will grow vigorously, and choke and smother the tenderer culti-vated varieties. In nature, every plant produces as many seedlings as possible, and in the wild, thousands of plants will struggle together, competing with each other to survive. Much of human intervention is to pre-empt the natural process of selection, then to eliminate competition in favour of the plants selected.

If our weeds are for recycling, then clearly the way we weed must leave the plants in a condition where they can be used. If the plants are covered with poison they cannot be used either to feed the land or people. Weeds that are destroyed by herbicides have to be burnt or thrown out, quite apart from the effects of the herbicides on the rest of the garden. If we are to garden without waste, then we want to ensure that our weeds are not contaminated, any more than the vegetables we eat are contaminated, by harmful chemicals.

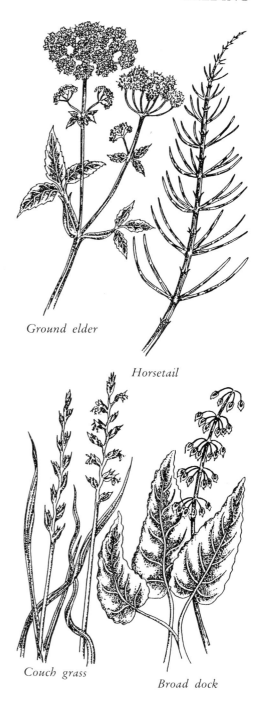

Ground elder

Horsetail

Couch grass

Broad dock

WEEDING

Many garden centres and shops will give us the impression that we need an armoury of chemicals to deal with weeds, implying that the use of these methods will relieve us of a huge and monotonous task. The reality is that weeding is not very daunting if we know how to set about it, and if we plant our garden to make it as labour-saving as possible.

In an established garden where the mass of perennial weeds have been eliminated long ago, weeds will either be annuals, or small perennials which have no sooner established themselves than they are removed again. There will be no vast root system of nettles or horsetails, and no huge tapering roots of dandelions or docks. In these circumstances the weeding should never assume immense proportions as long as it is done fairly regularly. By far the easiest way to cover the ground is to weed with a hoe. In the vegetable garden this is usually easy enough, as the vegetables are uniform and most often planted in rows, so the hoe can be run between them with little effort. You can hoe around shrubs in their beds, and a hoe can be used carefully between herbaceous plants. The important thing is not to disturb the root systems—hoeing should be a surface activity, and the hoe should be kept a respectful distance from small plants.

In dry weather hoed weeds can be left to dry out on the surface and die. In wet weather they are more likely to re-establish themselves. If there are masses of weeds which have gone to seed, everything is best removed immediately to the compost heap, as otherwise all the weeding will have done is to distribute the seeds nicely.

Obviously the less bare ground there is, the less weeding there is to do. Bare soil is not a natural phenomenon, and it does the soil itself no good. Nature will immediately seek to redeem things by filling it up as fast as possible. In our garden we will have areas of bare soil, in order to provide as much nutrition and light as possible for individual plants, and eliminate competition. But our aim should be to have as little bare ground as is compatible with providing the best for each plant.

Mulch is the obvious way to deal with large areas that would otherwise need constant weeding. The most effective mulch against perennial weeds is black plastic. This excludes both light and air, smothering the weeds beneath, until the root system can renew itself no longer. It is useful for controlling weeds around trees or shrub beds. When the plants themselves grow large enough to form an effective ground cover, the polythene can be removed. It is possible to cover polythene in an ornamental garden with a layer of woodchips or leafmould if it is too unsightly.

Other mulches are less drastic in their effect. Persistent weeds will in time find their way through bark chips, straw, leafmould, peat, grass mowings or anything else organic. In the end they, like the garden plants, will draw nourishment from the mulch itself, but continual application of mulch will smother the weeds in the soil and reduce the weeding problem to a minimum.

Sometimes handweeding is bound to be necessary, around bulbs or in rock gardens, and in between the vegetables within rows where the hoe cannot reach. Handweeding is best done literally by hand, with a handfork to help with deeper-rooted species. Once reduced to a minimum it is a pleasant job. It is important to move around as little as possible, as a human body is a large and clumsy thing to manoeuvre round delicate plants. Handweeding would ideally be done from a magic carpet suspended over the soil. The handfork is useful alongside the hoe to root out perennials with taproots before they have had time to establish themselves. It is no use hoeing the tops off dandelions and docks; they will merely send out more shoots from the piece of root left below the surface. Other deep-rooted weeds can be effectively hoed, such as hogweed, where if the crown is removed the long roots die away.

Gardeners faced with a new patch of land, or a garden quite overgrown with perennial weeds, will have to take a more drastic approach. Probably every garden has its *bête noire* among the perennial weeds, a species which is always there ready to take control again the moment an opportunity is offered. For some gardeners the scourge may be couch grass, whose white roots appear with every forkful of turned soil, strong enough to bore through a bulb or potato, and ready to form a complete underground mat of vegetation, very useful for holding down a sand-dune, but not so helpful among the shrubs and vegetables. For others the greatest affliction may be ground elder, whose sturdy pairs of green leaves threaten the vegetable patch from under every hedge and wall. Some may have cause to dread horsetails, whose roots go down eight feet, forming a massive underground network to catch the best nutrition the soil can offer. In places where there has been human habitation which has since gone to ruin, nettles and rose-bay willow-herb are a blessing for hiding desolation and dereliction, but become a nuisance when anybody tries to make a garden in that place again. Docks will rejoice in neglected cultivated ground, and hogweed will send up endless seedlings in soil that has once been dug. Faced with a problem like this, the gardener who does not want to poison the soil, leaving chemical traces that take years of organic gardening to eliminate, must look at other alternatives: to use a relatively safe poison like ammonium sulphamate, or to keep digging.

In an established garden one doesn't want to see a garden fork being used in beds and borders, or in fruit gardens among established root systems. Springtime forking over is best applied to open ground which has waited all winter for vegetables to be planted. Roots hate to be disturbed, and if the garden is weeded regularly it should never be necessary for weeding purposes. But on new or reclaimed ground the perennial roots need to be dug up, ploughed in, or chopped up as small as possible. This is the place for the mechanical rotavator, or failing that, for heavy spadework. That won't be the end of the story for the perennials that form widespread root systems. It will take years of clearing roots and slicing off new shoots to bring the perennial weeds under control. Eventually, continual removal of the green shoots will kill the root system beneath, and in more open ground, this is the only way to deal with ground elder when it has inextricably woven its way among the other plants. This is the place for the black polythene mulch.

Friends, Pests and Diseases

O universal mother, who dost keep
From everlasting thy foundations deep,
Eldest of things, Great Earth, I sing of thee;
All shapes that have their dwelling in the sea,
All things that fly, or on the ground divine
Live, move, and there are nourished—these are thine;
These from thy wealth thou dost sustain; from thee
Fair babes are born, and fruits on every tree
Hang ripe and large—revered divinity!

attributed to Homer
translated by Shelley
Hymn to Earth, Mother of All

Friends, Pests and Diseases

From time to time every gardener will discover holes in cabbage leaves, greenfly on roses, or a carrot crop whose leaves have turned yellow. *Don't panic!*.

First we had better consider why the plants are unable to resist the pests and diseases.

Plants, like humans, can suffer from various types of stress, which make them susceptible to illness. Sometimes, desperate to get started, we sow too early in spring—the soil is cold and wet and our seeds rot. Compacted soil can prevent roots getting down into the soil and shoots from reaching the surface. Overcrowding in seedlings can invite fungi, and in adult plants lack of light and nutrition lead to spindly growth. Starvation and lack of water will make a plant vulnerable to aphids, and bad drainage encourages fungal diseases. We can end up with rows of fungicides and pesticides simply because we grow our plants in soils deficient in humus and biological activity.

Too much sun, or too little, will upset different plants—and so will sudden changes in environmental conditions. An excess of nitrates, organic or inorganic, will encourage the lush growth favoured by sucking insects and fungi. We can upset our trees with unskilled pruning, and we can cause damage by planting the wrong plants next to each other. It is best for our plants and for ourselves if we learn to handle them gently, and find out more about their individual needs.

The best gardening, which cares for the plants and deals with unwanted organisms swiftly, gently and effectively, calls for maximum concentration, time, involvement and loving care. Practically, this may not be possible. Perhaps we won't get the magnifying glass out to look at the creatures on our fruit trees this year; perhaps next year we will. Maybe puffing derris powder rather than 'Long-Lasting Quick Death Spray' on the flea beetles eating the turnip seedlings is the best loving care we can offer just at the moment.

Pests and diseases specific to particular plants will be given in the plant lists. The list that follows in this chapter covers common problems that arise with more than one species, together with remedies that you can use to help your plants. The list also includes a number of 'garden friends' to cheer us up.

As you read this chapter, it will become clear that there is not much being said about flowering ornamentals. In general we will tolerate creatures eating our flowering plants so long as they are not spoiling the looks and the scent too much. But raspberries with grubs in them and lettuces covered with slugs are not at all appealing. In the ornamental garden there are seldom enough of the same species grouped together to allow pests and diseases to build up. In the vegetable garden, however, we almost inevitably have this problem; not only this, but we purposely breed vegetables for the size of their edible parts, which makes them particularly attractive to hungry creatures other than ourselves. If we keep an eye on our flowers, remove sickly ones, clear away dead leaves and stalks at the end of the season, and keep our plants well fed and watered, then greenfly may be the most serious problem we encounter.

We can give vegetables a helping hand to avoid pests and diseases by setting up a rotation system to prevent their occupying the same piece of ground more than once in three years. Correct feeding, watering, drainage and cultivation will reduce problems to a minimum even with vulnerable crops like potatoes, brassicas and tomatoes. These particular crops are subject to so many potential pests and diseases that a book with colour photographs of them all can be quite frightening. Take heart—they don't all happen at once, and precautions and vigilance will ensure that only a few pests and diseases enjoy our crops.

Even the best-kept garden, however, will suffer. Correct drainage will help to lower the slug population, for example, but even on beautifully-drained raised beds there can be enough slugs in early spring to devastate the struggling cloche-grown lettuce and carrots, or the newly-germinating runner beans. In recent years I have been desperate about the devastation, and have resorted to dangerous metaldehyde bait. True, I do not deserve the title 'organic gardener', but the slugs were just too quick and too many for me, and I promise I'll try Fertosan and beer traps again next year.

As a gardener I can never be careful or vigilant enough. Gardening teaches that there is a right moment to act, and for want of that action a crop or a plant can be lost. But there is always another season, another year in which to try again.

In order to identify pests and diseases quickly and correctly, use a well-illustrated and clear reference book. The Ministry of Agriculture, Fisheries and Food Bulletins published by HMSO, and the *Expert* series published by PBI are both excellent for diagnosis, but do not be fooled by their 'simple' chemical remedies. The effects of these chemicals are not simple and straightforward—it is only the mixing and spraying that are simple. These complex poisons have many obnoxious effects, causing harm in bodies from bacterial to human, virus to peregrine falcon. Who wants their babies to crawl on poisoned soil, or ducks and hedgehogs to eat poisoned slugs? Use these books to diagnose what is wrong, then consider a caring approach to putting things right now, and preventing the trouble arising again next season.

Though it may sometimes appear that way, pests and diseases are not out to get gardeners. However much chemical companies may foster the idea, we are not engaged in a war within our gardens, though nature is not going to do us any extra favours.

When we have to kill something, the substance used does some other harm, however slight, so it is best not to use any poisons casually or as a preventative. Even a heavy water spray on roses or fruit trees, at the wrong time, may wash away large numbers of beneficial insects, and leave the plants susceptible to fast-breeding plant eaters.

So we need to kill as little as possible, and try to create an ecosystem that works in our favour. Feed the birds in winter, and allow the garden to be attractive to hedgehogs, frogs and toads. Don't keep it so neat that there is nowhere for these helpful creatures to hide. If you fork gently around the raspberry canes in autumn and winter, pied wagtails and robins will pick out the chrysalids of the raspberry beetle (*Bytunus tormentosa*). On the edge of my vegetable garden there is a yew tree, and on the other side a big elder bush, both of which give berries and shelter for birds.

It is good to remember the creatures that live in our gardens, going about their business and helping us in the process. Lacewings and ladybirds are useful predators of aphids—there are 49 native species of lacewing and 39 of ladybirds. In addition there are sixteen species of capsid bug, which are predators of fruit tree red spider mite, and five species of anthocorid bug.

Ladybirds and their larvae are the most popular of the garden predators, although they are not the most efficient. It is rumoured that they can eat up to fifty aphids a day, but that would depend on the species of ladybird, the species of aphid, and the density of the aphid population. The fully-grown hoverfly larva can eat an aphid in about four minutes, and they are deliberately placed near aphid colonies at the egg stage. The larvae hunt out the aphids and, unlike the two-spot ladybird, are not permanently driven off a plant by ants.

During the winter it would be a good idea to read *Beneficial Insects and Mites* (published by HMSO), and Michael Chinery's *The Natural History of the Garden*. They will give you a different perspective on your pest problems. We are not alone—there is so much going on, secretly, in an organic garden. While you are doing some reading, try two of Lawrence Hills' booklets from the Henry Doubleday Research Association called *Vegetable Pest and Disease Control* and *Fruit Pest and Disease Control*—they are both very clear and detailed about what to do when problems arise. The Soil Association booklet, *Friend and Foe in the Garden*, is also both helpful and straightforward.

Friends, pests and diseases

F = Friend; P = Pest; D = Disease

ANTS P

Protect aphids against lacewing larvae, and tend also to drive hoverfly and ladybird larvae away from aphids. While ladybirds may desert aphid-infested plants as a result, hoverfly larvae will not. Also said to remove ladybird eggs.

Herbal remedy: Scatter pennyroyal or spearmint leaves.

Companion planting: Mint or tansy by the kitchen door stops ants from coming into the house.

Chemical control: Mix thoroughly equal parts of borax and icing sugar, and sprinkle where you see the ants, protecting from rain where necessary. A solution of pyrethrum and derris mixture poured into the nest will kill ants.

ANTHOCORID (ORCHARD) BUG F

Anthocoris nemorum appears abundantly in neglected orchards, or on fruit trees which are not drenched with pesticides. Some winter on the fruit trees, and some move to nearby hedgerows. Eats eggs of red spider mites found in fruit trees in autumn and spring, and on warm days in winter, so only use tar oil washes in January. An adult can kill about fifty red spider mites a day, and during its lifetime will consume 500-600 aphids.

Four other species are active in the garden, feeding on aphids and scale insects, apple suckers, capsid bugs, caterpillars, midges, mites and apple blossom weevil larvae and pupae.

APHIDS P

Very common, small, soft-bodied, pear-shaped insects which feed on plant sap.

Tricks and traps: Use organic feeds and not too much manure in order to produce less sappy growth.

Biological control: Encourage hoverflies and ladybirds, their natural predators.

Chemical control: Spray with soft soap, derris, pyrethrum or nicotine soap.

BATS F

Very useful creatures: each bat eats half its own weight in insects in a night. In Britain it is illegal to interfere with the resting places of bats.

BEES F

Bees—and other insects—pollinate our fruit and vegetables, so it is worth planting the flowers they feed on. Grow plenty of single flowers, as double flowers have less pollen.

Early bees enjoy aubretia, polyanthus, yellow alyssum and lungwort (*Pulmonaria*); summer bees like borage, hyssop, lemon balm, sage, annual alyssum, ageratum, lavender and thyme; autumn bees buddleia, Michaelmas daisies and the large pink stonecrop (ice plant).

BIRDS F and P

Birds pull up onion sets and white plastic labels, eat brassica plants, and can decimate fruit buds and fruit. But birds are useful in the garden. Robins and wagtails eat raspberry beetle grubs and caterpillars; nuthatches eat codling moths; tits and finches eat insects which live on buds; and starlings will feed on wireworms. If, however, the pests have been poisoned with organo-chlorine and organo-phosphorus pesticides, they can kill, maim or render infertile birds and their fledglings.

Pied Wagtail

A bird table and water supply will encourage birds. Bushes which are particularly attractive to birds include elder, wild cherry, dogwood, berberis and cotoneaster. Nesting boxes and thick hedges will also encourage birds.

To keep birds off crops, netting is the most efficient but most expensive method. Try cotton thread strung between the rows, or shiny, noisy bird-scarers (which you need to change every few months when they get used to them). A cat in the garden is very effective, but can also be a pest.

BLACKFLY P

This black aphid is a real problem on broad beans; also feeds on French and runner beans, beet, rhubarb, spinach, turnips, dahlias, nasturtiums, poppies, fat hen and thistles.

Tricks and traps: Keep soil cool and moist to help plants. When blackfly appear, cut off 3″/75mm of new growth from the broad bean, and eat it, burn it or compost it. November-sown longpods are tougher than spring-sown ones; a late Windsor variety sown in early June to crop in August and September will escape the blackfly, which will have flown off to its winter homes in spindle (*Euonymus*), viburnums and syringa (*Philadelphus*). In mild areas they can winter on shepherd's purse and other weeds, and so do not have to lay eggs.

Even if you eradicate all your host shrubs you can still inherit blackfly from your neighbours' gardens. Spray shrubs in spring with quassia, derris or nicotine before aphids transfer to flowering broad beans.

Herbal remedy: Garlic, stinging nettle and seaweed solution sprays help against aphids, but they are not certain preventatives.

Companion planting: Winter and summer savory are said to repel blackfly. In dry sunny areas, spinach between the broad beans helps keep the soil cool.

Biological control: Natural predators are ladybirds and the larvae of hoverflies. Hoverflies can be attracted by planting aromatic herbs at ends of rows.

Chemical control: Use sprays in the evening to spare the bees: soap or soft soap solution, quassia or nicotine. Try to resist pyrethrum, derris, or anything stronger.

BLACK-KNEED CAPSID F

Adults are 3/16"/5mm long, males being rich green with dark red eyes, females having paler bodies and eyes. Their knees are black. Nymphs are smaller and paler versions of the adults. They live on a wide variety of trees, and are at their most hungry nymph stage during June and July, the adults continuing to feed into October.

Black-kneed capsid adults and nymphs are voracious eaters of fruit tree red spider mite, plus leaf-hoppers, aphids, thrips and caterpillars, and sometimes each other. Females can eat 60-70 red spider mites a day; nymphs 5-40—black-kneed capsids can stabilize red spider mite populations.

Not affected by winter tar-oil washes as they do not winter on the trees, but killed by most summer insecticides. Safest sprays: soft soap, quassia chips, derris or nicotine.

BOTRYTIS D

A grey mould fungus. In a wet year spoils strawberries when it grows on leaves, stalks and fruit. Lettuce plants are infected through dead or damaged areas, leading to brownish-red rot when it reaches the stem. Tomato stalks develop grey furry patches; may spread to flower stalks causing fruit drop. Fruit stalks and leaves of cucumbers are affected, and greenhouse and tunnel-grown cucumbers are most likely to suffer. Red and white currants may suffer die-back of whole branches.

Tricks and traps: Encouraged by too much water and not enough fresh air—strawberry plants wrapped around with straw in a wet summer are the perfect environment. Plant strawberry rows 18"/45cm apart, and clear the bed very thoroughly in autumn. In a dry autumn burn off straw and strawberry leaves to kill fungus spores. If the straw never dries out, cut leaves off, remove all runners, rake or pull off the straw, and compost the lot. If all else fails, grow 'Red Gauntlet', which only has a moderate flavour, but is better than a mass of mouldy strawberries. Rotate strawberries and keep away from shady damp spots. Botrytis in lettuce, tomatoes and cucumbers is encouraged by cold weather, overcrowding, roughness in handling, overwatering, and inadequate ventilation in greenhouses and polythene tunnels. Badly-affected plants should be burnt or put into a polythene bag in the dustbin. Small winter greenhouse lettuce resist botrytis better than lettuces which are larger at the coldest period. When red and white currants suffer die-back, cut affected branch to healthy wood and burn it. Try a 30% urine and water spray in winter, and a seaweed solution sprayed every 2 weeks in summer.

Chemical control: Dust strawberry plants with flowers of sulphur; water lettuce with a solution of 1oz/30g of potassium permanganate dissolved in 2gall/9l of cold water, used when freshly mixed; try bicarbonate of soda in solution.

CABBAGE WHITE BUTTERFLY P

There are 3 cabbage white butterflies, but the green-veined white is more interested in various cruciferous weeds than in our cultivated brassicas and nasturtiums.

The large white female lays batches of conical yellow eggs on leaves of brassicas and nasturtiums during May. Yellowish-green caterpillars, splotched with black, feed voraciously in June. These then pupate, and an even larger generation start to feed in August and September, reducing cabbage and nasturtium leaves to a skeleton.

The small white lays her eggs singly, and they are much more difficult to see. The velvety-green caterpillars are also difficult to see, lying along the ribs of the leaves. They pupate at about the same time as the large white.

Tricks and traps: Inspect undersides of brassica and nasturtium leaves when white butterflies are hovering around them. Remove and crush any eggs. Try mixing ½ pt/300ml milk in 1gall/4.5l water, sprayed onto the leaves in May, and repeated every 3 weeks, hoping that rain does not wash it off in the interim.

Inspect leaves frequently for caterpillars. Look out also for the beige mottled cabbage moth while you are at it—there are not so

many of them but they can cause more damage than cabbage whites by eating into the heart of brassica plants.

Companion planting: Aromatic herbs and tomatoes grown near brassicas and nasturtiums may help to keep cabbage white butterflies away.

Biological control: Aromatic herbs and flowers will attract valuable ichneumon flies, which lay their eggs inside the bodies of the caterpillars of butterflies and moths, their larvae feeding on the caterpillars. *Pteromalus puparum*, one of the commonest chalcids, parasitizes white butterflies —a useful predator to encourage. Spray with *Bacillus thuringiensis*, taking special care to spray under the leaves. This bacillus is eaten by the caterpillars, and kills them without harming anything else.

Chemical control: Not usually necessary; if you feel you need one, use a pyrethrum-derris mixture or nicotine spray.

CANKER D

A general term for a diseased infectious area on the bark of trees and shrubs, a depression which is dead in the middle and rough round the edges. Cankers start from damage to the bark, sometimes from hailstones or children's feet, but usually from insect bites or scab fungus. A specific canker fungus grows on apple and pear trees; there are fungi specific to larch and poplar; and bacterial canker can have a disastrous effect on cherry trees. Some fungi attack a range of trees and shrubs. Many cankers are the result of both fungal and bacterial action.

Tricks and traps: There are a limited number of things you can do to help the plant, but they are effective. The most important is to grow varieties that are canker-resistant. If you inherit cankered fruit trees, especially well-established trees of varieties that you particularly like, cut out and paint the affected areas each year. Keep an eye out for sunken patches, using a hand-lens. Winter pruning will help. If neglected, the disease spreads down the branches with the rain. Cut out the diseased area to the living tissue; it may be useful to clean it out with a chisel. Cover the wound immediately with bituminous paint or a solution of *Trichoderma* powder.

Chemical control: If out of control, spray in January with Burgundy mixture.

CARROT FLY P

A greenish-black fly ¼"/6mm long. The larvae eat parsnips, parsley and celery as well as carrots. Its natural food is wild carrot and cow parsley. It lays its eggs near carrot seedlings in May and June, and the grubs can wipe out the whole crop. The second laying is in August and September; although the carrots and parsnips may look fine, carrot fly grubs will have made them useless for storage.

Tricks and traps: If carrot fly larvae have been in the crop, remove all the plants very carefully in the autumn, putting them right in the middle of a hot compost heap. If you cannot guarantee that your compost heap is hot enough, seal them in a plastic bag and put them in the dustbin. Dig over the ground 2 or 3 times in autumn so birds can find and eat larvae, or bring in chickens.

Sow carrot seed at ½"/12mm intervals, so you do not have to thin much; the smell of the crushed leaves attracts carrot fly from miles away. If you have to thin, do not leave thinnings on the soil, earth up remaining carrots, firm the soil by treading, and water with seaweed solution: carrot flies like to lay their eggs in disturbed soil. A fairly effective protection is old clear polythene used as a 3½'/1.2m high fence all round the carrot plot. Cloches of glass, polythene or Papronet will work best. To mask the smell, sprinkle paraffin-soaked sand along the rows, or hang creosoted rags or string. Lawn mowings are not as effective, but smell nicer, and an occasional sprinkling of lawn mowings can be added throughout the season, then dug into the soil. Avoiding action can be taken by sowing a quick-growing carrot like 'Early Autumn King' in May or June.

Herbal remedies: Sprinkle dried aromatic herbs or garlic powder when sowing, or give a garlic spray after sowing. These remedies are most effective if done when carrot fly are around—paint a board yellow and cover it lightly with tree grease, stand it near the carrots and parsnips, and see how many carrot flies stick to it each day. Start applying herbal remedies when flies appear in fair numbers.

Companion planting: Onions, garlic or leeks help mask the smell of carrots. The masking crop and the carrots should be planted in a 2:1 proportion, which makes life a bit difficult; the masking effect of onions is lost when the onions stop growing.

CENTIPEDES F

Above-ground species are speedy, shiny carnivorous insects, light brown with long flat bodies divided into segments, each segment bearing one pair of legs. Soil-living centipedes are thinner, longer and paler.

They eat insects, grubs, slugs, woodlice, mites and leatherjackets; also spiders, which is not such a good thing.

CHAFERS P

The problem chafers are the cockchafer or maybug, the garden chafer, and the rose chafer. All have large dirty-white larvae, fat and half-curled, which are often turned up when digging. They spend up to 3 years underground, eating the roots of grass, some herbaceous and alpine plants, dahlias, zinnias, potatoes, shrubs and fruit trees. Adults eat the leaves of these plants too, as well as rose and strawberry flowers, and the skins of young apples and pears.

Tricks and traps: A few chickens kept in a portable run will clear out most soil pests, including chafer grubs. Adults may be picked off small plants and roses, or shaken off fruit trees on to a sheet and given to the chickens. A mulch of oak leaves or crushed bark helps repel chafers, as well as cutworms and slugs. Forking over the soil in winter exposes the chafer grubs to birds and frost.

CHERRY BLACKFLY P

A black aphid which feeds on shoots and leaves of ornamental and fruiting cherries. It checks growth and dirties the leaves.

Tricks and traps: Can be discouraged by putting a grease band around the tree trunk to catch ants which would protect and encourage the aphids.

Chemical control: Spray with nicotine and soft soap early in the season, to keep the numbers down before predators like ladybirds and hoverflies arrive in July.

CHICKENS F

If you can keep chickens away from your vegetables and flowers, they are very useful friends to have in the garden, eating many soil pests. They should be moved fairly frequently, ideally in a mobile run or 'ark', and before they have a chance to create dustbaths or mudholes.

CORAL SPOT D

A fungus which produces pink spots or dark red cushions, usually on dead wood but sometimes on live growth. Lives on red and white currants, causing sudden wilting and death of whole branches when in full fruit. Also causes problems in ornamental trees and shrubs.

Tricks and traps: Burn any dead wood in the garden. When doing pruning or branch cutting, cut back to a joint or to the trunk —dead snags may allow an entrance for the disease. When cutting out infected wood, cut back to healthy wood. Paint wounds with bituminous paint within minutes, or *Trichoderma* paste within 48 hours. Do not feed currants or ornamentals with a lot of manure—use only compost or other low-nitrate organic mulch.

CUTWORMS P

Fat grey-brown caterpillars 1½-2"/35-50mm long, bigger than leatherjackets and without their funny wriggle. They are the caterpillars of the turnip moth, the heart moth, the dart moth and the yellow underwing. They work at night, eating through the stems of newly-planted cabbages, turnips, chrysanthemums, dahlias, asters, marigolds, zinnias, tomatoes and others, and hide in the soil by day.

Tricks and traps: Can be picked off the top of the soil at night; very early morning is best. Cut the top and bottom off milk cartons or tins, or use toilet roll inners, pushed into the soil to surround the seedlings—this will also help against leatherjackets, and a little against carrot fly. A mulch of oak leaves or crushed bark may help.

Biological control: A hedgehog in the garden will keep it free of cutworms.

Chemical control: Mix 1oz/30g borax, 1oz/30g icing sugar and 3lb/1.3k bran with enough water to moisten, and place under slates so you kill cutworms but not birds.

DAMPING OFF D

A fungus, causing seedlings to wither and blacken at the base before falling over and dying.

Tricks and traps: Indoors, use sterilized compost, sow thinly, water in the morning and do not over-water, ventilate well, and provide the right amount of heat. When giving a seed tray a soaking, do it with a seaweed solution, and water with seaweed solution when pricking out. Outdoors, do not sow in cold wet soil, sow thinly and do not overwater. Remove any fallen and blackened seedlings, and water the rest with seaweed solution.

EARTHWORM F

The gardener's best friend: soil would never have formed without the action of earthworms. Their tunnels form a network in the soil which allows air to circulate and excess water to drain away. This aeration helps the roots directly, and encourages the speedy decay of dead material and the release of plant nutrients. Wormcasts are very rich in nutrients and minerals which had been washed down to deeper levels.

EARWIG F and P

Chews up chrysanthemum and dahlia petals, but also eats scale insects, small flies and aphids. Sometimes eats leaves of beet-root, parsnips and carrots, and while hunting for insects on fruit trees will have a quick snack of leaves.

Tricks and traps: Place a half-closed empty matchbox or a plantpot filled with hay at the top of the chrysanthemum and dahlia canes. If wrecking a fruit tree, tie cloths around the branches and shake them out once a week—well away from the garden.

EELWORM (NEMATODE) P

There are millions of eelworms in the soil, and most never bother us. Some of these microscopic transparent creatures are parasites on the roots of potatoes, tomatoes, cucumbers, roses and chrysanthemums. When plants are bothered by eelworm, stems shorten and thicken, foliage becomes pale, and roots become galled, all as a result of sap being sucked out of the plant and poison being pumped in.

Tricks and traps: Best protection for vegetables is crop rotation to prevent a build-up of the cysts, which can stay sleeping in the soil for six years or more.

Companion planting: The *Tagetes* family exude a substance from their roots, said to kill eelworms. The most effective is *Tagetes minutae*, which is a huge plant best used in a whole patch in rotation. French marigolds (*T. patula*) have been used in rose-beds with success.

FIREBLIGHT D

A devastating bacterial disease of trees and shrubs of the *Roseacae* family, especially pears. Spreads via pollinating insects, and causes leaves and flowers to wither, but leaves do not fall. Spreads into twigs and branches, which often exude a bacterial slime; the tree or shrub then dies. Afflicted trees and shrubs should be pulled up and burned. The Ministry of Agriculture, Fisheries and Food should be notified.

FLEA BEETLE P

Makes holes in leaves, and may destroy seedlings of brassicas, radish, turnip and wallflowers.

Tricks and traps: Lawrence Hills describes a useful 'flea beetle trolley' in *Grow Your Own Fruit and Vegetables*.

Companion planting: Bergamot helps discourage flea beetle.

Chemical control: Dust with derris powder.

FUNGI D

The majority of fungi get their nourishment from dead material, but some eat living organisms. They cause many diseases, including damping off, wheat rust, smuts, wilts, mildews, club root, potato blight, botrytis, root rots, storage rots, scab, canker, silver leaf, peach leaf curl, honey fungus, coral spot and Dutch elm disease.

Tricks and traps: Build up soil fertility with organic materials, practise crop rotation, avoid planting and sowing in cold soil, and be careful not to overwater and overcrowd. Keep covered spaces well ventilated, and spray regularly with seaweed solution. If anything is badly afflicted, pull it up, and either burn it or put it in the dustbin in a sealed polythene bag.

GOOSEBERRY SAWFLY P

Eggs are laid on gooseberry, blackcurrant and whitecurrant bushes, and on the flowering *Ribes*. Lays its first batch of 20-30 white eggs per leaf in April or May, in rows close to the midrib. This generation lays in June, and their young lay in September. Caterpillars have black heads and green and black spotted bodies with orange marks. They are small but hungry creatures, and can strip a plant of its leaves very quickly. Other sawfly larvae eat the leaves of Solomon's Seal, and the larvae of several species eat rose leaves. Some of these larvae are called slugworms, such as the pear slugworm, which scrapes away the surfaces of pear and cherry leaves.

Tricks and traps: Look for eggs and young caterpillars before they spread out to strip the leaves. Pick off and burn affected leaves. It is impossible to spot them all, so spray as soon as you see signs of caterpillars.

Chemical control: Spray with derris or nicotine soap.

GREENFLY P

A green aphid: the one that bothers us most is the large rose aphid, which can multiply very quickly, spoiling rose flowers and leaves and weakening the whole plant.

Tricks and traps: Make sure plants are not suffering from stress: too much or too little food, too much or too little water, or not enough light.

Herbal remedy: Spray with nettle and seaweed spray.

Companion planting: Chives, parsley or garlic grown around rose trees may help repel greenfly. Poached egg plant (*Limnanthes douglasii*) or *Convolvulus tricolor* 'Blue Ensign' near roses or other infested plants will attract hoverflies; they will lay their eggs in the nearby aphids and destroy them.

Biological control: Hoverflies, lacewings and ladybirds will eat many greenfly. It may be necessary to get rid of any ants which are protecting the greenfly from predators.

Chemical control: Spray with soft soap or soapflakes and water. Soap takes the waxy coat off the greenfly and the insect will dry up. Wash sprayed plants with clean water soon after spraying, or the soap will clog leaf and stem pores. A home-made spray of rhubarb or elder leaves will kill greenfly. Pyrethrum, derris and nicotine sprays in summer will all kill greenfly—spray early or late in the day to avoid bees. In winter, spray rose stock with a tar-oil wash in December or January—this will kill the greenfly but not the lacewings, ladybirds and hoverflies, which all winter elsewhere. Only use chemical killers if you have to.

GROUND BEETLE F

The violet ground beetle is most common, black with iridescent violet margins to its wing-cases, but there are many other species, all useful to us. They are very active, and live in soil in damp shady places.

Ground beetles feed on cabbage root fly eggs; in a study it was found that of the 95% of cabbage root fly eggs that failed to produce flies, 90% were eaten by ground beetles. Some ground beetles eat slugs, and some are thought to eat lettuce root aphids.

HEDGEHOG F

A well-known if infrequent visitor to most people's gardens; it feeds on worms, slugs, beetles, cutworms, and millipedes. Milk in the autumn with bread soaked in it will help them gain weight for winter hibernation. Do not wake a hibernating hedgehog.

HONEY (BOOTLACE) FUNGUS D

Anthony Huxley in *Plant and Planet* calls this disease a 'dreaded tree killer'. The fungus kills trees and shrubs with a fan of white fungal growth below the bark near ground level and black 'bootlaces' on the roots; in the autumn, toadstools appear at the base. Wood affected by honey fungus is pale green and luminous in the dark. If you find honey fungus, the plant must be uprooted and burned and not replaced by another tree or shrub, since the black underground filaments can push through the soil for several yards in search of other root systems. Protect trees and shrubs by injecting *Trichoderma viride* pellets, especially trees and shrubs around one which has had to be destroyed.

HOVERFLY F

Synphus ribesii is one of the commonest black and yellow hoverflies, often found sunning itself on a wide variety of flowers.

Scaeva pyrastri is black and white, but still sufficiently wasp-like to stop birds from eating it. The larvae of *Synphus bolteatus* are able to get under the wool of woolly aphids and eat them, and will also eat large numbers of cabbage aphids. Planting certain flowers will attract hoverflies—Jim Hay recommends yellow flowers, *Tagetes* in particular; Lawrence Hills suggests poached egg plant (*Limnanthes douglasii*), *Convolvulus tricolor* 'Blue Ensign', and nasturtiums.

ICHNEUMON FLY F

Various sizes, but all slender with long legs. The female has a long ovipositar with which she lays eggs in the bodies of caterpillars. The grubs eat the caterpillars from inside, being careful not to kill them until ready to pupate. Eventually just the skin of the caterpillar is left, covered in yellow cocoons in which the ichneumon flies pupate. Leave these clusters alone.

LACEWING F

The most common are the green lacewings, of which there are 13 species. They have beautiful pale green gauze-like wings, and

the adults and larvae are ferocious eaters of greenfly and other aphids, mites, insect eggs and small caterpillars. The larvae are covered with bristles and hairs, and some species flick the skins of their prey onto their backs, making them look like a pile of rubbish moving over a rose bush.

LADYBIRD F

Probably our best-loved predator insect. The largest and most common is the 7-spot

ladybird. The 2-spot is smaller and its appearance can vary—usually it is red with two black spots, but it can be black with four red spots, or the spots may be linked together. The little 22-spot ladybird is black and yellow. The larvae are not so pretty—

they have been called 'little alligators'. Adults and larvae prey on aphids and scale insects in summer; in winter the adults hibernate in sheltered places.

LEAF MINER P

The larvae of several species feed on the tissues between leaf surfaces of chrysanthemums, cinerarias, pot plants under glass, beetroot, celery, and sometimes parsnips. Adult flies appear from April, and lay eggs on the underside of leaves. Grubs tunnel into leaves and cause white wavy marks. In severe cases, whole leaves can be destroyed.

Tricks and traps: Pick off and burn affected leaves. Chrysanthemum leaf miner also lives on sow-thistles, so these should be kept out of the garden. Deep digging will bury celery leaf miners.

Chemical control: Use nicotine and soft soap spray on badly-affected leaves, but not the day you are planning to eat the crop.

LEATHERJACKET P

The larva of the cranefly or daddy-long-legs—if these are in evidence one year, look out for larvae the next. Dark grey leathery-skinned grubs about 1"/25mm long,

moving with a strange wriggle. Eggs are laid in August-September and the grubs feed through winter and spring, eating plant roots. On warm, damp spring nights they come to the surface of the soil and bite through the stems of young plants.

Tricks and traps: If your lawn is badly affected during a dry summer, sprinkle with water and cover with black polythene for several hours; the leatherjackets will come to the surface, where they can be picked off or killed with a mower or roller—the birds will eat the remains. Put tubes round brassica plants as for cutworms.

Biological control: A chicken or two will help clear the soil.

MICE F and P

Field and wood mice in the orchard will eat grubs which are pupating on and just under the surface of the soil—stack a pile of logs to encourage them. On the other hand, mice are terrible for eating peas and broad beans early in the spring, when there is nothing much else to eat and the cat prefers to stay in the warm kitchen.

Tricks and traps: Swirling the seed in paraffin makes it taste nasty to mice, and holly or gorse in the seed trench frighten them away. You can also protect your peas by laying thick clear polythene flat on the ground until the pea shoots show through. The best thing is to sow later, when the mice are not so hungry.

MILDEW D

Many mildews live on plants, from peas and peaches to roses and michaelmas daisies. Powdery mildews make a white powdery mould on leaf and stem surfaces, and tend to be worse in dry seasons. Downy mildews are more felted and yellower, and are bad in cool wet summers.

Tricks and traps: Correct feeding, watering and drainage all help, and a mulch will help plants to keep cool and well-nourished. Some plants are weakened by direct sunlight, and would prefer a cooler and shadier life. Try to buy resistant varieties: old varieties of rambler roses are sometimes devastated by powdery mildew. Vegetables can be kept free of mildew by using rotations, not allowing the soil to get too acid, and keeping up the humus in the soil.

Herbal remedy: Marestail tea and elder leaf spray may safely be used.

Chemical control: The safest fungicides to use are Bordeaux mixture, Burgundy mixture, and flowers of sulphur. Some plants are harmed by copper and sulphur, so take care when choosing which chemical to use against mildew.

MILLIPEDES P

Millipedes may be confused with centipedes, but they are very different. The black millipede is most common, and has two legs to every segment, moves very slowly, and curls up stiffly when disturbed. They eat bulbs—lilies in particular—potatoes, carrots, germinating seeds of peas and beans, and many plant roots.

Tricks and traps: Millipedes reproduce slowly, so are worth trapping. Make a fine wire mesh cylinder or punch holes in a tin, attach a handle, fill with potato peelings or carrot pieces, and bury in the soil. Empty the contents once a week. Millipedes are often numerous in damp, acid, poorly-drained soils, and dislike soil which is disturbed, so could be a problem in a no-dig garden.

Herbal remedy: Sprinkle dried and powdered aromatic herbs or garlic on pea and bean seeds when sowing.

MOLES P

Moles are beautiful and secretive creatures; they eat leatherjackets, wireworms and millipedes, but also a lot of worms. As well as creating molehills on lawns, moles in the garden can cause difficulties when planting over their tunnels. I once planted a row of Brussels sprouts over and over again before moving the row away from the mole run.

Tricks and traps: Moles can be diverted by placing slates across their tunnels.

Herbal remedy: Put a twig of elder in each molehill.

PEACH LEAF CURL D

A fungus disease causing large red blisters on peach leaves, which then twist and distort. Cherries—both ornamental and eating—also suffer from their own type of fungal leaf curl, as do almond trees. Can be serious, since it causes early leaf fall and weakens the tree.

Tricks and traps: Take off and burn affected leaves.

Chemical control: After leaf fall, spray with Burgundy mixture, and spray again in January while the buds are still tight.

RUST D

Not a specific disease, but a descriptive name for many fungal diseases. Currant bushes suffer from rust in early summer, when foliage can wither and fall prematurely; the other hosts for currant rust are some pines. The alternative host for plum rust is anemones. Antirrhinums have been very susceptible to rust in the past, but rust-resistant strains are now available. Carnations, hollyhocks and some other perennials can suffer from a rust which produces numerous brown pustules—again rust-resistant varieties can be obtained. Roses may show signs of rust as dark yellow patches under leaves and powder on shoots, which may also be distorted. Sweet Williams have a rust which takes the form of pale green spots on upper leaf surfaces and brown spore masses underneath—red varieties are more resistant than others. Mint rust appears as light yellow or brown spots on leaves, usually when mint is crowded.

Tricks and traps: Most rusts are helped by liberal doses of well-rotted compost. With antirrhinum rust, pull out and burn infected plants. Water soil around perennials rather than leaves. Put in a sunny part of the garden, and avoid overcrowding. Thinning and dividing can help mint. With rose rust, pick remaining leaves in February, and spread 1"/25mm of peat, leafmould or compost under the plants to prevent re-infection from soil. Grow Sweet Williams in poor soil to avoid the soft growth which is susceptible to rust.

Chemical control: A Bordeaux mixture spray in late February or early March, after pruning, helps roses—it will also protect against black spot.

SAWFLY

see **GOOSEBERRY SAWFLY**.

SCALE INSECTS P

Most common is the mussel scale, which at adult stage looks like a tiny mussel shell, and lives on all fruit trees and bushes. Two other scale insects which feed on a variety of woody plants are brown scale and oyster-shell scale. Specific tree scales come in many shapes and sizes: beech scale produces woolly patches, yew scale looks like a red blob, and willow scale like whitewash.

Tricks and traps: If only a few are present, rub off with soapy water and a cloth. When they appear in large numbers they can suck a plant almost to death. After removing the scale, give the tree or bush a tonic mulch of compost or manure, spread from 6"/15cm from the trunk to the drip line of the branches, with 8oz/225g rock phosphate and 8oz/225g of rock potash per yd²/m². Spray leaves with seaweed solution.

Biological control: Ladybirds eat scale insects; *Anthocorus nemorum* even more.

Chemical control: The safest remedy is to paint with white spirit. A winter tar-oil wash will clear branches of scale, but also of a lot of friends. A lime-sulphur spray in spring will kill insects before they get hard shells, but will also kill anthocorid bugs.

SILVER LEAF D

A fungal disease, mainly of plum trees, but also affects almonds, apricots, apples, pears, cherries, currants, gooseberries, laburnum, willow and hawthorn. Spores enter through a wound, and the first sign is a silvering of the leaves. A brown bracket-fungus develops on the infected wood later in the year, and puts out spores to infect other trees between September and May.

Tricks and traps: Prune between the first week in May and the middle of July. Cut infected wood until there is no brown stain showing in the middle of the wood. Give a mulch of manure around the tree.

Biological control: Use *Trichoderma viride* pellets between February and April, or in August, both to cure the silver leaf in the tree and as a preventative if there is silver leaf in surrounding trees.

SLUGS P

In many ways slugs are useful—they are scavengers, removers of the dead and dying, prefering damaged and decaying vegetation rather than fresh. They can, however, cause a lot of damage, especially to seedlings. Slugs inhabit gardens in very large numbers; in an experiment, 27,500 slugs were taken from one small garden without effecting any noticable decrease in slug activity.

Tricks and traps: A mulch of oak leaves, sharp sand, wood ash and soot or slaked lime may help. Make beer traps, mixing beer and water with sugar and pouring into a wide dish: place with the rim flush to the soil surface, and remove slugs every morning. There needs to be a trap every few feet to be effective. Go out at night with a torch and pick slugs off the plants and soil surface; look under boxes, planks and stones in the daytime, removing any slugs you find. A good idea, though tedious, is to protect larger seedlings with milk cartons with the top and bottom cut out, or toilet roll inners. If you have a serious slug problem, germinate your runner beans in boxes inside, and only put them in the soil when they are strong.

Herbal remedy: Sprinkle southernwood or wormwood tea over the soil in spring and autumn.

Biological control: Ducks, hedgehogs, toads, frogs, centipedes, devil's coach-horse beetles and other small creatures enjoy eating slugs, as do blackbirds and thrushes; all these predators will be damaged or killed if the slugs have accumulated metaldehyde within them.

Chemical control: Fertosan slug killer is a contact killer, harmless to creatures other than slugs, including soil micro-organisms. It will kill some of the small slugs which are otherwise difficult to find.

THRIPS P

Small, slender black insect; also called thunderfly. They can pierce plant cells and suck out sap, though some feed on decaying materials, and some feed on red spider mites. Apple and pear thrips also feed on plum trees, sucking cell-sap from flowers and causing distortion, russetting of fruit, and sometimes preventing the formation of fruit.

Tricks and traps: On trees, a strong blast of water from a hose can get rid of some thrips. A pea bed that has had thrips should be well forked over, allowing the pupae to be eaten by birds. A chickens or two will help.

Chemical control: Apple and pear thrips lay their eggs in blossom, so it is best to spray with pyrethrum in the evening, to avoid bees. Onion thrips can be killed with liquid derris, and this is also effective for flowers in greenhouses.

TOAD AND FROG F

Good friends to have in the garden; though they eat worms, they also eat plenty of slugs, woodlice and flies. Encourage them by providing patches of long grass and a pond.

VIRUS D

Piercing insects such as aphids transmit virus from plant to plant. The original source of infection may have been infected stock or a dormant virus awakening in a sickly plant, or it may have been carried in from outside by birds, animals or humans. Viruses result in yield and quality loss, mottling, streaking, spotting, yellowing and curling of the leaves, and dwarfing of the whole plant.

Tricks and traps: Aphids should be killed so that they do not spread virus diseases. Pull out and burn affected plants. Buy virus-free stock from reputable dealers.

Herbal remedies: Spray with seaweed solution.

WASPS F and P

Useful for controlling flies. They like a little fruit and jam at picnics, but spend most of their time collecting small larvae and adult insects for their brood. In August there are no more wasp grubs to feed, so wasps go on a fruit-eating spree before the cold weather comes, when all except the queen die.

Tricks and traps: Half-fill a jam-jar with jam and water; add a paper or tin top with holes punched in it—the wasps crawl into the jar to find the jam and drown. If wasps are nesting in a hole, tip a load of grass cuttings over it; these will heat up and use up all the oxygen from the nest, thus suffocating the wasps.

Chemical control: Wasps in a hanging nest can be killed by putting a teaspoonful of derris into the entrance at night. Petrol, paraffin and ammonia may also be put in the nest, and the entrance plugged.

WEEVIL P

Long oblong insects with very pointed mouth parts. Pea and bean weevil is dealt with under 'Peas', but other weevils cause damage to fruit and ornamental trees. Apple blossom weevil lays its eggs in the unopened buds of apple blossom, causing the bud to stay closed while larvae feed on the stamens. Red-legged weevil feeds at night on the blossoms and developing fruit, leaves and shoot bases of cherries, trees of the peach family, plums, raspberries and gooseberries. It appears at the end of April or beginning of May, is ½"/12mm long, and black with red legs. The ¼"/6mm long clay-coloured weevil starts eating bark in March, and is found on raspberry canes.

Tricks and traps: If weevils are causing serious trouble on trees, put grease bands round trunks in summer; weevils drop from the branches in the morning and climb up the trunk at night. At night they can be trapped by putting newspaper with grease smeared round the edges under the tree. If a bright light is shone into the tree, the weevils will drop onto the paper, which can then be burnt. Grease-coated boards under gooseberry bushes have the same effect.

WHITEFLY P

Tiny moth-like creatures with white wings. The native species, cabbage whitefly, causes problems on brassicas; the introduced greenhouse whitefly feeds on tomatoes, cucumbers, greenhouse flowering plants and houseplants. They share the aphids' habit of sucking sap and exuding honeydew. Leaves become pale and curled, and black mould grows on the honeydew.

Tricks and traps: If the plant is robust enough, knock the whiteflies off or drown them with a jet of water. Remove and burn badly affected leaves and stumps.

Companion plants: Grow French or African marigolds with your brassicas and greenhouse crops. Dwarf nasturtiums and nicotiana may help vulnerable crops.

Biological control: For greenhouse whitefly introduce the parasitic wasp *Encarsia formosa* (see 'Remedies').

Chemical control: Use soft soap spray every two weeks, or nicotine spray if the whitefly are out of control.

WIREWORM P

The larvae of click beetles. The most common type is light brown, smooth and

slender. They start life eating dead vegetation in grass in fields or lawns, then move on to potatoes, carrots and other vegetables, lilies and other bulbs. Can be a big problem where potatoes and carrots are grown after grassland has been newly broken up.

Tricks and traps: If you find a lot of wireworms while you are digging up your grass, double dig, putting the turfs face down into the trench. Do not grow potatoes or carrots during the first season after digging. The opposite approach is to grow something they really like: sow agricultural mustard. Wireworms usually take 4-5 years to grow into click beetles, but if they feed really well they will only take 2-3 years, and will then fly all at once. If you sow mustard in April, dig it in and sow again in July—the clearance should then be very good. If the wireworms are in presently cultivated soil, try a trap similar to that for millipedes—a perforated tin with a handle, filled with vegetable scraps.

Remedies

Companion planting

Some plants enjoy having certain other plants living alongside them, while other combinations should be avoided. If crops are happy with their neighbours, they have more chance of withstanding pests and diseases. Planting aromatic herbs in the vegetable garden will help to repel pests, and if you plant simple flowers in the fruit and vegetable garden, they can help to attract useful predators, such as bees and hoverflies.

Introduce companion planting gradually, or add it to your present gardening methods where it seems appropriate. Don't be overwhelmed by any method, and whatever you choose to do, you don't need to do it all at once.

Plant basil, borage, hyssop, thyme, sage, rosemary and southernwood at the end of your vegetable beds—

anything that smells strongly can help repel pests. In cooler areas use calendula rather than basil, and be careful that your borage does not get out of hand. These aromatic herbs are particularly helpful in repelling cabbage white butterflies. Chives between roses will help to keep them clear of greenfly.

Garlic, leeks and onions between or around the carrots will help to mask the smell of the carrots and keep away carrot fly. Salsify and scorzonera can also mask the smell of carrots, but to do this effectively you will have far more of the masking plant than you need. Nasturtium, spearmint, stinging nettle, southernwood and garlic are all helpful in controlling aphids; nasturtiums will also control whitefly. *Convolvulus tricolor* 'Blue Ensign', *Limnanthes douglasii* (poached egg plant), and nasturtium are good to grow in the orchard, though not together, as they will crowd each other. They will attract hoverflies which will feed on their nectar, then lay their eggs on the fruit trees, where the larvae are ferocious feeders on aphids.

Mild herbal remedies

There are many herbal remedies, and people have experimented with making smelly mixtures of everything that comes to hand, from orange peel against ants to nettle liquid against aphids. At least you know that you are not harming your plants or the creatures that live around the plants, including us.

A simple herbal remedy is to make a spray from a tea of the leaves of a plant growing near the plants with a pest or disease problem. If the plant is healthy and smooth-leafed, its defence is possibly in its sap, so a tea of the healthy plant might upset the creatures or fungi on the diseased or infested plant.

To make a tea, cut up the part of the medicinal plant you are using and boil up a handful in a pint of water. Take the infusion from the heat when it has just boiled, and use when cool, sieved through a fine sieve or an old pair of tights, and diluted 1:4 with cold water, adding a dessertspoonful of soft soap or soapflakes which have been dissolved in warm water.

Another method of making herbal sprays is to take the same amount of plant and water as for teas, but liquidize them in a kitchen blender, leave them to stand for 48 hours, sieve, then use like the teas. Healthy bark can also be used in this way against scab and canker on trees.

GARLIC OR ONION SPRAY

Use against blackfly, carrot fly, wireworm, chafer grub, onion fly, moth caterpillar, pea and bean weevil, and slugs.

Chop 3oz/80g garlic or onion, soak in 2 teaspoons mineral oil (liquid paraffin) for 24 hours, then strain. Dissolve ¼oz/7g soft soap in 1pt/570ml warm water, and mix with the garlic/onion oil. To use as a spray, shake the mixture well and add 2 tablespoons to 1pt/570ml water.

Spray trees infected with peach leaf curl every day for a week with a solution of 6 crushed garlic bulbs to 5gall/23l water. Spray before fruit is swelling.

OAK LEAF MULCH

Use around seedlings and plants which are vulnerable to slug damage.

SEAWEED SOLUTION

Buy a gallon of this magic liquid and use it liberally all through the growing season. As well as adding potash and trace elements to the soil, seaweed helps against aphids, brown rot in fruit, potato scab and leaf-curl virus, botrytis in strawberries, damping-off in seedlings and tomatoes, big bud mite, potato and rose eelworms. It is more effective to use a weak solution of seaweed every other week throughout the growing season rather than 2 or 3 strong-solution sprays.

STINGING NETTLE TEA

Make in the same way as the other herbal

teas, and use against blackfly on broad beans and greenfly on roses.

Biological controls

These can be bought from the Henry Doubleday Research Association, whose address is given at the end of the book.

TRICHODERMA VIRIDE

A fungicide grown on cereal-based pellets, effective against silver leaf disease, Dutch elm disease and honey fungus. Holes have to be drilled in the trunk of the tree from February to April or in August, and the pellets pressed in. It is recommended to cover the holes with a bitumen paste to keep out mice and squirrels. Also available in powder form, which can be mixed with water to form a paste or spray for tree or shrub wounds, superseding bitumen and latex compounds.

BT 4000

A bacterial insecticide based on the bacillus *Thuringiensis*, sold dry in sealed containers, and made up into a solution to spray on to caterpillars on brassicas, fruit trees and ornamentals. The caterpillars that are killed may safely be eaten by scavengers, and the bacillus is killed by sunlight, so will not spread through the countryside.

PHYTOSEIULUS PERSIMILUS

A predatory mite sold on pieces of leaf, to be placed on plants being sucked by greenhouse red spider mite: very useful for peaches, nectarines and apricots grown under glass.

ENCARSIA FORMOSA

A small wasp parasite of whitefly, sold as a leaf covered with infected whitefly larvae. If the greenhouse is 55°F/13°C or above the *Encarsia formosa* will hatch out and parasitize the whitefly.

Stronger sprays and chemicals

These are usually for emergencies only, and should be handled and used with care. They should not be used as preventatives, or routinely. It is always best to use good cultivation, skilled pruning, traps, repellants, immune varieties, and the help of natural and imported predators wherever possible, but when blight threatens to destroy your potato crop, and aphids cover the rose-buds and are sucking them to death, you have to act fast, and apply a poison which will do as little harm as possible.

Fungicides

BORDEAUX MIXTURE

A mixture of copper sulphate and slaked lime which can be bought from a hardware shop or garden centre, effective against potato blight on potatoes and tomatoes, peach leaf curl, and canker, and reduces rose black spot, mildew and rust. Mix with water and use immediately.

BURGUNDY MIXTURE

Used for the same diseases as Bordeaux mixture. Dissolve ¾oz/22g copper sulphate in 2pt/1.1l hot water, and leave to cool overnight. Dissolve 1oz/30g washing soda (sodium carbonate) in 2pt/1.1l cold water, and mix the two solutions together. Do all the mixing in plastic buckets and spray straight away.

ELDER SPRAY

Effective against mildew, especially on roses, and also helps against black spot. It does not kill ladybirds or their larvae, or anthocorid bugs. Boil up 1lb/500g elder leaves with 6pt/3.4l water. Simmer for ½ hour, topping up water to keep it at original level. Sieve when cold. If sealed in bottles, will keep for up to 3 months.

URINE

Can be used straight on dormant fruit trees to control scab; best when buds are at their tightest in January. A 30% solution may be used against mildew, and there are reports of success against botrytis in greenhouses.

Pesticides

These are given in order of increasing strength. Use the weakest and least harmful chemical which you think will be effective. This means not always reaching for the derris when you see the first greenfly on the roses!

WATER

A heavy blast of water from a hosepipe with

a thumb over the end is enough to knock off and sometimes drown aphid, red spider mite, codling moth, and other troublesome creatures from robust fruit trees and ornamental shrubs and trees. Blasts of water should not be used routinely, because they get rid of beneficial insects too.

RHUBARB OR ELDER SPRAY

Use for killing greenfly and other aphids; will also kill small caterpillars. To make the spray more effective, add 1oz/30g soft soap to every 6pt/3.4l water.

SOFT SOAP

Buy this at your local hardware shop, garden centre or chemist, or from the HDRA. A better aphid killer than ordinary soapflakes or soapy water; destroys the protective wax coating on the aphids' bodies, but not on the bodies of ladybirds or hoverflies. If you have hard tapwater, use rainwater so that you do not waste the soap in making scum. Dissolve 1oz/30g soft soap in 6pt/3.4l of water.

QUASSIA CHIPS

Made from the wood of the tree *Picrasma quassioides*, and will keep indefinitely in a dry tin. An insecticide made from the chips will kill small caterpillars, sawflies, leaf miners and aphids, but will not harm ladybirds or bees. The mixture is very bitter, so should not be used on anything which is going to be eaten within a fortnight. Boil up 1oz/30g quassia chips with 2pt/1.1l water very slowly for an hour, topping up to maintain original quantity. Pour off and strain liquid when cool, and use 1 part solution to 4 parts water.

DERRIS (RETENONE)

A plant-derived insecticide which will kill all insects, fish and tortoises, although it is safe for human beings, birds and rodents. Effective against aphids, red spider mite and pea thrips, but it has to be used double strength against caterpillars.

FERTOSAN SLUG KILLER

A mixture of aluminium sulphate and herbs, which poisons small slugs on contact. It does not harm hedgehogs, birds, pets, earthworms and soil micro-organisms. It should be watered on to the soil, and kept away from seedlings and delicate leaves like lettuce.

PYRETHRUM

A relative of the chrysanthemum family which kills greenfly, blackfly, thrips and aphids. Its poison breaks down rapidly in light. Some sources say it is 'completely safe', others that it can be toxic to ladybirds and parasitic wasps, so like all poisons it should be used with care.

DERRIS AND PYRETHRUM MIXTURE

This is stronger than either of its constituents.

NICOTINE

I have tried boiling up old cigarette ends, but the smell was too awful for me to recommend it. A liquid nicotine soap may be bought from the HDRA. This is a powerful poison, so must be kept and used very carefully. Wear gloves to keep it off the skin. Nicotine will kill caterpillars when all else has failed, plus aphids, pea and bean weevils, scale insects and pea thrips. It is recommended for spraying euonymus hedges in spring, to kill the blackfly before they move to the broad beans and other vegetables.

Tools

Who goeth a borrowing,
    goeth a sorrowing.
Few lend (but fools)
    their working tools.

To borow to daie and to-morrow to mis,
    for lender and borower, noiance it is:
Then have of thine owne, without lending unspilt,
    what followeth needfull, here learne if thou wilt.

Thomas Tusser
September's Abstract

Tools

Good tools are simple, basic and strong. They fit well with the way our body works, so they become almost a physical extension of us. With a good tool you can, without effort and while keeping your hands at the other end of a six-foot shaft, hoe the weeds within an inch of your seedlings. Acquiring such skills has to be learned, however, and although it only takes two minutes to tell someone how to use a hoe, much more time is needed for your body to absorb that information. Eventually the use of the tool becomes second nature.

Your own tools become part of you in more ways than one. If you use the same tool for fifty years, and you may well, if you choose the best and care for it, then your body will bear the results. Gardeners are plagued by the fact that the ground where they work is beneath their feet, and so are liable to bad backs. This is why all the bigger tools have long handles, to minimize the bending over. Don't work bent double.

It is a myth that 'heavy' work has to be done by huge young men with bulging muscles. Anyone who is moderately fit can use all the basic tools effectively. Choose tools which are the right size and weight for you.

If you can afford it, buy stainless steel spades and digging forks and they will never bend or rust. Otherwise all hand tools need constant care. If they are left lying around, or are put away wet, they will rust. Dry your wet tools on a rag, and always, whether it is wet or not, brush off the clinging soil and wipe your tools with an oily rag. Old engine oil is fine. If you have a shed, put up hooks to hang your tools in a row. Then nothing will get lost or damaged, and you will be able to tell at a glance that they are all there. This attention may add a couple of minutes to the end of the gardening day, but will prolong the life of your tools for years. Few woodworkers or mechanics would treat their tools with the reckless abandon that is common to gardeners. Tools deserve respect.

Some tools require further maintenance, occasional sharpening or new handles from time to time. Most basic tools can be repaired at home without much difficulty. Simple sharpening should be done with oil and a whetstone. Unless you have proper shear sharpeners, take your shears to the shop, as it is easy to ruin the precision of a double-bladed tool if you are inexpert. Otherwise you can buy your own shear sharpeners and fix them to your workbench. With secateurs, take care to sharpen the blades on the sloping side, or they will no longer meet precisely. Check frequently-used secateurs often—they need to be kept sharp. A pocket whetstone is best for these, or alternatively you can get them sharpened professionally. It is essential to keep pruning tools sharp, or your pruning may do more harm than good.

The following list describes what to look for when buying each tool, how to use it well, and how to care for it. The hand tools are described first, then the simplest mechanical tools are covered —tools which may be realistic options for some gardeners.

Garden spade
Choose a good strong spade suited to your height and weight. Points to look

115

for are the type of handle—strapped or T-bar. A strapped handle is stronger, but both types will stand up to hard use if they are well made. Next, look at the way the shaft fits the socket—how the wooden handle fits the metal blade. The shaft should reach well down into the socket, fit well, and be securely riveted. Try to choose a spade with a flange on the top edge or you will ruin your boots when you press down on it.

Spades come with blades of varying widths and depths. The length of the blade is called the spit—the longer the spit the deeper you will dig. The cutting edge may be curved or square. It will need occasional sharpening, which you can do yourself with oil and a whetstone.

Like all long-handled garden tools, using a spade well is a matter of rhythm and balance. For basic digging it is your foot which provides the pressure. When you turn the soil use your stronger hand, with the other hand far enough down the shaft to act as a balance—this will involve the minimum strain.

Garden fork

Strain is always minimized when you use the right tool for the right job.

Garden fork   Manure fork

There are two kinds of digging forks, as well as pitchforks and manure forks which have quite a different function (see below). If you can only afford one

fork and have an ordinary multi-purpose garden, a strong digging fork will cover most purposes, but it will do the job of the manure fork badly. Conversely, you cannot dig with a manure fork. If you hold the two side by side you will see the difference—the tines of the digging fork are quite unlike the prongs of the manure fork, and the angle of the tool to its shaft is different.

The garden digging fork has rounded or squared tines, and the tines are almost in line with the shaft—like that of the spade, as its function is similar. Look out for the same features in a fork as in a spade.

The potato fork is used for lifting crops and has broad flattened tines, usually splayed out a little. In the small garden a digging fork will serve this purpose, but if you are harvesting a lot of root crops the potato fork is the right tool for the job.

Manure fork

The manure fork is related to the pitchfork, designed to lift material and throw it or load it somewhere else. It is the most useful tool for building compost heaps. You can use it to load seaweed into sacks on the beach, to throw muck into a trailer, to mix up your weeds and grass mowings into a good compost. You can use it with precision to build firm walls for your compost heaps, or, like a pitchfork, to spear a load of prunings to carry them to the burn pile. It is handy for feeding your bonfire and raking it back together. It is a pleasant tool to use properly, because when rhythm and balance are right there is very little strain involved. You can shift a ton of manure with no aches to show for it, and work comfortably all day with it at a steady pace.

Manure forks have four or five rounded prongs which curve upward, and the prongs are set at an angle to the shaft to assist the lifting movement for which it is intended. If you cannot find a manure fork at your garden suppliers, try an agricultural store.

Dutch hoe

This tool is your main support in dealing with weeds. Its blade is almost parallel to the shaft, and it comes in various widths. The shaft of the hoe is used quite differently from that of the spade or fork. It is much longer, because it is held flexibly in both hands and not grasped firmly or used with much pressure. Make sure you use it with your back straight; there is no need to bend over.

The Dutch hoe is used to weed between rows of vegetables, walking backwards and stirring up the soil surface by scraping the hoe to and fro so that the weeds are uprooted or sliced off. On a dry day you can leave the weeds to dry out on the soil surface. You can also hoe the beds around shrubs and herbaceous borders. The more of your garden that is practicable to hoe rather than handweed, the more you liberate yourself from endless weeding. Done regularly, your weeds will have less chance to settle and seed.

Draw hoe

The blade on the draw hoe is set at right angles to the shaft, and there are various types and designs. They are used for weeding in a rather different way from the Dutch hoe, chopping at the

Dutch hoe

Draw hoe

weeds from above and then drawing the hoe towards you rather than scraping to and fro below the surface. A draw hoe is useful in the vegetable garden for drawing seed drills and earthing up potatoes. The draw hoe is a more accurate tool for working round small plants than the Dutch hoe, and again, minimizes handweeding around rows of seedlings.

Garden rake

Buy a rake with strong iron combs. A rake in soft pliable metal will bend and eventually break. Make sure that the shaft is the right length for you, remembering that it is used similarly to

Garden rake

a hoe. The rake is used for collecting up stones from beds, and working surfaces to a fine tilth, particularly seed beds. Used well, it can create a fine level surface, as in preparing a lawn for sowing. It is also handy for odd jobs of clearing up around the compost heap or burn pile.

Lawn rake

The most usual design is the springbok rake, a fanned rake with twenty or so prongs which turn down at the end. This tool is used exclusively for raking lawns, and is specially designed to

Lawn rake

scarify a lawn without damaging it, which the garden rake is not. If you cannot afford a lawn rake a garden rake will do the job, but not as well or as easily.

Shears

If your budget is limited, get one good strong pair of garden shears, which can be used for edging lawns and trimming hedges. This is a tool that needs care.

Keep shears well oiled and have them sharpened when necessary. More shears probably end up on the scrap heap through neglect than any other garden tool, and yet the maintenance required is minimal. The screw needs to be adjusted so the blades fit perfectly —shears work by the way the two blades mesh snugly together, the cutting blade being one-sided—so make sure when you buy shears that they are strongly screwed together. If the blades wobble the shears won't work.

Lawn shears and border shears are long-handled shears suitable for sustained work on lawns. They all need maintenance, and one pair of well cared-for garden shears will be of more use than an assortment of blunt and rusted shears for every possible angle and situation.

Trowel

The short-handled tools are the basics with which we probably started. Children can use a trowel and a handfork in their own patch of garden. You need these tools if all you have is a window box or a two-foot-square herb garden in the back yard.

Trowels are used for planting. You can get special ones for different sorts of planting— bulbs, for example—but one strong basic trowel will do. Take care when buying a trowel: there are many cheap versions. The weak point is the neck, which in a badly-designed trowel will soon bend or break. Look too for the way the blade is attached to the handle. One small screw is not enough, nor is a blade let in to the handle without being firmly fixed. It will soon come loose. Make sure the whole blade is made of strong, fairly thick metal. Cheap thin blades will chip, dent, bend and break. The trowel is no more a cheap expendable tool than any of the others, and treated with the same care it too should last for ever.

Handfork

A handfork is used for fine weeding. There are areas which can never be suitable for the hoe—the rockery or small annual bed, or among tiny seedlings where you need your eye close to the ground. The handfork also roots out the small dandelions and docks, and infiltrating strands of couch grass and ground elder. The hoe won't deal with these perennial weeds because the roots will be left in the soil, and when they arrive in the garden they need to be dealt with before they establish themselves. You will spend quite a lot of time on your knees, handfork in hand. Choose a good strong handfork using the same criteria as you used in buying a trowel.

Handforks live in constant danger of disappearing into the compost at the bottom of a bucket of weeds. Buy scarlet ones or paint them bright colours, and keep your eyes open.

Dibber

This is a useful tool for planting long rows of seedlings, or masses of bulbs. It is essential for planting young leeks. The danger is that it is too easy to leave an air pocket below the plant, especially bulbs. Either buy a dibber with a rounded end, or make your own from a broken spade or fork shaft. For small quantities of plants, a trowel is perfectly adequate and easier to use correctly.

Secateurs

You can do more damage with a pair of secateurs used in ignorance than with almost any other garden tool. Be cautious. Secateurs are the tool for small pruning jobs. Use them for deadheading when you cannot pick the heads off easily. Never pull the heads off leaving a scarred and damaged stem—cut them. Secateurs are handy to carry with you to trim plants as necessary, and they are of course the tool for serious pruning.

It is worth investing in a good pair of secateurs. Ragged cuts will damage your plants. Look after this tool. It will require careful sharpening. The anvil type works on the basis of having one sharp blade which cuts down onto the opposing blunt side, while the scissor type works just like a pair of scissors. If you sharpen the wrong side of the scissor-type blade they will no longer meet properly, and the secateurs will be ruined. Keep secateurs oiled. They should snap open when not locked together.

Pruning saw
A pruning saw is a specialized tool and a joinery saw is not a substitute. The blade is slightly angled as you will seldom be able to work straight on.

Pruning saw

You can get pruning saws where the angle is adjustable. The blade and the handle are narrow enough to fit between close-growing branches. This is a tool that you may have to use with great precision while dangling from a branch, or wedged between the tree and the top of a stepladder. Make sure it is one you can rely on.

Lopping shears
This is an essential tool if you are undertaking serious pruning. It takes over where the secateurs leave off. The longer blades give greater purchase so that more of your strength is available to cut, and of course the longer reach brings more of the tree or shrub within range. If you are planning much tree pruning you may need tree-lopping shears with the greatest possible reach, but in most gardens this is unlikely to be a necessity. Loppers work on the same principle as secateurs. Don't be tempted to put great strain on the loppers to avoid using the saw.

Scythe and sickle
A scythe or sickle may be the answer if you have an extensive area of rough grass or patches of nettles or other weeds you want to prevent seeding. Scythed nettles make excellent compost.

A scythe needs to fit you. It is impossible to work with a scythe which is the wrong size. If you are not an expert, buy from somebody who can help you choose the right one.

Scything when done by an expert looks deceptively easy. Again it is a question of acquiring the knack—the right swing at the right angle. If you can, get someone who knows to show you. Wear boots to avoid cutting your legs. Once learnt, scything is one of the most meditative and satisfying of jobs, especially as it has to be done in the best of summer weather.

Shovel
A shovel differs from a spade as a manure fork differs from a digging fork, though in this case most people know the difference. A shovel is

Spade   *Shovel*

designed for shovelling, with built-up sides to contain material, and with the blade angled so the user has to bend as little as possible to bring it flush with the ground. A shovel may be needed for shifting sand or gravel or other material, and is useful for tidying up after compost making. Like the manure fork, it is a tool where correct balance will result in an immense saving of strain and strength.

Pick

The gardener who has to start work with a pick and shovel deserves sympathy—and good tools. A pick has two blades. It is used for breaking up ground and dislodging stones. You will need it to shift solid rubble, old concrete, or tarmac—some people will go to great lengths to produce a garden! Again, using a pick and shovel is a matter of rhythm and steady work rather than force.

Knife

Essential. Pruning used to be done with a sharp pruning knife—a more skilled operation than wielding secateurs, which have largely replaced it. You will still need it for cleaning up wounds on trees, for taking cuttings, layering, and budding and grafting if you do them. A knife is also used for multifarious other purposes from cutting twine to preparing radishes for instant consumption. Keep it on you.

Equipment

Every garden requires a basic stock of equipment. The most obvious item is the means of housing everything else— the garden shed. The type of space may vary, it may be attached to the house or part of it, it may be a free-standing shed or a brick outhouse. There may be no choice available, but you will need some space from which to operate, even if it's only the back of the garage.

Ideally, the tool shed or potting shed should be a pleasant place to be. There will be indoor work to do, and particularly in the absence of a greenhouse with a workbench, the shed may be the best space in which to do jobs such as sowing seeds, pricking out, potting on, mending tools, storing bulbs, studying seed catalogues and drinking tea. If you can afford a shed with a window and a work bench, then you are a fortunate gardener. Your tools can be hung on the opposite wall, and the space at the end can be used for the lawnmower and wheelbarrow. Shelves or a cupboard are essential for storing all the odds and ends the gardener will need. Every gardener will soon build up a store of necessary items. Good storage eliminates waste.

Keep food supplements and nutrients on one shelf, clearly labelled. Keep poisons locked away, or out of reach. Have a safe dry place for such maintenance tools as a gardener needs —hammer and nails, pliers, etc. Keep your trays and pots and potting soils where they are handy for the work bench. If necessary, large waterproof sacks of peat and compost can be stored outside. Keep a drawer or small shelf for odd items—twine and plant labels, tools for sowing and pricking out. You will need places for canes and stakes and netting, and hooks on the wall for sieves and coils of wire.

If your tool shed is also a potting shed, there will be plants being brought in and out. You will need a dry dim place to store away bulbs through the summer. It is of course essential to label bulbs and seeds clearly. Seeds can be kept cool and dry in an airtight box. You may repot and care for houseplants in the shed. Never leave diseased or infested plants lying about—cure them or burn them. Used flower pots and trays should be washed in hot soapy water before being used again. If you have plenty of pots, let the dirty pots collect in a box tucked away outside, and wash them all together on a wet day when you feel like it.

The largest single item of equipment is probably the wheelbarrow. Look for durability. Examine the welding, and beware of screws and bolts that will not take strain where it is needed. A contractor's barrow with a pneumatic tyre will last longest and take the greatest weights. However, there may be other factors to consider. It is no use having a heavy wheelbarrow that will carry several hundredweight if you can't lift it. If you have uphill journeys or have to negotiate steps or narrow planks, you may need something small and light. Make sure you can walk comfortably with your barrow without stooping or having to lift the handles too high to avoid scraping the ground. It is useful to have the sort of barrow where you can raise the sides with wooden extensions for light loads of weeds or grass. Make sure you choose a barrow that tips up easily when you empty it. It is hard to see how some designs of barrow can be tipped up at all. It helps to have a barrow that can easily be used with a shovel, which means a wide top and relatively shallow depth.

Store your wheelbarrow in the shed if you can. If you have to leave it outside, tip it up so the water doesn't collect inside and cause rust. Don't leave the barrow out for days with a pile of sodden weeds in it. Treat it as kindly as you treat your other tools.

Gardeners on the whole are hoarders and scroungers. They bring home wooden fruit-boxes for seedling trays and used plastic sacks and bits of wood that might be useful, or old tyres for planting next year's marrows in. They find old carpets in other people's dustbins and take them home for the compost heap, or appropriate old tin baths to make a noxious brew of comfrey or nettle water. They keep jars and milk cartons and egg boxes for seedlings and cuttings.

This is all good ecological practice. Money is best spent on the best tools and good equipment, but there are many bits and pieces we are now encouraged to buy which until recently no one dreamed of spending money on,

and there are many things thrown into dustbins which could be real assets to the well-run garden.

Garden machinery

If you have a large expanse of grass, an enormous hedge, and a big area to dig, or if you have limited time or energy, it can be very useful to have mechanical tools. We now accept lawnmowers as commonplace tools, rather as we take washing machines for granted, though it is still possible to scythe the grass and do our washing by hand.

Most of us do not need strimmers, hedge trimmers and cultivators, and when we do need one it is easier and cheaper to borrow from a friend, hire one, or buy one jointly with another gardener and share the use of it. Unlike a mower, these tools are not used every week of the growing season.

Before using any garden machinery, buy yourself some good earmuffs, and remember that your neighbours may not appreciate the noise of your engine on a peaceful Sunday afternoon.

One important choice you will need to make with any machinery you use is the sort of engine you want—battery-driven, mains electric or petrol-driven. For small jobs, the choice is usually between battery models, with their extra weight, and mains electric models, with their inconvenient and limiting cables. Although noisier, smellier, and usually more difficult to start than electric motors, petrol-driven machinery is tougher and much more versatile. If you decide to use petrol-driven machinery, you have the choice of 2- or 4-stroke. I admit to being rather prejudiced against 2-stroke engines, since they are noisier and higher-pitched than 4-stroke ones.

Mowers

Towards the end of a long summer it is easy to think of a lawn as never-ending work, but it can be a joy to the eye and a continuous source of compost and mulching material. Get a mower that suits your lawn and you. Maybe you can only afford a cheap second-hand mower, but it's still a lot easier than scything. If you can afford a shiny new mower, however, you have a variety to choose from.

My ideal mower would be an all-purpose 18″/45cm 4-stroke petrol-driven front-wheel-drive rotary mower. The cutting height would have a wide range so that it would be just as useful in the orchard, the vegetable garden, or in rough grass, as on the lawn. It would be able to handle any amount of long and wet grass, and it would have a big bag to collect up all the cuttings.

There is a great range of rotary mowers, from a 15″/37cm cutting width hand-propelled electric machine with a long cable, to a 36″/90cm 4-stroke petrol-driven monster like a tractor that you sit on. Take your choice.

Air cushion mowers are usually called 'flymos' (after the brand name), and range from 15″/37cm cutting-width babies with whisper-quiet electric motors to 21″/53cm toughies with a choice of loud 2-stroke or loud 4-stroke engines. I have never known air cushion mowers to float as well as the brochures suggest, and I like to be able to control the length of cut better than these machines allow.

A friend with a small lawn on a steep slope recently bought a small electric machine; she finds it quiet, convenient, easy to store, effective, and dangerous. She has to know exactly where the children and the cable are all the time. On the other hand, it handles long wet grass efficiently, and for more money she could also have bought a model which picks up the grass as it cuts it.

I once borrowed a tiny electric cylinder mower for a few months for mowing a small lawn, and found it both quiet and perfectly adequate for the job. Cylinder mowers are supposed to make the best lawns, but your lawn already has to be pretty good before a cylinder mower will do its job. They are not tolerant of bumpy surfaces or long wet grass, but they can cut smoothly and immaculately, leaving pleasing and very professional-looking stripes. Cylinder mowers also come in a range of sizes and with both electric and petrol-driven engines.

Strimmers

Strimmers are useful for cutting grass growing against walls and fences, and the larger ones are good for cutting bracken and bramble patches. They range from small electric single nylon-thread cutters with a long mains cable to magic machines with 37cc 2-stroke engines, special gearing, safety guard and harness, eight-toothed brush and bracken blade, four-reel nylon head, and optional saw blade and plastic blade. Pity it can't unblock the drains at the same time.

Strimmers are good at shooting grass, stones and twigs into your eyes and legs, so even on the hottest days goggles or sunglasses and trousers should be worn. The strimmer I used was a 30cc 2-stroke machine, and the noise it made was appalling. Wear ear muffs or you can damage your ears.

When I first used a strimmer I cut straight through a new rambler rose. They run away with you, and you need a lot of concentration and time to get an even cut, and to avoid slicing chunks out of the edge of the lawn or pieces out of the fence. For this reason it is unwise to use a strimmer around trees, bushes and hedges—you might not even notice what damage you were doing.

Hedge trimmers

If trimming a hedge of any size is a burden to you, consider using a hedge trimmer. A friend of mine has large hedges, and keeps them smooth and straight with her electric hedge trimmer. There are bigger models with 2-stroke engines for bigger hedges. Care should be taken not to cut the hedge when birds are nesting.

Mechanical cultivators

Do you really need to buy a cultivator? Could you borrow or hire one once or twice in a season? Could you try a no-dig method of gardening?

If your garden is absolutely huge, and you decide that you just must have a shiny new cultivator, again you have a whole range of models to choose from. The size of the machine will depend on the size of your garden and the amount of manual work you are able to put into it. Don't waste money buying something bigger than you really need.

The wheel-drive types of cultivator (such as the Rotovator) have wheels which support and drive the machine and blades which beat the soil. This is not very good for the soil, but the damage can be minimized by setting the blades at a slow speed. The wheel-drive makes the machine more manageable than cultivators which are driven by their blades or tines.

The type of cultivator I am most used to is a blade-driven machine with a 3½ or 5hp 4-stroke engine. Once you get the knack and don't fight it, it is pleasant and satisfying to use, and does a good job. This type of cultivator is better for the crumb structure of the soil than the wheel-driven species, and some of the awkwardness in handling can be overcome by having a reverse gear.

A good flower bed can be made by putting manure, wood ash and calcified seaweed on turf, then running the cultivator over the ground three or four times. Dig the edges nicely and cover with a hay mulch. Plant flowers and shrubs through the mulch. You will have an instant flower garden and the weeds will hardly get a look in.

The hired hand

As you get older, or when your health is not what it might be, you may decide to pay somebody to replace your own arms, legs, hands and feet. I hope you can find somebody competent who is pleasant to have in your garden. Once you have found such a person, hang on to them by showing how much you appreciate what they are doing. Pay them good wages—don't spend large amounts of money on machinery and then be mean towards somebody who is using their body on your behalf.

Respect your hired hand. Provide hot drinks in winter and cool ones in summer; occasional snacks are usually welcome. Paid helper and employer can often exchange useful information about gardening in general and your garden in particular.

Vegetables

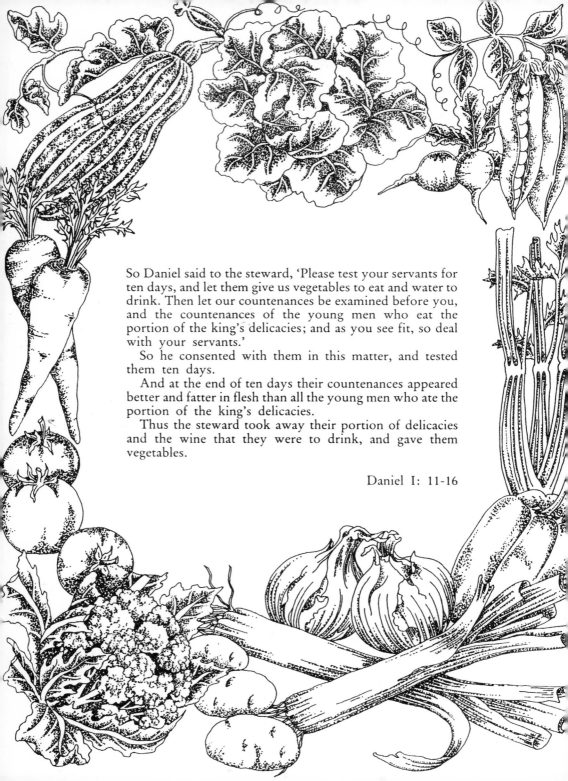

So Daniel said to the steward, 'Please test your servants for ten days, and let them give us vegetables to eat and water to drink. Then let our countenances be examined before you, and the countenances of the young men who eat the portion of the king's delicacies; and as you see fit, so deal with your servants.'

So he consented with them in this matter, and tested them ten days.

And at the end of ten days their countenances appeared better and fatter in flesh than all the young men who ate the portion of the king's delicacies.

Thus the steward took away their portion of delicacies and the wine that they were to drink, and gave them vegetables.

Daniel I: 11-16

Vegetables

We grow vegetables to feed ourselves and our families. In Britain this is a matter of choice; for less time and trouble we can in most places stock up at the greengrocer's, often with a wider and more predictable selection than we can produce from our own garden. So why bother?

First, because we want good food. Even if our own crop ends up looking grubbier, smaller and more chewed than the same thing in the shops, we know that it has not been sprayed with poisonous pesticides (the average commercial lettuce is sprayed fourteen times during its growing period), that it grew on a healthy organically-nourished soil containing no harmful chemicals, and that it is free from preserving methods that may range from wax or plastic coatings to radioactive rays. Growing your own crop *is* more unpredictable, but the successes can be as extreme as the failures, and our own crops will sometimes be wonderful.

Sometimes, however, we have as little control over pollution of crops in our own garden as we do over the food that arrives in the shops. If you suffer from heavy industrial or traffic pollution, your vegetables will absorb it—lettuces grown next to a main road will have significant traces of lead in them. If your soil has already been contaminated, it will take several years of organic gardening before the chemicals have broken down or been washed away: a garden must have been cultivated organically for three years before the Soil Association will certify it as an organic garden. The nuclear accident at Chernobyl in May 1986 has made us all aware that there is nothing we can do to protect our soil or plants from excess radiation. Your garden is not an island of purity and safety, but in most circumstances you can make it a healthier place to eat from than the alternatives.

Not only are we more sure that we are not eating anything poisonous if we grow our own vegetables; our crops will also have greater nutritional value, partly because they are eaten fresh. A salad from your own garden may have been growing less than half an hour ago, and retain all its vitamin C. Vegetables and fruit ripened by the sun are rich in vitamin E, which is unavailable in produce ripening in the hold of a ship. Food will also be nutritionally superior and better-tasting because you have chosen varieties for their flavour rather than their looks. Commercial varieties are selected primarily for their appearance (you don't choose vegetables in the supermarket by taking bites); their preserving qualities (largely irrelevant when you don't need to transport anything); and their uniformity in maturing (a positive disadvantage if you want to pick as you eat).

If you grow your own crops, it is worth thinking about how you intend to preserve them. A deep freeze can give you a wide selection from your garden all the year round with relatively little loss of taste or goodness, but there is a cost involved in buying and running it. Old-fashioned kilner jars are a neglected alternative, and other choices are pickling, jams, chutneys, and dry storage of roots. The choices are given under each vegetable.

Start harvesting your vegetables when they are young and small—they taste better and you will waste less in the long run. Before storing vegetables in a polythene bag in the fridge, wash them carefully and leave them damp. If you are using woodchips or sawdust to store root vegetables, make sure the wood is not fresh or resinous. For detailed information about preserving vegetables, see the HMSO book *Home Preservation of Fruit and Vegetables*.

Your own produce may be cheaper than shop-bought vegetables, but if you cost the labour you put into the vegetable garden you may consider yourself thoroughly exploited. Your own produce costs less money, but takes a lot more time, and you cannot guarantee the results. A garden will also take some initial investment in tools, equipment and supplements. Like most enterprises, it is only once you are well under way that you begin to notice the credits in the budget.

These are the personal gains of growing vegetables; there are also ecological advantages. If you are treating your own piece of land as well as you can, and producing food from it that has had nothing to do with exploitative agricultural practices or economies, then you know that you are doing no harm, either to land or people. Total self-sufficiency is hardly practical, either on an individual scale or as an overall goal, and is not necessarily a useful concept. When you consider the vast acreage of land that is cultivated by individual gardeners, however, food production from this source is by no means negligible, as became clear during the 'Dig For Victory' campaign in the Second World War.

It can be confusing when you start to grow your vegetables organically, so look for support and shared experience with other organic gardeners. Look for a Henry Doubleday Research Association or Soil Association gardening group in your area.

Finally, people who grow their own vegetables generally enjoy it, although it can be extraordinarily frustrating. There may be gardeners who are unfailingly successful in growing absolutely everything, whom disaster in the form of weather, pests or other problems never strikes, who have never drawn back the curtains on a June morning to find the ground white with frost or the potato patch full of frolicking cows, but I do not know these people.

Know your garden

There are very few vegetables which are indigenous, as you will see from the list. We have to modify the soil for cauliflowers and the climate for tomatoes if they are to thrive. We have to provide shelter, water, drainage and food for our fussy vegetables.

Every garden is different, so never assume that you can or cannot do what a book tells you. If the book says you can grow outdoor tomatoes in your sunniest bed, check where the author lives, find out where your cat sunbathes, and see if any of your neighbours grow tomatoes out of doors. You can always choose to provide the Mediterranean climate tomatoes love by investing in lots of glass and growing them indoors.

If you have read the chapter called 'Helping Your Garden Along', you will understand the importance of the soil testing kit in the vegetable garden. Used in conjunction with a survey of the weeds in your garden and advice from the neighbours, you should have a good idea about the state of your soil. If you go on to study rotations and the individual needs of each vegetable, you are ready to start providing for those needs.

Crop rotation

If you grow the same crops on the same soil every year, you will exhaust the soil and allow soil-borne pests and diseases to build up. This is particularly important for the health of potatoes, which can suffer from a build-up of eelworm, and for the brassicas, which will be devastated if clubroot gets a hold.

In terms of nutritional needs, vegetables can be roughly divided into four groups. Before planting or sowing, potatoes like a heavy feed of well-rotted compost or manure; peas and beans like a light feed of compost or manure; brassicas like a heavy feed of compost; carrots, parsnips and beetroots should have no manure. If the soil is not rich, add manure or compost the previous autumn for root crops. It is best to keep swedes and turnips with the brassicas: although they do not need the soil to be as rich, they share the same pests and diseases. Onions are grown with the carrots, although they need to have more food added to their patch. Lawrence Hills puts some strawberries into each group, but don't make the mistake of planting new strawberries where the last lot went. Replace a bed when it is 3-4 years old.

Rotation of vegetable crops helps the build-up of even fertility in the vegetable garden. Potatoes and brassicas are heavy surface feeders which is why they need plenty of manure and compost, some of which is left to be available for the following crops of roots and legumes. The legumes leave a legacy of nitrate-producing nodules on their roots for the benefit of the brassicas which follow.

Many soils need liming, and this is best done every 3 or 4 years after the potato crop and before the peas, so that the brassicas benefit from the highest pH and the potatoes get the lowest pH. Potatoes tend to develop scab if the pH is above 6.5. All vegetables suffer from a lack of available nutrients if the pH is lower than 5.5 or higher than 7.5. If you live on chalk, do not automatically assume that you have a high pH—calcium can be precipitated out of the soil very easily by the application of raw manure, chemical fertilizers or acid rain. On the other hand, if a gardener has been in the habit of applying hydrated lime every year, the soil could have a pH which is too high even in a predominantly acid area. Test the pH of the soil after each potato crop, and lime with ground limestone or magnesium limestone (dolomite) according to the instructions in your pH testing kit.

If you are not growing potatoes, you can use a three-course rotation of legumes, brassicas and roots. Draw a

Legumes	Potatoes
Light compost in autumn or spring. Peas Broad beans (+ *wood ash*) Runner beans French beans *followed by* Cabbage, spring cabbage, Brussels sprouts, broccoli, kale, winter cauliflower	*In heavy rainfall areas add rock phosphate and rock potash. In all areas add manure in autumn or spring, and seaweed solution in summer.* Early potatoes *followed by* Leeks *Lime in autumn after the crop if necessary.*
Brassicas	**Roots**
Heavy compost in autumn or spring. Cabbage family *from last year* + summer cabbage, cauliflower and early Brussels sprouts, turnip, swede. Lettuce and radish intercrop. *Green manure when winter greens finish if possible.*	*Compost for onion family in autumn or spring.* Onion, garlic, leeks. Carrot, parsnip, beetroot and other roots. *Green manure with vetches or rye grass and clover, not later than October to dig in spring if possible.*

Four course crop rotation

plan of your rotation each year, with details of what vegetables went where —do not rely on fickle memory.

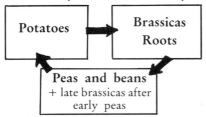

Three course crop rotation
Feed and lime as in four course rotation. Make sure brassicas and roots swap ends when they come back to the same section.

Green manure

In your vegetable garden you want to get as much food as possible from the space available and from the energy of the sun. To do this it is necessary to have as much of the garden as possible covered with green plants. Any green growth dug back into the soil will make extra plant nutrients available, particularly to poor thin soils which are lacking in humus. If you grow a green manure instead of leaving land fallow to grow weeds, you can choose plants which give the maximum amount of nutrition and humus, which grow fast, and will stop growing when you want them to. By digging in manure crops before they flower you can be sure that they will not seed themselves.

Summer green manure will be the most use in large gardens where fertility can be increased by having a manure crop in the rotation. Mustard is useful after an early potato crop for curing wireworm as well as adding fertility, but it can spread clubroot, so it should not be grown on land which has just had, or is about to have, the cabbage family grown on it.

No-dig gardening

This method of gardening is dear to my heart and to my back.

There are several reasons for not digging in the garden. If you bury manure or compost nine inches down in the soil you remove it from the oxygen and soil bacteria necessary to break it down into the nutrients which a plant can use. Thus the plant only benefits fully a year later, when the compost or manure is brought up to the top of the soil and more food is buried nine inches deep. Most of the plant's feeding roots are in the top three or four inches, and this is where eighty per cent of the useful soil bacteria live.

To retain moisture in the soil it is best to keep it firm. Capillary action bringing water up from the water table is disturbed by deep digging, and this can lead to the drying out of the top layers of the soil in the spring and early

Manure crop	Sowing time	Dig under	Sowing rate/yd² (m²)
Annual lupin	April-July	After 8 weeks	¼oz/6g; 1"/25mm deep;
	August	Before flowering	6"/15cm between rows
Mustard	April-July	When sappy, and flower buds showing	1oz/30g
Italian Rye + Late Red Clover	August- mid-October	In spring, when some growth has been made; useful before the potatoes	1½oz/45g
Hungarian Rye	August-early October	March-April when 2'/ 60cm high	1½oz/45g
Winter Tares	August-September March-April	March-April June-July	¼oz/6g; ½"/12mm deep; 3"/7cm apart, 6"/15cm between rows

summer. Another disadvantage of digging the soil is that every year new weed seeds are brought to the surface. It is also hard work.

'Firm' soil need not mean compacted soil. If a soil is kept well mulched and the surface kept warm, soft, damp, fine and friable, it will be just right for seeds and seedlings. The lack of disturbance under this surface layer and the available organic matter encourages worms. These worms will do our digging for us, their tunnels providing the right amount of drainage and aeration, and the worm casts giving us extra nitrates, phosphates and potash in the top layers of the soil. To avoid compaction, do not walk on the growing beds.

The difficulty of surface cultivation is the need for perfectly-rotted, fine, 100% weed-free compost and manure in large quantities. I have found three ways round that difficulty. The first is to have a very small garden, the second is black polythene, and the third is a hay mulch. Fairly good quality compost (or manure for potatoes) can be spread 3-4"/75-100mm deep on the soil when the crops are lifted, then covered with black polythene. Ask silage-making farmers if you can have the black silage bags when they have finished with them, or it can be expensive. Hold the polythene down firmly either with stones or wood, or by digging it in at the edges. Use weights in the middle to stop it billowing.

In spring, when the soil has warmed under the polythene and the weeds have grown and died, the soil is in perfect condition. Take off the polythene, fluff up the soil with a rake, and sow your seeds. As the plants get bigger, mulch with rougher compost and cover this with old hay, grass mowings, rotted sawdust, newspaper, or whatever other clean organic material you can get hold of.

Trenching

Growing certain vegetables over well-filled trenches can be very useful on poor soils, especially when there is not much compost and manure. Trenching is not recommended for clay soils or where drainage is a problem.

For potatoes, dig out trenches 8"/20cm wide by 8"/20cm deep, lay in 2-4"/50-100mm of well-rotted manure, compost and lawn mowings, then 1"/25mm of soil. Water the trench well if it is dry. Place the potatoes on top of the soil with their eyes facing upwards, cover them with soil, and rake the ground as flat as possible.

Peas and beans will appreciate a similar trench, filled during the winter and early spring with kitchen waste (not rat-attracting meat). For a spring trench, line it with newspaper, horsehair, or anything that holds moisture. Cover the trench with soil as soon as it is filled.

Cauliflowers need more refined treatment. Dig a trench 8"/20cm deep by 12"/30cm wide. Fill it with 6"/15cm of extra good compost and mix it with soil to fill up the trench. Use the soil left over to earth up and steady the magnificent cauliflowers as they get larger.

Winter celery trenches need to be 8"/20cm deep and 15"/37cm wide, with the rows about 3'/1m apart. The plants are set out on 4"/10cm of compost or well-rotted manure covered with 3"/75mm of soil. Earth up the plants in August.

If you have no convenient old compost or manure heap on which to grow marrows or courgettes, grow them above prepared holes or trenches. Make the trench 9"/22cm deep and 15"/37cm wide, and alternate 3"/75mm of well-rotted manure or compost with 3"/75mm of topsoil, trampling each layer well down and watering if it is not already damp. In the mound at the top, leave a depression for watering.

Mulches

One of the most important considerations when thinking about mulches for your vegetable garden is availability. I live near a livestock farm, so my favourite mulches are rotten hay and black polythene. Paper feed bags and newspaper can be useful; leafmould is like gold dust; grass clippings or spent hops are good when available. All mulches encourage slugs; straw more than others. Dead bracken is nice and airy for covering globe artichokes in winter, letting air through but protecting the plants against frost. Mulches keep the ground cold if put on too early; put them down in the second half of May.

For more about mulches in general look in 'Helping Your Garden Along'.

Raised beds and intensive cropping

The HDRA's *Raised Bed Gardening* is a good guide to raised bed cultivation and intensive cropping. Here I will give just a brief introduction to the subject.

In a raised bed system the garden is divided by narrow paths into beds 4-5'/1.2-1.5m wide. The beds should be short enough not to tempt anyone into walking over the bed because it is too far round. Make the paths to fit your feet, and the bed width to fit the length of your arms comfortably. Some paths will need to be wide enough for a wheelbarrow. Grass paths are not recommended—they look nice, but the grass competes with the crops in the beds. Keep the paths plant-free with a hoe, sawdust or woodchips.

The beds can be created in different ways—they may be deeply dug with lots of organic matter added, or made with a wood surround and extra soil and organic matter added. The method I used was to rotovate the soil and turf with supplements and manure as deeply as possible, then dig the paths out, throwing the path soil onto the beds.

The intensive-cropping raised bed system is a very old technique, row cultivation only being introduced when horse hoes began to be used in large fields. Where mulching and hand-weeding are possible, raised beds and intensive cropping can give higher yields than row cropping. Work and nutrients only go into the growing area, not into the walkways, and there is less weeding because plants on better soil can be grown closer together and smother out weeds. The size of individual plants can be controlled by careful spacing. Soil structure is more open because there is no need to walk on the beds, drainage is improved by lifting the beds, and the soil tends to be warmer, thus giving an earlier start to spring crops. Because of the closer planting, crops tend to finish earlier too. If the beds are quite high there is less bending over, and it is pleasant to work at a convenient level from a hard path.

A disadvantage of raised beds is that tall crops do not use the space economically. You may also find it hard to get non-hybrid compact forms of the vegetables you want to grow.

Lazy beds

This is a good method for reclaiming ground or in areas of bad drainage, traditionally used for growing potatoes. In autumn or spring, beds are marked out and manure or compost applied to the turf or soil. One barrow-load to 5yd^2/m^2 is good if you can get that much. The turfs in the path areas are then layered face down to the manure, and loose soil piled on top.

Leave the soil loose.

If you want to modernize this method, you can lay black polythene over the bed when the soil is damp. You can choose whether or not you want to leave the polythene on during the growing season.

Scots drills

This gardening technique has come from field cultivation, where horses were used to pull a drill plough, creating ridges on which seed, mainly turnip, was sown. A drill plough was also used in the 'big house' vegetable gardens, while in smaller gardens a draw hoe can be used to make the ridges. The ridge has a depression along its top into which the seed is sown, thus keeping the seed moist and protected.

The advantages of raised drills are ease of weeding and thinning, the plants are just knocked out with a draw hoe, and the raised soil will drain easily and warm up quickly in spring, even where the soil and climate are wet and cold.

Biodynamic vegetable gardening

In his introduction to Philbrick and Gregg's *Companion Planting*, H.H. Koepf uses the Goethe quotation we have borrowed for the back cover of this book: 'Nothing happens in living nature that is not in relation to the whole.' This is one of the fundamental ideas behind biodynamic gardening.

In the garden biodynamic theory is put into practice through the use of well-planned rotations; companion planting; sowing, planting and harvesting by the moon and stars; using biodynamic preparations on crops and soil; improving biological activity in the soil by good cultivation; and particularly by adding biodynamic compost.

Biodynamics are based on the teachings of the Steiner movement, and cannot easily be summed up in a short paragraph. The address list at the end of this book gives sources for more information.

Companion planting

This is a subtle and sensitive approach to gardening, and although it is part of biodynamics, it can be used independently. As you will already know if you have read the 'Friends, Pests and Diseases' chapter, 'companion planting' is a general term for growing plants together which are mutually advantageous. This may be a simple relationship, like the protection from wind that a row of Jerusalem artichokes will provide for a row of lettuce. At a more complex level, broad beans will provide shade for spinach, and spinach in turn will keep the ground cool between the broad beans and discourage blackfly from sucking the beans.

Again this is a complex subject, and books about companion planting are listed in the bibliography.

Planting by the moon and stars

This is a discipline practised by many ancient civilizations. In 1924 Rudolf Steiner pointed to the significance of stellar events and rhythms in his lectures on agriculture which formed the basis of the biodynamic movement. In 1952 Maria Thun began experimental work to develop the science of timing in agriculture.

There is a beautiful Kimberton Hills Agricultural Calendar which gives a detailed guide, down to the specific hours, when particular plants should be sown, planted and harvested. This timing is according to the phases of the moon and the juxtaposition of the moon and certain constellations. Maria and Matthias Thun have also produced the same information in booklet form. Details and an address are given at the end of the book.

Permaculture

'Permaculture' is a word coined by Bill Mollison and David Holmgren in their scheme for a perennial agriculture described in their book *Permaculture One*, published in Australia in 1978. Though the work was pioneered in Australia, the techniques apply world-wide. The authors describe permaculture as 'an integrated evolving system of perennial or self-perpetuating plant and animal species useful to man.'

The system seeks to use indigenous species and varieties of plants and animals, and is based on the use of trees to provide food and shelter for human beings, integrated with the farming and gardening of annual plants.

For more information about permaculture, see the bibliography.

Vegetables

ARTICHOKE, JERUSALEM

Helianthus tuberosus   *N America*

Origins and history: In 1613 tubers were sent to Europe from Ter Neusen, a village in North America, which is one suggestion for the origin of the name. John Parkinson (1569-1629) named them 'Potatoes of Canada'. The name may also derive from the Italian 'girasole articiocco' or 'sunflower artichoke', under which name it was distributed from the Farnese Garden in Rome soon after its introduction to Europe.

Description: Like a knobbly potato with a pungent earthy taste. Stalks and leaves like sunflowers, to which they are closely related; plants grow to 10'/3m. A good windbreak, but can shade other plants. Will spread if tubers are not cleared out in March.

Varieties: Choose the smoothest from your greengrocer or your own stock. If ordering from a catalogue, 'Fuseau' is smooth-surfaced, long and white, with a plant growing to only 5-6'/1.5-2m; 'Boston Red' pretty, but knobbly.

Site and soil: Tolerant; can be grown on most soils. Lime if the soil is very acid. If the soil is short of humus, dig in some compost or manure. pH 6.5-7.5

Propagation:

	J	F	M	A	M	J	J	A	S	O	N	D
Planting			░	░								
Harvest	░										░	░

Planting and harvesting times

Tubers should be the size of small eggs; take 2-4 weeks to sprout after planting.

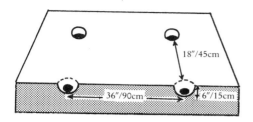

Planting diagram

Care and cultivation: When plants are 12"/30cm high, ridge them up like potatoes; in a windy spot put posts or canes at each end of the row with string or plastic-covered wire each side of the plants. Cut off flower buds.

Harvesting: In autumn cut stalks 12"/25cm above soil level. Smash stalks for compost or strip and dry for support sticks. Dig up tubers as required during winter. Clean out the bed and replant in March, or take what you need and cut the vegetation twice a year for compost. If you cut the plants more often they will die. Time from planting to producing: 7 months. Yield/plant 3-5lbs/1.4-2.3kg.

Kitchen: Cut thin and eat raw with lemon juice. Cook in any way that you would potatoes. Clean well and boil for 20-25 minutes. If you are going to peel them do it after cooking. Artichoke and potato soup is very good and not as strongly-flavoured as the artichoke on its own.

Keeping: Tubers keep fresh for up to 2 weeks in a polythene bag in the fridge.

Pests and diseases: Rarely suffer from pests and diseases. Sclerotinia Rot: stems attacked by fluffy white mould; black cysts develop inside the stem. Lift and burn diseased plants. Root Aphis, Slugs.

Companion planting: Good windbreak and shade for lettuce and spinach.

BEAN, BROAD

Vicia faba   E Mediterranean

Origins and history: Found near Bronze Age sites in Britain; in Egypt seeds have been dated to 2400BC. In the Middle Ages beans were a staple in Britain. They were an ideal crop to store as dried beans for the winter and spring. Broad beans have begun to be eaten green only since canning and freezing became commonplace.

Description: Standard varieties grow about 4'/120cm tall, varying from a 15"/37cm pod with 8-10 green or white kidney-shaped beans, to the Windsors which have 4-7 round seeds within a shorter, broader pod. Bushy dwarf varieties grow to 12-18"/30-45cm high; good for windy gardens or growing under cloches.

Varieties: 'Aquadulce' (white) is hardiest for autumn sowing but not the best flavour; 'Seville Longpod' (white) for autumn sowing, tasty. 'Fenland White Longpod' combines Longpod hardiness with Windsor flavour. 'Green Windsor' and 'White Windsor' for spring sowing, slower to mature but better flavour; 'Sutton' (dwarf white) is the main dwarf variety, 12"/30cm high, requires no staking.

Site and soil: Fairly sunny site; any reasonable soil. Thrives on previously-manured soil, e.g. after potatoes, limed in autumn or winter. Likes lots of potash, so rake seaweed meal into the soil before sowing, put wood ash around the plants when 12"/30cm high, or give a liquid seaweed feed throughout the growing period. pH 6-7.5.

135

Propagation:

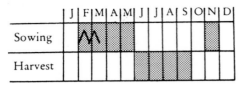

	J	F	M	A	M	J	J	A	S	O	N	D
Sowing												
Harvest												

Sowing and harvesting times

Lifespan of seed: 2 years. Sow at 4oz/120g seed/double 20'/6m row. Germination: 7-14 days. Sowing temperature 41-90°F/5-32°C. For the earliest crop, sow in November. Autumn-sown seeds are very vulnerable to bad weather and mice, so it is usually better to sow under cloches in February-March—even then field mice may eat the lot, especially in country areas—or sow inside and transplant. April is early enough for the main sowing; successional sowings can be made until the end of May. Spring-sown broad beans more vulnerable to blackfly. Sow extra beans at row ends for replacements in case of failures.

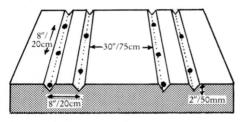

Sowing diagram

Care and cultivation: Hoe regularly and give extra seaweed solution to keep away the Chocolate Spot. If soil is dry when beans begin to form, water well. Tall-growing varieties need support. Drive a stake in at each corner of the double rows, put string along each side at knee height, and tie a short piece of string between the bean plants and the two long strings every 18"/45cm. When first beans are forming or plants are 3'/90cm tall pinch out the top 4-5"/10-12cm of stem to control blackfly, to help get an early crop, and to stop the plants flapping in the wind. When beans have been harvested, cut plants for compost and leave the roots in to provide nitrates from bacteria-holding nodules. It is a good idea to plant Brussels sprouts along these undug rows, though no later than July, as they like the extra nitrates and firm soil.

Harvesting: Yield: 30lb/14kg per double 20'/6m row. Time between autumn sowing and picking: 26 weeks; between spring sowing and picking: 14 weeks. Crop when young; they are not nice to eat when they are big and tough, though still good for soups. Take them first when they are 2-3"/50-75mm long, and later when the beans are showing through the skin of the pod and the joining scar between bean and pod is still green or white. Be careful not to break the plant while taking off the pods.

Kitchen: Small beans and pods may be cooked whole or sliced, boiled, steamed or fried; mature but still small and soft beans boiled for about 10 minutes and eaten with melted butter. Even more mature beans with black scars and leathery jackets can be puréed for soup. The pinched-out upper leaves can also be eaten.

Keeping: Broad beans keep fresh for 3-4 days in the open; up to 2 weeks in the fridge in a polythene bag. Good for freezing.

Pests and diseases: Blackfly: Often a serious pest. Chocolate Spot: Caused by lack of potash; when you see it it's a bit late to do anything. When 12"/30cm high rake in 4oz/120g wood ash per yd^2/m^2 carefully around the plants. Water with seaweed solution once a fortnight during growing season. Pea and Bean Weevils: Create U-shaped notches around the leaves, though broad beans are usually tough enough not to be badly affected (see 'Peas'). Seed Beetle: Discard any bean seeds which have little holes in them; the grubs may still be there. No flowers: Usually results from the soil being too rich with too many nitrates. Do not give manure.

Companion planting: Do well with carrots, cauliflowers, beet, leeks, celeriac and potatoes. Help cucumbers and cabbages. Inhibited by onions, garlic and shallots. Beans and fennel have a mutual dislike.

BEAN, FRENCH

Phaseolus vulgaris   S and C America

Origins and history: Radiocarbon dating shows that these beans were being cultivated in Peru in 8000BC. Reached Europe in the sixteenth century.

Description: Plants are bushy and short, the flowers red, pink or white, and the green pods 4-6"/10-15cm long. Climbing varieties will grow as tall as runner beans; also purple and yellow podded varieties.

sowing outside, wait till soil is well warmed. Plant beans 2"/50mm deep at same spacing as for seedlings, or in double rows 12"/30cm apart.

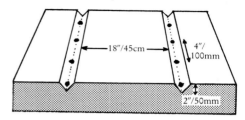

Sowing diagram

Varieties: Dwarf stringless varieties 'Sprite', 'Tendergreen' and 'Phoenix Claudia' good on sandy soils; 'Glamis' specially developed for Scotland. Flatpods include 'The Prince', 'Chevrier Vert', 'Masterpiece' and 'Kinghorn Wax' (yellow). 'Blue Lake' is a climber, and 'Comtesse de Chambord' for drying, both very tasty.

Site and soil: The site should be sheltered and sunny; the soil have enough organic matter not to dry out during the growing season. Lime if necessary in autumn. If potash is short, dig or fork in 4oz/120g wood ash per yd²/m². pH 6-7.5.

Propagation:

	J	F	M	A	M	J	J	A	S	O	N	D
Sowing			MMM									
Harvest												

Sowing and harvesting times

Lifespan of seed: 2 years. Sow at 3oz/85g per 20'/6m. Germination: 7-14 days. Sowing temperature: over 55°F/12°C. In cold areas sow in boxes or pots; plant out when all possibility of frost is over. If

Care and cultivation: Cloches are very useful over French beans while the plants are still small. Hoe regularly or mulch, and earth up like potatoes. Small twigs can be used to support the plants, or strings around the row with small stakes at the ends. Provide support for climbing varieties. Water well and regularly if soil is dry during or after flowering period. Can get caught by September frosts before cropping is finished, so cover late-sown crops with cloches. Can sometimes get a second crop of small beans if the plants are given a liquid feed after harvesting—worth a try.

Harvesting: Sowing to harvesting: 10-13 weeks. Yield per 20'/6m row: 16lb/7kg (dwarfs); 24lb/11kg (climbers). Start picking when bean pods are 4"/100mm long. Pick several times a week and do not allow the pods to grow enormous—this will stop new pods forming. It is safest to use scissors when picking, and the plants should not be loosened. Haricots (dried beans) are harvested when the pods are bulging and yellow. It is best to set aside part of the row to dry rather than leave the last of the beans. Finish off the drying indoors and store in airtight containers—reject any damaged or eaten beans.

Kitchen: French beans are at their best eaten young, straight from the garden. If you have missed this stage, pod them and cook the green beans like peas. Boil in slightly salted water for 5-7 minutes. Serve hot or cold. Cook dried beans in any way suggested for haricot beans, and serve hot, or cold with an oil and vinegar dressing.

Keeping: Fresh beans will keep in a polythene bag in the fridge for up to a week. They freeze well. Dried beans will keep almost for ever.

Pests and diseases: Once you get French beans to germinate they are not much troubled by pests and diseases. Slugs can be a problem.

Companion planting: Helps celery; and is mutually beneficial with cucumbers, cabbage and strawberries.

BEAN, RUNNER

Phaseolus coccineus   Central America

Origins and history: Cultivated for more than two thousand years in Mexico, runner beans reached Europe in the early sixteenth century, but for two hundred years were grown only for their decorative flowers.

Description: A popular crop, especially in the south of Britain, looking beautiful climbing up wigwams, poles, long sticks or plastic netting. Flowers range from white through pink to red and purple. The pods are flat and green, and the plants usually climb to 8-10'/2.4-3m; ground and dwarf varieties to 18-24"/45-60cm.

Varieties:

For poles or netting: 'Achievement' has

heavy crop of long straight pods; 'Enorma' very long pods—both have good flavour and are good for freezing. 'Painted Lady': red and white flowers, tasty beans, and plenty of foliage for a screen. 'Sunset': self-fertilizing, producing an early crop and recommended for freezing. 'Butler' and 'Polestar' are two new stringless varieties, but expensive to buy.

Ground and dwarf varieties: 'Scarlet Emperor' and 'Sunset' can be 'grounded' by pinching out growing points. 'Hammond's Dwarf Scarlet' grows to 24"/60cm.

Site and soil: Runner bean roots do not like to be too wet or dry, hungry or acid. Lime if necessary and incorporate plenty of compost or well-rotted dung deep into the bed or trench. Put in a sheltered position where their dense shade will not harm other plants (though it can help lettuces). pH 6-7.5.

Propagation:

	J	F	M	A	M	J	J	A	S	O	N	D
Sowing				M	M							
Planting												
Harvest												

Sowing, planting and harvesting times

Lifespan of seeds: 2 years. Sow at 1½oz/40g per 20'/6m double row. Germination 7-14 days. Sowing temperature: over 55°F/12°C. Sow seeds mid-April/end June, in ground or boxes of seed compost. If planting, use same distances as for sowing outside.

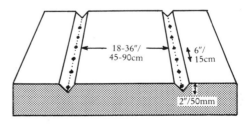

18-36"/45-90cm   6"/15cm   2"/50mm

Planting diagram

Care and cultivation: Early sowings in the north under cloches are likely to be decimated by slugs; always sow a few extra seeds at the end of the rows to fill in later. Put up poles when sowing to avoid disturbance later (or netting in June)—poles are rigid and easier to disentangle after harvesting, or grow them up sisal baler twine, then compost the lot. Water if dry, and mulch while soil is still damp. Pinch out shoots when they reach the top of the poles or net. If being grown without stakes, pinch out growing points as soon as they curl, and pinch out subsequent growth. Keep plants cropping well by giving seaweed solution feeds while beans are being picked.

Harvesting: Sowing to harvesting: 12-14 weeks. Yield: 120lb/55kg per 20'/6m double row. Start picking before they start to swell, when the pods are 6-8"/15-20cm long. Do not leave any to grow very big or the plant will stop producing. Pick 3 or 4 times a week. If any beans are to be dried for seed, choose a few plants and leave all their pods to ripen.

Kitchen: Top and tail pods, stripping strings from edges, and cut them diagonally into thin strips. Boil in a little water for 5-7 minutes, saving water for a soup or sauce. Drain and serve hot with a little butter.

Keeping: Will keep fresh in the open for 3 days; in a polythene bag in the fridge for a week. Runner beans freeze well.

Pests and diseases: Slugs.

Companion planting: As for other beans. Beets and kohlrabi grow badly if shaded.

BEETROOT

Beta vulgaris   Europe, E Asia

Origins and history: This root, native to Britain, was used to make medicines, the first recorded recipe being Roman from the third century. A German work of 1558 described the fat beetroot, then known as Roman Beet, but at that time it was rare.

Description: A root vegetable, usually round and red, though it can be white or yellow, long or cylindrical, with shiny green edible leaves.

Varieties: 'Cook's Delight' long, and bred for grating raw, does not have the usual earthy taste—has unfortunately been deleted under European regulations, and a substitute, 'Forano', is more easily available. 'Cheltenham Green Top' good storer, long, can be used from the ground in winter if protected. 'Avon Early' round, quick-maturing and bolt-resistant.

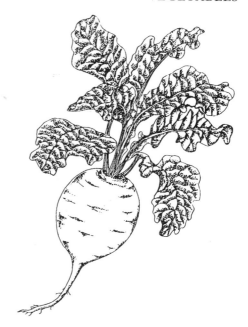

Site and soil: Sunny site and sandy soil high in humus. Keep beetroot in rotation with the other roots after the brassicas. pH 6-7.5.

Propagation:

	J	F	M	A	M	J	J	A	S	O	N	D
Sowing			M									
Harvest												

Sowing and harvesting times

Lifespan of seed: 4 years. Germination: 10-14 days. Sowing temperature: above 45°F/7°C. Sow salad beetroot in March-April under cloches, maincrop in May.

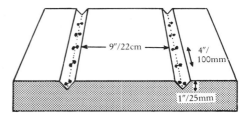

Sowing diagram

Care and cultivation: Thin each cluster of seedlings to one strong plant when plants are 1"/25mm high. Hoe to keep weeds down and mulch if necessary. Pull alternate plants when size of a golf ball—the ideal size for salads—and leave rest to grow to tennis ball size, or larger for storing.

Harvesting: Sowing to lifting: 11 weeks (globes); 16 weeks (longs). Yield per 20'/6m row: 20lb/9kg (globes); 35lb/16kg (longs). Maincrop ready for harvesting late September/October. Do not let frost catch them. Dig up carefully and twist off foliage, leaving 2"/50mm on the root. --

Kitchen: Beetroot is very nutritious, particularly when eaten raw. Tasty too as a hot vegetable, though many people only know it cold, cooked and sliced in vinegar. Good with a white sauce. Can make chutney and wine. Leaves can be cooked like spinach.

Keeping: Can be kept in the fridge for 2 weeks in a polythene bag. Easy to freeze when cooked and cut up. Store biggest and best in layers of sand, peat, sawdust or woodchips in a box, in a cool, dry, frost-free room.

Pests and diseases: Beet Leaf Miner (Mangold Fly) tunnels in leaves of beetroot early in season. Take off leaves and burn them or put them in the dustbin. Give crop a boost with dried blood or liquid feed. Blackfly

Companion planting: Best near French beans, kohlrabi and onions; suffer near runner beans, spinach and tomatoes.

BRASSICAS

The Brassicas or Cabbage Family include cabbages, Brussels sprouts, cauliflower, broccoli and kale, which all follow in alphabetical order within this section. Technically some root crops are also brassicas, but I will use the term in the way it is usually used, which is to cover the green leafy vegetables.

Keep brassicas in strict rotation, not allowing them to grow in the same plot more often than one year in three, to avoid a build-up of the pests and diseases to which the family is prone.

Grow brassicas on a firm, rich, moisture-retentive soil with a pH of 6.5-7.5. Most brassicas need to be sown in a seed bed, sowing temperature 41-90°F/5-32°C, and then transferred to their permanent home when 3-6"/7-15cm high, 5-7 weeks after sowing. Transplant firmly with lowest

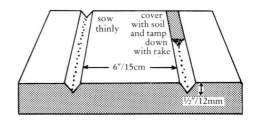

Seed bed sowing distances and technique

leaves just above soil surface; if you pull a leaf the plant should stay in the ground. Put water in the hole just before transplanting, and water immediately afterwards, preferably with seaweed solution. Putting toilet roll inners over young plants, buried ¾"/18mm in the soil, discourages soil pests. Earth up when growing well.

Pests and diseases: The brassica list of pests and diseases may well put you right off growing them, but be willing to try again. Birds can be a big problem in winter or spring, and the plants may need netting. Cabbage Root-Fly: first signs are tinged leaves and a proneness to wilt in hot weather; young plants collapse and die, older plants grow very slowly. Cauliflowers fail to form decent-sized heads and cabbages fail to heart. Put collars of roofing felt, plastic or linoleum on the soil surface tight around the stem of the plant to prevent flies laying eggs above the roots, though this can attract slugs to shelter there early in the season. To discourage maggots once on the roots, put a piece of rhubarb down the planting hole. When transplanting, take drastic action and wash them thoroughly in clean water. Sprinkle dried blood around plants and draw the soil up around the stalks to help them make new roots and grow on. If all else fails, get new plants. Club Root (Fingers and Toes): signs and symptoms much the same as for Root-Fly, but when you pull up the plants, roots are fat and distorted. The disease is caused by a slime fungus which can get into your garden in the groundwater or via boots, wheelbarrow wheels or introduced plants. Burn the plants. Prefers damp acid conditions, so the situation can be helped by good drainage and correct liming. If club root is severe, brassicas should not be grown on the site for 9 years.
Cabbage Caterpillars: risk period is April to

October. Holes appear in leaves and you can find and pick off fat green caterpillars of the Small Cabbage White Butterfly, or stripy hairy caterpillars of the Large Cabbage White. Cabbage Moth caterpillars tend to feed in the centre of the plants. Flea Beetles attack seed-leaves and eat holes in leaves. Can destroy a crop before it has got going.
Cabbage Aphids: can move in on unhealthy plants and make them unusable.
Old brassica stalks should always be dug up, smashed, and used under the compost or in pea and bean trenches. For a diagnosis of brassica troubles, see D.G. Hessayon's *The Vegetable Expert*, but do not use his chemical remedies.

Companion planting: Late brassicas and early potatoes do well together. Brassicas like dill, chamomile, sage, rosemary and mint. To repel Cabbage White Butterflies plant tomatoes, sage, rosemary, hyssop, thyme, mint and hemp. Brassicas dislike strawberries and onions. Red cabbage and tomatoes are incompatible.

Purple sprouting broccoli

BROCCOLI

Brassica oleracea italica — *Mediterranean*

Origins and history: Name means 'little shoot' in Italian; introduced into Britain in the mid sixteenth century.

Description: Sprouting groups of flower buds on a hardy 3'/90cm high plant. Calabrese, the green sprouting variety, is harvested in autumn, and purple or white sprouting broccoli the following spring.

Varieties:
Calabrese: 'Green Comet' F_1, rather like a green cauliflower; 'Autumn Spear' small shoots September-November.
Purple Sprouting: 'Christmas Purple Sprouting' difficult to grow in the north; 'Early Purple Sprouting' most popular, more compact than other spring broccoli.
White Sprouting: 'Nine Star Perennial': heads appear in April-May for many years if you cut all the flowers and mulch feed in spring. Some resistance to club root.

Site and soil: Soil should be reasonable and firm, and the site sunny. Plant after the peas and beans in a rotation. pH 6-7.

Propagation:

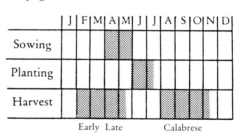

	J	F	M	A	M	J	J	A	S	O	N	D
Sowing												
Planting												
Harvest												

Early Late   Calabrese

Sowing, planting and harvesting times

Lifespan of seed: 4 years. Germination 7-12 days.

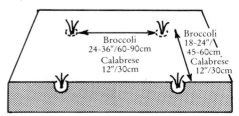

Broccoli
24-36"/60-90cm
Calabrese
12"/30cm

Broccoli
18-24"/
45-60cm
Calabrese
12"/30cm

Planting diagram

Care and cultivation: May need staking. Mulch around plants when soil is damp. Broccoli, along with kale, is the easiest of the brassicas to grow successfully.

Harvesting: Sowing to harvesting: 12 weeks (calabrese); 44 weeks (sprouting varieties). Yield/plant: 1½lbs/700g. Start to cut when spears or flower buds are well formed but not yet opening; becomes tough and tasteless when it begins to flower. Cut central spears first and then side shoots.

Kitchen: For best flavour, steam spears for 15 minutes soon after picking. Eat hot with butter; cold with vinaigrette. Try raw in salads.

Keeping: Keeps in a polythene bag in a fridge for 3 days. Freezes well.

BRUSSELS SPROUTS

Brassica oleracea gemmifera *Europe*

Origins and history: Developed from a sport which appeared in Belgium about 1750; not grown in Britain in any quantity until 1850s.

Description: Sprouts appear as small cabbage-like growths on main stem, in the leaf axils. Plants 18-36"/45-90cm high.

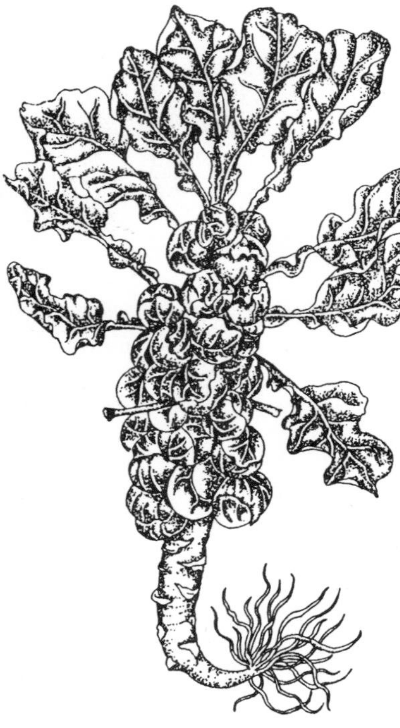

Varieties: 'Early Half Tall' compact, crops September-midwinter; 'Bedford Fillbasket' mid-season, large sprouts and heavy yields. 'Bedford Asmer Monitor' more compact, mid-season. 'Roodnerf' and 'Rubine' late red varieties with good flavour.

Site and soil: Firm fertile soil; need not be as rich as for cabbages and cauliflowers. Site should be reasonably sunny and sheltered. Fork compost into soil in autumn before crop is planted, preferably after legumes.

Propagation:

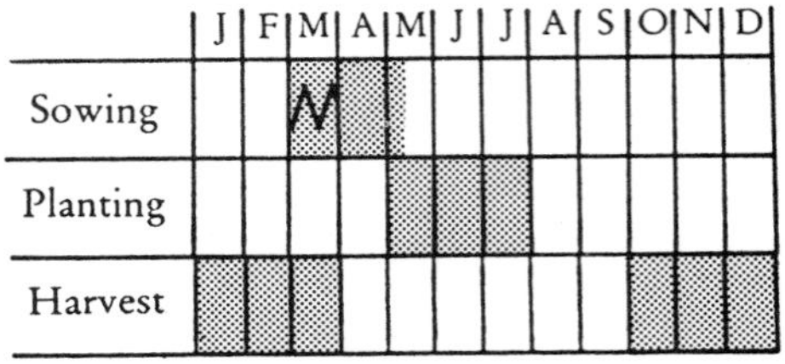
J F M A M J J A S O N D
Sowing
Planting
Harvest

Sowing, planting and harvesting times

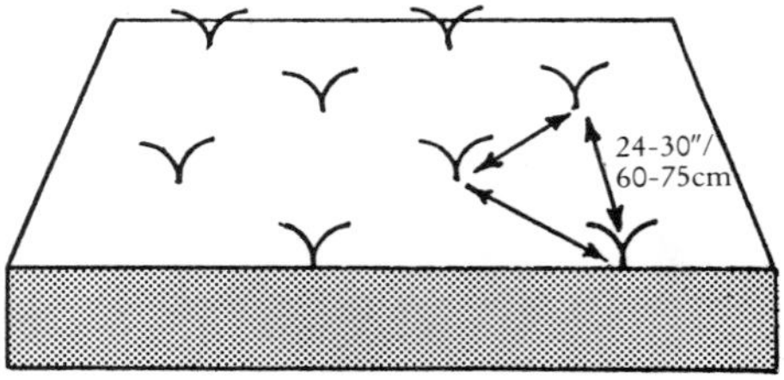
24-30"/
60-75cm

Planting diagram

Care and cultivation: Hoe regularly, and water young plants. Stake tall varieties.

Harvesting: Sowing to picking: 28 weeks (earlies); 36 weeks (lates). Yield/plant: 2lb/900g. Start to pick when sprouts at bottom of stem are eating size and still tightly closed. Cut with a knife or push downwards, using sprouts from each plant at each picking rather than taking all from a few plants. Remove blown sprouts and yellow leaves. When all sprouts have been eaten, stem top can be eaten as cabbage.

Kitchen: Do not boil to a yellow mush. Very good cut up or grated in a salad, or boiled for 7-8 minutes in an inch of water.

Keeping: Not more than 3 days in a bag in the fridge. They freeze well.

Pests and diseases: Brussels sprouts are the particular favourite of pigeons.

CABBAGE

Brassica oleracea capitata
Europe, W Asia

Origins and history: The wild cabbage has a loose leafy head; it was only under cultivation that the hard-headed varieties evolved. The name possibly derives from the Latin 'caput' or 'head'—the botanical name certainly does.

Description: Layer upon layer of leaves wrapped tightly together; apart from the stalk the whole plant is edible. Although usually spherical, cabbages can also be pointed or long. Categorized by harvesting season into summer, winter and spring varieties. Chinese cabbage is in a category of its own.

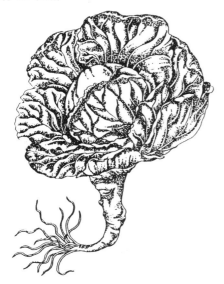

Varieties:
Summer varieties (sown under glass in February/March or outside April/May): 'Greyhound' (pointed) sold in many garden centres, very quick to mature; 'Golden Acre' (round) also very popular; 'Minicole' F$_1$ (round) will stand for 3 months without splitting; 'Red Drumhead' a hardy solid red cabbage, good for pickling or storing; 'Dwarf Red Dutch' a small, hardy red, sow in autumn and overwinter; 'Summer Monarch' for cooking and salads, recommended by Lawrence Hills, but difficult to find except through the HDRA.
Winter varieties (sown April/May): 'January King' has red-tinged leaves like a savoy, but less curled; 'Holland Late Winter' a white cabbage for coleslaw and storage; 'Best Of All': savoy (large crinkly leaves), cut in September; 'Ormskirk Rearguard' very hardy and late savoy, lasts into March or April; 'Aquarius' F$_1$ savoy has compact habit for close planting; a weak starter.
Spring varieties (sown July/August to provide spring greens—collards—or left to mature into conical heads; in cold areas overwintered under cloches or in a cold frame and planted out in spring): 'April' recommended for flavour, very early, compact and reliable; 'Harbinger' matures over a long period.
Chinese cabbage (*Brassica pekinensis*: look more like cos lettuces than ordinary cabbages): 'Sampan' F$_1$ good bolt resistance, sown from April onwards; 'Pe Tsai' sown July/August, pale green and up to 2'/60cm tall; 'Two Seasons' F$_1$ suitable for both April and July sowing.

Site and soil: Dig or fork in compost in autumn. If not following legumes in a rotation, lime. Unshaded site. pH 6-7.5.

Propagation:

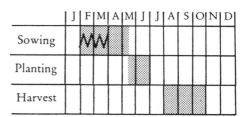

SUMMER CABBAGE

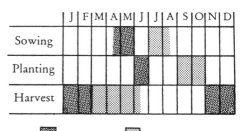

| | winter | | spring |

WINTER AND SPRING CABBAGE
Sowing, planting and harvesting times

Lifespan of seed: 5 years. Germination 7-12 days.

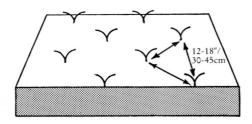

Planting diagram

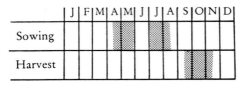

	J	F	M	A	M	J	J	A	S	O	N	D
Sowing												
Harvest												

Sowing and harvesting times (Chinese cabbage)

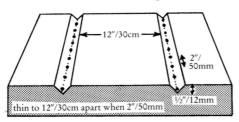

Sowing diagram (Chinese cabbage)

Care and cultivation: Hoe until plants are growing well and then mulch. Water if necessary and give a liquid feed when the heads start to go into a ball. Tie heads of Chinese cabbage with raffia or string in August.

Harvesting: In early spring, greens can be taken from rows of spring cabbage, with plants left at 1'/30cm intervals to grow on. Can get secondary crop of little cabbages from stumps left between by cutting a ½"/12mm deep cross on the stump.

Kitchen: Eaten raw in coleslaw or in a vinaigrette dressing, pickled in vinegar or made into sauerkraut. Cooked, cabbage can be boiled, stir-fried, baked, made into soup, casseroled or braised.

Keeping: Cabbages are usually cut and eaten immediately, but red and winter white cabbages can be cut in November and stored in a straw-lined box in a cool dry place. Most cabbage will keep for a week in a fridge in a polythene bag; Chinese cabbage for several weeks. It is possible to freeze cabbage after blanching it.

CAULIFLOWER

Brassica oleracea botrytis
E Mediterranean

Origins and history: Known and eaten by the Romans. Gerard (1597) called it 'Cole Flowery'. Grown widely after the late seventeenth century. Purple and red types were once common.

Description: A single stem bearing a large roundish flower-head, called the curd, made up of underdeveloped white or creamy-white flower buds. Sits within strong pointed leaves, which in summer cauliflowers are spreading or erect, and in winter and spring cauliflowers are wrapped over the curd.

Varieties:
Summer varieties (sown under glass in February or outdoors in April): 'Snowball' good early variety; 'All The Year Round' a versatile cauliflower; 'Alpha' an early cauliflower which can cope with difficult conditions.
Autumn variety (sown outside April-May): 'Veitch's Self-Protecting' large, frost-resistant.
Winter varieties (sown outside in May): 'Northern Star' very hardy, recommended for north of Britain, heads in May; 'Purple Cape' hardy, produces purple curds in March/April.

Site and soil: Cauliflowers are the *really* fussy members of the brassica family. Choose a fairly sunny site and work one bucket per 2yd² (m²) of compost into the soil in autumn. Lime new ground in winter, or follow well-limed legumes in a rotation. Be careful not to over-lime as cauliflowers, like turnips, are very susceptible to boron deficiency (boron is locked up in very alkaline soils). Make sure soil is firm. pH 5.5-7.5.

Propagation:

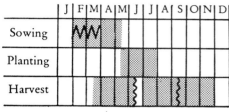

	J	F	M	A	M	J	J	A	S	O	N	D
Sowing												
Planting												
Harvest												

winter   summer   autumn

Sowing, planting and harvesting times

Lifespan of seed: 5 years. Germination 7-12 days.

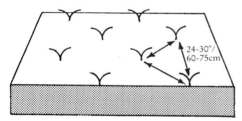

24-30"/ 60-75cm

Planting diagram

Care and cultivation: If plants are not growing away 3 weeks after transplanting, scatter 2oz/yd² (60g/m²) of dried blood to perk them up. Keep weedfree by hoeing and then giving a good mulch. Make sure soil does not dry out or plants will quickly make very small curds, and feed the plants with liquid manure until end of July. Protect curds against sun and snow by breaking leaves over them. Push plant over to delay harvest.

Harvesting: Sowing to harvesting: 18-24 weeks (summer and autumn varieties); 40-50 weeks (winter varieties). Yield/plant 1-2lbs/500-900g. Start taking cauliflowers to eat before they are full-size to avoid a glut. Will spoil if florets start to separate. A few leaves broken over the curd will keep a growing cauliflower back a few days.

Kitchen: Cook cauliflower carefully to keep it firm and tasty. Good with a white, brown or parsley sauce; perfect with cheese sauce. Looks nice cooked whole, but easier cut into sprigs. Good cut up in a salad.

Keeping: Will keep up to 3 weeks if hung up by their roots in a cool shed and misted occasionally with water. In a polythene bag in the fridge will keep for a week. Cauliflowers can be frozen, but are disappointingly tasteless when defrosted.

Pests and diseases: Boron deficiency shows up as brown patches on curds, and is caused by overliming (see 'Brown Heart' under 'Turnip'). Pigeons.

Companion planting: Good near celery.

KALE (BORECOLE)

Brassica oleracea acephala
E Mediterranean

Origins and history: The name kale was originally used, like the German cognate 'kohl', to cover most of the cabbage family. Today the name is used for those brassicas which have crinkly leaves and do not form a head, for which the more precise name is borecole, a name which comes from the Dutch word 'boerenkoel', or peasant's

cabbage. The rape-kales are descended from the wild *Brassica campestris*, the ancestor of turnips and swedes.

Description: Range from dwarf and curly kales like parsley on stalks, to pale green plain-leaved kales, to the strange-looking and delicious purple of Ragged Jack.

Varieties:
Rape-kales (not to be transplanted): 'Asparagus Kale' delicious, but not easy to obtain; 'Ragged Jack' very prolific and easy to grow, available from HDRA (will transplant); 'Hungry Gap' easily available.
Borecoles: 'Dwarf Green Curled' hardy, can be picked from November; 'Tall Green Curled' rather tough and bitter; 'Thousand-Headed Kale' has delicious young shoots and can be picked from February onwards; 'Pentland Brig' has curly-edged leaves to be eaten in November, shoots in early spring, and broccoli-like flower spears later.

Site and soil: Kales do not like rich feeding, and are best planted on a soil cleared from a previous crop of peas and beans. Do not need transplanting until July, so possible to put them in after early legumes. Keep ground firm, clip off bean or pea plants, pull out weeds, and rake ground flat. pH 6-7.5.

Propagation:

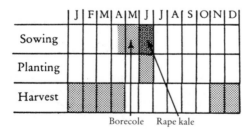

	J	F	M	A	M	J	J	A	S	O	N	D
Sowing												
Planting												
Harvest												

Borecole   Rape kale

Sowing, planting and harvesting times

Lifespan of seed: 4 years (borecole); 5 years (rape kale). Germination: 7-12 days.

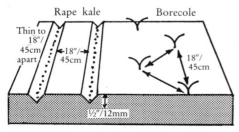

Rape kale   Borecole

Thin to 18"/45cm apart   ←18"/45cm→   18"/45cm

½"/12mm

Sowing and planting diagram

Care and cultivation: Stake tall varieties and plants that have fallen over. In February give liquid manure to help shoot growth.

Harvesting: Sowing to cutting: 30-35 weeks. Yield/plant: 2lbs/900g. Curly-leaved varieties can be eaten in the autumn, clipping off only young leaves. When fresh shoots come between February and May, pick before they get too big: 4-5"/10-12cm long is best.

Kitchen: Use raw in salads, or cook for 5-8 minutes in a little boiling water.

Keeping: Kale can be frozen. Can be stored in a fridge in a polythene bag for 3 days.

CARROT

Daucus carota sativa   *Mediterranean*

Origins and history: In Germany and France carrots were being grown in fields and gardens by the thirteenth century, and in the sixteenth century botanists described red and purple carrots in France and orange carrots in England. Carrots have been widely used as a sweetener, as recently as the Second World War when sugar was scarce.

Description: Vary from golf-ball and finger-sized earlies to giant long-rooted varieties. All a fairly uniform orange colour with fern-like leaves.

Varieties:
Earlies (sown under glass in February/March; April/July outdoors in succession): 'Amsterdam Forcing' the usual finger-sized early carrot; 'Early French Frame' round and fast-developing; 'Early Nantes' quick to mature.

Maincrop (sow outside April-June): 'Autumn King' good for storing and hardy, slightly carrot fly resistant; 'Regulus Imperial' a good keeper; 'James Scarlet Intermediate' half-long, broad and tapered; 'New Red Intermediate' very long, best for sandy soil, keeps well.

Site and soil: Sunny site, and a soil manured or composted for the previous crop, preferably brassicas. Do not like heavy or stony land, but stump-rooted varieties will manage. pH 5.5.-7.

Propagation:

	J	F	M	A	M	J	J	A	S	O	N	D
Sowing			M									
Harvest												

for young crop in Nov/Dec sow early variety in August; cover with cloches from October

Sowing and harvesting times

Lifespan of seed: 4-5 years. Germination 17-20 days. Sowing temperature: over 45°F/7°C. Useful to cover bed with black polythene, which will kill germinating weeds, stop bed getting too wet or too dry, and help warm soil. Rake seed bed into a fine tilth. Mix dry sand with seed to sow thinly.

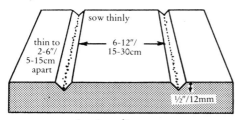

sow thinly

thin to 2-6"/ 5-15cm apart

6-12"/ 15-30cm

½"/12mm

Sowing diagram

Care and cultivation: If your hand slipped when sowing, you will need to thin, muttering incantations to ward off carrot fly. If 1-2"/25-50mm apart leave and thin when harvesting. Burn discarded seedlings. Water seedlings that are left with seaweed solution or sprinkle 1oz/yd^2 (30g/m^2) of dried blood. Earth them up: dry earth and exposed root tops will leave them more vulnerable to carrot fly. Hoe between rows until foliage is thick enough to shade out weeds. If soil is dry, water regularly; a large amount of water on a dry soil will cause carrots to split.

Harvesting: Sowing to harvesting: 12 weeks (earlies); 16 weeks (maincrop). Yield/20'/6m row: 8lb/3.6kg (earlies); 20lb/9kg (maincrop). Pull up or dig small early carrots as required for eating. Harvest maincrop carrots for storing in October. Lift carefully with a fork on a sunny day. Gently rub off surface soil checking for damaged or diseased carrots: only perfect carrots more than 1"/25mm diameter at the top should be stored. Cut foliage off an inch from the root top.

Kitchen: Carrots are very versatile. Can be eaten raw, either whole, chopped or grated. Liquidized cooked carrots make a delicious soup. Carrots can be added to stews, cut into matchsticks for stir-fries, steamed, or boiled in a little water for 15 minutes.

Keeping: Will keep in the refrigerator for 2 weeks if stored in a polythene bag. If freezing carrots, choose small young ones. There are many ways of storing carrots for long periods without freezing: easiest for the small garden is a box of sand, peat, sawdust or woodchips. Carrots are stored in layers *not* touching each other, and the box kept in a cool, dry, mouse- and frost-free place. Check occasionally and remove rotten carrots before they infect adjacent ones.

Pests and diseases: The awesome carrot fly is the scourge of every gardener; in some areas the situation is so bad that it is hardly worth growing carrots. See under 'Friends, Pests and Diseases' for remedies. Carrot Aphid may turn leaves red or yellow; if you run your hand along the foliage and it feels sticky with honeydew it is the feeding ground of aphids, particularly if the plant is stressed due to lack of water. Look under 'Aphids'.

Companion planting: Grows well with lettuce and chives; helps growth of peas.

CELERIAC

Apium graveolens rapaceum
Europe, W Asia

Origins and history: Derived from wild celery; probably an eighteenth century variant of celery.

Description: A very knobbly swollen root-

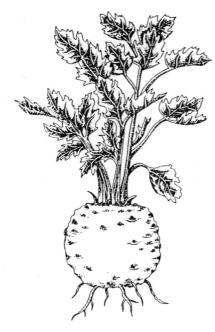

like stem about 4-5"/10-12cm in diameter with a flattened base, brownish with white flesh. The leaves are slender and bitter.

Varieties: 'Tellus' quick-growing and smooth-skinned; 'Marble Ball' medium-sized and round with a good strong flavour, stores well in winter.

Site and soil: Needs a very fertile soil. Fork in manure or compost in autumn or spring. pH 6-7.

Propagation:

	J	F	M	A	M	J	J	A	S	O	N	D
Sowing			W									
Planting												
Harvest												

Sowing, planting and harvesting times

Lifespan of seed: 5 years. Germination: 12-18 days. Sow under glass in March at 60-65°F/15-18°C, preferably in peat pots. Sow 3 to a pot and later remove weaker

seedlings. Harden off before planting out in May or June, when plants have a slight swelling at base. Swelling should sit on top of soil.

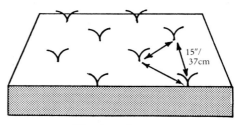

Planting diagram

Care and cultivation: Hoe regularly and mulch in early summer when soil is moist. Feed with liquid manure every 2-3 weeks from 6 weeks after planting to end of July. Earth up in early September.

Harvesting: Sowing to harvesting: 30-35 weeks. Yield per 20'/6m row: 14lb/6kg. Best to harvest the whole crop at maximum size, since taste does not deteriorate nor does flesh become tough and stringy with age. In cold areas lift in October-November; in mild areas cover roots with straw and lift as required until early spring, like parsnips.

Kitchen: Grate or cut into strips for a winter salad, or boil in cubes for half an hour in water to which a little salt and lemon juice have been added.

Keeping: Cut off roots, twist off tops, and store in sand or peat in boxes in a cool, frost- and mouse-proof place. Can be frozen in cubes.

Pests and diseases: Slugs; Celery Fly (see under 'Celery').

Companion planting: Good with leeks. Helps protect brassicas from caterpillars.

CELERY

Apium graveolens   Europe

Origins and history: A ninth century French poem talks of the medicinal value of the plant, and in sixteenth-century Italy celery was still only being used as a medicine. By the mid-eighteenth century the cultivation of celery had evolved to create a less bitter stalk, and it became a culinary delicacy all over Europe.

Description: Biennial plant, stalks of which are eaten in first year. Leaves light green; stalks may be white, pink, yellow or green.

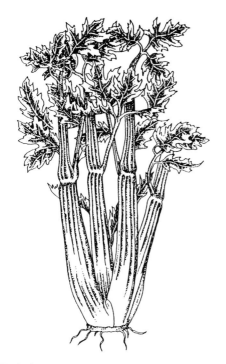

3 to a pot, later removing weaker seedlings. Harden off and plant out after danger of frost.

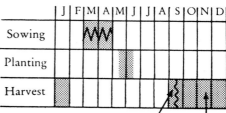

	J	F	M	A	M	J	J	A	S	O	N	D
Sowing			〰	〰	〰							
Planting							▒					
Harvest	▒								〰	▒	▒	▒

Self-blanching Trench

Sowing, planting and harvesting times

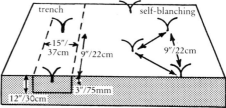

trenches 36″/90cm apart

Planting diagram

Varieties:

Trench varieties: 'Solid White' to eat from October to Christmas; 'Dwarf White' needs less earthing up; 'Solid Pink' hardiest variety; 'Wright's Giant Red' lasts until the end of February.

Self-blanching varieties: 'Golden Self-Blanching' most popular, reasonable flavour, ready to eat in August; 'Avonpearl' less stringy than others; 'American Green' has solid hearts, pale green stalks, crisp and stringless.

Site and soil: Not too sunny, and soil very fertile and moisture-retentive. The celery trench should be dug in April, the bottom of the trench well forked, a layer of manure or compost well trodden in, and covered with soil to within 3″/75mm of the top. Self-blanching varieties should be grown in blocks to give a little shade to the inner plants. Dig in a bucketful of manure per 2yd^2 (2m^2) in spring. pH 6-7.

Propagation: Lifespan of seeds: 5 years. Germination: 12-18 days. Sow seeds of both trench and self-blanching varieties indoors in March at 60-65°F/15-18°C,

Care and cultivation: Harden off and plant out late May-mid June. Do not let plants get dry or crowded as this will make them bolt later. If buying plants, get them from a good nursery at planting time. After planting fill the block and the trench with water. Celery needs lots of water and a lot of extra food. Give liquid manure every fortnight until the end of August. Blanch trench varieties, which should be about 1′/30cm high, in August: remove side shoots, wrap newspaper or cardboard around stalks, tie loosely, and fill trench with soil. 3 weeks later pile earth right up to leaves, taking care not to get soil into heart. Firm ridges with back of spade. If likely to be frost, cover with straw. Hoe between self-blanching varieties and tuck straw between outside plants to assist blanching.

Harvesting: Sowing to harvesting: 24 weeks (self-blanching); 40 weeks (trench). Yield per 20′/6m row: 25lb/11kg. Harvest self-blanching varieties before hard frosts arrive; try not to disturb neighbouring plants. Lift trench varieties before Christmas if white, and in January/February if pink or red. Take plants from one end of the row, always carefully covering up next plant each time.

Kitchen: Usually eaten raw in sticks or cut up in salads. Best to eat inner stalks raw and use outer ones cut up in stews, soups or stir-fries. Celery hearts can be braised.

Keeping: Will stay fresh in a refrigerator in a polythene bag for 3 days. Can be frozen if cut up and blanched; use in cooked dishes.

Pests and diseases: Celery Fly (Leaf Miner) grubs make winding tunnels and blisters in leaves from May onwards. Pick off affected leaves; if a lot of leaves are taken off give 2oz/60g dried blood per 10'/3m of row. Celery Leaf Spot: brown spots appear on leaves and spread over the foliage. Treatment as for Celery Fly. Celery Heart Rot: heart of celery is found to be shiny and rotten when plant is lifted, caused by bacteria entering through a wound. Celery should not be grown on affected soil next season. Slugs. Split stalks can be caused either by dry soil or by an excess of nitrates in the soil. Plants should be kept moist, and given a high-potash feed in the summer.

Companion planting: Mutually beneficial to leeks; helped by tomatoes and French beans.

CUCUMBER

Cucumis sativus   *Central Asia*

Origins and history: Emperor Tiberius ate cucumbers, as did Charlemagne in the ninth century. They were first grown in England in the fourteenth century.

Description: Long green vegetables which grow on vines. Inside the green skin the flesh is white, watery and translucent. Cucumbers consist mostly of water, often as much as 97%. Can either be grown outdoors or in a greenhouse or frame, and different varieties are used with different propagation and cultivation techniques.

OUTDOOR CUCUMBER

Green fruit relatively short, fat and warty; also yellow 'apple' varieties, and long smooth green varieties recently developed. Outdoor cucumbers are less work and more tasty than indoor cucumbers—but much later harvesting.

Varieties: 'Burpless Tasty Green' F_1 the best, sweet and digestible; 'Long Green' heavy cropping.
Gherkin variety (short, used for pickling): 'Venlo Pickling' usual variety.
Apple variety: 'Crystal Apple' prolific and easy to grow.

Site and soil: Like sunshine and protection

from strong winds. Soil must be well drained and rich in humus. pH 5.5-7.5.

Propagation: Lifespan of seed: 7 years. Germination: 6-9 days. Sowing temperature: over 56°F/13°C. Grown on mound or ridge formed by digging a hole 12"/30cm³ or a trench 12"/30cm wide and 12"/30cm deep, filling it with alternate layers of soil and compost. Last layer should be soil, left in a mound or ridge. Tread each layer down, and water if dry. Sow 3 seeds in middle of mound, or every 24"/60cm along ridge, 1"/25mm deep and 2"/50mm apart, laying edgewise

	J	F	M	A	M	J	J	A	S	O	N	D
Sowing				▲								
Planting						▓						
Harvest								▓				

RIDGE CUCUMBERS

	J	F	M	A	M	J	J	A	S	O	N	D
Sowing												
Planting												
Harvest												

GREENHOUSE CUCUMBERS
Sowing, planting and harvesting times

in soil. Cover with plastic, cloche or jar, especially in cold areas. Can sow seeds indoors in April at 70-80°F/21-27°C and transplant in June after hardening off gradually.

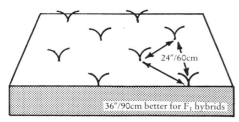

Planting diagram (ridge and greenhouse)

Care and cultivation: Thin to most vigorous when have first pair of true leaves. When plants have 7 true leaves pinch tip out to produce side shoots, which can trail over the ground or be trained up mesh. Keep the plants watered round bases, making sure not to get water on leaves or stalks; water in the morning. Black polythene round plant will retain moisture, protect fruit from rot, and keep down weeds. Do not remove male flowers as female flowers must be fertilized to produce cucumbers (except for a few newly-developed all-female varieties). Once first fruits are swelling give a high-potash liquid feed, or top-dress with 3"/75mm of compost around the plant.

GREENHOUSE CUCUMBER
Varieties:
Unheated greenhouses (remove male flowers): 'Telegraph' late Victorian variety, still good and popular, up to 18"/45cm long; 'Butcher's Disease Resisting' rougher skin but more prolific; 'Conqueror' a heavy cropper with outstanding flavour.

Heated greenhouses (all-female F₁ hybrids; do not have to have male flowers removed, are more disease-resistant and more prolific, but high temperature is needed to keep them happy): 'Femspot' F₁ early maturing, disease resistant; 'Pepinex' F₁ (formerly 'Femina'), first of F₁ all-female cucumbers; 'Petita' F₁ will stand cooler temperatures; 'Uniflora D' F₁ has no male flowers and no side shoots longer than 6"/15cm: they stop themselves—amazing!

Site and soil: Either grow in bags or pots, or directly in greenhouse soil. If using border soil practise a 3-4 year rotation or change the top 9"/22cm of soil every year. Add plenty of well-rotted manure or compost. Cucumbers benefit from special compost:

4gall/20l moss peat (medium grade)
2gall/10l well-rotted manure or compost
1½gall/7l sharp sand
3oz/85g fine-ground calcified seaweed or hydrated lime
9oz/250g blood, fish and bone
3oz/85g dried seaweed meal or dried wood ash

Propagation: Lifespan of seed: 7 years. Germination: 3-5 days. Sow early March (heated greenhouse) or late April (cool greenhouse). Germination temperature: 70-80°F/21-26°C. Can buy ready-germinated ('chitted') seeds from catalogues. Sow single seed edgeways in above compost ½"/12mm deep in 3"/75mm peat pots.

Care and cultivation: Plant out late March (heated greenhouse) or late May (cool greenhouse), 24"/60cm apart in soil, 1 per pot or small growing bag, or 2 per large growing bag. Water well, keeping water off stem. Growing temperature: 60°F/15°C (ordinary varieties); 70°F/21°C (all-female varieties). Water often to keep soil or compost moist but not too wet. Atmosphere should be humid; when watering, spray water on the floor of the greenhouse, taking care to keep water off leaves and stems. Train up wire or cane, and pinch out the growing point before it reaches roof. Pinch out side shoots 2 leaves beyond 2 female flowers: these have little cucumbers behind them. Male flowers have thin stalks and should be removed. Pinch out tips of flowerless side shoots when 2"/50mm long; also tendrils and sublaterals. When first fruits have started to swell, feed every 2 weeks with high potash feed.

I₅₁

Harvesting: Sowing to harvesting: 14 weeks (outdoor); 12 weeks (greenhouse). Yield/plant: 8 cucumbers (outdoor); 20 cucumbers (indoor). Pick continuously; if left to grow big will stop new fruit developing, and big cucumbers do not taste as good. Cut with knife or secateurs, and strip the plant if a frost is expected, using small cucumbers for pickling.

Kitchen: Usually served raw, sliced thin in sandwiches or in chunks in salads and yogurt. Pickled cucumbers—gherkins —taste good, especially pickled with dill.

Keeping: Can be kept wrapped in poly-thene in the fridge for a week. Cannot be frozen, except as soup.

Pests and diseases: Slugs and Snails; Botrytis; Powdery Mildew.

Companion planting: Good with lettuce, radish, celeriac and French beans. Appreciate the shade of alternate rows of sweetcorn or sunflowers.

GARLIC

Allium sativum   Central Asia

Origins and history: Popular in Ancient Egypt, and now used widely, especially in Mediterranean countries. It is believed to ward off evil spirits, and is used medicinally as an antiseptic as well as in cooking.

Description: In some gardening books garlic is described as a herb, and in others not mentioned at all. It is so easy to grow that it seems a pity not to include it, as its distinctive taste can make many dishes particularly tasty. Garlic bulbs look like small onions, but unlike onions grow underground. The leaves are strap-like, and the bulb becomes white and papery when dry.

Varieties: Can use cloves from a bulb bought in a shop—make sure they are French or Italian—buy from a seed catalogue, or save your own from one year to the next.

Site and soil: Grow in the onion bed, around the carrots. Make sure it is well drained.

Propagation: Plant out March-April. Cloves should be planted pointed end up, 2"/50mm deep and 6"/15cm apart.

Care and cultivation: Hoe to keep free from weeds.

Harvesting: Harvest in August, or when leaves turn yellow. Dig up bulbs and dry them in an airy place out of the rain.

Kitchen: Use either as a flavouring or as a flavour enhancer in a flan or quiche with onions, cheese, eggs and tomato. Also good crushed in an oil and vinegar dressing.

Keeping: String like onions and store in a cool, dry place. Will keep until your next crop is ready to harvest.

Pests and diseases: White Rot (see under 'Onions').

Companion planting: Garlic and roses help each other. Will inhibit peas and beans.

LEAF BEET

Beta vulgaris cicla   Europe, Asia

Origins and history: Aristotle mentions red chard in 350BC. The Romans ate chard and spinach beet, and they were extensively used in the Middle Ages.

Description: The easy-to-grow chards and spinach beets look good in the flower garden. Swiss Chard grows to 18"/45cm high with thick white leafstalks and veins, and bright green leaves. Ruby Chard has red stalks and veins, while Rainbow Chard has red, purple, yellow or white stems. Spinach beet or perpetual spinach looks more like spinach, being bigger than the chards and having narrower leaves.

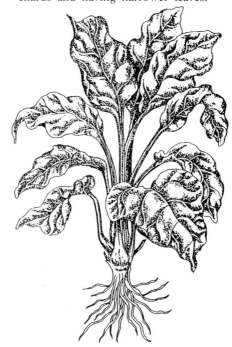

Varieties:
Swiss Chard (Silver Chard; Seakale).
Ruby Chard (Rhubarb Chard).
Rainbow Chard.
Spinach Beet (Perpetual Spinach).
Site and soil: Enjoy sun or light shade and will tolerate fairly dry conditions. pH 6-7.5.
Propagation:

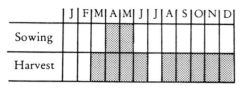

	J	F	M	A	M	J	J	A	S	O	N	D
Sowing												
Harvest												

Sowing and harvesting times

Lifespan of seed: 4 years. Germination: 10-14 days. Sowing temperature: over 45°F/7°C.

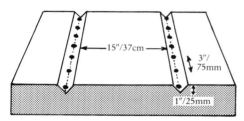

Sowing diagram

Care and cultivation: Thin to 9-12"/22-30cm when seedlings have 3 strong leaves. Hoe regularly and nip off bolting heads; keep moist and mulch if necessary.

Harvesting: Sowing to harvesting: 13-15 weeks. Yield per 20'/6m row: 14lb/6kg. Harvest carefully and regularly. Take leaves before maximum size, and leave central leaves and root undisturbed.

Kitchen: Use like spinach, though a little stronger-tasting. Chard stalks may be cooked separately like asparagus, steaming for 20 minutes, or chopped and boiled for 15 minutes.

Keeping: Leaf beets do not store well.

LEEK

Allium ampeloprasum porrum
Europe, Asia, N Africa

Origins and history: The Romans thought the best leeks were grown in Egypt. The 'Welsh onion' is a variety of leek, *A. fistulosum*, and more popular than the leek in the

Orient. The name 'leek' is Teutonic in origin, the word 'laec' appearing in an Anglo-Saxon document of 1000AD. In fact 'laec' referred to the whole onion family: leeks were 'porleac'. Until the sixteenth century leeks were more popular than onions.

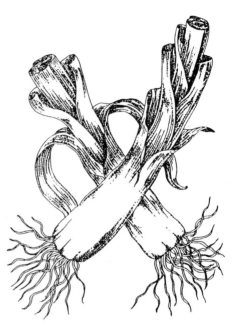

Description: A shank of rolled leaves, white at the bottom, rising to become green with cascading pointed strap-like leaves.

Varieties: 'Lyon Prizetaker' for cropping September-November, long thick stems and a mild flavour; 'Early Market' large early variety but not winter hardy; 'Musselburgh' hardy reliable and fine-flavoured for December-February cropping; 'Winter Crop' very hardy late-season (February-April), good for exposed northern sites; 'Royal Favourite' a giant winter variety, fine-flavoured, late maturing and hardy.

Site and soil: Open, sunny site. Greedy feeders, though not as fussy as onions. Dig in well-rotted compost or manure in autumn or spring. It is possible to get late leeks in after early potatoes in late July or August. pH 6-8.

Propagation: Lifespan of seed: 3 years. Germination 14-18 days. Sowing temperature: 45-75°F/7-24°C. Sow in tray in seed compost in early March, and prick out

153

	J	F	M	A	M	J	J	A	S	O	N	D
Sowing												
Planting												
Harvest												

Sowing, planting and harvesting times

1"/25mm apart into boxes of potting compost. Keep at 50-60°F/10-15°C. Harden off and plant out in June. Late varieties best sown in seed bed ½"/12mm deep in rows 6"/ 15cm apart, thinned to 1"/25mm and planted out in July-August. Young plants are usually available very easily.

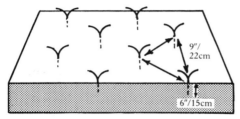

Planting diagram

Care and cultivation: Plant out when 8"/20cm long and as thick as a pencil. If seedbed or box is dry, water the day before planting out. Make holes 6"/15cm deep with a dibber. Fill the holes up with water, *not* soil. If soil is dry after planting out, keep watering. If you want a longer white stem, blanch by drawing soil up around plants. Feed with liquid manure from 6 weeks after planting until end of August. Hoe throughout growing season.

Harvesting: Sowing to harvesting: 30-45 weeks. Yield per 20'/6m row: 20lb/9kg. Start to lift when still small; do not wait until they are at optimum size or you will waste some at the end of the season. Lift with a fork; pulling usually breaks them. If frost threatens to clamp leeks into the ground, put straw around them or dig some up and store them in cool dark place.

Kitchen: Wash leeks well—cut lengthwise first. Eat the nutritious leaves cut thinly in a thick soup or stew; leek and potato soup is delicious. Leeks in white sauce is another traditional dish, and they are good in a leek flan.

Pests and diseases: Leeks are strong and usually stay clear of pests and diseases. The problems they do have they share with onions, and these can be avoided by rotation. Leek Moth (*Acrolepia assetella*) lays its eggs on leaves of leeks, onions, shallots and garlic near ground level April-early May. Caterpillars eat long tunnels in the leaves, robbing the plant of strength. Moths emerge in July. Can be killed in the plants with a nicotine spray. As the leeks are used, the soil should be forked over to encourage birds to eat the chrysalids.

Companion planting: Leeks and celery grow well together. Masks scent of carrots to help against carrot fly.

LETTUCE

Lactuca sativa   Asia Minor

Origins and history: Cultivated in the royal gardens of Persia more than 2,500 years ago. Lettuce was well-known in medieval Europe. The firm-headed lettuce was developed in Europe in the fourteenth and fifteenth centuries. The botanical name, and perhaps the common name too, derives from the Latin word for milk, referring to the milky juice of the plant.

Description: A green leafy plant, essential to summer salads. Lettuces vary from the upright Cos, through the cabbage lettuces, to the curled leaves of the salad bowl types. Though they are usually green, there are some red-tinged varieties.

Varieties:
Spring/summer varieties: 'Tom Thumb' a good butterhead lettuce for a small garden, fine flavour; 'Continuity' another butterhead, with red-tinged leaves. 'Webb's Wonderful' a crisphead lettuce which grows well and stands without bolting for a long time, even in a hot summer; 'Windermere' similar but can also be sown under glass in October for a May crop; 'Lobjoit's Green' a large and crisp cos lettuce, does not need tying up; 'Little Gem' a quick-maturing cos, small and compact; 'Salad Bowl' has loose leaves—cut and come again.
Winter varieties: 'Imperial Winter' will survive the winter in favoured spots and produce large heads in May; 'Arctic King' more compact; 'Premier' for growing in the greenhouse, cold frame or cloche—gives large pale green hearts in April; 'Winter Density' a winter cos.
Site and soil: Soil should be well fed, moist, and not too acid: the brassica patch is ideal. Sow seeds in pots, a seed box, or straight into the bed. Winter/spring lettuce have to be grown under protection or in a warm, well-drained spot. Do not do well in shade or bright sunlight; shade from growing brassicas is ideal. pH 6-7.
Propagation:

	J	F	M	A	M	J	J	A	S	O	N	D
Sowing		⋀	⋀		⋀					⋀		
Planting			⋀	⋀								
Harvest												

Sowing, planting and harvesting times

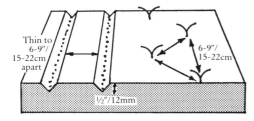

Sowing and planting diagram

Lifespan of seed: 4 years. Germination: 6-12 days. Sowing temperature: 32-84°F/ 0-29°C. Indoors, sow 3 seeds to a tiny peat pot, thin to 1 plant, harden off and plant out. Outdoors, sow every 3 weeks, making sure to sow the right amount each time so you do not have a summer glut. Lettuce do not grow so well if transplanted after June.
Care and cultivation: Transplant seedlings when they have 2 true leaves, between the peas, beans or brassicas at 9-12"/22-30cm intervals, or thin non-transplanted seedlings to same distance. Take care not to bury lower leaves. Keep hoeing—lettuce are easily swamped by weeds—and keep soil damp. Water in the morning if soil is dry. If plants grown under glass or in a cloche, ventilate when necessary; soil should be drier than when plants are grown outside.
Harvesting: Sowing to harvesting: 10 weeks. Yield per 20'/6m row: 30 heads (30lb/14kg). Wait until they have a solid centre, which you can check by pressing very gently—squeezing the plants will damage the leaves. Pull plants or take leaves in the morning when they are cool and sappy.
Kitchen: Usually used in salads. Wash well, dry, and chill in the fridge. Shred with mint; try lettuce soup and stir-fried lettuce. Lettuce braised with peas and onions tastes like spinach.
Keeping: Will keep 3-4 days if kept damp in a polythene bag in the fridge.
Pests and diseases: Slugs; Root Aphids; Botrytis.
Companion planting: Good with carrots and radish. Likes strawberries.

MARROW
Cucurbita pepo   Central America

Origins and history: Early explorers brought them to Europe where they became a culinary delicacy. Marrows appeared in Britain at the end of the eighteenth century, when they were called vegetable marrows to avoid confusion with bone marrow. By Victorian times marrows were very popular. In the past 30 years courgettes or zucchini, which are baby marrows, have become popular. Though less versatile than full-grown marrows, they are tastier.
Description: Fruit of a vine-like plant, with soft pale flesh inside a more or less tough skin which can be green, yellow, white or orange. Plants may be bush-like or trailing —courgettes are usually grown on bushes.

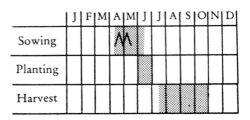

	J	F	M	A	M	J	J	A	S	O	N	D
Sowing				⋀⋀								
Planting												
Harvest												

Sowing, planting and harvesting times

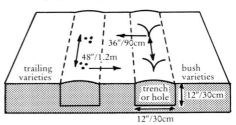

Planting diagram

Varieties:
Marrows: 'Long Green' and 'Long White Trailing' very big marrows which store well; 'Early Gem' F₁ bush, early and prolific; 'Green Bush' a good all-rounder which can be picked early for courgettes or left to produce dark green striped marrows. Courgettes: 'Zucchini' produces many dark green fruit; 'Golden Zucchini' has yellow fruit.

Site and soil: Sunny sheltered site, soil rich in humus and well-drained. Grow well on old compost heaps, or prepare holes or ridges as for cucumber. pH 6-7.5.

Propagation: Lifespan of seed: 6 years. Germination 5-8 days. Sowing temperature: over 56°F/13°C. Start seeds inside, sowing a single seed on its edge ½″/12mm deep in a 3″/75mm pot in May. Plant out (under cloches if danger of frost) second week of June. At end of May sow 3 seeds 1″/25mm deep and 2″/50mm apart at centre of each mound, or at appropriate intervals along trench (3′/90cm for bush; 4′/120cm for trailing). Make sure soil is damp, and place a cloche or jar over the seeds.

Care and cultivation: When seedlings are crowding each other, remove weak plants, leaving 1 to grow on. It is as well to leave cloches over the plants until they are trying to get out of them. Trailing varieties need growing tips pinching out when 2′/60cm long. Keep soil moist, but do not wet leaves or stem of growing plants. Mulch with compost when fruiting starts, and put hay over compost so fruit have clean surface to lie on. Keep free of weeds.

Harvesting: Pick courgettes when about 4″/100mm long and marrows at 8-10″/20-25cm. Leave storing marrows to mature and develop a strong hard skin before harvesting, but remove before frosts begin.

Kitchen: Stuff marrow and bake in the oven: a rice stuffing is very tasty. Courgettes are good sliced and boiled in ½″/12mm of water with peas, beans, carrots and a little onion and garlic. Good fried, and in salads. Marrows can be used for wine, jam, pickles, chutney and marrow rum.

Keeping: Marrows will keep in a cool dry place for several months. Courgettes will stay fresh for about a week in a polythene bag in the refrigerator, and freeze well if sliced up.

Pests and diseases: Slugs and snails are

particularly hungry when marrows go into the ground, and can completely destroy them. Withering of young fruit can be caused by over-watering. If plants give very few fruits or none at all, it may be because there are not enough insects to pollinate the fruit. On a dry morning take a male flower (the male flowers have no fruit at the back of them) and put it into a female flower; use only one male flower per female.

ONION

Allium cepa   *Central Asia*

Origins and history: The Ancient Egyptians used onions, and the Israelites in the wilderness longed for onions, leeks and garlic, which they had eaten while living in Egypt. Shallots (*A. ascalonicum*) come originally from Israel, and are said to have been introduced into Britain by the Crusaders.

Description: An onion bulb is usually pale cream in colour—although some are red outside and pink inside—and has the well-known layers, the outer layer being dry and darker in colour. Some varieties are round, and some longer and flatter.

Varieties:
Onion sets: 'Stuttgarter' mild and flat, keeps well; 'Rijnsburger Wijbo' and 'Sturon

Autumn Gold' keep until May, large, pale yellow globes.
Shallots: 'Hative de Niort' very uniform; 'Dutch Yellow'; 'Dutch Red'.
Bulb onions from seed: 'Bedfordshire Champion' a good keeper, heavy and globe-shaped, susceptible to downy mildew; 'Ailsa Craig' large but not a good keeper; 'Autumn Green' has flattish bulbs for keeping, can be sown in spring or autumn; 'Mammoth Improved' huge and delicious; 'Mammoth Red' best mammoth for keeping.
Japanese onions: 'Kaizuku Extra Early' sow in August for following July, flat bulbs ripening to a pale yellow, will not keep, not for northern Britain.
Spring onions: 'White Lisbon' quick-growing and silver-skinned; 'Ishikura' long thin white stems with no bulbs.
Pickling onions: 'Paris Silverskin'; 'Quicksilver' fast maturing.

Site and soil: Onions from seed need very high fertility and extra phosphate. Follow brassicas in rotation and grow with carrots. In autumn dig in half a bucketful of well-rotted manure or compost per yd^2/m^2, then on a dry day in spring fork in 4oz/110g ground limestone and 4oz/110g seaweed meal, *or* ½lb/225g wood ash, per yd^2/m^2. Then rake or fork into the surface a mixture of 4oz/110g salt, 4oz/110g fish meal or bone meal, and 4oz/110g soot per yd^2/m^2. Mid-April, when soil is fairly dry, tread and level with a rake until there is a good surface tilth. Onion sets, spring onions, pickling onions and shallots do not need such fancy soil treatment. The soil should be firm, but need not be so fine. pH 6-7.

Propagation: Lifespan of seed: 4 years. Germination of seed: 21 days. Sowing temperature: 45-77°F/7-25°C. Time for sets to sprout: 11-14 days. When sowing onion seed under glass, sow thinly ½"/12mm apart in February/March in potting compost. Firm and cover seed with ¼"/6mm fine compost, damp but not waterlogged, at a temperature of 60-65°F/15-18°C. Put boxes outside at least 2 weeks before transplanting. Plant about ½"/12mm deep, vertically in the holes, and firm well so the tips don't touch the ground or start to rot. August-sown Japanese onion seeds should be sown 1"/25mm apart and ½"/12mm deep in rows 9"/22cm apart.

Care and cultivation: When outdoor-sown seedlings are ½"/12mm tall, thin to

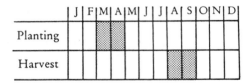

	J	F	M	A	M	J	J	A	S	O	N	D
Planting			▨	▨								
Harvest								▨	▨			

Planting and harvesting times (sets)

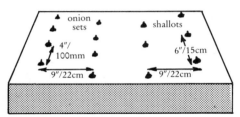

	J	F	M	A	M	J	J	A	S	O	N	D
Sowing	◊◊◊	▨	▨					▨				
Planting				▨	▨							
Harvest								▨	▨	▨		

Sowing, planting and harvesting times (seed)

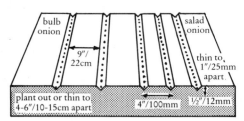

Planting diagram

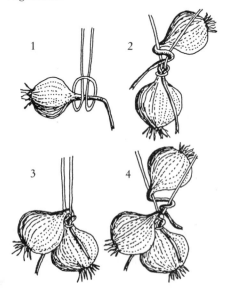

Sowing diagram

2-6"/50-150mm and water if necessary. In spring seedlings of Japanese onions should also be thinned to 2-4"/50-100mm, depending on how big you like your onions (in a cold damp area put a cloche over them for the winter). If you have bought sets and the ground is too cold or wet, open the packet and spread them out in a cool well-lit place to stop sprouting. Wait until the ground has warmed up before planting out onion and shallot sets. When planting, cut or twist off dry tops, so there is nothing for the birds to pull on; plant with the tips just covered. Keep hoeing and hand-weeding. Sets will need pushing back in if the frost has lifted them. Give autumn-sown onions liquid manure in spring; the rest of the crop in May and June. In July give a high potash liquid feed, or spread wood ash between the plants, and spray with seaweed solution. If onions bolt, break off flower stems.

Harvesting: Planting to harvesting: 20 weeks (sets); 18 weeks (shallots). Sowing to harvesting: 45 weeks (August-sown); 24 weeks (spring-sown). Yield per 20'/6m row: 18lb/8kg (sets); 20lb/9kg (seed). Mature onion bulbs go yellow at leaf-tips, and leaves fall over. If still green in mid-September, push stems over in an attempt to ripen bulbs. Dig bulbs up on a sunny day 2-3 weeks after leaves have fallen over. Rub soil off carefully and dry in a light airy place. When dry, can be stored after inspection for damaged, diseased or thick-necked bulbs. Autumn-sown onions do not store well, but use them in July before other onions are ready. Use spring onions a few at a time March-October.

Kitchen: Try baking in their jackets like potatoes, then peel just before serving. Lawrence Hills gives many good recipes at the end of *Grow Your Own Fruit and Vegetables*.

Keeping: Store on strings (see diagram opposite), in trays, or in net bags or old tights. Rope and tray methods are best because you can sort and use onions which are going off. Keep in a dry and well-lit place. Salad onions can be kept in a polythene bag in the fridge for up to a week. Blanched or lightly-fried onions freeze well.

Pests and diseases: Keeping onions strictly in rotation will keep most pests and diseases at bay, and growing from sets makes plants almost immune to Onion Fly. The preventative for Onion Fly is 1oz/30g flowers of sulphur to 3yd/1m of furrow, scattered after covering seed, or raked into soil after sets have been planted out.
Onion White Rot: white fluffy mould in base and roots; leaves turn yellow and wilt. Burn affected plants. Practise strict rotation. Bolting can be a problem. Thick-necked onions are a sign of an imbalance of nutrients, usually too many nitrates and not enough potash. Wood ash, seaweed, meal and seaweed solution feeds should cure this condition the next year.

Companion planting: Do well with beetroot, early lettuce and summer savory. Mask carrot scent and inhibit Carrot Fly as long as fly is not already in garden. Inhibit growth of peas and beans.

PARSNIP

Pastinaca sativa   Europe

Origins and history: In the sixteenth century one of the staple foods of Europe's lower classes, by which time several fleshy parsnip varieties had been developed. The Latin name is derived from a verb which means to dig and trench the ground.

Description: A root vegetable, usually pale in colour and long, rather like a fat carrot with celery-like leaves. Has a distinctive flavour which people tend to either love or hate.

Varieties: 'Tender and True' very long; 'Avon Resister' small roots, canker-resistant; 'White Gem' short and fat, good for shallow stony and clay soils, canker-resistant; 'Student' medium-sized, best flavour.

Site and soil: Unforked parsnips need a well-dug, stone-free soil manured from a previous crop, ideally brassicas. Benefit from 2oz/60g seaweed meal per yd^2/m^2 spread on the soil after digging and before covering for the winter. pH 5.5-7.

Propagation:

	J	F	M	A	M	J	J	A	S	O	N	D
Sowing												
Harvest												

Sowing and harvesting times

Do not keep seed. Germination: 10-28 days. Sowing temperature: over 45°F/7°C. Do not sow too early.

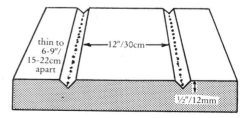

thin to 6-9"/15-22cm apart

12"/30cm

½"/12mm

Sowing diagram

Care and cultivation: Sowing radishes thinly between the parsnips provides a clear line for hoeing before parsnips germinate. Thin plants when they have first pair of true leaves. Hoe regularly, being careful not to damage roots.

Harvesting: At optimum size when leaves are starting to lie down and die. Usually dug up when wanted for eating; if not lifted and stored in sand or peat in November there is a danger of losing them to canker over the winter.

Kitchen: Give them a good scrub and cut away any bad bits. Cut into chip-sized pieces and roasted in oil until they are golden and crispy. Also good mashed with carrots, butter and nutmeg.

Keeping: In a polythene bag, parsnips will refrigerate for about 2 weeks.

Pests and diseases: Canker is caused by various fungi invading cracks and wounds in the top of the parsnip root; the result may be black or red rot. Sowing in late April helps prevent the condition; it also helps to make sure the soil is not too acid. Celery Leaf Miner can cause blisters on the leaf, and leaves which are affected should be removed. Carrot fly.

PEAS

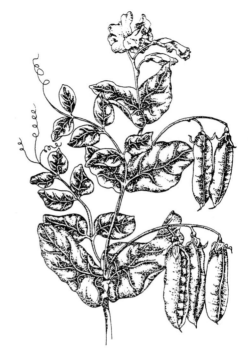

Pisum sativum
Probably E Asia; no known wild ancestor

Origins and history: Peas have been a staple food for thousands of years. Seeds of primitive peas have been found preserved in mud where lake dwellers lived 5,000 years ago in what is now Switzerland. Until recently peas were grown mostly to be dried for winter use, and were generally smaller and browner than modern peas.

Description: Peas grow on long trailing vines, and the part which is eaten is the seed, which grows inside long pods which develop from the female flowers. Sometimes both peas and pod can be eaten. Vary from autumn-sown dwarfs with a round pea, to the 5'/1.5m tall sugar-snap, whose pods are eaten whole.

Varieties:
Early varieties:
Round-seeded, extra hardy:
'Meteor' 12"/30cm high, will produce even in cold, exposed sites; 'Feltham First' 18"/45cm high.
Wrinkled-seeded, sweet:
'Kelvedon Wonder' 18"/45cm high,

mildew-resistant and good for successional sowing April-July; 'Early Onward' 24"/60cm high.
Second early: 'Hurst Greenshaft' 30"/75cm high, long-podded and heavy-cropping; 'Onward' easy to grow even in wet summers; 'Miracle' 4'/1.2m high, big pods, but too tall for windy sites, and liable to downy mildew in wet conditions.
Maincrop: 'Senator' 36"/90cm high, good for yield and flavour; 'Alderman' 6'/1.8m high, ridiculously tall but heavy cropping, good for a big garden.
Petits pois (very small sweet peas): 'Waverex' 24"/60cm high, most common variety.
Mange tout: 'Sugar Snap' 6'/1.8m high, delicious, seed expensive; 'Oregon Sugar Pod' 3½'/1m tall, a better height but still expensive; 'Asparagus Pea' not easy to find.

Site and soil: Like an open sunny spot, and should ideally be kept in rotation after the potato crop. Peas like a well-limed soil, so if you put kitchen waste in pea trenches, sprinkle hydrated lime before replacing top 2"/50mm of soil and sowing. Lawn mowings are useful in the trenches, but for early peas kitchen waste and well-rotted compost will provide the moist conditions needed for good peas. On open sandy or gravelly soils line trench with a few layers of newspaper. pH 6-7.5.

Propagation:

	J	F	M	A	M	J	J	A	S	O	N	D
Sowing		⋀⋀							⋀			
Planting												
Harvest												

Sowing, planting and harvesting times

Lifespan of seed: 2 years. Germination: 7-10 days. Sowing temperature: 41-90°F/5-32°C. If soil is sandy, cover seeds with 2"/50mm soil; if heavy clay with 1½"/32mm soil.

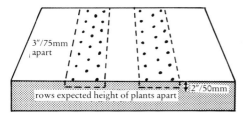

3"/75mm apart

2"/50mm

rows expected height of plants apart

Sowing diagram

Care and cultivation: Hoe, and after seedlings appear and before 3"/75mm tall put in supports. It is difficult to give good support to peas, and tall varieties take up a lot of space. In some ways it is more sensible to grow a dwarf pea like 'Kelvedon Wonder' in succession, but the tall-growing varieties are very beautiful and prolific. In a very wet season give up runner beans and train giant peas like 'Alderman' over bean poles and netting. Varieties up to 18"/45cm high can be supported with twigs; tall varieties are best on a rigid structure of high posts and 1½"/32mm mesh chicken wire, which should be a good foot higher than stated height of peas. Help them along with string if necessary. Peas like a moist soil, so water if dry and mulch around plants with hay, lawn mowings, or paper feed bags. Do not use straw as it will encourage slugs.

Harvesting: Sowing to harvesting: 32 weeks (autumn-sown); 11-12 weeks (earlies); 13-14 weeks (second earlies); 15-16 weeks (maincrop). Yield per 20'/6m row: 15lb/7kg. Pick regularly. Be careful when picking pods not to break plant: use two hands. When all peas have been picked, cut haulms off at soil surface, composting them and leaving roots in ground to give nitrates to the brassica crop which follows next in the rotation. Decide which peas you want to dry and leave on the plants. If peas mature on plants, fine, but if it is too wet for them to dry out properly, tie in bunches and dry in the kitchen. Mange tout varieties are eaten before pods are fully developed, and Asparagus Peas should be eaten very small.

Kitchen: Eat peas fresh from the garden, boiled for 10 minutes with a sprig of mint. Delicious in salads, cooked or uncooked. Mange tout can be chopped and eaten in salads, or boiled for 3 minutes. Sugar snap peas are delicious sautéed in a little butter. With small fresh peas it is sufficient to drop them into boiling water, and not actually cook them at all. Use dried peas in pease pudding.

Keeping: Will keep 2-3 days in their pods in a polythene bag in the refrigerator. Peas freeze extremely well.

Pests and diseases: Mice; Birds. Pea and Bean Weevils can destroy newly-emerging seedlings. At this stage you cannot see the typical notched leaves: seedlings just disappear, the weevils eating everything, including the seed. Hoeing along rows and winter digging can both help. On well-grown plants an attack often does no harm, but at the first sign on seedlings, spray with a nicotine mixture, both on plants and on soil. Soldier beetles can control them. Pea Thrips (Thunder Flies) cause dead silver patches on pods and leaves. Use nicotine spray unless eating very soon, in which case use derris and pyrethrum mixture. Pull up badly-affected plants, and give birds a chance to eat thrips by digging over surrounding soil. Tend to be more thrips in dry weather. Maggotty peas due to the maggots of the Pea Moth are more common in the south of Britain. The pea moth lays its eggs between June and August, and if maggots become a big problem you will have to use only March-sown peas and eat beans for the rest of the year. In time moths will die out with help of shallow digging in winter to allow birds to eat white cocoons.

Companion planting: Good with radishes, carrots, cucumbers, sweetcorn, beans and turnips. Inhibited by onions, garlic, shallots and chives.

PEPPER

Capsicum frutescens (hot, chili)
C. annuum (sweet)
S and Central America

Origins and history: Cultivated peppers were introduced to Spain in 1493, and were known in England by 1548.

Description: Peppers grow on upright plants 2-3'/60-90cm high; the fruit has a shiny skin, which is the same colour as the flesh and can be green, red, orange or cream. The inside of the fruit is hollow, and the seeds form immediately below the stalk. Chili peppers are thin, pointed and hot. Can irritate hands and lips.

Varieties: (peppers grown in Britain are usually F_1 hybrids bred for our climate) 'Worldbeater' high yielding; 'Gypsy' F_1 early, deep red when ripe; 'Canapé' F_1 early maturing with small fruit; 'New Ace' F_1 early and high-yielding; usually only one variety of chili pepper available.

Site and soil: Outdoor peppers need a well-drained fertile soil in a sunny, sheltered position, preferably against a south-facing wall. Indoor peppers can be grown with tomatoes in a greenhouse or on a sunny windowsill. They can grow near the glass without shading. Grow in rich compost or fertile greenhouse soil. pH 5.5-7.

Propagation:

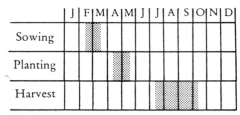

	J	F	M	A	M	J	J	A	S	O	N	D
Sowing		▓	▓									
Planting					▓	▓						
Harvest								▓	▓	▓		

for outdoor crops do everything 2 weeks later

Sowing, planting and harvesting times

Lifespan of seed: 5 years. Germination: 14-21 days. Raise seedlings inside at 60-70°F/15-21°C, sowing 2 seeds in each potting-compost-filled pot.

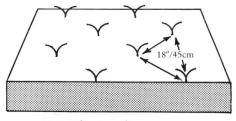

18"/45cm

Planting diagram

Care and cultivation: Harden off outside plants and plant 18"/45cm apart each way. Plant greenhouse plants at same distance or in bags or 9"/22cm pots; water in with seaweed solution. Mist regularly in dry weather to help fruit set and discourage red spider mite. Keep soil moist but not sodden. Give high potash feed when fruit begin to develop.

Harvesting: Sowing to harvesting: 18-20 weeks. Yield/plant: 6-10 fruits. Cut when you want to eat them; they should be fat and shiny.

Kitchen: Good in salads, in tomato sauce, on pizzas, in vegetable stews, and stuffed.

Keeping: Blanched peppers will freeze well, and peppers can be kept fresh in a polythene bag in the fridge for at least ten days.

Pests and diseases: Aphids; Red Spider Mite; Blossom End Rot (see 'Tomatoes').

POTATO

Solanum tuberosum   S America

Origins and history: Cultivated in the Andes in prehistoric times. The first potatoes brought to Europe in the sixteenth century did not thrive, but earlier, heavier-cropping varieties had become a staple by 1800, especially in Ireland. In 1845 crops were destroyed by blight, causing mass starvation and emigration.

Description: The part we eat is the underground tubers. The leaves taste bitter, and the green tomato-like fruits following the white, purple and yellow flowers are poisonous.

Varieties:
First earlies: 'Epicure' round with white flesh, good flavour, deep-eyed so hard to clean, but quick to grow; 'Sharpes Express' kidney-shaped with white flesh, will go on to grow large for a baking potato; 'Foremost' or 'Sutton's Foremost' oval with white flesh, delicious, good cropper; 'Pentland Javelin' oval and white-fleshed, eelworm-resistant, some resistance to scab, heavy-cropping and a good keeper, boring flavour; 'Ulster Chieftain' a very early early with an instantly forgettable taste.
Second earlies: 'Catriona' kidney-shaped with cream-coloured flesh, a yellowish skin and purple patches round eyes, crops well; 'Duke of York' kidney-shaped with yellow waxy flesh when cooked (easily overcooked), stores well. 'Red Craig Royal' red, oval, good crop and flavour.
Maincrop: 'Desirée' oval with pale yellow flesh and a beautiful metallic deep pink skin, drought-resistant, heavy cropper, versatile, good flavour, vulnerable to scab; 'Golden Wonder' kidney-shaped with yellow flesh, good flavour, grows well in Scotland but difficult to buy; 'Kerr's Pink' round with white flesh and pale pink skin, very good for chips, and tall thick stems good at supressing weeds; 'Pentland Dell' kidney-shaped with white flesh and skin, heavy-yielding, does not like a cold spring; 'Pink Fir Apple' oval with yellow flesh and pink skin, good in salads, low yield.

Site and soil: Will grow on any soil as long as well-manured and not waterlogged. Should be kept in a 3 or 4 year rotation, and never grown year after year on the same ground. Good at killing other vegetation with their dense leaf canopy, so can be used in newly-cleared ground. Avoid frost pockets and choose a sunny spot. Shade earlies from early morning sun, as this is when frost kills. Do not add lime as this encourages scab. Add well-rotted manure in autumn or spring, dug into trenches or forked into surface. $2oz/yd^2$ ($55g/m^2$) seaweed meal will help provide a balanced diet. A no-labour-in-spring method is to spread seaweed and dung in the autumn and cover with black polythene, holding down edges with stones or earth and planting in April or May through 'X's' cut in the polythene. This is very good for areas where winter rain leaches nutrients away, and when you can get old black polythene from silage heaps. pH 4.5-6.

Propagation:

	J	F	M	A	M	J	J	A	S	O	N	D
Planting			▲									
Harvest												

Planting and harvesting times

Potatoes required for 20'/6m row:
⅓oz/10g at 12"/30cm spacing: 7oz/200g
1oz/25g at 12"/30cm spacing: 20oz/550g
1oz/25g at 15"/37cm spacing: 16oz/450g
2oz/50g at 12"/30cm spacing: 40oz/1.1kg

Get seed potatoes in February and set out in open boxes—egg trays are good—with eyes looking up. Put in a light place where they will not be touched by frost. Shoots should be sturdy and greenish-purple; each potato should have only 2-3 shoots. With early potatoes you can get limited shoots by putting in light and warmth in September-October. When sprouted put in cool dark place until spring. Can rub out sprouts, but plant has already used energy to produce them. This 'chitting' promotes faster growth when potatoes are in the soil. Maincrop seeds should be small with 2-3 eyes, to prevent potatoes crowding, which pushes potatoes to the surface, where they become green and useless.

If short of manure or compost, put leaves or lawn mowings in bottom of trenches, then manure, then 2"/50mm earth. Lay in potatoes and cover with soil. Can be done under black plastic or on flat dug ground, where you can use a big dibber or trowel, putting potatoes at bottom of 6"/15cm holes and filling with compost or manure.

John Bleasdale suggests planting very small maincrop potatoes about ⅓oz/10g each 4"/100mm deep and close together, since extra space for earthing up is not needed between rows. It is possible to cut large potatoes to produce the same result, but this involves more seed and more work.

Classic planting distances for potatoes, all planted 4-6"/10-15cm deep, are earlies: 12"/30cm apart, 24"/60cm between rows; maincrop: 15"/37cm apart, 30"/75cm between rows.

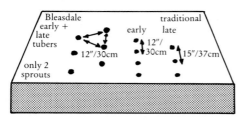

Planting diagram

Care and cultivation: If danger of frost, cover young plants with soil or hay. If growing on bare soil, keep well hoed and earth up when 9"/22cm tall, unless growing them by the Bleasdale method. A hay mulch will keep weeds down and stop potatoes greening. If ground gets very dry, water once tubers have started to form.

Harvesting: Planting to lifting: 12 weeks (earlies); 25 weeks (maincrop). Yield per 20'/6m row: 25lb/11kg (earlies); 40lb/18kg (maincrop). Use earlies as needed. Dig with a potato fork if possible to avoid spearing. Harvest maincrops on a sunny day, drying on soil surface. Make sure all tubers are removed: the smallest ones can grow into big disease-carrying weeds in your next year's pea crop.

Kitchen: New potato skins will come off with a good scrub, and new potatoes are usually boiled with a sprig of mint and eaten with butter. Potato salad is good too. Maincrop potatoes can be boiled, mashed, roasted, baked or chipped, and can be combined with other ingredients in hundreds of dishes.

Keeping: Store dry undamaged potatoes in a hessian or woven plastic bag, or in a good wooden box, somewhere dark, dry and frost-free. Before storing, separate out potatoes needed for seed, and inspect in January and March, rubbing sprouts from eating potatoes. Maincrop potatoes will store until spring, and new potatoes will store for a few weeks, though their flavour is always best straight out of the garden. New potatoes will freeze after blanching in water, and chips in oil, but it is hardly worth taking up freezer space.

Pests and diseases: From July onwards be on the lookout for brownish-grey patches of Potato Blight on leaves. As a preventative, spray with Bordeaux Mixture every fortnight from early July in the south and mid-July in the north. 'Pentland Dell' is resistant to one strain of blight, but was attacked in Cornwall in 1968. Early potatoes are less likely to contract blight because they finish growing by late July. Bury diseased haulms or put in the dustbin; they are difficult to burn and should only go in the middle of the hottest compost heap. Common Scab will occasionally appear if the soil is too limey. Always lime after potatoes in the rotation. Also appears when soil has been dry for a long time. The fungus will just scrape off. Good supplies of humus and crop rotation will help with most potato diseases. Viruses can be controlled by using certified seed. Slugs can be a problem. A good guide to what is wrong with your potatoes (or to frighten yourself by discovering what could go wrong!) is D.G. Hessayon's *The Vegetable Expert*, with vivid and alarming colour pictures, but use HDRA's *Potato Growing for Gardeners* for remedies.

Companion planting: Early potatoes grow well with beans. Hemp helps protect against blight. Dead nettle and nasturtium grown nearby are beneficial. Resistance to blight lessened if grown near sunflower, tomato, apple, cherry, raspberry, pumpkin and cucumber.

RADISH

Raphanus sativus   *W Asia*

Origins and history: The Romans grew radishes, but the small varieties we use now were developed by the French in the eighteenth century.

Description: Root vegetable, usually with a pinkish-red root and dark green leaves. The salad radish is a quick-growing annual; winter varieties are big, with black or white skins and an even stronger flavour than summer radishes.

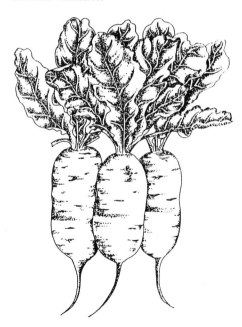

Varieties:
Spring/summer varieties: 'Cherry Belle' the recommended salad radish, remains in the ground for a few weeks without growing pithy; 'Scarlet Globe' a very speedy radish, good for early sowing under a cloche; 'French Breakfast' red skin, white at root end, good flavour, but will not stand long; 'Large White Icicle' long and white.

Winter varieties: 'Long Black Spanish' crisp and good for grating in salads; 'Black Spanish Round' good for cooking or raw in a salad; 'China Rose' white flesh and strong flavour.

Site and soil: Enjoy a fertile well-drained soil, so put in the brassica patch with the lettuces. The cloche for early salads should be in a bright sunny spot. pH 6-7.

Propagation:

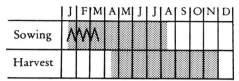

Sowing and harvesting times

Lifespan of seed: 4 years. Germination: 4-7 days. Sowing temperature: 41-90°F/5-32°C. Summer radish best sown in small amounts at 14-day intervals. Winter varieties are sown in July or August.

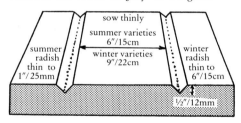

Sowing diagram

Care and cultivation: Hoe along rows when they appear. Thin crowded seedlings to 1″/25mm (summer); 6″/15cm (winter).

Harvesting: Sowing to harvesting: 25-40 days (summer); 10-12 weeks (winter). Yield per 20′/6m row: 8lb/3.6kg (summer); 20lb/9kg (winter). Start pulling summer varieties when red bodies start pushing out of soil. Lift winter varieties in November.

Kitchen: Used in salads and as salad garnishes.

Keeping: Radishes can be kept in a polythene bag in the refrigerator for a week. Store winter radishes in sand or peat.

Pests and diseases: Flea Beetle can destroy seedlings—watch for holes in leaves.

Companion planting: Good with peas, lettuce, cucumber, nasturtiums, chervil. Antagonistic to hyssop.

SPINACH

Spinacea oleracea   SW Asia

Origins and history: Cultivation had spread in China by 647 AD, and the Moors brought it to Spain from North Africa in 1100. Prickly-seeded winter spinach was grown in European monasteries by the fourteenth century. Round-seeded spinach was first described in this country in 1522.

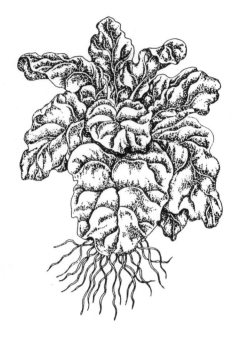

Description: Both summer round-seeded and winter prickly-seeded have lush, mid-green triangular leaves. The leaves of winter spinach are slightly bigger than those of the summer variety. New Zealand Spinach (*Tetragonia expansa*) is not related to the other spinaches—a spreading plant with small soft fleshy bright green leaves.

Varieties:
Summer round-seeded: 'Monatol' low in oxalic acid, available from HDRA; 'Sigma-leaf' long cropping time before running to seed, may also be sown in autumn as a winter crop.
Winter prickly-seeded: 'Broad-leaved Prickly' has dark leaves, slow to bolt.

Site and soil: Likes rich damp soil with plenty of organic matter. New Zealand

Spinach will tolerate less fertile soil. Summer spinach will benefit from light shade; winter and New Zealand Spinach like a sunny place. pH 6-7.5.

Propagation:

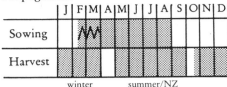

	J	F	M	A	M	J	J	A	S	O	N	D
Sowing		MM										
Harvest												

winter   summer/NZ

Sowing and harvesting times

Lifespan of seeds: 2 years. Sow at ½oz/15g per 20'/6m row. Germination: 12-21 days. Sow summer varieties in succession March-May; winter varieties in September. Sow New Zealand Spinach in peat pots under glass in March and plant out 24"/60cm apart each way late May, under a cloche if there is any danger of frost.

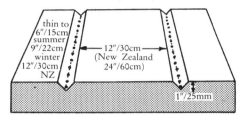

thin to
6"/15cm
summer
9"/22cm
winter
12"/30cm
NZ
12"/30cm
(New Zealand
24"/60cm)
1"/25mm

Sowing diagram

Care and cultivation: Thin plants promptly, to 3"/75mm at first and then to 6"/15cm, using thinnings in salads. Keep hoeing, and water well if dry. Winter spinach will need cloches.

Harvesting: Sowing to harvesting: 8-14 weeks (longest for New Zealand spinach). Yield per 20'/6m row: 15-20lb/7-9kg. Pick continually to encourage new growth; do not take more than half the leaves from any one plant at a time.

Kitchen: Use very young leaves in salads, then cook. Contains oxalic acid, which locks up calcium and iron, so avoid in large quantities. Very good in lasagne between layers of pasta and cheese sauce, as a filling for pancakes, and as filling for a quiche. Steam leaves, or boil with a little butter or margarine and no water.

Keeping: Spinach will freeze well, blanching young leaves for 2 minutes. Will store in a refrigerator in a sealed polythene bag for 2 days.

Pests and diseases: Slugs and Snails.
Companion planting: Likes growing near strawberries.

TOMATO

Lycopersicon esculentum   S America

Origins and history: When introduced into Europe via Italy in the sixteenth century it was thought of as a poisonous decorative plant, and was called 'Pomo d'Oro', 'Love Apple' and 'Peruvian Apple', but it soon began being eaten. It spread throughout Europe and further afield a century ago, rapidly becoming the big business it is today.

Description: A weak-stemmed perennial grown as an annual. Its natural shape is a straggling, spreading bush. Tomatoes are usually red, though the originals were yellow, and tomatoes can be yellow, orange or striped, cherry-sized, plum-shaped, medium round, or large and knobbly.

Varieties:
F_1 hybrids (good growers, disease-resistant, heavy-yielding and thick-skinned, minimal flavour): 'Pixie' F_1 an exception to the rule, tasty and thin-skinned early outdoor bush variety.
Ordinary varieties (cordon, greenhouse or outdoor): 'Alicante' heavy-cropping, greenback-resistant, early fruiting, thin-skinned, good flavour; 'Gardener's Delight' small and tasty, cropping heavy; 'Harbinger' early, thin-skinned, good flavour; 'Ailsa Craig' early, good taste, susceptible to greenback.
Bush varieties (for outdoor growing only): 'Red Alert' a new variety, very early, with delicious small fruit; 'The Amateur' has medium-sized fruit, easily available; 'Tiny Tim' a window-box tomato with fine-flavoured tiny fruit.
Large continental varieties (grown as cordons): 'Marmande' outdoors or indoors, fleshy fruit with few seeds, flavour not as good as on the Continent because it really needs more sun.

Site and soil: Tomatoes are greedy feeders, but do not overdo the nitrates—they like plenty of potash. The following trench technique will work indoors or outdoors: take out $12 \times 12''/30 \times 30cm$ trenches $24''/60cm$ apart, and fill with well-rotted compost or manure—pig, horse or goat rather than cow. Place straw on top of muck, then wilted comfrey leaves and wood ash, then soil, mounded slightly to aid soil warming. Water at least a fortnight before plants go in. If you grow tomatoes in the same place each year sterilize your border soil or grow the plants in pots or gro-bags using the compost recipe given under 'Cucumbers'; it is difficult to grow tomatoes well in bags, pots or ring culture because the nutrients in comfrey liquid high potash feed are not as immediately available as those in a chemical feed. pH 5.5-7.5.

Propagation: ▼ sowing Y planting

	J	F	M	A	M	J	J	A	S	O	N	D
Heated greenhouse	▼	YY										
Cold greenhouse			▼▼	YY								
Outdoors				▼▼	⋀⋀Y							
Harvest												

Sowing, planting and harvesting times

Lifespan of seed: 3 years. Germination: 8-11 days. Seeds need $65\text{-}70°F/18\text{-}21°C$ to germinate, and $60\text{-}65°F/15\text{-}18°C$ to grow on. Either sow seeds thinly in a shallow box of seed compost and prick out into 3″/75mm pots when first true leaves come, or sow 2 seeds directly into a 3″/75mm pot, removing weaker seedling when 1″/25mm high. Hybrid tomatoes are very sensitive to temperature falls, and if too cold leaves of all tomato plants will turn blue and plants will stop growing. Unless growing large numbers of tomatoes it is best to get plants from a nursery or friend.

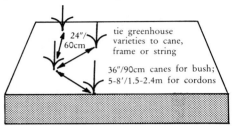

24″/60cm

tie greenhouse varieties to cane, frame or string

36″/90cm canes for bush; 5-8′/1.5-2.4m for cordons

Planting diagram

Care and cultivation: When pricking out or planting seedlings, bury plant up to its first leaves, as roots will grow from the stem and make the plant more sturdy. As cordon plants grow, tie loosely to canes or wind round slack strings tied loosely round base of plant. When side shoots appear in leaf axils, gently pull them sideways and they will break at their base. Bush tomatoes need less support and no taking out of side shoots. Use a sharp knife or secateurs to remove yellowing leaves below fruit trusses. Some green leaves may be cut out to help ventilation below the bottom truss.

Regular watering and feeding is very important. Water with comfrey liquid every week—a useful source of potash. Do not let soil or compost dry out—may have to water night and morning in hot weather if growing plants in pots, and wet leaves and greenhouse paths early in the morning before the sun gets hot. Irregular watering can cause Blossom End Rot and split fruit.

Tap or shake plants to help pollination. When nearing roof of greenhouse or plants have about 7 trusses each, pinch out top shoot 2 leaves above last truss.

Ventilation is important—tomatoes like a buoyant atmosphere but not a draught. Tomato leaves and fruit scorch easily in full sun; if necessary shade or whitewash glass. In early spring, heat can be conserved by lining with thin polythene or bubble film.

Give bracken or comfrey mulch in July.

Harvesting: Pick when ripe. Don't wrench fruit off the plant—there is a swelling on the stalk which will snap if you hold the fruit in your hand and press the swelling with your thumb. If tomatoes have not ripened by end of season, put unripened ones in a drawer with some ripe ones or with an apple and use them as they ripen, always leaving a ripe one with the unripe.

Kitchen: A warm tomato straight from the truss is delicious, as are fresh tomatoes sliced with lettuce, either as they are or in a light oil-and-vinegar dressing. Tomatoes, cooked and uncooked, go well with basil. Large tomatoes may be stuffed and cooked. Tinned tomatoes are so cheap and good that it seems a shame to use home-grown ones to make spaghetti sauce. Green tomatoes are good in stews, chutneys and pickles.

Keeping: In a polythene bag in the fridge tomatoes will keep for about a week.

Pests and diseases: Outdoor tomatoes are generally untroubled apart from blight. Greenhouse Whitefly; Virus: diseased plants should be burned; Botrytis; Potato Blight (see 'Potatoes'); Root Rot causes wilting in hot weather—plant may be saved by mulching around stem to allow new roots to grow; plants should not be grown again in the same soil; Foot Rot is usually seen in seedlings due to infected soil and overwatering—plant may be saved by mulching around stem; Stem Rot is like a canker, and can be cut out if found early enough. Change soil or compost for next crop, and do not let secateurs or fingers spread infection—clean with meths. Disorders caused by infrequent or insufficient watering include Blossom End Rot, a leathery sunken patch at the base of the fruit, Blossom Drop, and split fruit.

D.G. Hessayon's *The Vegetable Expert* has a good section on tomato troubles.

Companion planting: Good with asparagus, early cabbage, parsley, stinging nettle. Antagonistic to kohlrabi and fennel.

TURNIP AND SWEDE

Brassica rapa and *B. napus napobrassica*
W Asia, E Europe

Origins and history: The turnip has been eaten by human beings and their domesticated animals since at least the first century AD, being one of the staple vegetables for poor people until replaced by the potato. The swede is possibly a hybrid of wild cabbage and turnip, discovered in Bohemia in the late Middle Ages and introduced to Britain from Sweden in 1770.

Propagation:

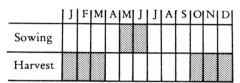

	J	F	M	A	M	J	J	A	S	O	N	D
Sowing								for tops				
Harvest				tops only								

Sowing and harvesting times (Turnip)

	J	F	M	A	M	J	J	A	S	O	N	D
Sowing												
Harvest												

Sowing and harvesting times (Swede)

Lifespan of seed: 2 years. Germination: 6-10 days. Sowing temperature: 41-90°F/5-32°C.

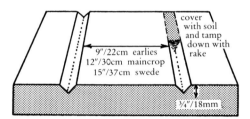

9"/22cm earlies
12"/30cm maincrop
15"/37cm swede

cover with soil and tamp down with rake

¾"/18mm

Sowing diagram (Turnip and Swede)

Description: The turnip has rough hairy leaves, and the flesh is usually white; the swede has smooth cabbage-like leaves and yellow flesh. Swedes are sweeter and more hardy than turnips, and good for storing. Turnips are at their best when young. Can also be used for spring greens.

Varieties:
Turnip: 'Purple-Top Milan' early, flat and tasty, good under a cloche; 'Snowball' white-fleshed, globular and quick-growing, eat while young; 'Manchester Market' maincrop keeper with white flesh; Golden Ball' a yellow turnip.
Swede: 'Marian' good flavour, high yield, some resistance to clubroot and mildew; 'Acme' purple-topped, small and sweet, quick-growing.

Site and soil: Need a sunny spot and a fertile adequately-limed soil which will retain moisture in the summer. Soil should be firm and ground composted or manured the year before. Early turnips like a richer soil, and turnips and swedes like 1lb/450g fishmeal per 4yd²/3.5m². If surface of soil is loose, tread down and rake. pH 6-7.5.

Care and cultivation: Thin in stages when large enough to handle. Thin turnips to 2"/50mm, then to 5"/12cm for earlies, 9"/22cm for maincrops and 9"/22cm for swedes, eating thinnings. Thinning not necessary with turnips grown for spring greens. Keep hoed, and water if the soil becomes dry. Some people believe that yields are higher when swedes are grown in blocks rather than rows.

Harvesting: Sowing to harvesting: 6-12 weeks (turnips); 20-26 weeks (swedes). Yield per 20'/6m row: 14lb/6kg (early turnips); 24lb/11kg (maincrop turnips and swedes). Turnips for spring greens can have leaves cut in March-April and will resprout several times. Pull early turnips when small, either for eating raw or cooking. Start to harvest the maincrop turnips and swedes in early autumn. If soil is light and climate not too cold and wet, swede and turnip can be left in ground until midwinter.

Kitchen: Grate early turnips for mixing into salad, or boil whole for 25 minutes and soothe their peppery taste with butter or potato. Large turnips and swedes can be cut up and used in vegetable stews or Cornish pasties. Swedes are usually cooked and mashed; if cooked with potatoes you will get a creamier texture.

Keeping: To store over winter twist leaves off and pack in a strong box between layers of sand or peat.

Pests and diseases: Flea Beetle; Clubroot (see under 'Brassicas'); Soft Rot and Black Rot: roots can only be taken out and burned; Brown Heart: brown or grey areas in the flesh which later decay. Caused by boron deficiency, to which swedes are particularly sensitive. Use ground limestone, chalk or dolomite (not hydrated lime) on acid soils to raise pH. For a temporary cure mix 1oz/30g borax to 2 gall/9l water and spray over 15yd²/m², using a fine rose.

Companion planting: Good with peas.

Herbs

An extensive range of herbs can be grown in the garden and used for culinary and medicinal purposes. This section just covers the most common herbs; for more information read *Planning the Organic Herb Garden* by Sue Stickland.

From the cook's point of view, the best place to grow herbs is as close to the kitchen as possible. Both for their beautiful colours and scents and as companion plants, herbs can be grown all over the garden. I grow thyme, sage, rosemary and marjoram in the flower garden, and cannot bring myself to cut them for drying until they have flowered, which is all wrong for preserving. Flowering herbs also help in the vegetable garden around the brassicas and root vegetables. They create a balance, and help protect the vegetables from pests.

If you want to dry herbs, cut them just before they flower on a sunny day after a dry spell. Their essential oils are then at their strongest. Let them wilt in the sun or in an airing cupboard after cutting, then hang them in the kitchen in paper bags with holes in for 2-3 weeks. Crush them and put into clean dry jars when they are crisp.

You can also preserve herbs in cubes of ice in the freezer. Chop the herbs finely, and fill the divisions of an ice cube tray. Pour on boiling water, let it cool, then put the tray to freeze. Use the cubes in cooking as needed.

When making herb teas, chop the fresh herbs finely and cover the tea while it is infusing.

As in the flower lists, the following abbreviations will be found under 'Description': HA hardy annual; HHA half hardy annual; B biennial; P perennial.

BASIL

Ocimum basilicum
Tropical Asia, Africa, Pacific

Origins and History: Pliny wrote about basil in the first century AD. Became very popular in Tudor times as more varieties imported from India.

Description: HHA Delicate, erect habit, about 18"/45cm tall with fairly large stalked oval aromatic pale green leaves.

Site and soil: Best grown in a greenhouse, cold frame, or cloche in north of Britain, sheltered spot in full sun in south. pH 5.5-6.5.

Propagation: Sow under cover March-April ½"/12mm deep. Plant out 6"/15cm apart in May under cover, or when all risk of frost is over. For winter pickings, make a second sowing in June or July and pot up when large enough to handle. Keep the pot on a warm kitchen windowsill.

Care and cultivation: Keep free of weeds and do not allow to dry out. Pinch out growing tips to promote bushiness and discourage flowering.

Harvesting: Gather leaves as required. If wanted for preserving, pick leaves before flowering.

Kitchen: Use in soups, stews, sauces, salads and drinks. Particularly suited to tomatoes. Preserve by the ice cube method.

Pests and diseases: Greenfly.

Companion planting: Beneficial to tomatoes, and repels flies and mosquitoes. Antagonist: Rue.

BAY

Laurus nobilis   Mediterranean

Origins and history: Came to Britain with the Romans.

Description: Tender P Evergreen shrub or tree growing up to 30'/9m. Killed by hard frosts. Aromatic tough oval dark green leaves 2-4"/50-100mm long.

Site and soil: Grow outside in sheltered sunny position. In northern Britain best grown in a tub and moved inside in winter. pH 6-7.5.

Propagation: Difficult to propagate. Buy a small pot-grown plant in spring.

Care and cultivation: Move indoors in winter if necessary. If shaping, clip in May.

Harvesting: Gather leaves as required. Use prunings for drying. Dry at room temperature.

Kitchen: Tomato dishes, tomato sauce, stews, custards and rice dishes. Basis for bouquet garni.

CHERVIL

Anthriscus cerefolium   W Asia

Origins and history: Introduced to Britain by Romans; now naturalized.

Description: HA An umbellifer, slightly hairy, 12-24"/30-60cm high, with delicate deeply-cut 3-pinnate leaves and a mild aniseed flavour.

Site and soil: For summer crop grow in fertile moist soil in a shady position. Do the same for a winter crop in mild areas, otherwise grow under cover. pH 5-6.5.

Propagation: Sow seeds ½"/12mm deep February-April for summer; August for spring crop. Thin to 4"/10cm.

Care and cultivation: Remove most of flower heads to promote leaf growth. Leave a few for next year's self-sown crop.

Harvesting: Gather leaves as required, taking from the outside of the plant.

Kitchen: Delicate flavour—add to soups, eggs and salads just before serving.

Companion planting: Beneficial to radishes.

CHIVES

Allium schoenoprasum   N hemisphere

Origins and history: British native. Cultivated variety introduced by Romans. Used in cottage gardens under the name 'rush-leek'.

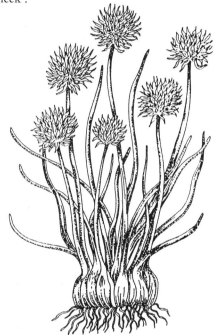

Description: P Member of the onion family, grows in tight clumps. Grass-like cylindrical leaves 6-10"/15-25cm long, with pale purple or pink globe-like flowers.

Site and soil: Sunny site and fertile well-drained soil. pH 6-7.5.

Propagation: Sow chives April-May as for onions. Transplant 2-3 seedlings together 9"/22cm apart. Divide clumps every 3-4 years in spring or autumn. If you are lucky you can get plants from friends or neighbours.

Care and cultivation: To encourage vigorous growth, cut back to the ground twice a year, unless growing for the pretty flowers. Foliage dies down in winter; if you want chives in winter, use cloches. Good as an indoor pot plant, or in a window box.

Harvesting: Gather leaves as required, cutting from the base of the plant.

Kitchen: On or in potatoes, soups, sauces, omelettes, salads and cottage cheese. To preserve, use the ice cube method.

Companion planting: Beneficial to carrots.

DILL

Anethum graveolens   Europe

Origins and history: Mentioned in ancient Egyptian, Greek and Roman texts as a medicinal herb. Though not native to Britain, was cultivated here by 1570.

Description: HA Smooth-stemmed umbellifer about 24"/60cm high. Finely-divided leaves, like fennel. Yellow flowers borne in umbels (flat clusters) 2-6"/5-15cm long, seeds elliptical, slightly flattened and ridged, brownish-yellow, about 1/8"/3mm long. Seeds mainly used, sometimes foliage.

Site and soil: Sunny well-drained site. pH 5-6.

Propagation: Sow seeds April-May where plants are to grow. Thin to 12"/30cm apart.

Care and cultivation: Water in dry weather, keep free of weeds.

Harvesting: Gather leaves as required. For seeds, cut heads when brown.

Kitchen: Use leaves in yogurt and vegetable dishes; seeds in pickling vinegar, cakes, bread and rice. Dry the seeds in their flower heads upside down in bunches in a paper bag in a warm place.

Herb tea: For flatulence and colic, especially for children and babies. Infuse 1-2 teaspoonsful slightly crushed seeds in 1 cup of boiling water for 10-15 minutes. Take before meals or as required.

Companion planting: Beneficial to cabbage; antagonistic to carrots.

FENNEL

Foeniculum vulgare   Mediterranean

Origins and history: The Romans ate the young stalks. Medieval herbalists recommended it for eyesight. Introduced early into Britain, it was an important ingredient of the wine called sack. Now grows wild in sea cliffs in England, Wales and Ireland.

Description: P 24-48"/60-120cm high umbellifer with blue-green feathery foliage and small yellow flowers in umbels. Seeds are oblong or oval brownish-yellow, 1/6"/4mm long.

Site and soil: Sunny site, well-drained soil. Good in a herbaceous border. pH 5-6.

Propagation: Sow seed April-May where plants are to grow, in seed bed or pots. Thin or transplant to 15"/37cm apart.

Care and cultivation: Weed; pinch out tops of tallest shoots to encourage more leaves and support with sticks if necessary.

Harvesting: Gather leaves as required. For seeds, cut heads when brown.

Kitchen: Strong aniseed flavour: use in soups, sauces, vegetables and salads. Seeds used in pickling vinegar. Dry seeds as for dill.

Herb tea: Stimulates digestion and appetite, relieves flatulence and colic, calms coughs. Infuse 1-2 teaspoonsful lightly-crushed seeds in 1 cup of boiling water for 10 minutes. Take 3 times a day, half an hour before meals.

Companion planting: Antagonistic to most plants.

LEMON BALM

Melissa officinalis   Middle East

Origins and history: Introduuced by Romans; often found as garden escape in southern England. Was important in monastic apothecary gardens.

Description: P 12-24"/30-60cm tall. A vigorous plant with long-stalked toothed oval leaves, smelling and tasting of lemon. Inconspicuous white flowers.

Site and soil: Likes sun or shade and soil which is moist but not rich, pH 5.5-7.5.

Propagation: Sow seeds in nursery bed every 4 years when the plants are getting tired and woody. Sow thinly 1/2"/12mm deep. Thin to 6"/15cm apart when small, and move as replacements in September/October.

Care and cultivation: Hoe to keep free of weeds.

Harvesting: Cut when wanted for everyday use. For drying, cut just before flowering.

Kitchen: Use in salad or with peas, beans and potatoes.

Herb tea: Helps digestive problems, lightens depression, helps feverish conditions like 'flu. Infuse 2-3 teaspoonsful dried (6-9 of fresh) herb in a cup of boiling water for 10-15 minutes. Take morning and evening or when needed.

Companion planting: Beneficial to all plants.

MARJORAM

Origanum spp   *Europe*

Origins and history: O. *majorana* (Sweet Marjoram) came with the Romans; O. *onites* (Pot Marjoram) came from Sicily in 1759. O. *vulgare* is native to dry chalk soils of southern England.

Description: P Sweet or Knotted Marjoram is a bushy plant 9-18"/22-45cm high, with stalked elliptical slightly hairy grey-green leaves, ¼-1"/6-25mm long. Tender perennial grown outside as annual. Pot Marjoram is a robust perennial with oval hairy leaves very like Sweet Marjoram but tougher. Flowers whitish. Good as a pot plant. O. *vulgare* P is larger than the other marjorams, 12-24"/30-60cm high with oval leaves ½-2"/12-50mm long; purple/pink flowers.

Site and soil: Sunny spot with fertile well-drained soil, or plant in a pot or window box. Pretty in the flower garden. pH 6-8.

Propagation: Sow Sweet Marjoram thinly, indoors in March or outdoors April-May. Thin or transplant 6"/15cm apart. Sow Pot Marjoram outdoors as above. Or, take softwood cuttings in early summer. Or, divide plants in autumn. O. *vulgare* treat as Pot Marjoram. Seed catalogues usually only offer Sweet Marjoram.

Care and cultivation: Keep free of weeds.

Harvesting: Gather leaves as required. Harvest for drying before flowering.

Kitchen: Use all marjorams in the same way, in omelettes, salads, stuffings, sauces, and sprinkled over soups before serving. To preserve, dry the leaves.

Herb tea: For colds or 'flu, coughs and headaches. Infuse 1 teaspoonful dried (3 fresh) herb in 1 cup of boiling water for 10-15 minutes. Take 3 times a day.

Companion planting: Generally beneficial.

MINT

Mentha spp.   *Asia*

Origins and history: Introduced by Romans; mint sauce—to stimulate the appetite—was first mentioned in Britain in the third century AD.

Description: There are many different types of mint, each looking and tasting slightly different. They all have very vigorous invasive white roots, like a cross between nettle and couch grass roots. Apple mint is tall with large round fluffy grey-green leaves, while my favourite, spearmint, has pointed mid-green leaves and the best flavour. There are crinkly-leaved mints and variegated-leaf mints. Taste your mint before growing it.

Site and soil: Thrives in most garden soils in sun or shade. pH 5.5-7.5: add well-rotted manure or compost.

Propagation: Plant pieces of root 2"/5cm deep and 9"/22cm apart in autumn or spring.

Care and cultivation: Keep weed-free, and keep in check by growing it in a container sunk into the ground or surrounded by slates or metal or plastic sheet. Top dress with compost or well-rotted manure in autumn. Divide and move every 3-4 years.

Harvesting: Use the leaves when required. For drying, cut the mint at its base before flowering. To preserve, dry in a warm place.

Kitchen: Use in the water when boiling potatoes and peas, and in salads.

Pests and diseases: Mint rust—small orange spots on swollen shoots. Lift and burn. Plant new stock in new fertile position. Unlikely to appear if kept moist and well-fed.

Herb tea: Garden mints aid digestion and allay flatulence. Infuse 1 teaspoonful dried (3 fresh) herb in 1 cup of boiling water for 10 minutes. Drink as often as required. Can be depressive.

Companion planting: Beneficial to brassicas: helps repel cabbage white caterpillars. Good with tomatoes.

PARSLEY

Petroselinum crispum   *S Europe*

Origins and history: To the Greeks, parsley was a symbol of death, and in medieval England curly parsley was associated with black magic.

Description: B In the first year produces a rosette of long-stalked bright green leaves, either fern-like or closely curled, 6-11"/15-27cm long. In second year produces umbels of yellow flowers on stems 24"/60cm long. Dies in severe winters.

Site and soil: Sunny or partially-shaded position, fertile moisture-retentive soil. pH 5-7.

Propagation: Sow seeds ½"/12mm deep in April-May for summer, and July-August for winter or spring. Thin to 6"/15cm apart. Germination can take 4-6 weeks. Do not sow in cold wet soil. Accelerate germination of seeds by watering drill with boiling water *before* sowing, or try fluid sowing. Keep moist until seeds have germinated. Seed sown indoors germinates faster. Parsley grows well in pots for winter supply.

Care and cultivation: Keep weed-free and water when dry. In winter protect with bracken or a cloche.

Harvesting: Use the leaves when required. Growth is stimulated by cutting back to ground level not more than twice a year.

Kitchen: Use as a garnish with most dishes, and in sauces, soups and stews. To preserve, use the ice cube method, or dip in boiling water for 2 minutes, shake dry, then crisp in a warm oven. Keep in an airtight container.

Pests and diseases: Carrot Fly—yellowing of the leaves. Aphids—yellowing of the leaves and stickiness. Severe stunting is sometimes caused by Motley Dwarf Virus transmitted by aphids: burn affected plants.

Herb tea: Eases flatulence and stimulates menstruation. Infuse 1-2 teaspoonsful dried (2-6 fresh) herb in 1 cup of boiling water for 5-10 minutes. Take 3 times a day.

Companion planting: Beneficial to tomatoes and roses.

ROSEMARY

Rosmarinus officinalis
Asia Minor and Mediterranean

Origins and history: The name is from the Latin 'dew of the sea'. Introduced by Romans; mentioned in an eleventh century herbal as a way of discouraging moths in clothes chests. Cottage garden plant.

Description: Tender evergreen P Erect bushy shrub up to 7'/2.1m tall in favoured areas. Narrow needle-like leaves, dark green above, white and hairy beneath.

Spikes of blue-white flowers in May. Very aromatic.

Site and soil: Light, sandy soil in sunny position. pH 5-6.

Propagation: Sow seed in nursery bed April/May. Thin to 4"/100mm. Plant in final position following spring 15"/37cm apart. In north of Britain, sow under cover and pot on. Quickest to grow from stem cuttings taken in August.

Care and cultivation: Protect plants from frost, or pot up and keep indoors over winter.

Harvesting: Use leaves as required. For drying, cut off shoots before flowering.

Kitchen: A strong, aromatic flavour, used in savoury dishes, especially with meat, and in salads and fruit salads. Dry to preserve.

Herb tea: Good for the heart and circulation. Infuse 1-2 teaspoonsful dried (3-6 fresh) herb in 1 cup of boiling water for 10 minutes. Take 3 times a day.

Companion planting: Beneficial to beans, cabbage, carrots and sage. Deters Carrot Fly and Cabbage Moth.

SAGE

Salvia officinalis   *S Europe*

Origins and history: Used by Greeks, Romans and Arabs. Used medicinally in Britain in the Middle Ages.

Description: P A low-growing shrub 12-18"/30-45cm high with pointed oval long-stalked greyish-green hairy wrinkled leaves which are very aromatic. Spikes of violet-blue flowers June/July.

Site and soil: Sunny site on light well-drained soil. pH 5.5-6.5.

Propagation: Sow seed in nursery bed April/May, thin to 4"/100mm apart, plant in final position following spring 15"/37cm apart. Or, take stem cuttings in spring or early summer. Plant out in spring. Grows well in pots.

Care and cultivation: Keep weed-free. Prune lightly after flowering, not later than the middle of August, to keep bush in shape.

Harvesting: Use leaves as required. For drying, cut off shoots before flowering. Dry to preserve.

Kitchen: A little goes well with bean and tomato dishes, and in cheese dishes. Use in sage and onion stuffing. Good as an

antidote to fatty meats like pork and goose.

Herb tea: Useful for mouth and throat conditions and dyspepsia; stimulates the uterus and should not be used during pregnancy. Infuse 1-2 teaspoonsful dried (3-6 fresh) herb in 1 cup of boiling water for 10 minutes. Take 3 times a day.

Companion planting: Beneficial to cabbage, rosemary and carrots. Deters cabbage moth and carrot fly. Antagonistic to cucumber.

TARRAGON

Artemesia dracunculus   S Europe

Origins and history: Cultivated, especially in France, for many centuries. Both Latin and English names mean 'little dragon', referring to the belief that it could cure bites and stings. Mentioned in Gerard's *Herball* of 1597.

Description: Tender P Bushy plant 2-4′/ 60-120cm high with slender branching shoots and smooth narrow olive-green leaves.

Site and soil: Sheltered site on well-drained soil. pH 5.5-7.

Propagation: Buy plants of French Tarragon, not Russian Tarragon which is nearly tasteless. Plant in early spring or autumn. Take cuttings in June or sever rhizomes in March and replant 2-3″/50-75mm deep.

Care and cultivation: Keep weed-free. Remove flowering shoots to produce more leaves. Not completely hardy, so cover with ash, straw or bracken in winter.

Harvesting: Use leaves as required. To dry leaves, cut before flowering.

Kitchen: Use the leaves fresh or dried in omelettes, salads, sauces, and in wine vinegar to create tarragon vinegar.

Companion planting: Beneficial to all plants.

THYME

Thymus spp   *Mediterranean*

Origins and history: Introduced by the Romans. Grown in gardens for many centuries, and in classical and medieval times it was thought to be a source of inspiration and courage.

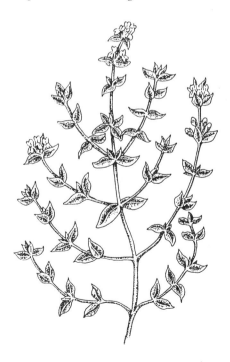

Description: P A small bushy shrub 6-18"/15-45cm high, with small grey-green aromatic leaves and small pretty pink flowers. There are over 100 kinds of thyme. Common thyme (*T. vulgaris*) has the strongest flavour; Lemon Thyme (*T. citrodorus*) less strong and lemony. Wild Thyme (*T. serpyllum*) is low and creeping, and less pungent.

Site and soil: Dry well-drained sunny position. Grow near the kitchen door, in flower beds, in the vegetable garden, in pots and window boxes. pH 5.5-7.

Propagation: Easy to raise from seed. Sow April-May ½"/12mm deep in nursery bed. Thin to 4"/100mm. Plant out 12"/30cm apart in September. *Or*, take stem cuttings in April-May. *Or*, divide old plants in autumn. *Or*, layer low branches in autumn.

Care and cultivation: Keep weed-free. If not already trimmed, prune after flowering to keep bushy.

Harvesting: Use leaves as required. For drying, pick before flowering when the plant is dry.

Kitchen: Use in tomato dishes, soups and stews. Dry to preserve.

Herb tea: Useful for respiratory and digestive difficulties. As a gargle, eases throat infections. Infuse 2 teaspoonsfuls dried (6 fresh) in 1 cup of boiling water for 10 minutes. Take 3 times a day.

Companion planting: Beneficial to brassicas: helps repel cabbage root fly. General good influence.

Fruit

'Come buy our orchard fruits,
Come buy, come buy:
Apples and quinces,
Lemons and oranges,
Plump unpecked cherries,
Melons and raspberries,
Bloom-down-cheeked peaches,
Swart-headed mulberries,
Wild free-born cranberries,
Crab-apples, dewberries,
Pine-apples, blackberries,
Apricots, strawberries;—
All ripe together
In summer weather,—
Morns that pass by,
Fair eves that fly;
Come buy, come buy:
Our grapes fresh from the vine,
Pomegranates full and fine,
Dates and sharp bullaces,
Rare pears and greengages,
Damsons and bilberries,
Taste them and try:
Currants and gooseberries,
Bright-fire-like barberries,
Figs to fill your mouth,
Citrons from the South,
Sweet to tongue and sound to eye;
Come buy, come buy.'

Christina G. Rossetti
Goblin Market

Fruit

As with vegetables, when you grow and eat your own fruit you know roughly what has gone into the making of that fruit. You do not have to worry about the possible effects of fertilizers and pesticides, or whether fungicides or radiation treatment have been used to give the fruit a longer shelf life. You can choose to grow varieties with thin skins, soft texture and juiciness—varieties that commercial growers cannot use as they do not transport well. These are often the varieties with the best flavour and the most vitamins. If you eat your fruit straight off the tree, it will not only be fresh, but you can also pick when the fruit is perfectly ripe, whereas commercial growers have to pick theirs slightly under-ripe. Fruit will not usually gain its full flavour when it ripens off the plant.

Growing fruit is even more cost-effective than growing vegetables. Buying your stock may be expensive, but the plants will almost certainly repay that cost in their first full fruiting year, and the next twenty, thirty, or even a hundred years' crops will all be profit. If well looked after, most soft fruits will produce for twenty years, apples as much as fifty years, and there are cherry trees in Kent that are still producing after a hundred years.

Site and soil

Frost is a big danger to fruit. One frosty night in spring can kill the fragile blossoms, and without flowers there will be no fruit. Avoid frost pockets, or find varieties which are less prone to frost damage than others, or which flower later. Small trees, cordons and bushes can be protected with sacking supported on a wooden framework, and the odd blackcurrant bush can have a light cotton sheet thrown over it. Be grateful for a late cold spring: blossom will be late and less likely to be caught by frost.

Pears and dessert plums need the sunniest and most sheltered part of the garden. North of a line between Chester and Lincoln they are best grown against a high south or west facing wall. Dessert apples are hardier, but still choose your site with care if you live north of this line. Damsons will make a good windbreak in most areas of Britain; cooking apples will do so in the south. Peaches, nectarines and apricots will fruit well in a sunny sheltered spot in the south, but will need to be under glass in the north.

Tree fruit will grow well in most kinds of soil, but they prefer a fairly deep (9"/22cm) well-drained medium loam, with a pH of 6.5 for apples, 6-7.5 for pears, and 7 for cherries, plums, peaches, nectarines and apricots. Dessert apples, plums and pears need the best soil and drainage. Cooking varieties are generally more tolerant than dessert varieties, and apples are more tolerant of dry conditions than pears.

Heavy (clay) soils will provide good crops as long as they have been well cultivated, plenty of organic matter incorporated, the subsoil broken up, and the drainage attended to. Light (sandy) soils can be difficult, and need plenty of organic matter, including long-lasting materials like shoddy and horsehair, dug in before planting.

Gravel and chalky soil will need trenching down to the subsoil, and plenty of long-lasting organic matter added. This preparation should be done at least three months before planting, preferably in summer.

Soft fruits prefer cooler, damper, more acid conditions than tree fruit, and can therefore be given the second-best sites in your fruit garden.

If your soil is poor, delay planting for one year. Lime in autumn if necessary, then sow a green manure like Italian ryegrass with red clover (at $1\frac{1}{2}$oz/yd^2 (45g/m^2)) in October—earlier in the north of Britain. When this is 6-9"/15-22cm high in late spring, dig it in with well-rotted manure or compost at about 1 barrow-load per 12yd^2/11m^2. Now sow agricultural lupins or vetch and dig in again with compost or manure; then if you have time do the same with a mustard crop. By autumn the plot will be transformed. Check the pH again, and bring it up with ground limestone if necessary. Cover it with black polythene until the plants arrive, and you may be able to plant them immediately. For information on planting fruit trees, see 'Helping Your Garden Along'.

Watch your fruit trees for early signs of mineral deficiencies, though if you mulch every year with organic material this is unlikely to arise. If you inherit a neglected garden, feed well with mulch, and spray with seaweed solution once a fortnight during the growng season. For information about mineral deficiencies, see Lawrence Hills' *Grow Your Own Fruit And Vegetables*, and the Royal Horticultural Society's book, *The Fruit Garden Displayed*.

Companion planting

To encourage hoverflies around the orchard, which control aphids and keep red spider mite in check, grow nasturtiums, poached egg plant (*Limnanthes douglasii*) or *Colvolvulus tricolor* 'Blue Ensign'.

Choosing your plants
TREE FRUIT
Many fruit-tree varieties are grafted on to the rootstock of another variety to obtain optimum growth characteristics. Choose a tree which has a rootstock suitable for your purposes: for a small garden you will want dwarf rootstocks; for standard trees choose a vigorous rootstock; for big trees on exposed sites choose a very vigorous rootstock. Rootstocks have no effect on the fruit produced, but control the growth of the tree and the time it takes to come into fruit. A dwarf rootstock has fibrous roots with no taproot, so the tree will always need support and feeding; a vigorous rootstock has a long taproot, so the tree will become well anchored in the ground and after eight years will need no support. Trees on a dwarf rootstock will start fruiting in 3-6 years, whereas trees on a vigorous rootstock will take 8-12 years.

Most fruit trees need a pollination partner, so take care to buy at least two trees that flower at the same time. If you are buying pear or plum trees, make sure the trees are compatible as well as flowering at the same time. Some varieties, like 'Bramley Seedling' apples, are triploid—such varieties produce no viable pollen, so its partner will need another pollinating partner; you will have to buy three trees which flower at the same time. Use the pollination tables at the end of *The Fruit Garden Displayed*.

SOFT FRUIT
Strawberry plants and raspberry canes are very susceptible to virus diseases, so it is important to buy virus-free stock. If possible, buy stock which has been certified under the Ministry of

Agriculture Certification Scheme. If you use your own or other people's stock, make sure it is healthy. All soft fruits set their fruit alone.

Support and protection

Tree fruits need good stakes for support when planting (see tree planting in 'Helping Your Garden Along'). Blackberries, loganberries and raspberries need strong posts and wires to support them. The posts should be 2×2″/50×50mm, and about 8′/2.4m long, which will allow for 18″/45cm underground and a similar amount above the top wire to carry the bird netting. Three parallel wires starting 24″/60cm above the soil will be sufficient for raspberries, but loganberries and blackberries are better with five. Make sure the posts have been soaked in a preservative which is not poisonous to plants—creosoted wood should be left to weather for a month before using. Use thick strong wire—not the thin plastic-coated type, which rusts and breaks very easily.

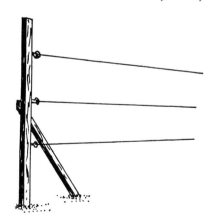

Support for cane fruit

In some areas, birds can do a great deal of damage to fruit buds. Bird scarers and cats can help, but the only

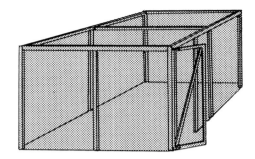

A fruit cage

effective control is netting. Netting is essential for cherries. Ideally, grow your soft fruit together and build a cage over it (see Lawrence Hills' *Grow Your Own Fruit and Vegetables*). Use nylon netting or chicken wire, but not galvanized wire mesh, as the zinc will be transferred to the fruit. Uncover the fruit during the pollination period, as insects do not like flying through mesh.

We have no space here to write specifically about peaches, nectarines, apricots, grapes or walnuts—do not let that put you off trying them!

Pruning

Basic instructions for pruning are given under each fruit. The following diagram shows the important distinction between spurs (the short growths on which the fruit is produced), fruit buds (which will first produce blossom and then fruit), and growth buds (which produce new shoots).

There are specific reasons for pruning fruit trees and bushes, namely:
—to produce fruit each year (many trees naturally fruit only one year in two).
—to produce fruit early in the life of the tree.

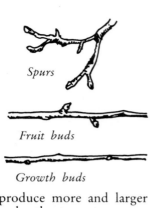

Spurs

Fruit buds

Growth buds

—to produce more and larger fruit.
—to make the tree strong enough to carry extra fruit.
—to produce the shape we want.
As far as shape is concerned, cordon, pyramid and espalier are the most suitable fruit tree shapes for a small garden. Where space is available, bush, half standard and standard will give larger crops per tree, and are easier to handle.

Spindle

Bush

Pyramid

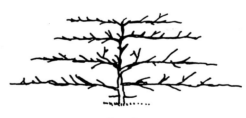

Espalier

Cordon

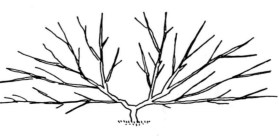

Fan

Tree fruit

APPLE

Malus domestica   *Caucasus, Turkestan*

Origins and history: More than twenty varieties were known to the Romans, who also knew about grafting. Varieties recorded 400 years ago are still grown today, including 'Court Pendu Plat' and 'Nonpareil'.

Description: Apple trees can be trained in many shapes, both as free-standing bushes, pyramids, spindles, half standards and standards, and against walls, fences or wires in fans, espaliers or cordons. Blossom late April-May; fruit August-December. Early apples tend to be softer. Fruit can be sweet or acid; yellow, green, red or russet; more or less spherical.

Varieties: There are so many varieties it is useless to be given a list, so I will just give hints on what to look for when selecting apple varieties. It is good to grow your local varieties—such as 'South Lincoln Beauty', 'Beauty of Bath' and 'Cornish Gillyflower' —both for genetic diversity and because the area will suit them. The Royal Horticultural Society operates an apple variety identification service; their address is at the back of the book.

Points to consider:
Hardiness: 'Cox's Orange Pippin', the most popular dessert apple, cannot stand cold and wet, and should not be grown north of the Chester/Lincoln line because it will be prone to canker. 'James Grieve' is called the Cox of the North, but has a tendency to canker in mild wet areas. It is best not to have early-flowering or late-fruiting varieties in the north of Britain, because they may be spoilt by frost; latest-flowering varieties include 'Crawley's Beauty' (dessert) and 'Edward VII' (cooker). For some resistance to frost on blossom, choose 'James Grieve', 'Laxton's Epicure' and 'Worcester Pearmain' (all desserts), and 'Lane's Prince Albert' (cooker).
Vigour: Do not buy a very vigorous tree like 'Bramley's Seedling' for a small garden.
Pollination: For cross-pollination you must have varieties whose flowering times overlap. I have only read of one self-fertile apple tree—'Allington Pippin' ('South Lincoln Beauty'). For pollination tables see the Royal Horticultural Society's *The Fruit Garden Displayed*.
Cooker or eater: take your choice; some varieties are both.
Flavour: Taste is partly dependent upon environment. You are safer with local varieties.
Nutrition: 'Ribston Pippin' (dessert) is the best for vitamin C. 'Sturmer Pippin' and 'Adams Pearmain' (dessert) and 'Belle de Boskoop' (cooker) also have high vitamin C. All are unsuitable for the north of Britain.
Storage: Early varieties do not store well.
Shape and size: Depends on rootstock (see under 'Propagation').

Site and soil: Apple trees must not be planted in wet soil; varieties susceptible to canker and scab will suffer more in damp conditions. Trees on acid soils will need two handfuls of crushed shells in their planting holes. Use heavy mulch on alkaline soils. pH 5-6.5.

Propagation: Apple trees are propagated by grafting or budding. Most are grown on 'Malling' (M) or 'Malling Merton' (MM) rootstocks, which have predictable effects on growth:
Dwarfing: Malling 27 (M27) 4'/1.2m tall, correspondingly compact; needs good

cultivation and staking all its life.
Malling 9 (M9) 7'/2.1m tall; very common.

Semi-dwarfing: Malling 26 (M26) 9'/2.7m tall.
Malling Merton 106 (MM106) 10'/3m tall; sturdier than other dwarfs.
Vigorous: Malling Merton 111 (MM111) 13'/4m tall; better choice in poor soils.
Very vigorous: Malling 25 (M25) for well-anchored large trees.

A complete list of rootstock numbers is given in Simmon's *Manual of Fruit.* Instructions on grafting and budding are given in *The Fruit Garden Displayed.*

Care and cultivation: Keep soil clear as far as branches extend, and keep grass under the tree mown—vigorous trees can be slowed down by long grass. Keep grass and mulches away from the trunk—they encourage collar rot. Mulch to feed tree and attract beneficial insects like rove and ground beetles which eat some apple pests. If not thriving, give extra manure in spring. If flowers suffer a frost, spray with cold water before sunrise: it is the quick morning thaw that kills them, and a slower thaw may save them. In a very dry June, water heavily to stop excessive shedding of fruitlets. If the crop is very heavy, thin the fruit to give bigger and better fruit, stop strain on the tree, and discourage biennial bearing. Remove any small or misshapen apples and the centre (king) apple from each cluster. After the natural June drop, leave only one or two of the best in each cluster, depending on the vigour of the tree.

Pruning:
Young trees: Fruit trees are usually sold when 3 years old, with the first pruning already done. Instructions for early pruning of your own 'maidens' (one-year-old trees), and details of how to train young trees into cordon, fan, espalier and tree forms will be found in *The Fruit Garden Displayed* and *Grow Your Own Fruit and Vegetables.* Too heavy pruning in the early stages causes too much growth and delayed fruiting. Too little or no pruning causes fruiting too early and too heavily, with long whippy growth which may break under the weight of the fruit.

Maintenance pruning:
FREE-STANDING TREES (OTHER THAN PYRAMID-SHAPED TREES):
Usually only need winter pruning in November or February. Shorten leader by two-thirds of its new growth, and prune laterals back to third or fourth bud pointing away from centre (if tree has spreading habit, choose an upward-pointing bud). If branches are crossing or rubbing together, cut out weakest and cover the wound with *Trichoderma viride* or a pruning paste. Some of oldest growth may be removed or cut back to encourage new growth. Very vigorous or tip-bearing trees (like 'Bramley's Seedling') only need summer pruning (see below).

CORDONS, ESPALIERS, FANS AND PYRAMID-SHAPED TREES:
Need regular summer pruning if they are growing correctly. Summer pruning reduces the leaf area and stimulates the tree into making fruit buds rather than more growth. In July or early August, shorten the leaders by a quarter of their new growth, and the laterals by a third of their new growth. The following winter take off all the new growth since the summer pruning, plus one bud of the older growth. Do not prune the leader of a cordon or pyramid. Thin fruiting spurs if old, large or overcrowded.

GENERAL:
Winter pruning in February helps to avoid scab, canker and brown storage rot; summer pruning will get rid of quite a few aphids. Neglected trees may be worth saving, but taste the fruit first. Renew them over a period of years; do not prune excessively all at once. Remove all dead and diseased branches and thin out crowded growth. In summer, pinch out or prune unwanted growth from old branch cuts. Shorten very tall extended branches to a new sideshoot in winter. Thin out congested spur systems. If a tree has been poorly fed and is stunted it will appreciate harder cutting, as long as the soil is well drained and well fed. Give all neglected trees extra manure or compost. If trees are hopelessly old and diseased, pull them up and use them for firewood.

Harvesting: Early varieties start in late July, the latest will be ready in December. Test for ripeness by lifting fruit and giving it a slight twist—when ripe it will come away from the spur easily. Handle with great care; if bruised they will not store. Pick all the apples; any left on the ground or on the tree spread pests and diseases.

Kitchen: Delicious raw and cooked. Eat whole, chopped up or grated in salads or muesli, cooked in pies and crumbles, as apple sauce, or stuffed and baked.

Keeping: Can be kept without any special method of preserving, but only unblemished fruits of late varieties. Store in 150 gauge polythene bags, or wrap individually in oiled paper or newspaper, preferably in slatted wooden boxes. Keep store room cool and rodent- and frost-proof—do not use the loft of a centrally-heated house. Check periodically and remove rotting fruit. Each variety has a different storage life. Early varieties can be bottled or frozen. Use a juice extractor and freeze or bottle the juice, or boil the apples to a concentrate which can be used as a jam substitute.

Pests and diseases: Scab: olive-green blotches on leaves, which fall early; on shoots as blisters; on fruits as brown or black scabs or cracks. Control by pruning and removing diseased leaves; if out of hand in a wet year, spray in January with Burgundy mixture, Bordeaux mixture or neat urine.
Canker: Sunken grey patches on branches; can kill whole branches if they are girdled.
Apple Powdery Mildew: fruit will not set, leaves and blossom covered in white powder, and often wither and fall. Cut out affected branches as soon as possible, winter prune and use Burgundy mixture in January.
Brown Rot: fungus entering through wounds in apple, causing brown spots which grow until whole apple is brown. Remove and burn affected fruit, take care when picking apples not to puncture skin; spores survive in apple stores so keep storage materials scrupulously clean.
Codling Moth: produces most of maggots in apples. Use grease bands in summer to trap caterpillars crawling up trunk and branches, or put 1"/25mm of a 10:1 water/treacle mix into jamjars, cover them with netting to keep out bees, wasps and hoverflies, and hang them in your apple trees. Pick up all fallen fruit.
Apple Sawfly: tunnel into fruit earlier than Codling Moth, leaving droppings around tunnel entrance. Spray with nicotine and soft soap or derris immediately after petal fall, and remove apples from ground.
Apple Aphids: treat as aphids just before petals show pink, except for Woolly Aphid or American Blight, which causes damage to woody stems and branches. Paint patches with a 2:1 mix of paraffin and methylated spirit.
Apple Capsids and Apple and Pear Sucker: former makes small brown holes in leaves followed by damaged shoots, blossom and young fruit; latter looks rather like frost scorch, with damage to leaf buds and blossoms. Use grease band, then hose tree vigorously with water, or use a nicotine and soft soap spray at first sign of damage.
Winter Moths: wingless females lay eggs in winter which hatch to become brown or green 'looper' caterpillars, feeding on opening buds and young leaves—grease band between October and April, or spray with *Bacillus thuringiensis* when caterpillars are feeding from April onwards.
For other pests see the HDRA leaflet *Fruit Pest and Disease Control.*

CHERRY

Prunus avium (Sweet Cherry); *P. cerasus* (Sour Cherry)   *W Asia, Europe*

Origins and history: *P. avium* a British native; most cultivated cherries originated in Greece and Turkey. Grown in ancient Egypt. Tradescant's catalogue of 1634 listed 15 varieties growing in Britain; there are now 300 varieties, and worldwide there are more than a thousand forms of sweet cherry alone.

Description: Sweet Cherry is a tall spreading tree up to 35'/11m high; Sour Cherry is smaller. Long leaves pink in early spring, mid green later. White flowers in early spring, followed by round fruit on long stalks, yellow to almost black, July-September.

Varieties:
Sweet:
'Merton Favourite' black cherry, good crop mid-July, strong-growing; 'Merton Glory' large sweet white fruit mid-July, vigorous, crops early in life; 'Stella' self-pollinating, dark red cherry late July, moderate flavour, good crop, upright tree.
Dessert/Cooking:
'May Duke' dark red fruit end July, rich flavour, fairly vigorous growth, upright and compact, slightly susceptible to canker, hybrid (partially self-pollinating, but better with a morello); 'Late Duke' another self-pollinating hybrid, late-flowering, red fruit in August, rich flavour, moderate cropping.
Sour/Cooking
'Morello' self-pollinating, dark rather bitter red to black fruit August-September, small tree, vigorous when young, suitable for training against wall, canker-resistant, susceptible to Silver Leaf and Blossom Wilt. Usually needs cross-pollinating varieties to fruit successfully (see *The Fruit Garden Displayed* for a pollination chart).

Site and soil: Sweet cherries need a sheltered site. Sour cherries can be used for wind protection and on north-facing walls. Will not tolerate acid soil, damp climate, or bad drainage. pH 6-7.5.

Propagation: Stake when planting. Rootstocks:
Gean or Wild Cherry: Gives tall vigorous tree.
Mahleb: Used on some sour varieties, slightly dwarfing, dependable.
Mazzard: Vigorous and adaptable to most soils.
Malling 12/1: Uniform size, vigorous, some resistance to canker.
Colt: New, slightly dwarfing, for sweet cherries.

Care and cultivation: Cultivate as for apples, though substitute hay or straw for manure as mulch. If trained against a wall, may need watering before the June drop. Net against birds.

Pruning: Prune as little as possible. Saw out broken, dead or sickly branches in June. Do not cut in winter, when fungi spores are at their most active. To fan-train sweet cherries: tie in any sideshoots, pinch out shoots growing away from wall, and remove 3"/75mm of growing tips in summer. Treat Dukes in the same way.

Sour cherries tend to fruit on previous year's growth. In late spring a few shoots should be cut back to a growth bud on the older wood to encourage new growth.

Harvesting: If cherries are not cracking they can stay on the tree until fully ripe. Sour cherries should have stalks cut with scissors.

Kitchen: Eat sweet cherries fresh, or in pies or crumbles.

Keeping: Sour cherries make very good jam, and bottle and freeze well.

Pests and diseases: Bacterial Canker: causes flattened dead areas on branches which exude gum, prevents leaf development and branches may die back (see 'Canker'). Silver Leaf, Brown Rot (see under 'Apple'); Birds, Cherry Blackfly.

DAMSON

Prunus domestica ssp *insititia*
E Europe, W Asia

Origins and history: Reputedly brought from Damascus to Italy in 114BC—hence the name 'Damascene Plum'. Used medicinally in the sixteenth century; now naturalized in British hedgerows.

Description: Small compact tree, sometimes shrub-like. Mass of white blossom in spring, followed by small oval purple acid fruit. Leaves long and oval, mid-green. Makes good windproof hedging.

Varieties: 'Farleigh' early-flowering, rich-flavoured fruit in early September, partially self-fertile (best with other damsons), good as hedge; 'Merryweather' early flowering and self-fertile, plum-like fruit in September, vigorous spreading habit; 'Prune' ('Westmorland Damson', 'Cheshire Damson', 'Shropshire Damson') early-flowering self-fertile dense twiggy tree, prolific blossom on bare branches, best flavoured fruit late September; 'Bradley's King' mid-period flowering (good for northern areas), large sweet fruit with heavy crop late September, vigorous upright habit.
Some varieties need pollination partners (see *The Fruit Garden Displayed* for a pollination chart).

Site and soil: Any reasonable soil. Withstands north winds, but blossom may be caught by hard spring frosts. pH 6-7.5.

Propagation: Stake when planting. Rootstocks: *St Julien A* or *K*, or own roots.

Care and cultivation: Keep soil cultivated 30″/75cm around tree. Mulch to keep soil moist and weed free.

Pruning: Buy 3-year old trees ready pruned, or train your own maidens. Damson do not need maintenance pruning. Cut out crowded branches and dead wood between early May and mid-June. Clip hedges in summer.

Harvesting: Pick in September/October when soft. For preserving gather while still firm, but an even purple.

Kitchen: Too acid to eat raw, but makes delicious pies and puddings.

Keeping: Makes excellent jam and wine. Bottle and freeze well.

Pests and diseases: Usually trouble-free. Occasionally problems with Silver Leaf, Aphids or Canker.

PEAR

Pyrus communis   W Asia

Origins and history: Homer called the pear 'fruit of the gods'; in the first century AD Pliny recorded 35 varieties. There were extensive orchards of British varieties in the middle ages, but French and Belgian pears started to be imported in the seventeenth century, and now only specialist nurseries supply British varieties.

Description: Upright growth, 10-40′/3-12m high. Clusters of white flowers in early spring; long glossy mid-green leaves. Fruit ready to pick October-November; there are soft melting dessert and hard cooking varieties.

Varieties: Try to find varieties suitable for your area. If you have room, choose pears for succession, as they remain perfect for dessert only for a short time. 'Beurre Hardy' dessert, pick late September to eat in October, strong grower and heavy cropper, slow to start bearing; 'Doyenne de Comice' dessert, pick in October to eat November-December, large fruit with very good flavour, vigorous, trains well, scab-resistant; 'Glou Morceau' dessert, pick mid-November to eat December-January, good flavour, needs south-facing wall to finish ripening, moderate spreading habit; 'Conference' self-pollinating dessert, pick late September to eat October-November, reliable cropper, bears early in life, upright growth, good for bottling, prone to scab and canker; 'Fertility Improved' self-pollinating dessert and cooking, pick late September to eat in November, round good-flavoured fruit, upright moderate habit.

Most varieties need pollinating partners (see *The Fruit Garden Displayed* for a pollination chart).

Site and soil: Pears do best in a warm dry climate, and are not recommended north of the Chester/Lincoln line. They flower early and blossom can get caught by spring frosts. Select a warm sheltered position, and fertile soil with good drainage. pH 6-7.5.

Propagation: Stake when planting. Rootstocks:
Malling Quince C: Semi-dwarfing for restricted forms. Bears early.
Malling Quince A: Semi-dwarfing, later bearing and more growth than Quince C.
Wild Pear: Gives very vigorous standard tree. Can be grassed down—grow grass up to 12″/30cm from trunk.

Care and cultivation: Mulch with 2″/50mm manure for 3 springs after planting. Then give light manure mulch each spring if not vigorous, and check the pH. Grass down if too vigorous.

Pruning: As for apples.

Harvesting: August-November, depending on variety. Some are difficult to remove—do not break spurs. Pick when slightly under-ripe—early pears lose flavour if picked when over-ripe; late pears don't gain full flavour if picked too early.

Kitchen: Delicious fresh when perfectly ripe, good with cheese. Stew and serve with chocolate sauce.

Keeping: Store as for apples. Each variety has a different storage life. Bottle well.

Pests and diseases: See under 'Apples'; also:
Pear Leaf Blister Mites: brown pustules on leaves. Handpick and destroy infested leaves in summer.
Pear Midge: small maggots feeding on young fruitlets cause distortion and premature dropping. Collect affected fruit and destroy.
Fireblight: Originally introduced on pears. Flowers blacken and shrivel; leaves wither and go brown.

PLUM, GREENGAGE
Prunus domestica   N hemisphere

Origins and history: Cultivated plums are derived from several species, including one British native, *P. insititia*. Domesticated since about 1000BC. In 1640 John Tradescant named 64 varieties; the ubiquitous 'Victoria' originated around 1840. Greengages were imported from Italy to the French royal gardens in the sixteenth century, and were used in British walled gardens by the eighteenth.

Description: Vigorous tree up to 20'/6m high, though can be kept smaller with dwarfing rootstock and careful pruning. White flowers in early spring followed by purple, red or mottled fruit in August; long medium-green leaves. Greengage less vigorous; round green, yellow or translucent fruit with richer taste than plum.

Varieties: 'Victoria' best known and very tasty, vigorous, heavy cropper, self-fertile and good pollinator for other plums, frost-resistant, matures early, prone to Silver Leaf; 'Transparent Gage' fine flavour, strong sturdy tree, needs shelter; 'Czar' a self-fertile cooking plum, thrives on north walls; 'Kirke's Blue' delicious, but crops badly in north, dwarfish spreading habit, fruits mid-September; 'Quetsche' ('Carlsbad Plum') for stewing, bottling and wine, vigorous upright habit, self-fertile, good crop end-September, hardy as damson; 'Myrobalan' ('Cherry Plum', *P. cerasifera*) grows to 18'/5.5m, attractive bushy tree, beautiful early blossom vulnerable to frost, small red or yellow fruit delicious when ripe.
See *The Fruit Garden Displayed* for a pollination chart.

Site and soil: Delicate varieties need south or west-facing wall. Victorias, Carlsbads and cooking plums are tougher. Fertile well-drained soil. pH 6-7.5.

Propagation: Stake when planting. Rootstocks:
St Julien A: Semi-dwarfing, compatible with most varieties.
St Julien K: Dwarfing.
Pixy: Most dwarfing; needs good soil and cultivation.
Brompton: Sends up few suckers; helps trees grow on and recover after silver leaf disease.
Myrobalan: Vigorous strong-rooted standard, not suitable for greengages. Tolerates wide range of soil and climatic conditions. Resists crown rot.

Care and cultivation: Maintain compost mulch six inches from trunk out to drip line. If soil is acid, scatter 2lb/1kg magnesium limestone or ground limestone around the tree every second autumn. If fruit is small, give trees manure. If the crop is heavy, thin and give branches padded support. If branches break, paint with *Trichoderma viride* to prevent Silver Leaf disease. Disturbing soil round tree encourages suckers, so rely on mulch to keep weeds down. If dry, water heavily before fruit ripens.

Pruning: With young trees, prune new growth on leading shoots to 15-21"/37-53cm and on laterals to 6-9"/15-22cm in April-May.

Maintenance prune as little as possible. Cut out dead, diseased, weak or crossing wood in May. If tree is very vigorous and not fruiting, prune in late June, taking new growth on leaders to 12"/30cm and on laterals to 6-9"/15-22cm. May need root pruning, or digging up and replanting if not too big.

Plums on walls should have sideshoots pinched out to 3-4 leaves in summer. May need root pruning every five years. Scrape away soil from roots, and cut out thick roots 24"/60cm from trunk, leaving any fibrous roots.

Harvesting: For dessert, pick when soft and juicy. For cooking and preserving, pick when fully coloured but still firm. In rainy seasons splitting of the skin is common, and fruit should be picked quickly before flies and wasps get at it.

Kitchen: Eat fresh, or cook in pies and puddings.

Keeping: Bottle or use for jam.

Pests and diseases: Silver Leaf: most important disease of plums.
Canker, Powdery Mildew, Birds.
Gummosis: gum on fruit caused by bad drainage and shortage of lime.
Leaf-curling Aphids: prune off affected shoots May-July; spray with pyrethrum.
Plum Gall Mites: overwinter in bud scales and make galls on foliage. Pick leaves off and burn, then check remaining leaves weekly.

Soft fruit

BLACKBERRY, LOGANBERRY
Rubus sp.   *N hemisphere*

Origins and history: Blackberry (*R. ulmifolius*) is a British native, cultivated in garden hedges by the sixteenth century. Serious cultivation started in the early nineteenth century in North America, where most varieties have been developed. Loganberry (*R. loganobaccus*) discovered in 1881 in California; introduced into Britain about 1899.

Description: Blackberry is an invasive climbing plant with long prickly arching stems and compound light green toothed leaves; pink or white clustered flowers in June-July followed by characteristic knobbly black fruit. Loganberries grow like blackberries, but produce long dark red fruit.

Varieties:
BLACKBERRY:
'Oregon Cutleaf Thornless' best flavour, fruits in August; 'John Innes' also thornless, fruits in August; 'Bedford Giant' best flavoured thorned variety.
LOGANBERRY:
'Loganberry LY59' good flavour, moderate

vigour; 'Thornless Loganberry L654' a sport of 'Loganberry LY59'.

Site and soil: Grows in any soil in sun or partial shade; no manuring. Grow on wires over walls, arches or fences. pH 5-6.

Propagation: Dig in 1lb/450g of 1:1 bonemeal/hoof and horn mix to every yd^2/m^2 of bed. Plant October-March; loganberries and thornless blackberries 8'/2.4m apart, thorned blackberries 12'/3.6m apart, in rows 6'/2m apart. Spread roots out well. Leave new shoots but cut old stems to 9"/22cm. To increase, layer in July, and sever and plant out the following spring.

Care and cultivation: Keep weeded, and mulch with old straw or hay in summer.

Pruning: The year after planting, tie new growth along wires 12"/30cm apart (see beginning of fruit section for details). Cut out most old canes as soon as they have fruited, and tie up new ones. Fruit on both old wood and new, so some 2-3-year-old canes can be left. If thorned shoots appear on thornless varieties, remove from the root (like all suckers).

Harvesting: Blackberries August-October; loganberries July-September.

Kitchen: Raw on breakfast cereals, cooked with apples in puddings.

Keeping: Preserve in jellies and jams, bottle or freeze, or make wine. Keep flavour well.

Pests and diseases: Mildew if too dry around roots. Loganberries can get Cane Spot and some virus diseases (see under 'Raspberries').

BLACKCURRANT

Ribes nigrum   Europe, Asia

Origins and history: Native to Britain, and recorded in seventeenth century herbals. In 1836 there were still only 6 varieties; now there are about 35.

Description: Rounded bush 4-6'/1.2-1.8m tall with 3-lobed mid-green leaves. Distinctive smell. Inconspicuous greenish flowers in early spring, followed by small round black fruits in clusters (strigs) July-September. Very rich in vitamin C. Late varieties are less likely to have blossom damaged by frost.

Varieties: 'Baldwin' highest in vitamin C, compact, late fruiting, needs fertile well-drained soil; 'Westwick Choice' late fruiting, resists Big Bud Mite; 'Wellington XXX' fruits mid-season, vigorous grower.

Site and soil: Any moist well-drained soil in sun or partial shade. Dig in extra compost or manure on sandy soil. pH 6-8.

Propagation: To give long-lasting nitrogen, dig in old feathers or shoddy before planting (or use 2lb/1kg hoof and horn per yd^2/m^2), plus a barrowload of manure per $5yd^2/4m^2$ and 1lb/450g bonemeal per yd^2/m^2. Plant 4-5'/1.2-1.5m apart, depending on variety. Make hole wide enough to spread roots, and deep enough just to cover previous soil mark. Firm in carefully. They will fruit well for about 10 years. To increase, take 6-8"/ 15-20cm stem cuttings in September when pruning, insert in nursery bed, and transfer to permanent positions the following autumn.

Care and cultivation: Mulch lightly with manure in winter or spring, and with lawn mowings or straw in summer. Do not over-manure—resulting soft growth is susceptible to disease. Keep weeded. Net when fruit starts to appear.

Pruning: After planting cut back to 3-4 buds above soil on each stem. Fruit grows best on 1-year-old wood, so cut out most of old wood down to base or to a new strong shoot as soon as bush has fruited. As the bush gets older, you will be cutting out between ⅓ and ¼ of the old wood each year.

Harvesting: If you have masses to pick, cut out fruiting branches and pick them on the kitchen table like the professionals. It is best, however, to pick from the bushes, so as to catch early and late ripeners.

Kitchen: Good raw if very ripe. Cook in tarts, pies, puddings.

Keeping: Make juice, syrup or jam. Bottle. Freeze very well.

Pests and diseases: Leaf Spot Fungus: a problem in wet seasons, leaves fall and fruit withers. Burn leaves and spray branches with Burgundy mixture; use compost in spring instead of manure as excess nitrogen makes plant more susceptible.
Gooseberry Mildew: result of too much nitrogen. Reduce manure; cut out tips to 3″/75mm and burn; spray with 4oz/125g soft soap and 8oz/250g washing soda to 2½gall/12l water; spray again next spring and when bushes have just set fruit.
Reversion: virus disease which changes shape of leaves, making them longer and narrower, eventually killing whole bush—dig up and burn.
Big Bud Mite: produces enlarged buds and helps spread viruses. Spray with derris/pyrethrum mixture when leaves have just appeared and flowers nearly opened; cut out any overlarge buds during pruning and burn them. 'Seabrooks Black' is resistant to mite and virus; 'Goliath' very susceptible to mite.
Currant Aphis: curls up new leaves and stunts new growth. Tar oil wash in February.
Magpie or Currant Moth Caterpillar: yellow stripes down sides, black and white markings, strips leaves at speed. Spray with liquid derris/pyrethrum mixture. Birds.

GOOSEBERRY

Ribes grossularia   Europe

Origins and history: British native; earliest record of cultivation thirteenth century. 23 varieties were recorded in 1778, 300 in 1821. In the nineteenth century gooseberry clubs held competitions, and before long there were more than a thousand varieties, most of which have since disappeared.

Description: A bush 24-48″/60-120cm high; also grown as a cordon. Upright or drooping habit, prickly spines on stems, 3-lobed mid-green leaves, inconspicuous reddish-green flowers followed by green, white, yellow or red fruit which can be smooth or hairy May-July.

Varieties: Choose upright varieties for a small garden. 'Whitesmith' early flowering, pale fruit with excellent flavour in mid-season, upright growth, resistant to American gooseberry mildew; 'Langley Gage' dessert, very early flowering, delicious large pale yellow fruit in mid-season, habit and resistance like 'Whitesmith'; 'London' used to win all prizes for size, smooth red skin with good flavour in mid-season, spreading bush.

Site and soil: Sun or partial shade. Will not tolerate poor drainage. pH 5-6.5

Propagation: Prepare soil as for blackcurrants. Choose 2-3-year-old bushes with a good 6-9″/15-22cm 'leg'. Plant when dormant 4-5′/1.2-1.5m apart; cordons 12″/30cm apart. To increase, take

12"/30cm stem cuttings in autumn, insert in nursery bed, and plant out next autumn.

Care and cultivation: Keep weeded. In April apply 1lb/500g wood ash per yd²/m². Mulch with mowings, hay or straw. Longer-lasting potash can be provided by putting comfrey leaves under the mulch every year, or adding rock potash at 2lb/1kg per yd²/m² every 5 years. Do not use manure.

Pruning: Aim to have bushes with open centres so that sun can ripen fruit and you don't scratch your hands when picking. Prune in March, as for apples.

Harvesting: Pick hard and green for bottling; large and soft for eating raw.

Kitchen: Delicious raw when fully ripe; excellent for pies, tarts and fools.

Keeping: Good for bottling, freezing and making jam.

Pests and diseases: American Gooseberry Mildew: treat as for blackcurrants; use resistant varieties.
Gooseberry Sawfly: main gooseberry pest, can strip a bush in days.
Birds.

RASPBERRY

Rubus idaeus   Europe

Origins and history: British native, used medicinally since classical times. First recorded cultivation in 1551. Old stock has not survived because of weakening effects of virus disease and continuous vegetative reproduction. Many new virus-resistant varieties bred since 1950.

Description: Bushy plants with biennial canes, 5-8'/1.5-2.4m high. Prickly stems, compound mid-green leaves, inconspicuous white flowers followed by red fruit (sometimes yellow) July-September; autumn-fruiting September-October. Productive life: 10 years.

Varieties: Choose for succession so that most of the fruit can be enjoyed fresh. 'Malling Promise' early, good flavour, vigorous, fairly tolerant of virus; 'Malling Exploit' early, good for preserving; 'Malling Jewel' midseason, very good flavour, tolerant of mosaic virus; 'Lloyd George' midseason, short canes, smaller fruit but with excellent flavour, can also fruit in autumn; 'Golden Everest' mid-season, sweet yellow-orange fruit; 'Norfolk Giant' late, vigorous, good for preserving;

'Lord Lambourne' late, vigorous, good flavour.

Site and soil: Fertile soil in sun or partial shade. Will not thrive in poor soil; dislikes lime. pH 5-6.5.

Propagation: Prepare soil as for blackcurrants. Plant ideally in November, though possible until April. Dig trench 12"/30cm wide and 3"/75mm deep. Plant 12"/30cm apart, with 4-6'/1.2-1.8m between rows. Cover roots carefully and firm. Shorten cane to 12"/30cm. To increase, propagate from suckers.

Care and cultivation: In spring, mulch with 4oz/125g wood ash per yd²/m² or comfrey leaves, together with manure or compost, then cover with lawn mowings. If soil is rich, manure every other year. Hoe away new growth between rows and pull out weak growth. After pruning fork mulch into soil surface, taking out any weeds; fork again in winter to expose raspberry beetle maggots to birds. For details about support, see the introduction to the fruit section. Try planting carrots or lettuce between the rows in first year.

Pruning: Cut old grey canes close to ground after fruiting. Retain up to 8 new canes per plant, keeping the strongest; do not keep canes thinner than your little finger. Tie new canes 3-4"/75-100mm apart, using soft string: slope or bend over very long canes. Cut all canes of autumn-fruiting raspberries to ground in February, as these fruit on new growth.

Harvesting: Pull fruit from core ('plug') very gently when ripe, holding truss with your other hand to stop stalks breaking. It will come easily if ripe.

Kitchen: Delicious raw, or in puddings and sponges.

Keeping: Bottle, freeze, or make delicious jam.

Pests and diseases: Compost, good drainage and liming will cure most problems.
Cane Spot: purple spots on young canes. Cut out badly-affected canes; spray with Bordeaux mixture when buds are opening and again ten days later.
Spur Blight: dark blotches at cane joints. Treat as for Cane Spot.
Raspberry Beetle: lays eggs in flowers, and grubs feed on fruit. Dig over soil under canes in winter to expose grubs; spray with derris ten days after start of flowering, and again ten days later.
Virus: important disease for raspberries; leaves yellow, mottled and blotched. Plant new raspberries in another site.
Birds.

REDCURRANT, WHITECURRANT

Ribes sativum   Europe

Origins and history: Cultivated varieties first mentioned in Germany in the early fifteenth century. Grown in Britain by the late sixteenth century, and became common in cottage gardens.

Description: Vigorous bushes 3-5'/ 1-1.5m high. Maple-like mid-green leaves, inconspicuous white flowers in early spring followed by small red or white fruit growing in strigs from spurs of 1 to 10-year-old wood in July. Grown in bush or cordon form. Productive life 25 years.

Varieties:
REDCURRANT:
'Laxton's No. 1' flowers late so avoids frost, heavy crop midseason; 'Red Lake' flowers late, fruit with thickish skins midseason, vigorous; 'Rondom' late flowering, acid fruit late in season, resistant to leaf spot, not very juicy.

WHITECURRANT:
'White Versailles' early, sweet, can be eaten raw.

Site and soil: Do not need such a rich soil as blackcurrants. Grow happily against east or north wall. Some varieties have brittle branches: protect from wind. pH 5.5-7.

Propagation: Prepare soil as for blackcurrants. Need less manure and compost than other soft fruits. Plant when dormant, preferably October-November. Get 2-year-old bushes or cordons. Plant bushes 4'/1.2m apart; cordons 15"/37cm apart; wall fans 3'/1m apart. To increase, take 12"/30cm stem cuttings in autumn, insert in nursery bed, and plant out in 2 years.

Care and cultivation: Weed. Mulch with lawnmowings or hay. If necessary, water well when berries are swelling. Net when fruit starts to appear.

Pruning: Prune as apple.

Harvesting: Leave redcurrants for a few days after they turn red for maximum flavour. Can hang for up to 2 weeks. Pick fruit with strigs to avoid crushing berries and harming fruiting spurs.

Kitchen: Eat raw when ripe; good in tarts, pies and puddings.

Keeping: Freeze well; contain pectin so make a good jelly, useful for helping strawberry jam to set.

Pests and diseases: See 'Blackcurrant'. Also Coral Spot Fungus, Botrytis, Dieback.

RHUBARB

Rheum rhabarbarum   *E Asia*

Origins and history: Imported from China in the sixteenth century; by the end of the eighteenth century rhubarb was being forced for the London market. In the nineteenth century it became a common garden plant.

Description: Not really a soft fruit, but not really a vegetable either! A perennial plant 3-5'/1-1.5m high with poisonous large wavy green leaves and edible red or green fleshy stalks. Tall creamy flowers in summer. Can harvest long before soft fruit, so very useful. Productive life: 10 years.

Varieties: 'Hawkes Champagne' best flavour; 'Timperly Early' good for jam and bottling.

Site and soil: Sunny site; best in well-drained rich loam. pH 5.5-7.

Propagation: Prepare soil by digging in 2lb/1kg coarse bonemeal, 1 barrowload manure or compost, and 1 barrowload shoddy or feathers per 2yd²/m². Buy crowns, or take best from old clumps when dormant. Set out 30"/75cm apart (3 crowns will be enough for a family). Plant upright with bud just above soil surface.

Care and cultivation: Force rhubarb by covering with bottomless buckets in early spring—remove buckets as plants grow. Do not pick after beginning of July—the leaves are necessary to strengthen the plant. Cut off flower stalks. Don't clear away stalks and leaves until quite dead. In November mulch with 8oz/250g bonemeal per yd²/m², plus 12"/30cm of leaves held on the bed with ½"/12mm mesh.

Harvesting: Do not harvest in first year, and do not force in second year. In subsequent years pull stalks when reaching top of bucket—break from base of plant.

Kitchen: Good in crumbles, pies, and stewed. High in oxalic acid.

Keeping: Stewed rhubarb can be bottled or frozen. Use in jams, chutneys and wine.

Pests and diseases: Very hardy.

STRAWBERRY

Fragaria × *ananassa*   *Europe, N America*

Origins and history: Wild strawberries are *F. vesca*, a British native, cultivated for centuries. Alpine strawberries, also *F. vesca*, were first cultivated in the mid-eighteenth century. The first American species, *F. virginiana*, arrived in Europe in 1556; *F. chiloensis* (cultivated by native Americans) arrived in the early eighteenth century. Modern large-fruited strawberries are hybrids of *F. virginiana* and *F. chiloensis*. First hybridized in France, then in England in 1821. 'Royal Sovereign' produced by Laxton Bros. in 1892. Most other old varieties died out from disease. New varieties since developed.

Description: A perennial herb with a crown of dark green palmate leaves. Small white flowers followed by pale to dark red fruit.

Varieties:
MAINCROP (large-fruited garden varieties, fruit ripens June-July, multiply by runners, most productive in first 4 years):

'Royal Sovereign' early, best flavour, light bearer, susceptible to disease; 'Cambridge Rival' early, good flavour, upright habit, mildew resistant, good under cloches; 'Redgauntlet' midseason, little flavour, heavy bearer, botrytis resistant; 'Cambridge Late Pine' midseason to late, delicious flavour, fairly heavy cropping, virus resistant; 'Talisman' late, moderate flavour, resistant to root rot and mildew, a little susceptible to botrytis.
PERPETUAL (crosses between maincrop and alpine, ripening July-October):
'Hampshire Maid' good flavour; 'La Sans Rivalle' very good flavour, will tolerate light and chalky soils.
ALPINES (small fruit, starting to ripen in June, continuing until first frost, upright, multiplies by seed):

'Baron Solemacher' most common.

Site and soil: Fertile, well-drained soil; can tolerate sun or shade. Renew strawberry plants every 4 years, preferably growing them in rotation with vegetables; have one bed in each section, and each year renew the bed that has been grown with the potatoes, but in a different part of the section. pH 5-6.5.

Propagation: Add 1 barrowload manure or compost plus 2lb/1kg bonemeal per 4yd^2/m^2 at least a month before planting. Best to plant in August, so plants have time to settle before winter. Strawberry runners are usually easy to come by, but it may be safer to buy virus-free stock. Plant 12"/30cm apart with at least 24"/60cm between rows. Make sure crowns are not buried. Firm well and water in with seaweed solution. To increase, choose best runners, sever and transplant in August.

Care and cultivation: Hoe between plants in spring. Mulch with peat, pine needles, straw, woodchips or black polythene; polythene or straw may encourage slugs. Use compost under mulch on poor soil. Net when fruit starts to appear. After fruiting, burn or cut back leaves to discourage botrytis. Clear off mulch, and compost (but not woodchips—or polythene!).

Harvesting: Maincrop June-July; perpetuals and alpines until October or November.

Kitchen: Eat fresh—high in vitamin C if eaten within 3 days of picking.

Keeping: Do not keep well, except as jam, which can be difficult to set. Frozen or bottled strawberries are only good for puddings.

Pests and diseases: Alpines and perpetuals stronger than maincrops.
Botrytis: most common disease—brownish-grey fluffy mould. 'Redgauntlet' is resistant.
Virus, Aphids, Birds, Slugs.

Nuts

You could think about growing nuts as well as fruit. If you live in the south of England, you might choose sweet chestnut or walnut; hazel will grow anywhere.

HAZEL
Filbert, Cobnut   *Europe, Asia*

Origins and history: British native, found at altitudes of up to 2000'/600m. Nuts have been widely harvested since prehistoric times. The hazel tree is sacred to the Norse god Thor, and the wood was still being used to make cudgels in the seventeenth century.

Description: Small tree or shrub up to 19'/6m tall, grown for nuts or for ornament. Thicket-forming. Catkins in early spring, followed by inconspicuous female flowers. Showy leaves; nuts encased in decorative covers.

Varieties: 'Lambert's Filbert' ('Kentish Cob') has large long nut with good flavour; 'White Filbert' a later development; 'Red Filbert' similar, but with a red skin. Needs cross-pollinators, so choose at least two compatible varieties.

Site and soil: Any well-drained soil in sun or partial shade. Does well in exposed places. pH 6-7.

Propagation: Grow from seed, or layer in autumn.

Care and cultivation: Mulch.

Pruning: If developing a single trunk on a young tree, select 4-6 main branches. During training period, prune shoots to half their new growth. Remove suckers all year round. Can leave unpruned to form thicket. Nuts are borne on last year's wood. Thin branches slightly every year to encourage new growth. Hazel can be coppiced.

Harvesting: Gather nuts when they are loose in their covers, or after they have fallen. A mature tree can yield a 25lb/11kg crop. Hazels usually bear crops biennially.

Kitchen: Tasty as a snack, in a stuffing for green peppers or other vegetables, or in nut loaves, cakes, biscuits, salads and muesli.

Keeping: Store in a cool, dry, rodent-free place.

Pests and diseases: Squirrels, mice.

Flowers

Nay, more than this, I have a garden plot,
Wherein there wants nor herbs, nor roots, nor flowers,—
Flowers to smell, roots to eat, herbs for the pot,—
And dainty shelters when the welkin lours:
    Sweet smelling beds of lilies and of roses,
    Which rosemary banks and lavender encloses.

There grows the gillyflower, the mint, the daisy
Both red and white, the blue-veined violet,
The purple hyacinth, the spike to please thee,
The scarlet-dyed carnation bleeding yet,
    The sage, the savory, the sweet marjoram,
    Hyssop, thyme, and eye-bright, good for the blind and dumb;

The pink, the primrose, cowslip, and daffadilly,
The harebell blue, the crimson columbine,
Sage, lettuce, parsley, and the milk-white lily,
The rose, and speckled flower called sops-in-wine,
    Fine pretty kingcups, and the yellow boots
    That grow by rivers, and by shallow brooks;

And many thousand more, I cannot name,
Of herbs and flowers that in gardens grow,
I have for thee; and conies that be tame,
Young rabbits, white as swan, and black as crow,
    Some speckled here and there with dainty spots;
    And more, I have two milch and milk-white goats.

Richard Barnfield
Daphnis to Ganymede

Flowers

Garden flowers, as opposed to shrubs, have leaves and stems that die back in winter and grow again in spring, either from seed or from their roots.

The lists are divided into annuals and biennials, perennials, and bulbs—convenient working classifications for the gardener.

Annuals and biennials

These flowers are bright and colourful, temporary, and for the most part well known and loved. All the annuals and biennials in this list are suitable for outdoors, being hardy annuals (HA), half hardy annuals (HHA) or hardy biennials (HB): no tender plants for the house or greenhouse are included, though some of these might successfully be grown in some gardens, and some garden annuals and biennials listed will grow happily in the house or greenhouse. The classifications are by no means rigid. Some perennials are usually treated as annuals or biennials because their best blooms are produced in the first or second year, but if left to themselves in less formal gardens, many will become sturdy plants and go on flourishing. Some of our favourite 'annuals' (like pelargoniums and begonias) are in fact tender perennials, which can be grown in the greenhouse and bedded out as annuals in summer. Their cycle of care and cultivation in this case is similar to that of half hardy annuals, and they will be found in the annuals list.

A plant may be treated as a hardy annual in Cornwall, whereas in the north of Scotland it would never germinate outside in time, and must be started indoors as a half hardy annual.

Many annuals are of tropical origin, and since their seed cannot germinate early enough in our climate, they are classified as half hardy in temperate zones. Most of these flowers rely on the brilliance of their blooms rather than their scent to attract pollinating insects, which is why they make such a show in our gardens. Some hardy annuals are less flamboyant and have more fragrance, like the old-fashioned mignonette and night-scented stock.

Annuals and biennials flower profusely because their lifespan is short. An annual germinates from seed, grows, flowers, produces seed and dies within one season. To survive, it has to attract pollinators quickly, and send out as many seeds as possible. Persistent deadheading will cause most annuals to flower again and again in their effort to set seed, so that the garden can have a continual show of flowers, often right through to the first frost.

Being temporary has certain advantages. Almost all gardeners make use of annuals and biennials to fill up gaps in beds and borders, and add a bit of summer colour without disrupting any long-term plans. There are times in most gardeners' lives when a temporary garden is all that is available, and annuals can transform a garden very rapidly. They are also invaluable in a new garden, for use around the permanent features that have not yet grown to their full stature. They do well in tubs, window boxes and balconies, and climbing annuals will provide an instant screen during the months when it is pleasant to sit outside. These arrangements can even be portable—a small tub or hanging basket can be put wherever you want it.

Annuals are pretty tolerant, usually only needing adequate sunlight and tolerable soil. In a dark wet summer they will not do well. In general a better soil will produce better results, though sometimes too good a soil produces more foliage than flowers. There are annuals which will cope with almost anything. A mass of calendula, cornflower and candytuft will enliven places where nothing more exotic would dare put out a shoot. Annuals have shallow roots, which means that they are tolerant of thin soil, but they must be given water when they need it since they have no deep reserves to draw on. They are excellent for children who are beginning to garden—the results are quick, spectacular, and (with a little help) easy.

Another advantage of these short-lived plants is that they are resistant to pollution. They have little time to be overcome by poisons from earth, air or water. Pests and diseases are of less concern, too. These have little chance to establish themselves, and even if they do you can start with something different next year. Annuals tend to be troubled by aphids, and sometimes by cutworms or red spider mite. Rust, wilt, leaf spot and powdery mildew are the commonest ailments, but they are not the problem they are in the vegetable garden. Some plants have been bred to resist diseases—for instance snapdragons, which used to be susceptible to rust, are now often sold in rust-resistant varieties.

One home for annuals and biennials is in the formal bedding scheme. Half hardy annuals are most suited to this, or hardy annuals brought on in a greenhouse as if they were half hardy annuals. A bedding plant is not a type of plant, but a use to which it is put. Bedding plants can be as diverse as fuchsias and forget-me-nots, pelargoniums and sweet peas—all they have in common is that they have been planted out in early summer in a formal bedding arrangement.

Try to avoid planting in straight lines—even in formal schemes random placing looks better; edges of species beds, however, give a crisper appearance when in a straight line. Spring bedding schemes usually consist of bulbs, wallflowers and other early flowerers, followed by a summer bedding scheme which might include half hardy annuals and tender perennials. A bedding scheme of this sort needs a well-stocked greenhouse in the background, and is usually only found in parks and the gardens of greenhouse enthusiasts.

Most gardeners use annuals and biennials less formally, but not necessarily haphazardly. Some are traditional garden flowers—foxgloves, hollyhocks, calendula, poppies and candytuft. Hardy annuals may seed and return year after year. Some, like poppies, can rapidly become invasive, but with constant removal of seedheads and weeding they can be welcomed every year. New seeds will usually be more prolific and diverse, and provide a greater show.

The cultivation of these plants is not difficult, but it requires labour. All are grown from seed, although you can buy seedlings or young plants from a nursery or garden centre ready for planting out.

Hardy annuals are the easiest. They prefer to be sown where they are to flower. If this is not practical, they can be brought on early in the greenhouse. Depending where you are, seeds are usually sown outside in March-May, though some can be sown in August-September, overwintering and blooming early in the spring—these are described as 'winter annuals'. When the seedlings have two pairs of leaves they can be thinned.

Half hardy annuals usually require a temperature above 55°F/13°C to germinate, but this varies, and will be given on seed packets. Seeds are sown in seed boxes, and when two pairs of leaves have appeared they are pricked out into larger boxes with potting compost. They are grown on, hardened off, and planted out in May or June. Thereafter they need the same care as hardy annuals. To grow a few half hardy annuals you don't need a greenhouse—a warm sunny windowsill is quite adequate.

Hardy biennials have a different rhythm. They are usually sown outdoors in a seedbed in June or July. They are pricked out into a nursery bed when the seedlings have two pairs of leaves, and grown on until September-October, when they are planted out where they are to flower. They are composted after flowering, usually in June or July of the year after they were sown.

Care and cultivation is similar for all these plants. In general, annuals and biennials are very tolerant, though it is necessary to choose the right plant for the soil, and this is indicated in the lists. Some bushy varieties, such as snapdragon and wallflower, will benefit from pinching out—removing the growing point and encouraging side shoots to develop, thus making a bushier plant with more blooms. Tall plants will probably need staking, especially on exposed sites, and regular deadheading is necessary to prolong flowering. When all flowering is over, they should be pulled out and composted.

Perennials

Herbaceous perennials are one of the great delights of British flower gardens. They are plants that have persistent roots that grow together in clumps, and deciduous stems and leaves that die back to the crown every year. Not all perennials fit this description—some have evergreen leaves which last all winter, even if only at the base of the plant. The term 'hardy perennial' (HP) is used to cover all these plants.

Hardy perennials are found in the temperate regions of the world, where the seasons are sharply differentiated, so they have become adapted to cold winters and warm summers, dying back to the roots every winter and lying dormant, then returning again in the spring. Most of the wild plants of Britain are hardy perennials, as our climate favours them, and some of our own natives have been improved into garden species, for example columbine, globe flower, purple loosestrife, meadow cranesbill, thrift. All these are familiar cottage garden flowers.

There are hardy perennials suitable for almost every soil, and as long as they are given sufficient nutrition, water, sun and shelter, they will thrive. Since the environment here suits them, they are not much troubled by pests and diseases. Any trouble is usually due to aphids, blackfly or greenfly, or leaves being eaten by caterpillars, slugs and snails. Root predators are likely to be cutworms or garden swift moth grubs. They seldom suffer diseases, the most likely being mildew or mould.

Perennials are permanent and yet adaptable. They are easy to propagate. They are cheap, especially as new plants are often passed on by giving or exchanging them—anyone who grows perennials is bound to have a surplus at dividing time. They are versatile and can be used in almost any garden scheme—there are almost certain to be some that are suitable for your conditions. Above all they are beautiful, offering a choice of colour, shape, foliage and flowering time which can be the focus of the flower garden almost all the year round.

With such attractions, it is not surprising that hardy perennials were the basic flower stock of cottage gardens for centuries. Most cottage garden varieties only exist now in a few old gardens, and we are only likely to get them as gifts from neighbours with such gardens. If we can acquire the old pinks, hollyhocks, columbines, European peonies and the rest, we will find they have drawbacks. The flowering times seem relatively short; there may be a smaller display of blooms than we are used to; and more seriously, we may find them less pest and disease resistant than the modern varieties. In recompense we may have flowers with a scent seldom found today, with delicate shades of colour, seeds that breed true and plants that seed themselves without effort. Old varieties of hardy perennial such as phlox were often left for years without lifting or dividing, and though hollyhocks and columbine were shortlived, they came back from seed. Original cottage garden varieties do not need replenishing from shops or garden centres, but they are hard to find, even difficult to identify, often being referred to by their species name alone.

Our greatest nineteenth century bequest in the cultivation of hardy perennials is the herbaceous border. It was developed by Gertrude Jekyll, in the movement to reinstate the old perennial flowers which had lost favour with the arrival of annual bedding schemes. Both she and William Robinson also used recently-introduced perennials from abroad which could flourish without artificial conditions in the British environment.

In Jekyll's time the rules were strict: the border was strictly for perennials only, and the designs were planned to the last detail. In contrast to the primary colours of the bedding schemes, Jekyll's herbaceous borders were usually studies in one or two colours, with a sensitive use of white and foliage plants. Hardy perennials are not as bright as annuals; their hues are subtler, certainly in the old varieties—and Gertrude Jekyll concentrated on delicate gradations of shade from one end of a bed to the other. Account was also taken of different flowering times, shapes and heights.

Such careful planning was costly and labour-intensive, which explains why none of Jekyll's borders survive in their original form, but the descendants of her borders still epitomize British flower gardens at their peak of perfection, and the formal herbaceous border can still be seen in all its glory in some of the great flower gardens of the country, from Hampton Court to Inverewe.

If you plan to have a herbaceous border there are several things to take into account. Aspect is important, and the bed should ideally face south to give maximum choice and scope, though there are tough shade-loving perennials that will happily face any way, including north. Borders are best viewed lengthways from the house, so that the inevitable seasonal gaps are hidden, and can either be straight or curved to fit the surrounding features. Your bed is unlikely to have the breathtaking sweep of flowers seen in the great gardens, but even if it is only a few yards long there is plenty of scope. A more restricting limitation is width: the bed should preferably be ten feet or more from front to back to allow gradations of height and pattern. Shelter is also important. Borders traditionally backed on to walls, hedges, or banks of shrubs. Tall species particularly require wind shelter, though overhanging trees are obviously not an advantage. Perennials are increasingly being planted in island beds, a practice made popular at Bressingham in Norfolk in the 1950s.

Nowadays the rules are more relaxed. The mixed border has become more common, and in small gardens is a great deal more practical. Hardy perennials are interspersed with shrubs, bulbs and annuals. The shrubs provide a permanent structure around which to plan, and require less maintenance. The main criticism of the herbaceous border is the labour it requires to maintain it.

Take the chance to dig well while the bed is empty, as perennials hate to have the soil disturbed once they are planted. Dig at least one spit deep, or in very heavy soil double dig, and remove all perennial weeds. Perennial weeds left in a border of hardy perennials are a real nuisance. They become intertwined with the plants and cannot be eradicated until the time comes to rework the bed again. Dig in well-rotted manure or compost. Mulch is excellent around perennials, as it feeds the soil without disturbing it and keeps down the weeds.

A border should not be a random hotchpotch of anything that comes to hand; it is better to choose a few plants that go well together, and take plenty of each. Survey your plants, then take a piece of squared paper and decide what is going to go where. The things you will need to take into account include:

Height: You want tall plants at the back and small ones at the front, but not moving from step to step in serried ranks. Be careful not to hide your shrubs. Vary the heights and let the level flow from front to back.

Shape: Some flowers are flat, some spiky. Some leaves are big and broad, some small and intricate. Think about what the plants will look like during the considerable time that they are not flowering. Different types of flower will also serve to break up a straight line of plants of the same height.

Colour: We may not be as strict as Jekyll, but we can be subtle. Perennial colours lend themselves to intricate changes of shade. Make use of foliage plants as a foil to bright blooms.

Flowering time: With careful planning you could have a mixed border with drifts of colour from February to December in the south, rather less in the north, though inevitably there will be gaps. If you go away every summer, plant early and late perennials so the gap happens while you are away. With small borders, go for a shorter flowering period to prevent a scrappy look.

Mass: Don't dot plants around; set them in groups of three to five, depending upon their individual size. Jekyll talked of 'drifts of flowers'. Repeat groups along the length of the border. Plant them with their ultimate spread in mind—remember that perennials reproduce by vegetative spreading, and after three years each plant will be covering much more ground. As a general rule, use half the ultimate height of the plant as its planting distance. Some perennials flourish so well that they become invasive, and you will have to stop them overspreading.

The ideal planting times are September-October or March-April. In early autumn there will still be some warmth in the soil to help the plants settle, but on clay soils spring is a better time, when the frost has broken up the soil. With plan in hand, set your plants in their planting positions out on the newly-prepared bed; if this is going to take some time, heel them in. When you come to plant, make a hole for each plant slightly bigger than the rootball, with a mound in the middle to support the crown. Water the hole, then set the plant in the hole with its crown about an inch below the soil surface, the roots splayed out around it. Fill in with compost or soil, making sure there are no air pockets around the roots, firm the soil, and water the plants in.

After this initial effort your herbaceous border should present few problems. Weed with a hoe, and be scrupulous about eliminating baby perennial weeds. Mulch in spring or autumn. You will have to stake tall varieties. The key to successful staking is to do it soon enough, before the plants begin to fall over. Use canes for the tallest plants, and peasticks or twiggy sticks for the smaller ones, and tie them up with garden twine at regular intervals as they grow. Alternatively you can use metal rings, available in garden shops, which the plants grow through, or black garden net stretched on canes. After the plants have flowered they will begin to die back. Dead head early flowerers like lupins after flowering, but do not be tempted to cut live stems and leaves before the autumn. They can be cut back in autumn to within a few inches of ground level. Leaving an inch or two of stem will provide some frost protection over the winter. In very cold districts you can delay cutting back until the spring for maximum shelter from frost. Alternatively, lay dead stems or leafmould over the crown for frost protection.

Every two or three years most plants will need lifting and dividing, again in September-October or March-April. This is your chance to rework the bed and eliminate any earlier mistakes. Some hardy perennials, like peonies, hate to be moved, but most need to be divided, or they will begin to die back at the centre until you have a straggly

ring. After cutting back, dig the plant up carefully, shake away the excess soil, and divide it, using two forks back to back.

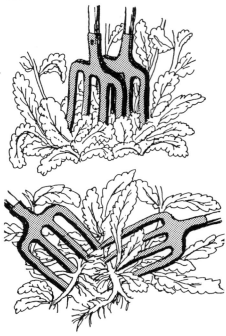

You can also grow perennials from seed, saving your own seed or buying it. If you want to save seed, remember to buy strains that will breed true. Most perennials do not need high temperatures to germinate; some need to be frozen as seeds. It is easiest to allow nature to take its course and let the seeds lie in the soil over winter to germinate in the spring when they are ready. Most hardy perennials are started in seedbeds or cold frames, transplanted to nursery beds, then planted out in the late summer where they are to flower the following year. Some perennials can also be propagated from cuttings—this is mentioned in the list.

There are perennials suitable for almost every purpose. For example, bergenia and geranium make excellent ground cover; dianthus and gaillardia are suitable for very dry places; caltha and hostas make good bog plants for moist places. The list indicates when a plant is useful for a particular purpose.

Bulbs

Nearly all gardeners rely on bulbs to provide the first colour in spring, and some use them for renewed cheer in autumn. Bulbs produce attractive and luxuriant flowers and there are species adaptable to almost all gardens.

The word 'bulb' is usually used to refer to bulbs proper, corms, and tubers, all of which are parts of a plant that swell in order to store food so the plant can survive adverse conditions in a dormant state. Bulbs used as food, like onions and fennel, are therefore very nutritious. Bulbs are not a kind of plant, they denote a method of survival used by many different species scattered across most plant families—for example, some begonias are tuberous and some are not; anemones form corms but not all other ranunculi do.

A bulb is a swelling of the leaf or stalk bases of a plant.

In a corm, the swollen part is the base of the stem, which forms a single swollen organ, as in crocus and gladioli.

A tuber is formed either from an underground stem (a rhizome), or from a swollen root. This is the most widespread form of swelling; familiar tubers are Solomon's seal, iris, winter aconite and dahlia.

Bulbs are a response to a particular environment, one in which there is a short season favourable to growth, and a long period during which dormancy is neceessary. Wild bulbs tend to come either from a Mediterranean climate, where the short moist spring is followed by a hot dry summer, or a continental climate, where there is a short wet spring between a cold winter and a hot summer. Some bulbs are alpines, coming from areas where snow lies for much of the year, with a brief period of wetness when the snow melts, and a short hot summer. A temperate climate like ours is not ideal, and most of our bulbs tend to do particularly well after an exceptionally cold and snowy winter, or after a dry summer. The worst problem faced by British bulbs is the damp, and those on the east coast tend to do better than those on the west. In too wet a soil, bulbs will rot, and wet conditions will also favour slugs, snails and fungal diseases. There are exceptions, however, and there are bulbs like water irises that demand a wet habitat.

Bulbs characteristically grow very fast as soon as the temperature and moisture are right, sending roots surprisingly deep, quickly followed by leaves, stems and flowers. They tend to produce attractive blooms, since there is only one opportunity for pollination, and they are very reliable in the flower garden. After flowering, the leaves pass nutrients back into the bulb, which swells again as the leaves die back. This is why the leaves of bulbs must never be cut or removed until they have withered completely, otherwise the bulb has no way of replenishing its stores for next year.

Many of our modern varieties are the result of breeding, but wild species are also very popular. Besides our native species, and the naturalized crocuses and daffodils bequeathed to us by the Romans, wild bulbs have been collected from most parts of the world. Because they are so easily collected, the Victorians imported wild bulbs on a large scale—we now grow a far smaller range of bulbs in our gardens than was common a hundred years ago.

Many people think that bulbs are

foolproof, and so they are—for one year. This is because you buy bulbs complete with an embryo plant and stored nutrients, and all you have to do is plant it. Success in subsequent seasons depends on the environment and the gardener.

Bulbs need a fairly rich, well-drained, sandy soil, well dug before planting. If your garden is very wet, make raised beds bordered with brick or stone for better drainage. Tree roots are also good for absorbing excess moisture. Keep the soil well fed with compost or leafmould. Don't use manure, as it contains too much nitrogen for bulbs, and you will get too much foliage at the expense of flowers. Compost can be dug in where bulbs are to be planted, or used as a mulch. Mulch is the best way to feed bulbs, in fact for lilies it is essential, and keeps the weeds down without disturbing the bulbs. Bonemeal is an excellent food. It can be hoed into beds in December or January, or it can be mixed with the mulch, or dug into new areas with compost.

No one garden will supply the right conditions for all bulbs, since some like sun and some shade, some acid soil and some alkaline. Almost all need shelter from excessive wind, and in general they prefer bare ground, as too much vegetation encourages the dreaded slugs, though naturalized bulbs do well in grass or among ground cover.

Given the right conditions, bulbs need little maintenance. Unless they are used for spring bedding schemes they can be regarded as a permanent feature, only needing to be moved when they get very crowded. During their growing period they may need watering—water the soil rather than the plant—and tall species such as gladioli and lilies may need staking. Flowers should be deadheaded after blooming, other-

wise energy will go into forming seeds rather than next year's bulb. Let stems and leaves remain until they have withered away, and if necessary keep them watered, for this is the important stage of forming a new bulb. Since the dying leaves must be left intact, think in advance how you will deal with them, covering them with an edging of summer flowers or interspersing them with annuals. Bulbs in grass should be planted in areas which are not mown until mid-June.

Propagation is easy, since bulbs will increase quite naturally in the right conditions. They do not like to be disturbed too often, but every few years will show signs of overcrowding. Flowers will get smaller and fewer, bulbs will fail to develop shoots, and bulbs may appear at the soil surface.

When this happens, wait until the bulbs have died back, but there is still a trace of foliage, and lift them carefully with a garden fork, inserting the fork a few inches away from the clump and digging deeply. Separate the bulbs gently by hand, otherwise the tender roots can easily be destroyed. If the clump has become so impacted that it won't break apart in your hands, leave it in a cool place until the soil dries out, then lever the bulbs gently apart. Soft, damaged or diseased bulbs should be burnt.

Some bulbs, such as snowdrops, should be replanted straight away. If you want to store bulbs and replant them in the autumn, heel them into soil and water them until the foliage has died away, then clean them and store them spread out in flat boxes in a cool, dry, airy place.

Bulbs are not like seeds, and cannot be stored indefinitely. If they miss a season they will dry up and shrivel away. Remember to label them.

If you are buying new bulbs, get

good ones. They should be firm and plump, with the outer skins intact (apart from tulips, which often shed their papery skin). The best time for planting spring bulbs is September, though tulips can happily be planted until November. Autumn-flowering species need to be planted in March or April. If bulbs have been divided, put some back in the places where they obviously thrive. It is better to scatter the bulbs at random rather than laying them out in serried ranks—for the easiest random effect, scatter them on the soil surface, then plant them where they chance to lie.

Bulbs can be planted with a trowel or with a bulb planter, a tool worth having if you have many bulbs to plant. Alternatively, you can dig a wide hole and place the bulbs in position together, then firm the soil over them all. If you use a trowel, avoid leaving an air pocket under the bulb. When planting in grass use the wide hole method—lift the turf carefully, dig in the compost and bonemeal, and replace the turf over the bulbs.

A rough rule is that bulbs like to be planted at about twice the height of the bulb, though they need to be deeper in

Depth in inches

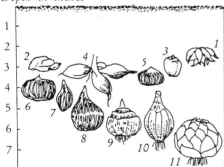

Bulb planting depths: 1: Ranunculus; 2: Anemone; 3: Scilla; 4: Dahlia; 5: Crocus; 6: Gladiolus; 7: Bulbous Iris; 8: Tulip; 9: Hyacinth; 10: Narcissus; 11: Lily

lighter soils and shallower in heavy ones. Using their contractile roots, bulbs will actually move to the optimum depth, some burying themselves surprisingly deep to find the right moisture conditions. It is always better to plant bulbs too deeply rather than too shallow.

Bulbs can be propagated from seed, but this is a slow business, taking up to seven years, and when division is so easy only real enthusiasts are likely to undertake it. The danger is that cultivated species will not breed true. Seed-grown bulbs are only worth it if you want varieties which are not available in the shops.

The worst problems for bulbs are slugs and snails. Aphids, cutworms and red spider mite are also common pests. Mice eat bulbs, especially crocus. Moles break roots and shift bulbs around, and birds, especially sparrows, eat the flowers, particularly of yellow crocuses. Common diseases are virus and fungi which attack leaves and bulbs, particularly when conditions are too wet.

Perhaps the simplest and most attractive way to use bulbs is to naturalize them in drifts in grass. Smaller species are delightful in thin grass, but daffodils and narcissus are the obvious choice for tougher conditions. Woodlands and orchards also lend themselves to naturalized bulbs. Remember that grass cannot be cut until mid-June. In 'wild' areas, meadow flowers planted in the grass follow on well from naturalized bulbs.

Tulips and hyacinths are traditional favourites in spring bedding schemes, but this is a very labour-intensive way of using bulbs. Bulbs have no place in formal herbaceous borders—hoeing becomes difficult, and bulbs do not appreciate the thick mulch enjoyed by hardy perennials. Roses and bulbs do not enjoy close proximity. Rock gardens are ideal for some dwarf bulbs: the well-drained soil is right for them and the bulbs extend the season of colour in the rock garden.

For most gardeners, bulbs will join perennials, annuals and shrubs in the mixed border. Bulbs and shrubs supply the first colour in spring and the last in autumn, and the bulbs are dormant while the annuals and perennials are doing their bit. Plant the bulbs last, so that you do not inadvertently dig them up again, and it is a good idea to label clumps of dormant bulbs. Try putting spectacular and scented bulbs where you sit out.

Together with annuals, bulbs are plants to turn to when you don't have much of a garden at all. They thrive in tubs and window boxes. They are also tolerant of pollution, coming up fresh every year, though a poor soil will not nourish them in successive years.

Other types of flower garden

There are many kinds of flower garden, and we have touched on several of them. The possibilities range from naturalized flowers in a wild garden to a tub on the terrace. There is no space in this book to do more than indicate some of the choices, and sooner or later you may find yourself drawn into a speciality of your own. It may be a particular type of garden—a Japanese garden, a water garden, a bog garden, an edible landscape. It may be one species of flower, and you will end up growing prize dahlias or chrysanthemums.

Though we cannot look at the whole spectrum of flower gardens, you can still be aware of what is possible. You can choose to go in any direction from here. I would like to mention two specialist sorts of flower garden, the rock garden and the wild garden.

The rock garden

Alpines or rock plants come from the mountainous regions of the world. They are all perennials, since annuals are virtually non-existent at high altitudes. Since very few gardens in Britain offer a remotely similar habitat, the creation of suitable conditions and the raising of these plants can be an absorbing occupation.

Much of the fascination of alpines is that on the whole they are still wild species. With some exceptions, notably in the saxifrage family, they have not been bred for cultivation, and until recently their seeds were gathered in the wild, though now they are more often propagated in alpine nurseries. Rock plant explorers are still collecting the seeds of new species. Conservation and export laws now protect most species, but amateur alpine collectors can still see their plants in their native habitats in the Alps and the Pyrenees.

The definition of rock plants has broadened to include many other dwarf perennials whose larger relations feature in our beds and borders. There is no strict dividing line between herbaceous perennials and rock plants, other than that a rock plant is small, compact and neat, and grows relatively slowly. Most rock gardens contain plants which are not herbaceous perennials at all: they have bulbs, miniature shrubs and dwarf conifers. The true alpine rock garden is a much more specialist affair.

A rock garden can be made almost anywhere. Because the plants are so small, a stone or concrete trough, or even a windowbox, can contain a variety of alpines: the provision of the right soil for such a small garden creates no problem. On a slightly larger scale, a raised bed creates a larger version of the trough.

A full-scale rockery is a more

ambitious project, requiring thought and construction skills. You will need to acquire stones, which can be expensive if you live in an urban lowland area, and good stonework requires expertise and strength—it cannot be undertaken lightly. An alternative is to build your alpine garden out of solid blocks of peat. Choose local rock where possible to blend in with your surroundings.

Think about aspect. A rock garden built on a flat site has the advantages of providing several aspects and micro-climates, otherwise the garden should ideally face south or west. The site needs to be open and airy, well away from trees—rock plants hate to be smothered by autumn leaves and dripped on by overhanging branches.

The main requirement is that it should be very well drained, hence the necessity for raised beds or rockeries on almost all sites. In a heavy soil a drainage layer of stones or broken brick will have to be laid about 18"/45cm below the soil surface of the rockery. For surface drainage use a thin layer of stone chippings or grit, as rock plants do not like moisture round their stems. An alternative to a rock garden is a scree garden, a mixture of soil and rock chippings.

On a new site it is vital to get rid of perennial weeds before you build, let alone plant. A rockery should ideally be built in the autumn, left to settle over winter, and planted in the spring. Weeding must sometimes be done not only by hand, but with a knife and even tweezers. Watering must be done with a mistlike spray, and alpines may need to be protected from too much moisture during wet winters. The site needs to be kept very clean, and watch kept for slugs, snails, mice, birds and aphids.

Rock gardens are not for *laissez-faire* gardeners, but the rewards are many. The plants are small and delicate and beautiful, and with careful selection you can have flowers from one year's end to another.

The wild garden

In the wild garden we are creating an ecosystem that belongs to the place where we are. The plants we choose may be native, but not necessarily so. If we are gardening on chalk soil we may decide to grow the flowers of the chalk downs rather than enriching the soil with compost and manure; if we are gardening on peaty soil we may supplement what is already there with heathers and azaleas; if part of our garden is wet and marshy we may encourage kingcups and irises to naturalize among the reeds. If we have inherited a copse of trees we may use the flowers of the woodland—primroses, anemones and bluebells in spring, foxgloves and lilies-of-the-valley in summer. Sometimes a wild garden is simply offered to us as a gift we can have the humility to accept.

A common reason for opting for a wild garden is to provide a sanctuary for plants and animals which live under threat in an increasingly polluted and diminishing countryside. Flowers which our ancestors took for granted are disappearing. We may remember meadows full of cowslips, banks of primroses, woods filled with bluebells, cornfields with poppies and corn-flowers, hedges bright with campion, vetches and ladies smock, and the rare and lucky discovery of a bee orchid or mountain primula. More and more gardeners are becoming aware of their new role as conservationists, whether it be of old varieties of flowers and vegetables, or of wild species and habitats that are under threat. There are companies that specialize in wild flower seeds, and books that supply the information needed to create a 'wild' ecosystem in your garden. Wild or naturalized plants need to be helped to find their niche. Seeds can be raised by the gardener in the usual way before they take their place in a new system. Grass is helpful to flowers in the wild, giving natural support equivalent to staking in the border, but it can also choke new seedlings to death. We need to tip the balance of nature in favour of the plant we want to flourish, even though the ultimate aim is a system that will largely take care of itself. A wild garden will attract insects, and then birds and small animals. This is eventually what we want, but in the early stages we will need to interfere a little.

How to use the flower lists

The list of flowers that follows should include the flowers that you are most likely to come across, but we are almost certain to have excluded somebody's favourite; nor can we say everything about each species.

Remember that the descriptions are general, and you will sometimes find great variations in the different varieties—we have given ranges of height, colour, etc., but there is no space to describe every available variety separately. Rather than list a few varieties, we have indicated what to look for and how to make choices, rather than making choices for you. Remember, too, that trying to grow named varieties

from seed is risky—the next generation may revert to the original species.

The flowers are all listed under their Latin names (see 'The naming of plants' to find out why), but if you only know the English name of a flower you can easily find it by looking up the English name in the index, where it will give the Latin equivalent and the page reference.

The flower lists, like this introduction, are divided into annuals and biennials, perennials, and bulbs, though do remember that some families have species in more than one category. All the plants are hardy, meaning that they can be grown out of doors in Britain.

Under 'perennials' are a few plants which are often found in the rock garden, and are not usually classed as herbaceous perennials because they are too short. You will find arabis and aubretia and cerastium, because even if you have no rock garden you may have the edges of paths and steps, or perhaps the top of a wall, where these plants would be just the thing. Do not use these in a specialist rock garden, however, as they can be very invasive. Many herbaceous perennials have related rockery varieties.

Abbreviations used in the flower lists are:

HA   Hardy annual
HHA   Half-hardy annual
HB   Hardy biennial
P   Perennial
HP   Hardy perennial

Annuals and biennials

AGERATUM

Floss Flower   *Mexico*

Origins and history: Name from the Greek 'a-'—not, and 'geras'—old; i.e. lasts for a long time. Introduced in nineteenth century.

Description: HHA Clusters of blue, white, pink or mauve flowers. Good for edging, carpeting, filling bare patches. Height 5-12"/12-30cm.

Flowers: June to September.

Site and soil: Sheltered, sunny site, or light shade. Moist soil.

Propagation: Sow seeds thinly (very small) February-April, 60-65°F/16-18°C, depth ⅛"/3mm. Do not cover. Germination 10-14 days. Prick out and harden off. Plant late May or early June. Space 6"/15cm apart.

Care and cultivation: Dead head frequently. Keep soil moist.

ALTHAEA

Hollyhock   *Europe, Asia*

Origins and history: Traditional cottage garden flower; the name is from the Greek 'althaea'—to cure. 'Hoc' is the Anglo-Saxon for Mallow; 'holy-hoc' may be because it was brought home from East by pilgrims. Modern varieties have changed very little from the originals.

Description: HP, usually grown as HB. Original colour pink; now tall spikes of red, yellow, pink or white single or double flowers with light green hairy leaves. Suitable for the back of borders. Height 6-9'/2-3m. Also dwarf varieties.

Flowers: July to September.

Site and soil: Any reasonable soil in a sheltered sunny spot.

Propagation: Sow seeds January-February at 50-60°F/10-16°C at ¼"/6mm depth. Germination 14-21 days. Prick out and harden off. Plant out seedlings 15"/37cm apart. *Or*, sow seeds May-June where they are to flower, and thin to 24"/60cm apart.

Care and cultivation: Needs training against wall. Water if dry. Deadheading not necessary.

Pests and diseases: Caterpillars, slugs, snails; rust.

ALYSSUM

Sweet Alyssum   *Europe*

Origins and history: Edging plant in cottage garden flowerbeds. Has naturalized on sandy soils.

Description: HA Small cushions of white, mauve or pink sweet-scented flowers. Greyish-green leaves. Very popular for edging, rockeries, walls and paving, tubs. Height 3-6"/75-150mm.

Flowers: June to September.

Site and soil: Any well-drained soil in a sunny position. Tolerates light shade.

Propagation: Sow seeds February-March 55-60°F/13-16°C, depth ¼"/6mm. Germination 7-10 days. Prick out and harden off. Plant out in May. Space 8-10"/20-25cm.

Care and cultivation: Dead head for continuous flowering.

Pests and diseases: Aphids.

AMARANTHUS CAUDATUS

Love Lies Bleeding
Asia, Americas

Origins and history: Cottage garden flower, mentioned by Gerard in the seventeenth century.

Description: HA Drooping tassels of tiny red flowers and large light green leaves. One variety has pale green flowers. Used as feature in bedding schemes. Cut and dried flowers last well. *A. hybridus* and *A. hypochondriacus* have upright plumes of red flowers. Height 36-40"/90-100cm.

Flowers: July-October

Site and soil: Likes full sun and rich well-manured soil, though tolerates poorer soils.

Propagation: Sow seeds in March at 55-60°F/13-16°C. Germination 14-21 days. Prick out and harden off. Plant out in May, 18"/45cm apart. *Or*, sow where they are to flower in April-May, and thin

seedlings out to 18"/45cm apart.

Pests and diseases: Aphids.

ANTIRRHINUM

Snapdragon   *Mediterranean*

Origins and history: Introduced from southern Europe, it was well established by the sixteenth century. Often naturalized in Britain. Old varieties much hardier than modern hybrids. Used to be used as perennials.

Description: HP used as HA or HB, usually grown as HA Very popular, highly colourful, sometimes strong-scented spikes of flowers. Usually treated as annuals and used in bedding schemes or to fill gaps in borders. Comes in sizes from dwarf to giant (6-48"/15-120cm), though intermediate varieties most often grown.

Flowers: July-October (first frost).

Site and soil: Any well-drained soil, but prefers light-medium and stony soils, enriched with well-rotted manure. Prefers sun. Likes rocks and walls.

Propagation: Sow seeds January-March 60-65°F/16-22°C at ⅛"/3mm depth. Germination 10-14 days. Prick out

and harden off. Transfer to flowering positions April-May. Space 9-18"/22-45cm apart, depending on height. Can sow outside July-September at ¼"/6mm depth. Thin seedlings to 9"/22cm and grow until spring. Protect with cloches on exposed sites in winter. It is possible to root cuttings, but seeds are easier.

Care and cultivation: Encourage bushy growth by pinching out growing points. Dead head to prolong flowering.

Pests and diseases: Rust—buy rust-resistant strains. Damping off: do not use peat compost—cover with fine grit or sand. Leaf spot and stem rot in north.

BEGONIA

Tropics and sub-tropics

Origins and history: Introduced relatively recently. Begon was the patron of an expedition to the Antilles in the early eighteenth century, where begonias were first collected. Became popular hothouse plants in the nineteenth century. Outdoor varieties more recent, from *B. semperflorens.*

Description: P (tender), but often treated as HHA Bright glistening green or variegated leaves; white, pink and red flowers. Each plant bears male and female flowers—male more showy, can see winged ovaries on females. Height 6-24"/15-60cm.

Flowers: June to September.

Site and soil: One of few annual bedding plants that likes shade under trees. Thrives on light soil, preferably enriched with peat or leafmould.

Propagation: Hard to grow from seed—usually bought as bedding plants. Seeds tiny—sow thinly on loamless compost February-March. Do not cover with compost. 68-78°F/20-26°C necessary for germination. Place sheet of glass over seed trays to prevent drying out. Germination 14-28 days. Prick out and harden off. Plant out early June. Begonias propagate well from cuttings.

Care and cultivation: Water when dry.

Pests and diseases: Damping off; grey mould.

CALENDULA

Pot Marigold   *S. Europe*

Origins and history: Was kitchen herb and

used in salads, hence 'Pot' Marigold. Name is from the Greek 'kalends', implying that the plant could be found flowering on the first day of every month. Introduced to Britain in the sixteenth century. Also used as a medicinal herb. Ubiquitous in cottage gardens.

Description: HA Long, narrow, light green leaves, daisy-like flowers bright orange or yellow. Grows to 12-24"/30-60cm.

Flowers: May to October (first frost).
Site and soil: Thrives in any soil and conditions. For best results use medium well-drained garden soil in sunny position.

Propagation: Sow seeds March-May at ½"/12mm depth where plants are to flower. Germination 10-14 days. Thin out to 12"/30cm apart. *Or,* sow August-September for late spring flowering. Will re-seed itself.

Care and cultivation: Dead head for continuous flowering. Pinch out growing points to encourage bushiness.

CAMPANULA MEDIUM
Canterbury Bell, Cup and Saucer
S Europe

Origins and history: Old cottage garden flower, originally brought from Europe in the sixteenth century. *C. medium* is believed to have originated in the Pyrenees. Sometimes found naturalized in England.

Description: HB Long bright green hairy leaves and spikes of bell-shaped flowers in blue, pink, violet or white. Height 15-36"/37-90cm. Blooms may be single, semi-double or double. Related to perennial campanulas.

Flowers: May-July.
Site and soil: Any well-drained fertile soil and sunny position.

Propagation: Sow seeds outdoors April-June in seed bed at ¼"/6mm depth. Germination 14-21 days. Thin to 9"/22cm apart. Transplant to final flowering position in September 12"/30cm apart.

Care and cultivation: Stake stems. Dead head.

CENTAUREA CYANUS
Cornflower   *Europe*

Origins and history: A native of Britain, adapting itself to growing in cornfields until

the introduction of herbicides. Sometimes used to be called 'Hurt-sickle' because the tough stems damaged reapers' sickles.

Description: HA Developed from common farmland weed. Grey-green leaves and wiry stems bearing sprays of pink, red, purple, white, or the original blue flowers. Height 9-36"/22-90cm.

Flowers: June-September.
Site and soil: Any fertile well-drained soil in sunny position.

Propagation: Sow seeds March-May where plants are to flower. Germination 10-14 days. When second true leaf appears thin to 9-15"/22-37cm. *Or,* sow seeds August-September for spring flowering.

Care and cultivation: Staking necessary for tall species. Dead head.

CHEIRANTHUS
Wallflower   *S Europe*

Origins and history: Introduced long ago for its sweet scent. Was called 'Gillyflower' and used in nosegays as protection against the plague. Often naturalized on dry walls and in crevices. Same family as brassicas—*crucifera.*

Description: HP, usually grown as HB Deservedly popular spring-flowering plants, sweetly-scented flowers in red, yellow, orange, white, pink or bi-coloured on spikes amid mid-green foliage. *C. cheiri* most often grown, in beds and borders. Height 12-24"/30-60cm, but also dwarf varieties 8-12"/20-30cm suitable for rock gardens. *C. allionii* (Siberian Wallflower) yellow or orange 15"/37cm high.

Flowers: *C. cheiri* April-June; *C. allionii* May-July.

Site and soil: Any well-drained soil in sunny position. Acid soils may need more lime.

Propagation: Sow seeds May-June at ¼"/6mm depth in seed bed. Germination 10-14 days. Thin to 6"/15cm apart, transplant to flowering site September-October, spacing 10"/25cm apart depending on height of variety.

Care and cultivation: When plants 5-6"/12-15cm high pinch out tips before transplanting.

Pests and diseases: See under brassicas.

CLARKIA

W North America

Origins and history: Discovered by Lewis and Clark and named after Clark in 1805.

Description: HA Double flowers on upright spikes in red, pink, purple, orange or white. Height 18-24"/45-60cm. *C. elegans* has bigger blooms than *C. pulchella*. Used in borders, best in groups.

Flowers: July-October.

Site and soil: Medium to light soil. Likes it slightly acid, in sunny situation. Avoid heavy feeding.

Propagation: Sow seeds March-June where they are to flower at ¼"/6mm depth. Germination 10-14 days. Thin to 12"/30cm apart. *Or*, in sheltered areas or under cloches, sow in September for spring flowering.

Care and cultivation: May need staking with twigs.

CONVOLVULUS

S Europe

Origins and history: *C. tricolor* native to Mediterranean. A cottage garden flower, cultivated for centuries in Britain, and often naturalized near settlements.

Description: HA Dark green foliage and trumpet flowers in bright colours with yellow, gold or white throat. Short-lived, hence sometimes called Morning Glory; not to be confused with *Ipomoea purpurea*. Height 12-15"/30-37cm.

Flowers: July-September.

Site and soil: Any well-drained garden soil in a sunny position.

Propagation: Sow March to May where plants are to flower at ½"/12mm depth. Germination 10-14 days. Thin out to 9-12"/22-30cm. *Or*, sow in September and overwinter under cloches for larger plants.

Care and cultivation: Dead head.

DIANTHUS

Carnation, Pink, Sweet William

Origins and history: Most annual varieties from European species, though some from East. Known in Ancient Greece, and traditional British garden flower since Elizabethan times—see under *D. perennials* for full history.

All annual species have the same

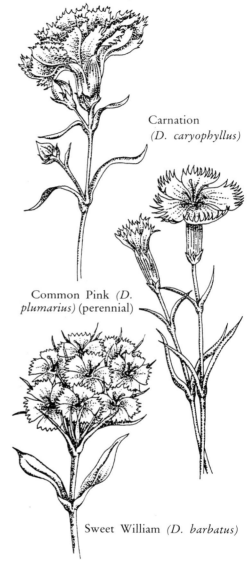

Carnation
(D. caryophyllus)

Common Pink *(D. plumarius)* (perennial)

Sweet William *(D. barbatus)*

requirements for site, soil, care and cultivation. For other details, see under separate species.

Site and soil: Any well-drained, preferably alkaline garden soil, sunny spot.

Care and cultivation: Like bone-meal, wood ash and plenty of grit. Don't give fresh manure.

D. BARBATUS

Sweet William   *Europe*

Description: HP usually grown as biennial. Dense flattened heads of many single or double flowers in crimson, scarlet, pink, white and variegated, sweet-scented, leaves mid-green unlike other pinks; many hybrids, some annual. Height 12-24"/30-60cm, dwarf forms 6-10"/15-25cm.

Flowers: June-July.

Propagation: Sow seeds May-June in seed bed ¼"/6mm deep. Germination 10-21 days. Thin seedlings to 6"/15cm apart. Transplant to flowering positions in October 8-10"/20-25cm apart.

Care and cultivation: Pinch out tips of main shoots above a joint to encourage side shoots. Dead head.

D. CAROPHYLLUS

Annual Carnation, Clove Pink, Gillyflower *Europe*

Description: HHA Colours include shades of red, pink and white. Excellent bedding annuals, but won't do well in the far north. Strong sweet scent. Grey-green leaves.

Flowers: July-October.

Propagation: Sow seeds January-March at 60-65°F/16-19°C   at   ¼"/6mm   depth. Germination 7-10 days. Prick out and harden off. Transplant to flowering position April-May 18"/45cm apart. *Or*, sow seeds outdoors April-July at ¼"/6mm depth. Germination 10-14 days, thin seedlings out to 18"/45cm apart.

Care and cultivation: Dead head. Stake tall varieties.

D. CHINENSIS

Indian Pink, Annual Pink   China

Description: HHA Looser flowerhead than European varieties, many colours and single and double flowers. Sweet-scented. Height 6-12"/15-30cm.

Flowers: July-October.

Propagation: Sow seeds January-March at 60-65°F/16-18°C at depth of ⅛"/3mm. Germination 7-10 days. Prick out and harden off. Transfer to flowering position in May, 6"/15cm apart. *Or*, sow in April where they are to flower at ¼"/6mm depth. Thin to 6"/15cm apart.

Care and cultivation: Dead head.

DIGITALIS

Foxglove   *Europe*

Origins and history: Very common native plant, especially in the west. Good in small doses for heart disease (otherwise poisonous), and still used in modern medicine.

Description: P treated as HB. Can be grown as perennial. Tall one-sided spikes of bell-like flowers. Familiar in woodland and garden, especially in shady places. Wild foxgloves pinky-purple, garden varieties white, yellow, purple, through to red, rosette of big downy leaves. Height 3-5'/1-1.5m. Good companion for other plants.

Flowers: June-August.

Site and soil: Any reasonably moist soil in shade or partial shade. Prefers slightly acid soil.

Propagation: Seeds very small. Sow May or June in pots of seed compost, barely covering them. Germination 14-21 days. Prick out and harden off. Transfer seedlings to nursery bed 6"/15cm apart. Move to final position in September, 12-24"/30-60cm apart. *Or*, sow outside in May or June, scattering and barely covering them with damp peat. Space out in nursery bed as above.

Care and cultivation: Remove central shoot after flowering to encourage side shoots. Cut back in October if leaving as a perennial.

ESCHSCHOLZIA CALIFORNICA

Californian Poppy•   *W North America*

Origins and history: Discovered by Charrisco on expedition to Pacific in 1815, and named after Dr Eschscholz, who was in the party. Introduced to Britain by Douglas.

Description: HA Very easy to grow. Bright-coloured orange, yellow, white or red poppy-type flowers with fine-cut blue-green leaves. Flowers shortlived and closed in cool weather, but appear continuously. Good for sunny banks and borders. Height 12-15"/30-37cm.

Flowers: June-October.

Site and soil: Well-drained soil, preferably sandy. Full sun.

Propagation: Sow March-May where plants are to flower at ¼"/6mm depth,

at 50-60°F/10-16°C and ¼"/6mm depth. Germination 14-21 days. Prick out and harden off. Transfer to flowering positions in May, 12"/30cm apart. *Or*, in mild districts, sow outdoors in April.

G. pulchella single

just covering them. Germination 10-14 days. Thin seedlings to 6-9"/15-22cm apart. *Or*, sow August-September to flower next year—may require cloche protection in winter on exposed sites.

Care and cultivation: Removing seed pods increases flowering, but if one or two left will self-sow extensively for successive years.

GAILLARDIA PULCHELLA

Annual Gaillardia, Blanketflower
N. America

Origins and history: First discovered by Lewis and Clark in 1805. Commemorates M Gaillard de Marantonneau, French patron of botany.

Description: P usually grown as HHA Red and yellow daisy-like flowers in various forms, some ball-shaped, some florets round central disc. Good for cutting. Good border plant, though untidy. Height 12-24"/30-60cm.

Flowers: June-September.

Site and soil: Any light, well-drained soil, sun or partial shade.

Propagation: Sow seeds February-March

Care and cultivation: Stake where necessary, especially tall plants with large flower heads. Dead head to prolong flowering into autumn.

Pests and diseases: Downy mildew.

GODETIA

W North America

Origins and history: Discovered by Douglas on his first expedition to North America in 1822.

Description: HA Very popular bright-coloured single or double flowers in crimson, pinks, white and orange on green spikes. Compact bushy green foliage. Good for cutting and garden display. Height 9-24"/22-60cm. Related to chrysanthemums.

Flowers: June-September.

Site and soil: Any well-drained, light, moist garden soil, preferably in full sun.

Propagation: Sow seeds March-April at ¼"/6mm depth where plants are to

flower. Germination 10-14 days. Thin seedlings to 6'/15cm apart. *Or*, sow in September to flower following summer. May need cloche protection in exposed areas.

Care and cultivation: Tall varieties require staking. Water in dry weather.

GYPSOPHILA ELEGANS

Baby's Breath   *E Mediterranean*

Origins and history: Name from the Greek 'gypso'—chalk, and 'phileo'—I love. Traditional cottage garden flower.

Description: HA Numerous small pink or white flowers in sprays, and small grey-green leaves. Excellent foil to brighter flowers in borders. Good for cut flowers. Height 12-24″/30-60cm.

Flowers: May-September.

Site and soil: Prefers lime or chalk soils, sunny position.

Propagation: Sow seeds March-May at ¼″/6mm depth where plants are to flower. Germination 10-14 days. Thin seedlings to 12″/30cm apart. *Or*, sow in September for spring flowering.

Care and cultivation: May need staking.

HELIANTHUS ANNUUS

Sunflower   *N America*

Origins and history: Sunflower seeds provide important crops of seed and oil, especially in the USA. Flowers used as dye. Introduced to Britain as a garden flower in the seventeenth century.

Description: HA Giant single daisy-like flowers up to 12″/30cm diameter, in shades of yellow. Central discs brown or purple. Smaller varieties now available. Height 3-10'/1-3m.

Flowers: July to September.

Site and soil: Any well-drained soil in sun, sheltered from wind.

Propagation: Sow seeds March-May ½″/12mm depth where they are to flower. Sow 2-3 in each planting position, 12-18″/30-45cm apart, and thin out to 1. *Or*, sow under glass in February or March at 60°F/16°C, prick out and harden off. Plant out in May.

Care and cultivation: Support with stout canes or stakes. Remove dead heads to prevent excessive self-seeding.

Pests and diseases: Botrytis.

HELICHRYSUM BRACTEATUM

Strawflower, Everlasting Flower
Asia, Australia

Origins and history: Name from the Greek 'helios'—sun, and 'chrysos'—gold. First cultivated species recorded 1619 in the botanical gardens at Padua.

Description: Flowers like daisies which dry to 'everlasting flowers' in white, yellow, pink, orange and red. Good in beds and borders. Height 1-4'/30-120cm.

Flowers: July-September.

Site and soil: Light, well-drained soil in sunny position.

Propagation: Sow seeds March-May in open ground at ¼″/6mm depth. Germination 10-14 days. Thin out seedlings to 12″/30cm apart. *Or*, sow in February or March at 60-65°F/16-19°C. Prick out and harden off. Plant out in May 12″/30cm apart.

Care and cultivation: Seeds sown in the open should be protected by cloches during frost. Pick central flower to encourage flowering on side shoots. For winter decoration cut flowers before they are fully open and tie into bunches. Hang upside down in a cool dry place away from the sun until dry.

HELIOTROPIUM

Cherry Pie, Heliotrope   *Tropics*

Origins and history: Very popular in Victorian gardens. Garden variety derived from Peruvian species discovered by Europeans in the nineteenth century.

Description: Tender P usually treated as HHA Fragrant small flowers on large flowerheads from dark blue and mauve to white. Dark green leaves. Height 15-18"/ 37-45cm.

Flowers: May-September.

Site and soil: Fertile well-drained garden soil in full sun.

Propagation: Sow seeds February-March at 60-65°F/16-19°C at ¼"/6mm depth. Germination 14-28 days. Prick out and harden off. Plant out late May or early June 12"/30cm apart. Take cuttings in July.

Care and cultivation: Large plants may need staking. Pinch out young plants to encourage bushiness.

HIBISCUS TRIONUM

Flower Of An Hour
Old World Tropics

Origins and history: One species listed in Gerard (seventeenth century), but he only had the seeds, and hoped they would mature.

Description: Dark green leaves and yellow, red, pink or white flowers with white centre. Individually shortlived but appear continuously August-September. Open only for a few hours in the morning, but new hybrids last longer. Followed by bladder-like seed pods. Height 15-24"/ 37-60cm.

Flowers: August-September.

Site and soil: Any well-drained soil in a sunny position.

Propagation: Sow seeds March-May at ¼"/6mm depth where they are to flower. Germination 14-28 days. Thin out seedlings to 12"/30cm apart. *Or*, sow in March at 55-61°F/13-16°C, prick out and harden off. Plant out in early May.

Care and cultivation: If allowed to seed will self-sow for following years.

Pests and diseases: Greenfly.

IBERIS

Candytuft   *Europe*

Origins and history: 'Iberis' indicates Spanish origins. An early introduction from southern Europe, now sometimes naturalized. Cottage garden flower.

Description: HA White, pink, red or mauve flowers, sweetly scented. Quick growing, spreads into thick border. Narrow leaves and numerous flowers. Height 9-18″/22-45cm.

Flowers: May-August.

Site and soil: Any well-drained garden soil in sunny position—suitable in towns as resistant to polluted air. Thrives on poor soil.

Propagation: Sow seeds September or March-May where they are to flower at ¼″/6mm depth. Germination 10-14 days. Thin to 6″/15cm apart. Successive sowing will extend flowering season.

Care and cultivation: Dead head.

IPOMOEA PURPUREA

Morning Glory   *Tropical America*

Origins and history: Introduced late sixteenth century. Some varieties listed by Parkinson (seventeenth century).

Description: HHA Climbing plant—wiry stems twine round supports. Large trumpet-shaped flowers, single or clustered, blue, red or purple. Heart-shaped leaves. Flowers last one day but grow abundantly. Height 6-12′/2-4m.

Flowers: July-September.

Site and soil: Well-drained soil, light but preferably rich, in sheltered sunny spot. Ideally unshaded wall or fence, or up poles or pea-sticks. Grow outdoors only in mild areas.

Propagation: Sow 2-3 seeds per pot March-April at ½″/12mm depth at 60-65°F/16-19°C and thin to 1. Germination 10-21 days. Plant out in June. *Or*, sow seeds where they are to flower in April-May at ½″/12mm depth, and thin to 12″/30cm apart.

Care and cultivation: Dead head.

Pests and diseases: Aphids; thrips.

LATHYRUS

Sweet Pea   *Mediterranean*

Origins and history: Sent from Sicily to the Headmaster of Enfield Grammar School in 1699. Different colours developed in nineteenth century. Modern varieties not bred until late nineteenth century. Range of colours and heights extended at expense of scent. Favourite cottage garden flower.

Description: HA Climbing plant with tendrils at end of some leaf stalks to twine around supports. Red, pink, white or purple sweet-scented flowers. Height 1-10′/30cm-3m.

Flowers: June-November.

Site and soil: Any well-drained garden soil in sunny position. Ideally slightly alkaline. Likes bulky organic matter added to soil, e.g. well-rotted manure. Provide support—canes or peasticks. Prepare site previous autumn. Add wood ash for alkali.

Propagation: Soak or nick coat of seeds to help germination. Sow seeds September or March where they are to flower at ½″/12mm depth. Do not water for two days after sowing, then soak thoroughly and keep moist until germination has taken place. Germination 7-21 days. Thin out seedlings to 10″/25cm apart. *Or*, sow September-March in long pots or tubes at 60-65°F/16-19°C. Harden off. Plant out September-sown plants in April, March-sown plants in May.

Care and cultivation: Pinch out tips of young plants when 4″/100mm high to encourage sideshoots. Dead head, and pick off seed pods. After flowering leave roots in the ground as they will release nitrogen into the soil.

Pests and diseases: See under peas in the vegetable list.

LAVATERA TRIMESTRIS

Mallow   *Europe*

Origins and history: British native. Traditional cottage garden plant.

Description: HA Big bushy plant, pale green leaves and pink, white or mauve trumpet-shaped flowers 4″/100mm across. Good to add colour at back of border, and for cutting. Height 2-4′/60-120cm. Can be used as temporary hedge.

Flowers: July-September.

Site and soil: Any well-drained garden soil in sheltered sunny position. Too rich soil makes plant leafy with fewer flowers. Good seaside plant—salt-resistant.

Propagation: Sow seeds March-May where they are to flower at ½"/12mm depth. Germination 21-35 days. Thin out seedlings to 18"/45cm apart. Self-seeds profusely.

Care and cultivation: Staking may be necessary. Dead head.

LINARIA

Toadflax   *Mediterranean*

Origins and history: Native toadflax (*L. vulgaris*) still common wild flower. Garden species an introduction from southern Europe centuries ago; have sometimes naturalized.

Description: Spikes carrying flowers like snapdragons in blue, yellow, red, purple and pink—each flower has white or yellow blotch on lower lip. Good for borders and edging. Light green leaves. Height 9-18"/27-45cm.

Flowers: June-September.

Site and soil: Any well-drained garden soil in sunny position.

Propagation: Sow seeds September, or March-May where they are to flower at ⅛"/3mm depth. Germination 10-14 days. Thin out seedlings to 6"/15cm apart if necessary. May self-seed.

LOBELIA ERINUS

S Africa

Origins and history: Named after the seventeenth century botanist de L'Obel. Discovered by Plumier in South America in the seventeenth century.

Description: Tender P, usually grown as HHA Very popular blue, white or red flowers with bushy light green foliage. Used as edging plants, or as summer bedding plants. Trailing varieties good for tubs and hanging baskets. Often alternated with alyssum in edging. Height 4-8"/10-20cm.

Flowers: May to September.

Site and soil: Likes rich, moist soil, in sun or partial shade.

Propagation: Sow seeds January-March at 60-65°F/16-19°C. Seeds very small. Sow thinly; do not cover. Germination 7-14 days. Prick out seedlings, a few together, and harden off. Plant out in May 4"/100mm apart.

Care and cultivation: Keep moist. To encourage bushiness pinch out seedlings when 1"/25mm high.

LUNARIA

Honesty   *Europe*

Origins and history: Named by Gerard in the seventeenth century, but was clearly already a familiar garden flower. The name, from the Latin 'luna', refers to the full-moon-like seed-pods.

Description: HB Purple, or occasionally white or pink 4-petalled fragrant flowers, followed by silvery seed pods which can be dried for indoor decoration. Height 2-3'/60-90cm.

Flowers: April-June. Seedpods June, cut in August.

Site and soil: Any well-drained, preferably light, garden soil in partial shade.

Propagation: Sow seeds May-June in nursery bed at ½"/12mm depth. Germination 14-21 days. Thin out seedlings to 6"/15cm apart. Transfer to flowering position in September at 12"/30cm apart.

Care and cultivation: Do not dead head, as seedpods are a feature.

Pests and diseases: See brassicas in the vegetable list.

MALCOLMIA MARITIMA

Virginia Stock   *Mediterranean*

Origins and history: First introduction not recorded, though it was growing in the Physic Garden at Chelsea in the eighteenth century.

Description: HA Very easy to grow. Red, mauve, pink or white flowers and sweet-scented grey-green leaves. Used for edging, borders and rock gardens. Height 6-9"/15-22cm.

Flowers: Blooms 4 weeks after sowing for 6-8 weeks.

Site and soil: Any soil or site. Prefers sunny position.

Propagation: Sow seeds March-September where they are to flower. Just cover. Germination 7-10 days. Thin out seedlings to 6"/15cm apart if necessary. Will self-seed profusely.

MATTHIOLA

Stocks   *Europe*

Origins and history: Latin name from Matthioli, sixteenth century Italian botanist. 'Stock' is Middle English for 'stem'. Native of Isle of Wight, but no further north. Used as gillyflowers, then in eighteenth century became florists' flower. Naturalized early in rest of Britain.

Description: HA, HHA or HB Belongs to *crucifera* family. Many different coloured spikes of flowers with grey-green foliage. Sweet-scented. Very popular.
Types:
(1) HA 10-Week Stock. Many varieties, including dwarf.
(2) HB Brompton Stocks. Bushy. Named after London nursery where first bred.
(3) HHA or HB East Lothian Stock. Suitable for north of Scotland.
(4) HA Night-Scented Stock (*M. bicornis*). Flowers close during day. Untidy but very sweet-scented at night—often grown near windows.
(5) HA Perpetual Flowering. Dense spikes of double white flowers.

Flowers: HA June-August. HB March-May.

Site and soil: Any well-drained not too acid garden soil, in full sun or partial shade. Helps to enrich soil with organic matter—compost or well-rotted manure.

Propagation: HA stocks: sow seeds in April where they are to flower at ¼"/6mm depth. Germination 7-10 days. Thin out seedlings to 12"/30cm apart.

HHA stocks: sow seeds February-March at 60-65°F/16-19°C at ¼"/6mm depth. Germination 7-10 days. Prick out and harden off. Plant out in May 12"/30cm apart.

HB stocks: sow seeds June-July ¼"/6mm depth in seed bed. Germination 7-10 days. Thin seedlings to 4"/10cm apart. Plant where they are to flower in October, 12"/30cm apart.

Care and cultivation: Dried blood in spring will encourage growth and flower size. Biennials wintering outside need cloche protection on exposed sites. Dead head.

Pests and diseases: See under brassicas in the vegetable list.

MESEMBRYANTHEMUM CRINIFLORUM

Livingstone Daisy   *S Africa*

Origins and history: Masson discovered them while exploring the Cape in 1772.

Description: Tender P, usually grown as HHA. Bright daisy-like flowers in white, red, pink and orange, with succulent leaves. Brilliant display in sun; flowers close when no sun. Suitable for rockeries and edging. Height 4-6"/10-15cm.

Flowers: July-September.

Site and soil: Any well-drained garden soil, preferably sandy. Full sun essential.

Propagation: Sow seeds February-April at 60-65°F/16-19°C at ⅛"/3mm depth. Germination 14-21 days. Prick out and harden off. Plant out in May or June 8"/20cm apart after last frost.

Pests and diseases: Rot in damp conditions.

MIMULUS

Monkey Flower   *Americas*

Origins and history: Having a strong musky scent, *M. moschatus* was the most popular cultivated mimulus when the species was first introduced to Europe in the nineteenth century, but around 1950 all the plants unaccountably lost their scent. Perhaps the scented variety was an aberration in the first place—who knows? Now *M. cupreus* is the originator of most garden species.

Description: P usually grown as HHA.

Low-growing plants with snapdragon-type open-mouthed flowers (likened to monkey's face, hence Monkey Flower). Useful for bedding in shady damp places where other annuals won't thrive. Height 9″/22cm.

Flowers: June-September.

Site and soil: Likes moist soil which will not dry out—bog plant, prefers shade.

Propagation: Sow seeds February-March at 60-65°F/16-19°C. Press seeds into surface of compost. Germination 10-14 days. Prick out and harden off. Plant out in May 9-12″/22-30cm apart.

Care and cultivation: Keep moist.

MYOSOTIS SYLVATICA

Forget-me-not   *Europe*

Origins and history: Native to British Isles, with ten species. Hybrids for gardens developed in the late nineteenth century, but has been grown as a cottage garden flower for centuries.

Description: HB Very familiar blue, sometimes pink small flowers with hairy leaves. Used in borders and beds. Much used in formal bedding schemes with tulips and wallflowers. Height 6-12″/15-30cm.

Flowers: May-June.

Site and soil: Any fertile well-drained garden soil. Prefers at least partial shade and fairly moist soil. Denudes soil of goodness —ground will need feeding afterwards.

Propagation: Sow seeds May-July in seed beds at ¼″/6mm depth. Germination 14-21 days. Thin out seedlings to 6″/15cm apart and transfer to flowering site in September at 6″/15cm apart. Will self-seed abundantly if old plants left in.

Care and cultivation: May need cloche protection in winter.

Pests and diseases: Powdery mildew.

NEMESIA STRUMOSA

S Africa

Origins and history: Fifty species, all from South Africa. First became popular in 1892 and 1893 when exhibited by Sutton and Sons at the Royal Horticultural Society. The huge range of bright colours attracted much attention.

Description: HHA Many multicoloured blooms in bright colours—yellow, red, blue, pink, orange, etc. Usually grown in mixtures. Good in beds, borders, tubs, windowboxes. Height 9-18″/22-45cm.

Flowers: June-September.

Site and soil: Any garden soil—prefers light and slightly acid soil with plenty of organic matter. Peaty soil is excellent. Sunny position.

Propagation: Sow seeds February-April at 60-65°F/16-19°C at ⅛″/3mm depth. Prick out and harden off. Plant out May or June 4-6″/10-15cm apart.

Care and cultivation: Pinch out tips to encourage sideshoots. Water if necessary. Cut back after first flowering to get second flowering.

NICOTIANA

Tobacco Plant   *Central and S America*

Origins and history: Named after Nicot, who introduced the tobacco plant to Spain in the sixteenth century. Garden species first introduced in the seventeenth century.

Description: HHA Tall stems with open flowers. Very strong scent, especially in the evening. Originally white, now yellow, pink, green and red varieties. Height 9-36″/22-90cm.

Flowers: June-October.

Site and soil: Any well-drained garden soil in sun or light shade. Prefers rich soil.

Propagation: Sow seeds February-April at 60-65°F/16-19°C at ⅛"/3mm depth. Germination 10-14 days. Prick out and harden off. Plant out from late May after last frost at 9-12"/22-30cm apart.

Care and cultivation: Stake tall varieties. Dead head regularly to maintain flowers through season.

Pests and diseases: Aphids.

NIGELLA DAMASCENA

Love in a Mist   *Europe*

Origins and history: Latin name comes from the tradition that the plant's black seeds were brought from Damascus in 1570. Introduced from the Mediterranean. Traditional cottage garden flower since Elizabethan times.

Description: HA Originally blue flowers hidden in a mist of bright green fern-like foliage, now multicoloured varieties. Useful for borders and cutting—dried seedheads used for decoration. Height 15-18"/37-45cm.

Flowers: June-September.

Site and soil: Any well-drained garden soil in sun or partial shade. Likes compost.

Propagation: Sow seeds March-May where they are to flower. Just cover. Germination 14-21 days. Thin seedlings out to 6"/15cm apart. *Or,* sow seeds in September for spring flowering. Will self-seed.

Care and cultivation: Dead head.

PAPAVER

Poppy
Europe, Iceland, Middle East, Asia

Origins and history: Many different areas of origin, and varieties. Common red poppy native to Britain since Tertiary period—30 million years ago. The red poppy loves disturbed ground, and before herbicides it was endemic in cornfields. Opium poppies come from the East, where they are often found growing wild.

Description: HA or HB. Ephemeral flowers on long stalks. Double and single varieties. Nowadays many colours. Old favourite. Comes in many varieties and species. Height 6-36"/15-90cm.

Types:

(1) *P. rhoeas* HA—red Corn Poppy of European countryside. Shirley Poppy derived from this by Rev. Wilks: 24"/60cm high, single and double forms—pink, white or red varieties.

(2) *P. somniferum* HA—Opium Poppy: pink, scarlet or purple, often with darker centre.

(3) *P. nudicaule* P best treated as HB—Iceland Poppy: red, orange, yellow, white. Height 18-30"/45-75cm.

(4) *P. alpinum* P best treated as HB—Miniature Poppy in red, orange, yellow and white, height 4-10"/10-25cm, good for rock gardens.

Flowers: May-September.

Site and soil: Any garden soil in sun or light shade.

Propagation: HA Sow seeds March-May where they are to flower at ¼"/6mm depth. Germination 10-14 days. Thin seedlings out to 12"/30cm apart. *Or,* sow in September to flower in spring. Self-seeds profusely. HB Sow seeds June-August in seedbed at ¼"/6mm depth. Germination 10-14 days. Thin seedlings to 6"/15cm. Plant where they are to flower October-April 8-12"/20-30cm apart.

Care and cultivation: Dead head to prevent excessive seeding.

PELARGONIUM ZONALE

Zonal Geranium   *Africa*

Origins and history: The name comes from the Greek 'pelargos'—stork; 'zonal' from the horseshoe markings or 'zone' on the leaves. 2 species recorded as being cultivated in Britain in 1690. Nineteenth century hothouses meant a huge expansion in the cultivation of tender perennials, so many more varieties were bred. This plant has nothing to do with the genus *Geranium* (see under *Geranium*). There are over 300 recorded species of pelargonium, mainly brought to Europe from different parts of Africa (and a few from Australasia) in the last 3 centuries. Original plants had very small flowers, but a vast number of colourful varieties have now been bred, mostly in the nineteenth century. These species are still used extensively for hybrids. The most common British species originated in S. Africa.

Description: Tender P grown as HHA Familiar bright 5-petalled red, white and pink flowers with deciduous or evergreen leaves, ubiquitous in borders and beds, greenhouses, porches and windowboxes. Numerous varieties. Some have strongly-scented leaves, and some have leaves which are edible.

3 main groups:

Bedding pelargoniums: With zoned leaves. Flourish outdoors.

Greenhouse pelargoniums.

Fancyleaf pelargoniums: Grown for their leaves rather than for blooms.

The varieties described here are Zonal Pelargoniums for outdoor bedding, or Ivyleaf varieties which can be used similarly.

Another plant for the specialist which is also highly rewarding for the amateur, both in house and garden. Success is easy. Height: 12-18"/30-45cm (Zonal); 3'/90cm spread (Ivyleaf).

Flowers: May-October.

Site and soil: Any well-drained garden soil in full sun. Dig in compost or well-rotted manure before planting. Likes sandy or gritty soils best. Plant Ivyleaf Geraniums (trailing varieties) in tubs or window boxes, or use as ground cover.

Propagation: In July or August take 3"/75mm long tip cuttings, and insert individually in pots of cutting compost. Will root in 2-3 weeks. Pot on rooted cuttings when ready. Pinch out tips when 6"/15cm high to encourage bushiness. Water sparingly during winter. Harden off in April in cold frame and plant out late May/June 12"/30cm apart. *Or,* sow seeds January-February at 68-78°F/20-26°C at ¼"/6mm depth. Germination 14-28 days. Prick out seedlings into individual pots and grow on. Pot on again when ready. Plant out end May/June at 12"/30cm apart.

Care and cultivation: *Summer (outdoors):* Only water in very dry weather. Dead head to prolong flowering.

Winter (indoors): Dig up plants carefully before frost in September or October. Shake off soil. Pot up singly in potting compost. Pot firmly, and do not use too large pots. Reduce height of stems by half, and cut off all yellowed leaves and dead heads. Keep in a cool place and water very sparingly. In spring increase light and water.

PETUNIA

Argentina

Origins and history: Sent back by James Tweedie, a botanist who emigrated to South America from Edinburgh in the nineteenth century.

Description: Tender P best treated as HHA Colourful trumpet-shaped flowers in pinks, reds, purples, blues and whites (including bi-colours) on sticky stems. Good for beds, borders, tubs and window-boxes. Height 6-18″/15-45cm. Some trailing and small-flowered varieties.

Flowers: June-October.

Site and soil: Any well-drained garden soil in sheltered, sunny position. Not too rich or moist, or will produce fewer flowers.

Propagation: Sow seeds January-March at 60-65°F/15-19°C. Leave uncovered. Germination 7-14 days. Prick out and harden off. Plant in flowering site in May at 6-12″/15-30cm apart.

Care and cultivation: Dead head.

Pests and diseases: Aphids.

PHLOX

Phlox   *Texas*

Origins and history: Sent back by Thomas Drummond from an expedition in the early nineteenth century.

Description: HHA Straight stems with light green leaves. Dense heads of flowers in whites, pinks, reds and purples. Good for beds, borders and rockeries. *P. drummondii* is annual species. 3 groups: *stellaris* 4-6″/10-15cm high; *grandiflora* 12-18″/30-45cm high; *nana compacta* 6-9″/15-22cm high.

Flowers: June-September.

Site and soil: Any fertile well-drained garden soil in sun or partial shade.

Propagation: Sow seeds February-April at 50-60°F/10-16°C at ¼″/6mm depth. Prick out and harden off. Plant out in May 8″/20cm apart. *Or*, sow seeds September-October in cold frame or greenhouse at ¼″/6mm depth to plant out in spring.

Care and cultivation: Dead head.

RESEDA

Mignonette   *Egypt*

Origins and history: 'Mignonette' is French for 'little darling'. In the seventeenth century it was sent to the Physic Garden in Chelsea by Dr van Royen, Professor of Botany at Leiden University. Traditional eighteenth century cottage garden flower.

Description: HA Small yellow cones of flowers and spreading light green leaves. Insignificant to look at, but lovely and distinctive scent. Will attract bees. Suitable for beds and borders. Height 12-30″/30-75cm.

Flowers: July-September.

Site and soil: Fairly rich well-drained alkaline soil in sunny position, though will manage on any tolerable garden soil. Add lime if too acid.

Propagation: Sow seeds March-May where they are to flower at ⅛″/3mm depth. Firm ground thoroughly after sowing. Germination 10-14 days. Thin out to 9″/22cm apart. *Or*, sow February-March at 55°F/13°C. Prick out and harden off. Plant out in May.

TAGETES

Tagetes, African Marigold, French Marigold

Mexico (not Africa or France!)

Origins and history: African Marigold reached Britain from Mexico via South Africa, where the seeds had arrived in fodder for animals in the Boer War. French Marigold reached Britain from North Africa via Paris in mid-sixteenth century.

Description: HHA Numerous varieties very widely used in borders and bedding out schemes. Yellow, red-brown and orange compact flowers, both single and double. Crushed leaves have a powerful distinctive smell. Very useful for companion planting among vegetables and fruit.
Types:
(1) *T. erecta*—African Marigold: dark green leaves and yellow flowers. Tallest, with largest flowers. Double blooms. Also dwarf varieties. Height 12-36″/30-90cm.
(2) *T. patula*—French Marigold: dark green leaves and yellow or red flowers. Shorter, with smaller flowers. Huge variety of colours. Height 6-12″/15-30cm.
(3) *T. signata*—Tagetes: small daisy-like flowers in orange, red or yellow. Height 6-9″/15-22cm.
Various hybrids from mixtures of the three groups.

Flowers: June-October.

Site and soil: Any garden soil, preferably full sun. Tolerates poor dry soils.

Propagation: Sow seeds February-March at 60-65°F/16-19°C at ¼"/6mm depth. Germination 7-10 days. Prick out and harden off. Plant out in May at 12"/30cm apart. *Or*, sow seeds where they are to flower April-May at ¼"/6mm depth. Thin out seedlings to 12"/30cm apart.

Care and cultivation: Dead head.

Pests and diseases: Botrytis.

TROPAEOLUM MAJUS

Nasturtium   *Peru*

Origins and history: 'Nasturtium' means 'watercress'. *Tropaeolum* was introduced to Britain as 'Indian Cress' by William Lobb in 1686; hence the confusion, as it was first cultivated as a salad vegetable.

Description: HA Smooth circular mid-green leaves and faintly scented flowers in yellow, red, pink or orange. Leaves, seeds and flowers are edible. Good for window-boxes and hanging baskets. Good for companion planting. Height 10"/25cm upwards; climbing varieties up to 6'/2m.

Flowers: June-October.

Site and soil: Thrives on poor dry or sandy soils. Prefers full sun, tolerates partial shade. Rich soils will produce fewer flowers.

Propagation: Sow seeds (very large) 12-18"/30-45cm apart according to variety April-May where they are to flower at 1"/25mm depth. Germination 10-14 days.

Care and cultivation: Dead head.

Pests and diseases: Aphids, cabbage white caterpillars.

VERBENA HORTENSIS

Vervain   *S America*

Origins and history: Discovered in the nineteenth century by James Tweedie, a landscape gardener who emigrated to South America.

Description: Tender P usually treated as HHA Bushy plants with brightly coloured clusters of flowers in reds, pinks, blue and white. Commonly used in beds and windowboxes, and in edging. Height 9-15"/22-37cm.

Flowers: July-September.

Site and soil: Any fertile garden soil—likes additional organic matter or peat. Prefers full sun.

Propagation: Sow seeds January-March at 60-68°F/16-20°C at ⅛"/3mm depth. Germination 10-21 days. Prick out and harden off. Plant out in May after last frost, at 12"/30cm apart.

Care and cultivation: Pinch out growing tips to encourage sideshoots.

VIOLA

Pansy, Heartsease   *Europe*

Origins and history: Garden pansies created in nineteenth century from several native species, especially *V. tricolor*. In 1839 the earliest blotched pansies were bred from native violets by William Thompson on an estate in Buckinghamshire. Viola created from *V. cornuta* and garden pansy in 1860s.

Description: HP Shortlived, usually grown as HA or HB. One of most popular garden plants, used for bedding, edging. 5-petalled distinctive open flowers, now in a great variety of colours. Often sweet-smelling. *Types:*
(1) *V. odorata*—Sweet Violet: purple or

white, sweet-scented. Spreads by runners. Height 4-6"/10-15cm.

(2) *V.x wittrockiana*—Pansy: large bright-coloured flowers in yellow, red, blue, white, purple. Height 6-9"/15-22cm.

(3) *V.x williamsii*—Viola: smaller than Pansy, equally wide range of colours. Height 4-6"/10-15cm.

Flowers: January-December (depending on variety).

Site and soil: Prefer cool moist position, with well-drained garden soil. Sun or partial shade.

Propagation: *V. odorata*: sow seeds September-November at ¼"/6mm depth and overwinter in cold frame or cool greenhouse. Will germinate in spring. Prick out and grow on till autumn. Plant out in September 9-12"/22-30cm apart. Pansy and Viola: Sow seeds June-July at ¼"/6mm depth in seed bed. Germination 10-21 days. Thin out to 4"/100mm apart. Plant out September-October 9-12"/22-30cm apart. *Or,* sow seeds January-March at 50-60°F/10-16°C at ¼"/6mm depth. Germination 10-21 days. Prick out and harden off. Plant out in May, 9"/22cm apart.

Care and cultivation: Dead head.

Perennials

ACHILLEA

Yarrow, Milfoil   *North temperate zone*

Origins and history: Native British flower that flourished from about 500BC when the first cornfields were opened up. Garden species gradually developed from these. Called after Achilles, who is said to have treated his wounds with it. Yarrow was a common medieval herb; still used today.

Description: HP Tiny flowers loosely or tightly clustered into large heads; fernlike leaves. *A. filipendulina* (E Europe) yellow; *A. millefolium* (Britain) white or pink; *A. ptarmica* (Sneezewort, Britain) white, can be invasive; rock garden varieties from *A. tomentosa*. Several species used in herbaceous borders. Height 2-8'/60-240cm according to variety.

Flowers: June-September.

Site and soil: Any well-drained soil in a sunny position.

Propagation: Sow seeds April-June at

ZINNIA

Mexico

Origins and history: First species was sent from America to the Chelsea Physic Gardens in 1753. The species we cultivate today arrived in 1796.

Description: HHA Bright large daisy-like flowers, single, semi-double or double, in white, pink, red, yellow, orange or purple. good for cutting and borders. Height 12-36"/30-90cm.

Flowers: July-October.

Site and soil: Rich well-drained soil in sheltered sunny position.

Propagation: Sow seeds March-April at 60-65°F/16-19°C at ¼"/6mm depth. Germination 7-14 days. Prick out and harden off. Plant in final positions in June at 12"/30cm apart. *Or,* sow seeds where they are to flower at ½"/12mm depth in May. Germination 10-14 days. Thin out seedlings to 12"/30cm apart.

Care and cultivation: Pinch out growing tips to encourage sideshoots. Dead head. Tend to be damaged by wind and heavy rain.

¼"/6mm depth in a seed bed. Germination 14-21 days. Thin out seedlings to 12"/30cm apart and grow on. Plant in permanent positions October-March with space for 30"/75cm spread (*A. filipendulina*) or 15"/37cm (others). *Or,* divide in March, each division having 4 or 5 young shoots.

Care and cultivation: Stake on exposed sites. Cut back to ground level in autumn.

ALCHEMILLA MOLLIS
Lady's Mantle
Middle East

Origins and history: The name is Arabic in origin, and indicates the plant's use in alchemy. Well known for centuries as a healing herb for women's disorders. Another species, *A. vulgaris*, is native to Britain.

Description: HP Large pale green soft leaves, silvery underneath. Small yellow star-shaped flowers on branched heads, good for cutting. Height 12-18"/30-45cm.

Flowers: June-August

Site and soil: Any moist but well-drained garden soil in sun or partial shade.

Propagation: Sow seeds in March in a seed bed at ¼"/6mm depth. Thin to 6"/15cm apart and plant out between October and March, spaced at 15"/37cm. Divide any time between October and March. Self-seeds profusely.

Care and cultivation: Stake when necessary. Cut back to 1"/25mm above ground in autumn.

ALYSSUM SAXATILE
Perennial Alyssum   *E. Europe*

Origins and history: 'Saxatile' is the Latin word for 'gold dust'. Introduced to Britain from Crete in 1710.

Description: HP Bright golden yellow flowers; evergreen greyish-green leaves. Good for edging and rockeries. Double-flowered and dwarf varieties available. Height 9-12"/22-30cm.

Flowers: April-June.

Site and soil: Any well-drained garden soil, preferably in full sun.

Propagation: Sow seeds in March in boxes in a cold frame or cold greenhouse at ¼"/6mm depth. Germination 7-10 days.

Prick out, harden off, and plant out in a nursery bed 4"/100mm apart. Plant where they are to flower in September at 15-24"/37-60cm apart. *Or,* take 2-3"/50-75mm long cuttings in June and insert in cutting compost in a cold frame. Pot on and grow on in the cold frame. Plant out following March.

Care and cultivation: Cut back hard after flowering to prolong life and keep the plant compact.

ANCHUSA
Alkanet, Bugloss, Oxtongue   *S. Europe*

Origins and history: *A. sempervirens* native to West Country. 'Blue-eyed Mary' and other species introduced centuries ago from southern Europe.

Description: HP Bright blue forget-me-not-like flower clusters on tall untidy stems with tough hairy leaves. Short-lived, but useful for early flowering in the herbaceous border. Height 18-60"/45-150cm.

Flowers: May-July.

Site and soil: Any fertile well-drained garden soil in a sunny position. It hates the soil being too wet—add sand to heavy soil to improve drainage.

Propagation: Sow seeds April-June in seedbed at ½"/12mm depth. Germination 14-28 days. Thin out seedlings to 6"/15cm apart. Transfer to permanent positions in October at 12-18"/30-45cm apart. *Or,* take root cuttings in January and February. Plant in cutting compost in a cold frame and move to the nursery bed in April or May. Plant out in October. *Or,* divide clumps in March.

Care and cultivation: Dead head. Cut back in October.

AQUILEGIA
Columbine, Granny's Bonnets
N hemisphere

Origins and history: Name from the Latin 'aquila', because the flower supposedly represents an eagle's claw. Native on chalk soils throughout Europe. Grown in gardens since Middle Ages. Used to be used medicinally, though poisonous. *A. vulgaris* is traditional cottage garden flower.

Description: HP Grey-green leaves and delicate spurred funnel-shaped flowers in white, pink, red and blue. Familiar in beds and borders. Flowers relatively short-lived.

Height 24-36"/60-90cm. Many dwarf varieties.

Flowers: June-July.

Site and soil: Well-drained moist soil in sun or partial shade. Mulch in late spring.

Propagation: Sow seeds April-June in seedbed at ¼"/6mm depth. Thin seedlings to 6"/15cm apart, and plant out in September-October at 12"/30cm apart.

Care and cultivation: Dead head. Cut back to ground level in autumn.

Pests and diseases: Leaf Miners.

ARABIS

Wall Cress, White Rock Cress   *Europe*

Origins and history: Native rock cresses rare now in wild. *A. caucasica* brought from southern Europe and often found naturalized. Cottage garden flower.

Description: HP Mass of white or occasionally pink cross-shaped flowers on evergreen greyish-green cushions of leaves. Excellent trailing plant for walls, stone borders and rockeries. Height up to 6"/15cm.

Flowers: March-June.

Site and soil: Any well-drained garden soil in sun or partial shade.

Propagation: Sow seeds March-April in boxes in a cold frame or cool greenhouse at ¼"/6mm depth. Germination 14-21 days. Prick out seedlings, harden off, and plant out where they are to flower in May at 12"/30cm apart. *Or*, sow seeds May-June where they are to flower at ¼"/6mm depth. Thin to 12"/30cm apart. *Or*, insert cuttings of non-flowering rosettes in cutting compost in a cold frame in June or July. Pot on rooted cuttings and plant out in March.

Care and cultivation: Dead head. Cut back hard after flowering has finished, and you may get a second flowering. Keep plant compact. Can become invasive.

ARMERIA

Thrift, Sea Pink   *Europe*

Origins and history: *A. maritima* is native British thrift, a common seaside plant. Used in Tudor knot gardens; its neat hummocks were ideal for edgings in cottage gardens.

Description: HP Small hummocks of grass-like leaves and globular heads of tiny pink, white or red blooms. Good for seaside

gardens, for the front of borders and especially for rockeries.

Flowers: May-July

Site and soil: Any well-drained garden soil in full sun.

Propagation: Sow seeds March-April in boxes in a cold frame or cool greenhouse at ⅛"/3mm depth. Germination 14-28 days. Prick out into boxes and grow on. Plant where they are to flower in September at 12"/30cm apart. Or, sow seeds in July where they are to flower at ¼"/6mm depth. Thin to 12"/30cm apart. Or, divide and replant roots in March or April. Or, take 2"/50mm long basal cuttings in July/August and insert in cutting compost in a cold frame. Pot on rooted cuttings and plant out following autumn.

Care and cultivation: Dead head.

Pests and diseases: Rust, Damping off.

ASTER NOVI-BELGII or NOVAE-ANGLIAE

Michaelmas Daisy   N America

Origins and history: 'Aster' comes from the Greek word for 'star', referring to the shape of the flowers. Called 'Michaelmas Daisy' because of flowering time. Brought back from North America in the eighteenth century, and sometimes found naturalized.

Description: HP Pink, white, blue or purple daisy-like flowers with slender leaves growing along long stems. Very hardy. Double, semi-double and dwarf varieties available. Height 24-28"/60-70cm.

Flowers: September-October.

Site and soil: Any well-drained garden soil in a sunny position.

Propagation: Sow seeds March-April at 60-65°F/16-19°C at ¼"/6mm depth. Germination 7-10 days. Prick out, harden off, and plant out in May 15"/37cm apart. Or, divide between October and March, preferably in March. For a quick increase in numbers divide into single shoots at 6"/15cm apart, otherwise re-plant in clumps. Because the plants increase rapidly they need dividing every 2 years.

Care and cultivation: Keep moist, especially at flowering time. Will need staking. Dead head. Cut back from October onwards. Mulch.

Pests and diseases: Slugs, Caterpillars; Powdery Mildew (common), Aster Wilt.

AUBRIETA

Rock Cress, Aubretia   E. Europe

Origins and history: First introduced in 1710 from Greek mountains. Named after Aubriet, a French missionary in China, who has no obvious connection with the flower!

Description: HP Mass of short red or purple flowers on a cushion of evergreen leaves. A spreading mat of trailing leaves and flowers, excellent for walls, stony borders and rockeries. Height 3-4"/75-100mm.

Flowers: March-June.

Site and soil: Any well-drained, preferably alkaline, soil in a sunny position.

Propagation: Sow seeds March-June in seedbed at ¼"/6mm depth. Germination 14-21 days. Thin out seedlings to 12"/30cm apart. Plant where they are to flower in September at 18"/45cm apart. Or, take cuttings when cutting back in June or July. Mound a cutting compost over the crowns and use new shoots for cuttings. Or, take 2"/50mm basal cuttings in August or September and insert them in cutting compost in a cold frame. Pot on the following March and plant out between September and the next March. Or, divide established plants in September.

Care and cultivation: Where compact growth is required, cut back hard after flowering. To encourage trailing on walls, only dead head. You may get a second flowering after cutting back.

BELLIS

Daisy   Europe

Origins and history: Name from the Latin 'beautiful'. Native plant, cultivated since Elizabethan times, bred from B. perennis, our common lawn daisy. 'Daisy' comes from 'day's eye', as it opens and closes with light.

Description: HP often grown as biennial. Well-known flower with many thin white, pink or red petals. Double and single varieties. Leaves pale green and downy. Height 1-6"/2.5-15cm.

Flowers: March-October.

Site and soil: Any garden soil in sun or partial shade.

Propagation: Sow seeds outdoors in seedbed May-June at ¼"/6mm depth.

Germination 10-14 days. Thin seedlings out to 3-4"/75-100mm apart. Place in permanent positions in September about 5"/12cm apart. *Or*, divide plants in spring.

Care and cultivation: Dead head.

BERGENIA

Large-leaved Saxifrage   *Asia*

Origins and history: Named after the eighteenth century German botanist Bergen. Discovered by Wallich in Nepal at the end of the eighteenth century. Used to be classified wrongly with the saxifrages, hence its English name.

Description: HP Large thick glossy evergreen leaves which sometimes turn russet in autumn. Good ground cover. Pink, purple or white bell-shaped flowers in large sprays. Height 9-18"/22-45cm.

Flowers: March-May.

Site and soil: Any well-drained garden soil in sun or partial shade. For maximum leaf colour in winter it needs to be in full sun.

Propagation: Divide in September-October or March.

Care and cultivation: Remove dead heads and stems.

CALTHA

Kingcup, Marsh Marigold
Temperate regions

Origins and history: Native waterside plant; used to be planted by water in cottage gardens.

Description: HP Marsh plant with dark green leaves and large bright yellow flowers. Very useful by pools, and in bog gardens and wet places. Not a bed or border plant. Height 12"/30cm.

Flowers: April-June.

Site and soil: Likes water up to 6"/15cm deep, depending on species. Sun or partial shade. If planted out of water the ground must be kept moist. Likes organic matter.

Propagation: Sow seeds when ripe, or in March, and stand pots or trays in water in a cold frame in partial shade. Prick out seedlings into boxes and immerse them in water. Plant out in September or October. *Or*, divide in June after flowering. Lift the plants, wash the soil from the roots and separate the crowns. Shorten the roots before planting.

Care and cultivation: Keep moist at all times. Remove decaying leaves.

Pests and diseases: Rust.

CAMPANULA

Bellflower, Harebell   *Europe*

Origins and history: 'Campanula' is the Latin for 'little bell'. Several species grow wild in Britain, and there are many garden escapes. Grown in cottage gardens since sixteenth century, at which time new species were brought from Europe.

Description: HP Blue, purple or white bell-shaped star-shaped or tubular flowers on spikes, single or double. A favourite in beds and borders, and there are rockery varieties. Good for cutting. Height 2-48"/5-120cm depending on variety.

Flowers: May-August.

Site and soil: Any fertile well-drained garden soil in sun or partial shade.

Propagation: Sow seeds February-June in boxes in a cold frame or greenhouse. Press the seeds into the soil surface. Germination 14-21 days. Prick out, harden off, and plant out in permanent positions in May, 12-15"/30-37cm apart for smaller varieties, 15-18″/37-45cm for taller ones. *Or*, insert cuttings 1-2″/25-50mm long from non-flowering basal shoots April-May in cutting compost in a cold frame, pot on rooted cuttings and treat as seedlings. *Or*, divide clumps in autumn or spring.

Care and cultivation: Dead head. Stake taller varieties.

Pests and diseases: Slugs, Rust.

CENTAUREA
Cornflower, Knapweed   *S. Europe*

Origins and history: The Latin name recalls the legend that a potion of the plant healed the wounds of Chiron the Centaur. Cottage garden flower referred to by Parkinson in the seventeenth century.

Description: HP Thistle-like flowers in blue, pink, red or white, often with silver foliage. Good for herbaceous borders and beds. Very good for cut flowers, the flowers being long-lived. Height 18-48″/45-120cm depending on variety.

Flowers: June-September.

Site and soil: Any fertile well-drained garden soil in sun or partial shade.

Propagation: Sow seeds in April in boxes in a cold frame or cool greenhouse. Germination 14-28 days. Prick out, harden off, and plant out in a nursery bed 6″/15cm apart. Plant where they are to flower in October at 18-24″/45-60cm apart. *Or*, sow seeds in seedbed April-May at ½″/12mm depth. Thin to 6″/15cm apart. Plant where they are to flower in September-October, 18-24″/45-60cm apart. *Or*, divide clumps in autumn or spring.

Care and cultivation: Stake on exposed sites. Dead head.

Pests and diseases: Powdery mildew, Rust.

CERASTIUM
Snow-in-Summer   *Europe*

Origins and history: Used in cottage gardens since the seventeenth century.

Description: HP Grey leaves forming a thick carpet with star-shaped white flowers. Very invasive, but a good thick cover for rough places and borders. Use it with care in rockeries; it can easily choke everything else. Height up to 6″/15cm.

Flowers: May-July.

Site and soil: Any well-drained, preferably gritty, garden soil in a sunny position.

Propagation: Sow seeds March-May at ¼″/6mm depth where they are to flower. Germination 10-14 days. Thin to 24″/60cm apart. *Or*, divide clumps in March and replant immediately.

Care and cultivation: Dead head. Keep spread under control.

CHRYSANTHEMUM
CHRYSANTHEMUM MAXIMUM
Moon Daisy, Shasta Daisy   *Pyrenees*

Origins and history: Name is from the Greek 'chrysos'—gold and 'anthemum'—flower. Chrysanthemums have largely ousted the old cottage garden marguerite—*C. leucanthemum*—the native daisy. *C. maximum* is the Moon Daisy of the Pyrenees.

Description: Large white flowers with a yellow eye and dark green toothed leaves. Popular in herbaceous borders. Height 24-36″/60-90cm.

Flowers: June-August.

Site and soil: Well-drained fertile soil in a sunny position. Add lime to the soil if it is too acid.

Propagation: Sow seeds April-July in a seedbed at ¼"/6mm depth. Germination 10-14 days. Thin out seedlings to 6"/15cm apart. Plant out in October 18"/45cm apart. Or, divide clumps every 3 years in spring. Or, plant 2-3"/50-75mm cuttings in a cold frame in March.

Care and cultivation: Dead head. Stake. Cut back to ground level in autumn.

FLORISTS' CHRYSANTHEMUMS
E Asia

Origins and history: All florists' chrysanthemums are derived from 2 species which originated in China and Japan—*C. indicum* and *C. morifolium*. Were grown as garden flowers 2,500 years ago, but the creation of so many new varieties is a twentieth-century Western phenomenon.

Description: A large many-petalled flower, which can be a spectrum of colours from white and yellow to red and gold, with deep green oval leaves cleft into rounded lobes. There are now over 200 species and innumerable varieties, with a complex system of classification. The specialist varieties are grown annually from cuttings to flower in the autumn. They can be grown by the amateur, but be aware that you are paddling at the edge of an ocean of expert knowledge! The numerous cultivated varieties come under 7 main groups, based upon the type of flower:
Incurved: In a globe.
Reflexed: Petals falling outwards, open.
Intermediate: Between the incurved and reflexed forms.
Single: Only a few rows of petals around the central eye.
Anemone-centred: Differs only slightly from single.
Pompons: Small globular blooms.
Other types.

Site and soil: Well-drained soil with plenty of organic material.

Propagation: Sow seeds January-February at 70-75°F/21-24°C. Germination 7-28 days. Prick out, harden off, and plant out in autumn 12-18"/30-45cm apart. Or, take basal cuttings from crowns in March, 2-2½"/50-60mm long. Insert in cutting compost 1"/25mm deep and 2"/50mm apart. Water thoroughly once, and keep at 50-60°F/10-16°C. Transfer to 3"/75mm pots. Plant out late April or early May in moist soil. Plant shallowly

12-18"/30-45cm apart. Water well after planting, then not for several days afterwards. You can use the divided crowns of some varieties again, but cuttings give more compact plants and better flowers.

Care and cultivation: Prepare the ground in spring with compost. Insert stakes when planting. Water regularly. Pinch out growing tips at 6"/15cm to produce flowering stems. Feed liquid manure every week until

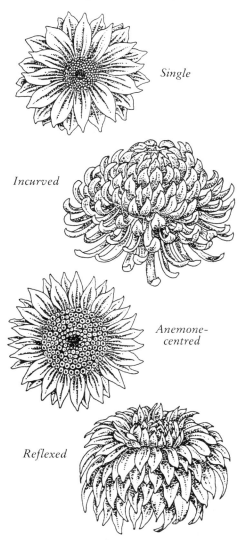

Single

Incurved

Anemone-centred

Reflexed

the buds show colour in early August. If you want large blooms leave only 1 bud on each stem at the end of July. In southern Britain the plants can overwinter outside. If leaving them outside, leave the stems over winter and cut back to 6"/15cm in spring. *Or*, lift the crowns and store them in a greenhouse. Water them into potting compost and water them again in spring when new shoots begin to appear.

Pests and diseases: Leaf Miner, Chrysanthemum Eelworm (see 'Eelworm'). Susceptible to many specific diseases because they are so highly bred, especially when many are grown together.

DAHLIA
See under 'Bulbs'.

DELPHINIUM
Europe

Origins and history: The name comes from the Greek 'delphin', a dolphin, from the shape of the flower buds. The first perennial delphinium was brought from Russia in the seventeenth century, and used as a cure for lice. Present garden species from late nineteenth century hybrids.

Description: HP Spikes of flowers up to 12"/30cm long in purple, blue, pink, red, yellow or white, on stems up to 8'/2.5m high. Mid-green deeply-dissected leaves. Popular at the back of borders. Height 18"-8'/45cm-2.5m depending on variety.

Flowers: June-August.

Site and soil: Deep rich well-drained soil in a sheltered sunny position. Enrich with compost or well-rotted manure. Dislikes too much acid.

Propagation: The seeds are short-lived— sow as soon as possible. *Or*, sow seeds May-July in seedbed at 1/4"/6mm depth, preferably in a shady position. Germination 14-21 days. Thin out seedlings to 12"/30cm apart, removing any flower spikes. Plant out in autumn 18-24"/45-60cm apart. *Or*, take basal cuttings 3-4"/75-100mm long in April. Insert in cutting compost in a cold frame. Plant out rooted cuttings in rows and transplant to flowering site in September. *Or*, divide and replant March-April.

Care and cultivation: Dig in manure or compost before planting. When dividing, compost deteriorated plants—delphiniums don't last for ever. Stake plants in April and keep tying as the stems grow. Remove some side buds from the longer shoots. Cut back flowerheads after flowering for a second flowering. Cut stems back to ground level in October-November. Mulch with compost during the summer. Water in dry weather. Protect the crowns in winter.

Pests and diseases: Slugs and Snails; Powdery Mildew.

DIANTHUS
Border Carnations, Pinks   *Europe*

Origins and history: Known since ancient Greece, the name is from the Greek 'dios'— god and 'anthos'—flower. Used by Greeks to crown heroes. 'Carnation' is corruption of 'coronation'. A traditional cottage garden flower since Elizabethan times. Like wallflowers, often called 'gillyflowers' because of their sweet scent. Maiden Pinks (*D. deltoides*) are sometimes naturalized in Britain. *D. armeria* used to be a common wild plant in south-east Britain, but is now rare. Cheddar Pink found wild and in cottage gardens in the West Country. Wild pinks and carnations are probably early introductions from France. The early nineteenth century was the peak of pink breeding, when there were 192 varieties.

Description: P Mat forming greyish leaves and single or double flowers, often patterned, in pinks, whites and reds. There is a great variety, and they can be used in many places in the garden. There are old-fashioned and modern pinks:
Old-Fashioned Pinks: From *D. plumarius*. Include old favourites and modern hybrids. They need renewing every 4-5 years, and are slow-growing. They have single flowers and a short flowering season. Height 9-15"/22-37cm (illustration under 'Annuals').
Modern Pinks: From *D.* x *allwoodii*. Crosses between old-fashioned pinks and perpetual-flowering carnations. Faster-growing with many more double flowers than old-fashioned pinks, and will usually flower again in September-October. Must be renewed every 3-4 years. Height 10-15"/25-37cm.
Border Carnations: Come from species native to southern France. Often scented. Best in groups, preferably in a raised bed in full sun. 'Cottage Carnations' are small border carnations. Flower in July-August. Height 24-36"/60-90cm.

Rockery Pinks: Come from the British *D. deltoides*—Maiden Pink, another cottage garden favourite, crossed with other species from the Alps. They have red, pink or white sweet-smelling flowers and mid-deep green leaves. Height 6"/15cm; flowers June-October. *D. alpinus* has larger flowers.

Dianthus varieties are classified by patterning of petals:

Selfs: One colour only.

Bi-colours: Mainly single colours but with a blotch of contrasting shade at base of petals.

Laced: Blotch at base plus petals edged with band of contrasting shade.

Fancies: Irregularly patterned.

Flowers: Old-Fashioned Pinks in June, Modern Pinks June-October.

Site and soil: Well drained preferably limey soil in full sun.

Propagation:

Pinks: Sow seeds March-April at 60-65°F/16-19°C at ¼"/6mm depth. Germination 7-14 days. Prick out and harden off. Transfer to flowering positions end May, 9-12"/22-30cm apart. *Or,* sow seeds April-July in cold greenhouse. Prick out and harden off. Plant when well-developed. *Or,* layer side shoots between June and August. *Or,* (the usual method) take heeled cuttings in August or in spring. Cut with a razorblade just below a node. Trim off lower leaves to 2 or 3 nodes.

Border Carnations: Sow seeds January-March at 60-65°F/16-19°C at ¼"/6mm depth. Prick out and harden off. Transplant to flowering positions April-May. Plant shallowly but very firmly, 12"/30cm apart. *Or,* layer non-flowering shoots July-August. Can transplant new plants in October.

Care and cultivation: Dead head. Stake carnations and remove side buds.

Pests and diseases: Numerous, as highly cultivated. Aphid, Carnation Fly; Leaf Rot and Spot, Mildew.

ECHINOPS RITRO

Globe Thistle   *S & E Europe, Asia*

Origins and history: Name from the Greek 'echinos'—hedgehog. Used to be cultivated as a crop in Spain: thistleheads used for tinder. Other varieties introduced later for ornamental purposes.

Description: HP Spiky spherical flowerheads resemble a rolled-up hedgehog,

covered with small blue flowers, followed by blue, silver, grey or brown seedheads. Grey-green thistle-like leaves can cause rashes when handled. Good for cutting. Flowers can be dried for winter. Height 36-48"/90-120cm.

Flowers: July-August.

Site and soil: Any well-drained garden soil in sunny position.

Propagation: Sow seeds in nursery bed April-June at ½"/12mm depth. Germination 14-28 days. Thin to 12"/30cm apart. Plant where they are to flower in autumn 24"/60cm apart. *Or,* divide plants between October and March.

Care and cultivation: Cut back stems in October. No staking required.

EUPHORBIA

Spurge   *Europe, Asia*

Origins and history: Named after Euphorbius, physician to King Juba of Mauritania. Several HP species are British natives. Cultivated as cottage garden flowers for centuries.

Description: Small insignificant yellow or green flowerheads, but often surrounded

by conspicuous bracts which look like petals, and decorative foliage. The stems contain a white milky sap which is highly irritating to sensitive skin or cuts. Good border plant. Height 12-48"/30-120cm.

Flowers: Varies—between June and September.

Site and soil: Any reasonable well-drained garden soil—will grow in sun or partial shade.

Propagation: Sow seeds in March at ¼"/6mm depth in boxes in a cold frame or cool greenhouse. Prick out, harden off, and plant out in a nursery bed 4"/100mm apart. Transplant to final position in October, 12-18"/30-45cm apart. Or, take 3"/75mm basal cuttings and insert in cutting compost in a cold frame April-May. Plant out when cuttings are well-rooted. Or, divide between September and April.

Care and cultivation: Cut faded flower stems to ground level to keep from becoming straggly.

Pests and diseases: Botrytis.

GAILLARDIA
Blanketflower   *N. America*

Origins and history: Named after M. Gaillard, a French patron of botany. Discovered by Lewis and Clark, and introduced by Douglas.

Description: HP Large red and yellow daisy-like flowers and grey-green leaves. Good for herbaceous borders because of its long flowering period. Useful for cutting. Height 18-30"/45-75cm.

Flowers: June-October.

Site and soil: Light well-drained soil in sunny position. Enrich soil with compost or well-rotted manure.

Propagation: Sow seeds June-July in nursery bed at ¼"/6mm depth. Germination 14-21 days. Thin to 4"/100mm apart. Plant where they are to flower in autumn, 18"/45cm apart. Or, divide clumps every 3 years.

Care and cultivation: Stake. Cut dead flowers back to base of stalk. In wet soil the plants may die in winter.

GERANIUM
Cranesbill   *Europe and Asia*

Origins and history: The name comes from the Greek 'geranos'—crane, because the seedpod resembles a crane's head and beak, hence also 'Cranesbill'. *Not* to be confused with pelargoniums. Some indigenous species, some brought from Europe.

Description: HP Free-flowering open flowers in shades of pink, purple, white or blue. Dense leaves in thick clumps—good ground cover. Varieties suitable for borders and rock gardens. Spreads rapidly. Height 18-30"/45-75cm.

Flowers: May-Sept. depending on variety.

Site and soil: Any well-drained garden soil in sun or partial shade.

Propagation: Sow seeds September-March in boxes in a cold frame at ¼"/6mm depth. Germination 14-21 days. Prick out and harden off. Plant out into nursery bed 4"/100mm apart and transplant in autumn to where they are to flower, 18"/45cm apart. Or, divide plants between September and March.

Care and cultivation: Tall varieties may need staking. Dead head. Cut back in autumn almost to ground level. May get second flowering.

GEUM

Geum   *Temperate zones*

Origins and history: Name from the Greek 'geno'—to taste good: refers to the aromatic roots of some species. *G. chiloense*, the usual garden species, collected in Chile by Alexander Cruikshank in 1820s.

Description: HP Bright saucer-shaped double or semi-double flowers in red, yellow and orange on wiry stems. Dense foliage forms thick clumps. Good ground cover. Height 12-24"/30-60cm; *G. montanum* (Alpine Geum) 9"/22cm.

Flowers: June-September.

Site and soil: Any well-drained garden soil in sun or partial shade. Likes soil enriched with leaf mould or peat.

Propagation: Sow seeds February-March or June-August in boxes in a cold frame or cool greenhouse at ¼"/6mm depth. Prick out and harden off. Plant in September where they are to flower 12-18"/30-45cm apart. *Or*, divide clumps in March or April every second year.

Care and cultivation: May need staking. Dead head. Cut back to ground level in autumn.

HELLEBORUS

Christmas Rose, Lent Lily
S Europe and W Asia

Origins and history: Name from the Greek 'helein'—to kill and 'bara'—food, because some species are poisonous. Various related native species. Lent Lily (*H. orientalis*) introduced from Mediterranean. Christmas Rose (*H. niger*) referred to in Ancient Greece, and was introduced into Britain long ago.

Description: HP Large 5-petalled saucer-shaped white, yellow, pink or purple flowers with a mass of golden anthers and smooth evergreen leaves which provide good ground cover. Good for cut flowers. *H. niger* very useful for winter show. Hardy and very long-lived. Height 18-24"/45-60cm.

Flowers: Christmas Rose: January-March; Lent Lily: February-April.

Site and soil: Deep well-drained moist soil in shady position. Add leaf mould or peat.

Propagation: Sow seeds June-July in boxes in a cold frame so they are exposed to frost. Should germinate in April, though can be longer. Transplant into nursery bed 9"/22cm apart. Will first flower at 2-3 years old.

Care and cultivation: Do not disturb once planted. Protect opening blooms with cloches. Water in dry weather.

HOSTA

Hosta   *China and Japan*

Origins and history: Discovered by Dr Franz von Siebold, one of the first explorers to obtain permission to visit Japan in the nineteenth century. He was eventually expelled from the country, taking *Hostas* home with him.

Description: HP Grown for its attractive large ribbed leaves, often variegated, and spikes of trumpet-like flowers, often scented. Foliage colour varies from yellow, through white and lilac, to nearly blue. Useful for shady borders and ground cover in woodland, and for planting by water. Height 15-36"/37-90cm.

Flowers: July-September.

Site and soil: Any reasonable moist soil, preferably in partial shade. Enrich soil with leaf mould, peat, or well-rotted compost.

Propagation: Divide plants in March.

Care and cultivation: Dead head.

KNIPHOFIA

Red Hot Poker   *S. Africa*

Origins and history: Named after Kniphof, a German professor of medicine. Brought to Europe from the Cape in 1707. Kept as greenhouse plant, and not planted outside until 1848 at Kew.

Description: HP Red, yellow or white torch-like flowers with open ends of flowerets pointing downwards, on erect stems with spiky grass-like leaves. Good for seaside gardens as they prefer the milder climate. Height 30-60"/75-150cm.

Flowers: June-August.

Site and soil: Any well-drained garden soil in full sun.

Propagation: Sow seeds in seedbed in April ½"/12mm deep. Thin to 6"/15cm apart. Plant out in final positions the following April. Or, divide clumps in spring.

Care and cultivation: Can leave undisturbed for years. May need winter protection in colder districts. Dead head.

Pests and diseases: Thrips.

LUPINUS

Lupin   *W North America*

Origins and history: The name is from the Latin 'lupus'—wolf; it was thought that the plants ravaged the soil by their invasiveness. Cultivated species come from North America, though some Mediterranean species have been used since Roman times for green manuring. The roots contain valuable nitrates. First American species brought back in 1637 by John Tradescant younger. Ancestor of most garden lupins is *L. polyphyllus*, brought from British Columbia by Douglas in 1826. In the 1930s the modern strain of Russell hybrids was developed, which was the start of garden lupins as we know them.

Description: HP Large pea-like flowers growing in long spikes in numerous shades—can be bi-coloured. Mid-green digitate leaves create a bushy plant. Very easy to grow, and spreads rapidly. Height 36-48"/90-120cm.

Flowers: May-October.

Site and soil: Any well-drained neutral or acid soil in sun or partial shade. Dislikes alkali. Lasts longer on a light soil, though will do well on a heavy soil for a shorter time. Likes bone meal but not manure.

Propagation: Seeds rarely breed true. Sow seeds April-June in boxes in a cold frame or cool greenhouse ¼"/6mm deep. Germination 21-28 days. Prick out and harden off. Plant in a nursery bed 6"/15cm apart. Transplant to flowering site in October, 24"/60cm apart. Or, take 3-4"/75-100mm long cuttings in April with a small piece of rootstock attached, and insert in sandy soil in a cold frame. Plant out in October. Lupins will self-seed freely, but may revert to blue.

Care and cultivation: Stake when necessary. Dead head to obtain second flowering and prevent seeding. Cut back to ground level in November.

Pests and diseases: Powdery mildew.

MECONOPSIS

Himalayan Poppy, Welsh Poppy
M. betonicifolia—Tibet
M. cambrica—Europe

Origins and history: Despite its common name, *Meconopsis* is *not* a poppy: *Papaver* is the true poppy. The name is from the Greek 'mekon'—poppy, and 'opsis'—like. Welsh Poppy is a traditional cottage garden flower, and the only species in the family to be found outside Asia—native to Wales and the West Country, though has spread throughout Britain. *M. betonicifolia* was brought from Tibet by Kingdon Ward in the 1930s.

Description: HP Numerous species, but only 2 are the originators of garden varieties. Himalayan poppy has brilliant blue flowers (occasionally purple) with oblong mid-green leaves. Many plants die off after only one flowering, but if the first year buds are picked off it will flower for 2 or 3 years. Height 24-48"/60-120cm. Welsh poppy has bright yellow or orange flowers and hairy mid-green leaves; it seeds freely and spreads rapidly, and is good for awkward places, stone walls and rocks. Varieties in many other colours. Height 12"/30cm.

Flowers: Himalayan Poppy: June-July; Welsh Poppy: June-September.

Site and soil: Welsh Poppy will grow anywhere; Himalayan Poppy needs a lime-free well-drained soil in partial shade.

Propagation:
Himalayan Poppy: Sow seeds September at ¼"/6mm depth, and leave outside in pots of seed compost until February, then bring them indoors. Germination 28 days onwards. Prick out and harden off. Plant in nursery beds 4"/100mm apart and grow on till autumn, then plant out where they are to flower at 12"/30cm apart.
Welsh Poppy: Sow seeds May-June in seedbed at ¼"/6mm depth. Thin out to 4"/10cm and plant where they are to flower in autumn at 12"/30cm apart. Self-seeds profusely.

Care and cultivation: May need staking. Dead head, especially Welsh Poppies, to prevent seeding. Cut back to ground level in autumn. Water Himalayan Poppy freely in summer, but needs dry soil in winter—in wet areas cover with cloches to keep dry.

MONARDA

Bergamot, Oswego Tea, Bee Balm, Horse Mint
North America

Origins and history: Named after the sixteenth century botanist Monardes. *M. didyma* sent to Britain by John Bartram in 1744 from Oswego on Lake Ontario, where it was used as a tea by the native Americans, hence 'Oswego Tea'. Cultivated since then as a cottage garden plant and herb. Favourite with bees and butterflies.

Description: HP Profuse spiky flowers clustered in whorls, originally scarlet, but now also in rose pink, white and purple. Hairy mint-like leaves. Both leaves and flowers are strongly aromatic, and the leaves can be dried for tea. Height 24-36"/60-90cm.

Flowers: June-September.

Site and soil: Moist soil in sun or partial shade. Mulch with compost or well-rotted manure in spring, plus bonemeal.

Propagation: Sow seeds in March at 60°F/16°C at ¼"/6mm depth. Prick out, harden off, and plant out in nursery rows at 9"/22cm apart. Plant where they are to flower in October at 15"/37cm apart. *Or*, divide roots in March and plant out 2"/50mm wide tufts from the outside of the clump and compost the centre. Division necessary every 2 years. Can become invasive.

Care and cultivation: Dead head and cut back in autumn to ground level. To dry the leaves, gather before the flower opens and dry as quickly as possible

NEPETA FAASSENII

Catmint   *Europe, Asia*

Origins and history: Garden catmints are hybrids from *N. mussinii,* brought from the Caucasus by a former Russian ambassador in 1803. *Nepeta* is its early Latin name. Called 'Catmint' because cats love it, and will roll in it luxuriously. Grown for its aromatic leaves and for its medicinal properties.

Description: HP Blue-grey leaves and spikes of lavender-blue flowers. Very aromatic. Good for borders. Very easy to grow and popular. Height 12-18"/30-45cm.

Flowers: May-September.

Site and soil: Any well-drained garden soil, preferably in full sun. Dislikes heavy or waterlogged soil.

Propagation: Sow seeds May-June at ¼"/6mm depth in seed bed. Germination 14-28 days. Thin to 6"/15cm apart and grow on until autumn. Plant out where they are to flower September or October at 12"/30cm apart; will flower the following year. *Or*, divide and replant March-April. *Or*, in April take 2-3"/50-75mm basal cuttings and insert in cutting compost in a cold frame. Pot on and harden off. Plant where they are to flower the following March or April.

Care and cultivation: Dead head. Do not cut back until the new shoots start to appear in spring. Will need dividing every 3 years.

OENOTHERA

Evening Primrose   *Europe, N America*

Origins and history: The name comes from the Greek 'oinos'—wine, and 'thera' —imbibing, since the roots were thought to induce a thirst for wine. Now widely naturalized in many parts of the world. Some native species; modern garden varieties from European and N. American species.

Description: HP Red buds open into scented golden flowers up to 3"/75mm wide which open in the evening and last several days. Spiky mid-green leaves. Height 1-2'/30-60cm.

Flowers: June-September.

Site and soil: Any well-drained garden soil in an open sunny position, preferably in full sun. Mulch with compost or well-rotted manure in spring.

Propagation: Sow seeds ⅛"/3mm deep in boxes in a cold frame or cool greenhouse in April. Prick out and harden off. Plant out

in a nursery bed 6"/15cm apart. Transplant to permanent positions in October, 12-18"/30-45cm apart. *Or*, divide clumps in March or April.

Care and cultivation: Water in dry weather. Cut back to ground level October-November.

PAEONIA

Peony   *Europe and Asia.*

Origins and history: The name comes from Paeon, a Greek physician, who is said to have first used the peony medicinally. Double varieties were developed from the single-flowered wild species. Naturalized since the Middle Ages, when it was introduced to Britain. Improved Dutch varieties were introduced to British gardens in the sixteeth century. Focus of much folklore because the phosphorescent seeds shine in the dark. Used medicinally.

Description: HP Huge double blooms up to 7"/17cm across, several on each stem, make peonies among the most dramatic shows in the flower border. Can be single, semi-double, double, even globular, in a large range of colours. Very good for cutting. Attractive leaves divided into leaflets of varying size and shape in different shades of green, sometimes tinted with bronze. Best grown apart from the herbaceous border, though it can be used there. Herbaceous peonies should be distinguished from tree peonies. *P. officinalis* grows wild in Europe and is a traditional cottage garden flower. Originally red, now varieties in different colours. Several species used to cultivate numerous varieties. This is another specialized field, but there are rewards for the amateur who follows the simple basic rules. Height 24-36"/60-90cm.

Flowers: Between April and July, depending on variety.

Site and soil: Any moist well-drained garden soil in open ground, in sun or partial shade. Choose a site out of early morning sun, as the young growth may be damaged by late frosts. Dig in well-rotted manure or compost at least 1 spit deep before planting. Add bonemeal.

Propagation: Seeds may not breed true. Sow seeds in September ¼"/6mm deep in boxes in a cold frame or cool greenhouse; may not germinate until next spring. Prick out, harden off, and plant out in nursery bed the next May, 9"/22cm apart. Grow on in nursery rows 3-4 years. Plant in final positions October or March.

Care and cultivation: Leave peonies undisturbed. Take 3 years to establish, and may live untouched for 50 years. Hate to be moved or divided. Water in dry weather. Will need staking. Dead head and cut back foliage in October.

Pests and diseases: Honey fungus, Peony wilt, Botrytis.

PAPAVER ORIENTALE

Oriental Poppy   *Asia Minor*

Origins and history: Many garden hybrids used in Britain since the nineteenth century.

Description: Flowers up to 6"/15cm across consisting of 4 scarlet petals with black bases and prominent black anthers. Coarse hairy deep-cut leaves. Garden varieties are double or single, pink, white or orange, as well as varying shades of original red. Height 24-36"/60-90cm.

Flowers: May-June.

Site and soil: Any well-drained garden soil, preferably in full sun. Dislikes too heavy soil.

Propagation: Sow seeds thinly June-August at ¼"/6mm depth in seedbed. Germination 10-14 days. Thin out seedlings to 6"/15cm apart. Plant where they are to flower between October and April at 20-24"/50-60cm apart. *Or,* take root cuttings and insert in a cold frame over winter.

Care and cultivation: Stake. Dead head. Cut back to ground level in October.

Pests and diseases: Downy mildew.

PHLOX

Phlox   *N America*

Origins and history: The name comes from the Greek 'phlox'—a flame. Introduced to Britain in the seventeenth century by Bartram, who sent back several species, including rockery species. Phlox has been established as a cottage garden flower ever since.

Description: Dense clusters of white, pink, purple or red flowers, which bloom prolifically. Narrow leaves, some evergreen varieties. Useful for beds and borders for late summer flowering. Height 12-48"/30-120cm. *P. subulata* most common rockery species: good for covering rocks and walls, with its dense flat masses of flowers in white, pink, blue, red and mauve, and moss-like leaves (height 3"/75mm; flowers April-May; many named varieties).

Flowers: May-September.

Site and soil: Any moist well-drained garden soil in sun or partial shade. Mulch annually with compost or well-rotted manure. The rockery species does best in full sun.

Propagation: Seeds may not breed true. Sow seeds in boxes in cold frame or cool greenhouse March-April at ¼"/6mm depth. Prick out and harden off. Plant in nursery bed at 6"/15cm apart. Plant out in autumn of following year where they are to flower, 18-24"/45-60cm apart. *Or,* divide in October or March. Compost the woody parts and replant side sections. *Or,* take stem cuttings 3"/75mm long from base of plant and insert in cutting compost in a cold frame in March. *Or,* take root cuttings February-March. Plant out rooted cuttings in nursery rows when at least 2-3"/50-75mm high. Plant where they are to flower at 18 months old.

Care and cultivation: Water in dry weather. Thin out weaker shoots on older plants. Dead head. Staking necessary. Cut back in October to just above ground level.

Pests and diseases: Eelworm, slugs; powdery mildew.

PHYSALIS

Chinese Lantern   *Japan, China*

Origins and history: The name comes from the Greek 'physa'—bladder, from the inflated calyx which also inspires the name 'Chinese Lantern'. Already a widespread cottage garden plant in the fifteenth century. Seeds used as medicine for gout.

Description: HP Flowers small and white, followed by bright orange papery calyces which can be dried for indoor decoration. Height 12-26"/30-65cm.

Flowers: July-August; seeds (lanterns) September-October.

Site and soil: Any well-drained garden soil in sun or shade.

Propagation: Sow seeds April-July in boxes in cold frame or cool greenhouse. Germination 14-21 days. Prick out and harden off. Plant out September-October at 18-24"/45-60cm apart. Can successfully grow named varieties true to type from seed. *Or*, divide plants March-April. Plant separate pieces immediately.

Care and cultivation: This is an invasive plant—cut away runners with a spade in the autumn and dig them out. To dry seed pods, cut stems when calyces begin to colour, hang stems upside down in a light, cool, airy shed. Pick off withered leaves when dry.

POLEMONIUM

Jacob's Ladder   *N. Hemisphere*

Origins and history: Native plant from the Pennines used in gardens since the sixteenth century. Now rare in the wild.

Description: HP Bright blue (or sometimes white) spikes or clusters of flowers, ornamental leaves divided into rung-like leaflets—hence 'Jacob's Ladder'. *P. caeruleum* is the traditional cottage garden plant. *P. foliosissimum* (from Rocky Mountains in USA) has a longer flowering period (June-September)—2 hybrids from this. Height 12-36"/30-90cm.

Flowers: April-August.

Site and soil: Any well-drained garden soil in sun or partial shade. Add compost as fibrous roots quickly exhaust the soil.

Propagation: Divide between October and March.

Care and cultivation: Cut back flower stems after flowering.

PRIMULA

Primrose, Cowslip, Auricula, Polyanthus, Primula
Temperate zones

Origins and history: 'Primrose' corruption of 'prima vera', the first flower of spring. The primrose (*P. vulgaris*) is a native, and a traditional cottage garden plant. The cowslip (*P. veris*), another native, is becoming rare in the wild. There are also native mountain primulas, like *P. scotica*, but they do not survive away from their native habitat. Wild primulas are very susceptible to pollution and the increased use of herbicides. Bred varieties were already common by the sixteenth century; double primroses existed in 1500. Polyanthus hybrids between primroses and cowslips have become extremely popular; they were originally known as False Oxslips, to distinguish them from wild oxslips. The first description of a true polyanthus comes from 1665, a plant derived from the False Oxslip. In the eighteenth century there was much breeding of primulas, including new species from abroad such as the Alpine primulas. Alpine primulas were a florists' speciality by 1860, and several hundred species were bred. Auriculas also come from the Alps, and became another florists' favourite, especially the bi-coloured varieties.

Description: HP The flowers are usually primrose-like, though sometimes bell-shaped. Very useful for small beds and borders, edgings and odd corners. All varieties described here are suitable for permanent life outdoors, though there are also half-hardy and greenhouse varieties. This is another area with scope for the specialist, yet much pleasure and reward for the amateur. For heights and flowering times see under each species. There are over 500 species of primula, many in cultivation. Some are suitable for rock gardens or bog gardens, others for ordinary beds and borders. The commonest types are:
Native Primrose, *P. vulgaris*, with varieties now available in orange, white, blue and

pink. Height 6"/15cm. Flowers March-April.

Native Cowslip, *P. veris*. Height 6"/15cm. Flowers March-April.

Polyanthus hybrids are extremely popular —the Pacific strain produces heads of bright-coloured flowers in blue, yellow, red, pink and white, all with yellow centres. The flowers are bigger and brighter than primroses. Height 12-18"/30-45cm; flower March-May.

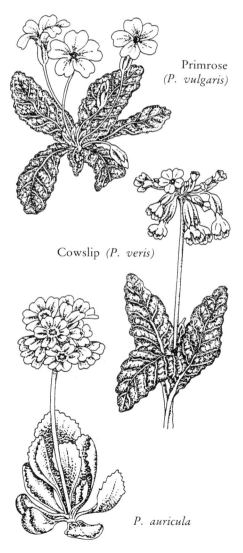

Primrose
(P. vulgaris)

Cowslip *(P. veris)*

P. auricula

P. aurantiaca (Candelabra) has dark red stems and yellow and orange flowers.

P. auricula, sometimes just called auriculas, are the traditional rock garden primulas, but there is no firm rule. Many kinds of primulas are suitable for rock gardens, and rock garden varieties are fine for edging and borders. Height 6"/15cm; flower March-May.

P. beesiana (Candelabra) has purple yellow-eyed flowers and rough-textured leaves. Height 24"/60cm; flowers June-July.

P. bulleyana (Candelabra) has light orange flowers and dark green leaves. Height 24-36"/60-90cm; flowers June-July.

P. denticulata (Drumstick Primula; China) is useful in bedding schemes and rock gardens, and for waterside planting. It has numerous small flowers in dense globular heads in pink, purple, white and red in varying shades. Height 12"/30cm; flowers March-May.

P. florindae (Giant Cowslip; China) has scented bell-shaped flowers in yellow, red or orange, on drooping stalks. Needs moist soil—good for bog gardens. Height 24-60"/60-150cm; flowers June-July.

P. helodoxa (China) has evergreen leaves and whorls of golden-yellow flowers. Height 24-36"/60-90cm; flowers June-July.

P. japonica (Candelabra Primula; Japan) is good for waterside planting. Whorls of short-lived flowers in various colours with pale green leaves. Height 18"/45cm; flowers March-July.

P. juliae, like the auriculas, is mainly for rock gardens. Creeping stems. Many hybrids. Height 3"/75mm; flowers March-May.

P. pulverenta (Candelabra) has white stems with whorls of crimson flowers. Several varieties. Height 24-36"/60-90cm; flowers June-July.

Site and soil: Most species will grow in any fertile moist garden soil, in sun or preferably in partial shade. Add peat, compost or well-rotted manure. Bog garden varieties like shade and damp soil. Rock garden varieties need good drainage and an open situation.

Propagation: Sow seeds when ripe (May-September) or straight after buying, in boxes in a cold frame or cool greenhouse, barely covering them. Germination 21-42 days—until then cover boxes with glass or polythene to keep moisture in. After germination keep compost moist and out of sun. Prick out and harden off. Plant out in nursery rows and plant in permanent positions in September or April. Planting distances: *aurantiaca* 9"/22cm; *beesiana* 9-12"/22-30cm; *bulleyana* 9-12"/22-30cm; *denticulata* 9"/22cm; *florindae* 9"/22cm; *helodoxa* 9"/22cm; *japonica* 9-12"/22-30cm; *pulverulenta* 9-12"/22-30cm; *veris* 9"/22cm; *vulgaris* 9"/22cm. *Or*, divide after flowering and plant immediately in new positions.

Care and cultivation: Keep moist. A peat mulch in spring will help to conserve moisture in summer. Dead head. Divide when crowded.

Pests and diseases: Caterpillars, Botrytis, Rust.

PULSATILLA

Pasque Flower   *Europe*

Origins and history: Called Pasque Flower because it flowers at Easter, and has always been symbolic of rebirth. Native of chalk soils of Britain, cultivated in cottage gardens since the sixteenth century.

Description: HP Often used as rock garden plant. Bell-like flowers open fully into pale purple, pink, yellow, red or white stars, followed by silky seedheads. Foliage

hairy and fernlike. Height 6-12"/15-30cm.

Flowers: April-July.

Site and soil: Any well-drained garden soil in open sunny position.

Propagation: Sow seeds in boxes in a cold frame or cool greenhouse in July. Prick out and pot on. Overwinter in frame. Water freely and plant out in September following year of sowing.

Care and cultivation: Protect buds from excessive damp with cloches.

PYRETHRUM

Caucasus

Origins and history: The name comes from the Greek 'pyr'—fire, probably because of its use in reducing fever. Important genus for organic gardeners, because the flowerheads can be ground into a powder which makes an effective insecticide not harmful to other animals. For this reason it is grown as a field crop in Africa and South America. Hybrids from *P. roseum* are garden varieties.

Description: HP Large daisy-like flowers, single, double or semi-double, in pinks, reds and white, with prominent yellow centres. Bright green feathery foliage. Good for herbaceous borders and for cutting. Height 24-36"/60-90cm.

Flowers: May-July.

Site and soil: Light well-drained soil in a sunny position.

Propagation: Sow seeds June-July at ¼"/6mm depth at 60-65°F/16-19°C. Germination 10-21 days. Prick out and harden off. Plant out where they are to flower in autumn at 16-18"/40-45cm apart. *Or*, divide every 3 to 4 years, in March or July. Compost woody root portions.

Care and cultivation: Stake early in May. Water freely. Cut back all stems as soon as flowering is over. May get second flowering early autumn.

RANUNCULUS

Buttercup, Batchelor's Buttons, Fair Maids of France
Temperate regions

Origins and history: A large and confusing family, including native buttercups and celandines. Garden varieties mostly foreign species. Fair Maids of France (*R. asiaticus*) introduced in sixteenth century to become familiar cottage garden flower. In the seventeenth and eighteenth centuries many new cultivated varieties were created by Dutch breeders. Became florists' flower; in 1792 there were 800 varieties, nearly all now lost.

Description: HP Profuse small yellow, red or white double, semi-double or single flowers with mid-green toothed leaves. Bushy habit. Good border plant and good for cut flowers. 2 common garden species: *R. aconitifolius* with white flowers and *R. acris* with yellow flowers. Dwarf buttercups are available for rockeries. Height 3-36″/7-90cm.

Flowers: May-August, depending on variety.

Site and soil: Any moist well-drained garden soil in sun or partial shade.

Propagation: Sow seeds March-June in boxes in a cold frame or cool greenhouse at ⅛″/3mm depth. Germination 21-42 days. Prick out and harden off. Plant out in a nursery bed 4″/10cm apart. Plant where they are to flower September or March at 18″/45cm apart. *Or*, divide in October or March.

Care and cultivation: Stake and dead head.

SAXIFRAGA

Saxifrage, London Pride
Mountainous temperate regions

Origins and history: The name comes from the Latin 'saxum'—stone, and 'frango' —to break. 'London Pride' is a name used for various garden species hybridized from Ireland and southern Europe. By the eighteenth century were a popular plant for edging borders.

Description: HP Star-shaped flowers in white, yellow, red and pink, on rosettes or mossy hummocks of leaves. Height varies from 2-12″/5-30cm. Most perennial species are evergreen. 3 main sections:
Euaizoonia (encrusted): Large silvery rosettes of leaves form carpet with large star-shaped flowers. Good for walls.
Dactyloides (mossy): Moss-like hummocks of deeply-divided leaves with clusters of star-shaped flowers.
Kabschia (cushion): Grey-green rosettes of leaves, but smaller and denser than Euaizoonia. Saucer-shaped flowers.
Some larger varieties from these groups are suitable for edgings and borders, e.g. *S. umbrosa*—London Pride. Most species are suited to rock gardens. Numerous varieties and many more hybrids. Choose carefully. Some are difficult to grow.

Site and soil: Must have well-drained soil; some like lime and plenty of grit. Needs some shade at midday in southern areas, but will tolerate full sun in the north.

Propagation: *S. cotyledon:* sow seeds March-July in boxes in a cold frame or cool greenhouse at 1″/25mm depth. Germination 21-42 days. Prick out and harden off. Plant out in nursery bed until autumn. Plant out September-October at 18″/45cm apart. Others: detach non-flowering rosettes in May or June and treat as cuttings. Insert in cutting compost and place in a cold frame. Soak pan after inserting, then water sparingly till April, after which water freely. In September pot individually, overwinter in a cold frame, and plant where they are to flower next September. *Or*, (all groups): divide after flowering and replant immediately.

Care and cultivation: Dead head.

Pests and diseases: Rust.

SCABIOSA

Scabious, Pincushion Flower
Europe, Caucasus

Origins and history: The name comes from the Latin 'scabies'—itch, for which the native species of this plant has been used as a cure for centuries. Pincushion Flowers (*S. atropurpurea*) came from Italy in 1591, where they are a wild species.

Description: HP Blue, white or purple 'pincushion'-like flowers. Good for beds and borders, and useful because of their long flowering time. Good for cutting and dried seedheads. Height 18-36″/45-90cm.

Flowers: June-October.

Site and soil: Any well-drained garden soil on open sunny site. Prefers chalk soil.

Propagation: Sow seeds February-March at 60-68°F/16-20°C at ¼″/6mm depth. Germination 14-21 days. Prick out and harden off. Grow on in nursery bed. Plant where they are to flower September-March at 18″/45cm apart. *Or*, take 2″/50mm long basal cuttings in March or April. Insert in pots of peat/sand mix and place in a cold frame. Plant out rooted

cuttings in nursery rows and transfer to flowering site between September and March. *Or*, lift and divide every 3 or 4 years in March.

Care and cultivation: Stake tall varieties, especially in wet weather. Cut stems after flowering at first joint. Cut back to ground level in November.

Pests and diseases: Slugs and Snails; Powdery Mildew, Root Rot.

SEDUM

Stonecrop   *Worldwide*

Origins and history: Several native species; *S. acre* the most common. Other natives rare in the wild but widespread in gardens.

Description: HP Fleshy cactus-like leaves and starry flowers in yellow, pink or white. Grown for the colours and shapes of the leaves and its attractive flowers and seed-heads. Liked by butterflies and bees. Suitable for walls and rockeries. *S. acre* and *S. albinum* tend to become invasive: choose other species, several of which come from Asia.

Flowers: Summer to autumn (depends on variety).

Site and soil: Any well-drained soil in full sun. Most sedums are resistant to drought because of their fleshy leaves.

Propagation: Sow seeds in boxes in a cold frame or cool greenhouse in March or April. Prick out and harden off. Grow on in nursery bed. Plant out in October where they are to flower. *Or*, divide and replant between October and March. *Or*, take stem cuttings 2"/50mm long and insert in nursery bed. Sedums are very easy to propagate.

Care and cultivation: Pick off dead stems in spring after flowering.

Pests and diseases: Slugs, Mealybugs, Aphids.

SEMPERVIVUM

Houseleek   *Europe*

Origins and history: 'Sempervivum' is Latin for 'ever living'. May have naturalized early in Britain as cottage garden escape. Used to be grown on roofs and stone walls, and above cottage garden doorways, hence 'houseleek'. It was supposed to bring good luck to the house.

Description: HP Rosettes of evergreen succulent leaves with sprays of star-like white, yellow, pink, red or purple flowers on thick stems. Height ½-3"/12-75mm.

Flowers: June-September.

Site and soil: Any well-drained garden soil in full sun.

Propagation: Remove rooted offsets and replant in autumn or spring. *Or*, sow seeds in March in boxes in a cold frame or cool greenhouse. Prick out and harden off. Grow on in nursery bed. Plant out where they are to flower from September.

Pests and diseases: Birds sometimes uproot newly-planted rosettes; Rust.

SOLIDAGO

Golden Rod   *Europe, N. America*

Origins and history: N. American species have replaced native varieties in gardens. Wild species used to be cultivated as a medicinal herb in cottage gardens.

Description: Plumes of bright yellow clustered flowers and narrow leaves. Familiar in beds and borders and good for cutting. Original garden species have given way to hybrids, which tend to be easier and more compact. Varying shades of yellow.

Giant and dwarf varieties available. Height 12-72"/30-180cm.

Flowers: July-September.

Site and soil: Any well-drained garden soil in sun or partial shade.

Propagation: Divide and replant roots between October and March.

Care and cultivation: Stake taller varieties. Cut down flower stems October or November.

Pests and diseases: Powdery mildew.

STACHYS

Lambs' Ears, Lambs' Lugs, Lamb's Tongue, Big Betony
Europe, Asia

Origins and history: The name comes from the Greek 'stachus'—a pointed spike, from its pointed flowers. Some native species; cultivated varieties from Middle Eastern species. Traditional cottage garden flower..

Description: HP *S. lanata* grey-leaved ground cover used as a summer bedding plant for its foliage. The grey leaves are covered with silky hairs, giving it a woolly appearance. Whorls or spikes of small tubular purple flowers. A non-flowering variety called 'Silver Carpet' is used as a carpeting plant. Another species in this genus is *S. macrantha* (Big Betony), with tall whorls of pink or purple flowers and pale green leaves. Height 6-24"/15-60cm.

Flowers: May-September.

Site and soil: Any well-drained garden soil in sun or partial shade.

Propagation: Divide clumps in autumn or spring.

Care and cultivation: Very invasive—cut back when necessary. Cut back in November.

VERONICA

N Hemisphere

Origins and history: Both common naturalized species come from eastern Europe and the Middle East. The taller garden varieties are longstanding cottage garden flowers.

Description: HP Spikes or single bright blue, pink or white flowers on erect stems. Good for beds and borders. Rockery varieties also available—can become invasive.

Height 12-60"/30-150cm according to variety.

Flowers: June-August.

Site and soil: Any well-drained garden soil in sun or partial shade. Enrich with compost or well-rotted manure. Do not allow to become waterlogged in winter.

Propagation: Sow seeds May-July at 1/4"/6mm depth in seedbed. Germination 14-28 days. Thin out seedlings to 9"/22cm apart and grow on until autumn. Plant where they are to flower in September at 24"/60cm apart. *Or*, divide plants in March or April.

Care and cultivation: Stake on exposed sites. Cut to just above ground level in November.

Pests and diseases: Powdery mildew.

VIOLA

Violet   *Europe*

Origins and history: Native plants; 1 rare species, the Teesdale Violet, is a relict from before the Ice Age. Violets used to be candied and eaten as sweets. Several native species cultivated since Middle Ages. Became florists' flowers in the eighteenth century, with numerous varieties. Very popular in the nineteenth century. New

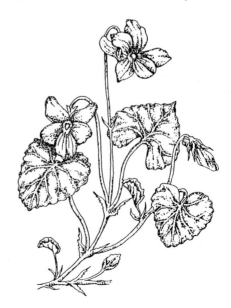

rust-resistant but scentless violets have recently been introduced.

Description: HP Usually sweetly-scented flowers in purple or white with mid-green leaves. Cottage garden flower. Good ground cover or edging. Good as carpeting under roses. *V. odorata* is the original of the florists' violets. Height 4-6″/10-15cm. All varieties are suitable for rockeries, but there are several special rockery violets: *V. aetolica* and *V. biflora* are both yellow, spring-flowering; height 2″/50mm. Also *V. gracilis*, height 4″/10cm, flowers April-June.

Flowers: February-September.

Site and soil: Any fertile, moist, well-drained soil, preferably in light shade.

Mulch in spring.

Propagation: Spreads by runners. Sow seeds September-November at ¼″/6mm depth in boxes and overwinter in a cold frame. Will germinate in spring. Prick out and harden off. Grow on in nursery bed until autumn. Plant where they are to flower in September at 12″/30cm apart (they will spread). *Or*, lift and divide in autumn. *Or*, take 1-2″/25-50mm basal cuttings in July and insert in cutting compost in a cold frame. Pot on when well-rooted, and plant out between September and March.

Care and cultivation: Water in dry weather. Dead head.

Pests and diseases: Pansy sickness, Rust.

Bulbs

ANEMONE
Windflower   *Europe*

Origins and history: *A. nemorosa* is our native wild plant. Crown anemone (*A. coronaria*, E Mediterranean) traditional cottage garden flower. Today's garden anemones come from French and Irish varieties descended from *A. coronaria*. with larger flowers in brighter colours.

Description: HP Windflowers suitable for naturalizing in open woodland and for rock gardens. Cup-shaped flowers which sometimes open right out, and deeply-cut mid-green leaves. *A. nemorosa* has white flowers, also varieties in pinks and blues. Height 6-8″/15-20cm; flowers March-April. *A. blanda* (from Greece) can be used similarly: blue, mauve, pink or white flowers. Height 6″/15cm; flowers February-April. *A. coronaria* varieties, De Caen and St Brigid, have brightly-coloured flowers in blue, red, pink, white and mauve. Height 6-12″/15-30cm. Florists' anemones poppy-like flowers with deeply-cut leaves.

Flowers: Wood anemones April-June. *A. coronaria* will flower most times of year depending when planted.

Site and soil: Rich well-drained soil in sun or partial shade. For *coronaria*, add leaf mould, peat or compost, also bonemeal and lime.

Propagation: *Coronaria*: plant 1-1½″/ 25-32mm deep, making sure they are right

A. blanda

way up (look for scar of last year's leaf stalk). Woodland anemones: separate offsets or divide rhizomes when growth has died down in summer.

Care and cultivation: In wet soils, lift *A. coronaria* in winter. Protect winter-flowering anemones with cloches from October onwards.

Pests and Diseases: Caterpillars, Cutworms, Aphids, Slugs.

BEGONIA
Tuberous Begonia
Tropics and sub-tropics

Origins and history: See under Begonia HHA. Introduced as British garden flower in the nineteenth century.

Description: Very diverse plants for different situations—pink and rose, scarlet and crimson, yellows and oranges. Used in summer bedding schemes. Tuberous begonias are all cultivated varieties, and can be traced back to 1860s. Vast choice—single and double flowers, large and small. Height 12-24"/30-60cm.

Flowers: June-October.

Site and soil: Moist soil in partial shade. Mulch to retain moisture. Dislikes lime.

Propagation: Practically every grower has different methods—here is one. Plant tubers indoors in April at 50-60°F/10-16°C in boxes of damp peat. Keep moist and shaded until 4-6 leaves have developed, and pot on in ¼ rich soil ¼ well-rotted manure and ½ peat, plus sprinkling of bonemeal at bottom of pot. Grow in shade at 60°F/16°C, and plant out after last frost. *Or*, plant out in June where they are to flower —will flower in August. *Or*, take stem cuttings. *Or*, divide tubers with a sharp knife—each piece must have an eye where the shoot will form.

Care and cultivation: Stake—large flowers on brittle stems. Keep moist—water soil, not plant. Lift in autumn, before first frost, dry off, and set tubers in boxes of peat. Store as bulbs.

Pests and diseases: Slugs, Eelworms, Weevils; Grey Mould, Powdery Mildew, Damping Off.

CHIONODOXA
Glory of the Snow   *Crete, Asia Minor*

Origins and history: Introduced to Britain in late nineteenth century.

Description: 6-petalled star-shaped pale blue, white or pink flowers with strap-like mid-green leaves. Good for naturalizing in grass and hedgerows, and for rock gardens and front of borders. Good in pots. Height 6"/15cm.

Flowers: February-April.

Site and soil: Well-drained garden soil in full sun.

Propagation: Plant 2-3"/50-75mm deep in large groups in autumn.

Care and cultivation: Lift and divide overcrowded bulbs when leaves begin to die back. Replant immediately.

Pests and diseases: Slugs. Smut.

COLCHICUM
Autumn Crocus   *Europe, Asia*

Origins and history: *Colchicum* is not related to *Crocus*, but to *Lilaceae*. Native species *C. autumnale*— meadow saffron from West Country, grown in gardens throughout Britain. Larger species *C. speciosum* introduced from eastern Europe in 1828.

Description: Cup-shaped flowers in pink or varying shades of purple, sometimes white, with glossy dark green leaves in spring. Height 3-8"/7-20cm depending upon species.

Flowers: September-November.

Site and soil: Rich well-drained garden soil in sun or partial shade.

Propagation: Plant 3-4"/75-100mm deep, either bought corms in August or September, or divided ones replanted as soon as leaves die back in July. Arrange in clumps. Separate offsets when lifting corms in June or July. Replant in flowering site or grow on for 1-2 years in nursery bed, then plant where they are to flower.

CONVALLARIA
Lily of the Valley
Europe, Asia, N America

Origins and history: Old cottage garden flower, called Wood Lily or Mugget. Used to be widespread in the wild, and used in arbours and shrubberies; now much rarer.

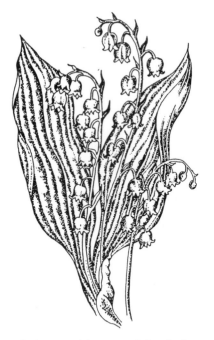

Description: White or pink single or double bell-like flowers in spikes on arching stems. Very sweet-scented, with pairs of mid-green leaves to each stem. Good ground cover; easily naturalized. Height 6-8"/15-20cm.

Flowers: April-May.

Site and soil: Any moist garden soil in shade, preferably partial. Add leaf mould or compost. Best under deciduous trees.

Propagation: Plant between October and March. Separate crowns and plant 3-4"/75-100 mm apart, with pointed end just below soil surface. Water in. Lift and divide rhizomes between October and March.

Care and cultivation: Water if necessary—must keep soil moist. Mulch soil annually with peat or compost when leaves die back.

Pests and diseases: Swift moth caterpillars. Grey mould.

CROCUS

Crocus   *Europe, Middle East*

Origins and history: Saffron crocus introduced by Romans, and reintroduced in the Middle Ages by the crusaders. Still grown commercially in Britain for saffron

in the eighteenth century. Other species introduced in later centuries. Nearly all autumn, winter and spring flowering species come from Spain and North Africa.

Description: Erect leaves, green with central white stripe, appear before flowers, which take form of long globular tube, borne singly on the stem. Open in sunshine. Good in beds and naturalized over large areas, or in rock gardens. Purple, blue, yellow, orange, white and bi-coloured. Garden varieties easier to grow than wild species. Very vigorous. 3 basic groups:
Winter flowering
Spring flowering: Dutch hybrids—very popular.
Autumn flowering
Height 3-4"/75-100mm.

Flowers: Autumn, winter or spring.

Site and soil: Rich well-drained soil in sun or light shade.

Propagation: Plant autumn flowering crocuses in July or August; winter and spring flowering varieties in August-September. Plant 2-3"/50-75mm deep and 2-4"/50-100mm apart. Lift and divide every 4th year.

Care and cultivation: Leaves die back inconspicuously, unlike daffodils. Leave until withered, and do not cut grass until they have died.

Pests and diseases: Mice, birds.

CYCLAMEN

Cyclamen   *Europe*

Origins and history: Name from the Greek 'cyclos'—circular, referring to the twisting of the flower stalk after fertilization, lowering the ripened seed to the ground. Cyclamens belong to *Primula* family. Came to Britain early; may have been 1 or 2 native species. Corms were once used medicinally in childbirth.

Description: Beautiful heart-shaped leaves on long stalks. Flowers with reflexed petals held above foliage. Good when naturalized under trees and shrubs; unlike most bulbs does well under conifers. Many sometimes sweet-scented flowers in pink, purple, red or white; foliage plain or variegated. There are many tender varieties as well. Height 3-6"/7-15cm.

Flowers: Late summer, autumn, winter or spring.

Site and soil: Well-drained, preferably

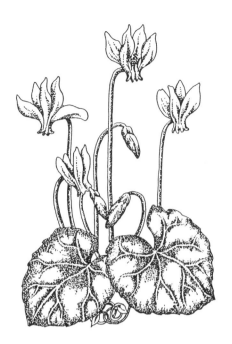

limey, soil. Enrich soil with leafmould and well-rotted manure. Partial shade. Shelter from wind.

Propagation: Autumn and winter flowering species planted July; spring flowering in October. Most species do not bloom in first season. Plant 2"/50mm deep and 2-3"/ 50-75mm apart. Plants cannot be divided.

Care and cultivation: Mulch with leafmould or well-rotted manure (not peat) after flowering.

DAHLIA

Border Dahlia   *Mexico*

Origins and history: Brought from Mexico to Spain and introduced into Britain by Lord Bute in 1789. The name commemorates the Swedish botanist Dahl, a pupil of Linnaeus. The tubers are edible, and it was first regarded as a vegetable rather than as a garden flower. In 1815 the first varieties with double flowers were bred in Belgium.

Description: HHP Useful in beds and borders to fill the late summer gap. A specialist flower easily grown by non-experts. Numerous varieties bred from 3 Mexican species—*D. pinnata*, *D. coccinea* and *D. rosea*. There are 2 main groups—

border dahlias grown from tubers and bedding dahlias grown as annuals from seeds. There are 8 groups of border dahlias:
Single flowered: 18-30"/45-75cm high.
Anenome flowered: 24-42"/60-105cm high, double, often bi-coloured.
Collarette: 30-48"/75-120cm high.
Peony flowered: 18-36"/45-90cm high.
Decorative: Many sizes of double bloom, 3-5'/90-150cm high.

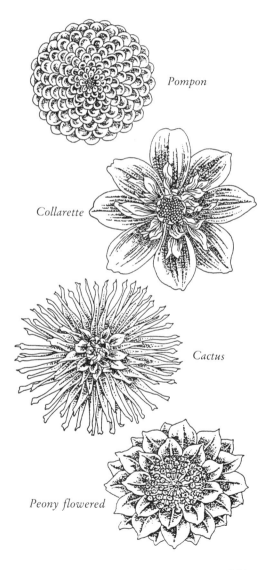

Pompon

Collarette

Cactus

Peony flowered

Ball: 36-48"/90-120cm high.
Pompon: 36-48"/90-120cm high.
Cactus and Semi-Cactus: Varying heights.
Many sizes and colours are available.

Flowers: August-October.

Site and soil: Well-drained, preferably
heavy, soil plus peat, compost or manure in
open sunny position. Dahlias are greedy,
and revel in rich ground. Ideally, give them a
bed on their own or put in large groupings.

Propagation: Plant unsprouted tubers in
May-June, 4"/100mm deep (2"/50mm
for dwarf varieties). *Or,* plant rooted
cuttings or sprouting tubers third week in
May if warm. Keep stored tubers moist,
and when the eyes on the crown start to
swell in March divide the tubers with a
sharp knife, making sure that each division
has an undamaged eye. Dust the cut parts
with flowers of sulphur and plant 4"/
100mm deep. *Or,* take cuttings of new
growths 3"/75mm long, cutting them off
the crown ¼"/6mm from the crown with
a sharp knife. Remove the lower leaves and
dip the base in hormone rooting powder.
Insert the cuttings round the edges of 3"/
75mm pots, 4 to a pot, in potting compost.
Keep moist at 60°F/16°C, out of full
sun. Pot on until ready to plant out.

Care and cultivation: Add peat or compost to soil, and rake in a handful of bone
meal at planting time. Insert a stake in each
hole *before* planting, and tie the stems to
the stakes at intervals as they grow. Pinch
out the leading shoots 3 or 4 weeks after
planting. If you want large blooms, disbud
all the side shoots instead. Dead head. After
the first frost cut the stems back to 6"/
15cm. Dig up the tubers with care, and
leave upside down for a week to dry. Store
in shallow boxes in damp peat, taking care
not to cover the crowns. Store in a cool
frost-free place.

Pests and diseases: Aphids, Caterpillars,
Earwigs; Botrytis.

ERANTHIS

Winter Aconite   *Europe, Asia Minor*

Origins and history: Name from the
Greek 'er'—spring, and 'anthos'—flower.
Not an indigenous flower, but introduced a
long time ago. Grown in gardens since the
sixteenth century.

Description: Golden buttercup-like
flowers set in rosette of finely-cut leaves
(not true leaves but bracts—true leaves

appear beside stalks when flowers open).
Good under deciduous shrubs and trees.
Very good naturalized and interplanted
with snowdrops (*Galanthus*). Spread
rapidly. Wild species (*E. hyemolis*) can
become invasive. Height 2-4"/50-
100mm.

Flowers: January-May, depending upon
species.

Site and soil: Gritty well-drained soil, but
needs to stay moist in summer. Shade or
partial shade is best (e.g. under deciduous
trees or shrubs)).

Propagation: Plant promptly in August-
September (don't like being out of the
ground). Plant 1"/25mm deep and 2-
3"/50-75mm apart in colonies. Often do
not bloom in first year. Can be difficult to
establish. Lift and divide every 4-6
years—replant at once.

GALANTHUS

Snowdrop   Europe

Origins and history: Name from the
Greek 'gala'—milk, and 'anthos'—flower.
Called Milkflower by Linnaeus. First
referred to as 'Snowdrop' by Gerard in
1633. Found in deciduous woodland all
over Europe; probably imported to Britain

from Italy in fifteenth century; naturalized rapidly.

Description: Familiar pearl-like buds pierce snow in winter and open out to bell-like single or double white flowers, each petal tipped with green. Very hardy—earliest flower in Britain in beds and borders. Excellent for naturalizing, especially with aconites and *Chionodoxa*. About 12 varieties in general cultivation. *G. nivalis* native snowdrop. Can be too invasive for beds, though excellent in woodland. Height 3-8"/7-20cm.

Flowers: January-April.

Site and soil: Cold, moist, preferably heavy soil, enriched with compost or well-rotted manure or leafmould. Deep-rooted, so needs well-cultivated soil. Sun or partial shade.

Propagation: Plant in September, 4"/100mm deep and 3"/75mm apart in small groups. May not bloom first year. Lift and divide every 3 to 4 years and replant 3 or 4 bulbs together immediately. Do not let bulbs dry out. Increase very rapidly.

GLADIOLUS

Sword Lily, Corn Flag
Europe, Asia, Africa

Origins and history: Name from the Latin 'gladiolus'—a sword. Native species now a protected wild flower. Used to be used medicinally. Garden varieties from South African species—first hybrids produced 1848.

Description: HHP Flowers on long spikes flowers all facing same way. Ribbed leaves have spiked point. Very useful plant for late summer and autumn, long-lasting, and in every conceivable shade. Good for cutting, beds, borders. Thousands of cultivated varieties, and new varieties constantly being introduced. Many systems of classification, by form, flower size and colour. Another specialists' flower, but ordinary gardener needs only to distinguish 4 groups:
(1) *Large-flowered* 36-48"/90-120cm.
(2) *Primulinus hybrid:* With hooded top petals on each flower. 18-36"/45-90cm.
(3) *Small-flowered.* 18-36"/45-90cm.
(4) *Butterfly hybrid.* Range of shades. 24-48"/60-120cm.
Height 18-48"/45-120cm depending on variety.

Flowers: June-September depending upon variety.

Site and soil: Any well-drained garden soil in sun or partial shade. Light sandy soil ideal. Work in bonemeal or compost while digging. Avoid windy sites.

Propagation: Species: Plant in late autumn. Hybrids: Plant corms after last frost. For extended flowering plant some at fortnightly intervals from mid-March to early June at 4"/100mm deep and 6-10"/15-20cm apart. Plant in groups.

Care and cultivation: Keep moist. Stake large-flowered varieties, especially in exposed positions. After flowering, lift when foliage turns brown. Cut off stem ½"/12mm above crown. Dry off and store until planting time. Cannot leave in ground over winter—not frost hardy.

Pests and diseases: Thrips; Core Rot, Gladiolus Scab, Dry Rot.

HYACINTHUS

Hyacinth   *Mediterranean*

Origins and history: Name from mythological youth Hyacinth, favourite of Apollo. Hyacinth craze in Europe when first brought from Asia Minor in sixteenth century. *H. orientalis* is wild originator, from Greece. Eighteenth century breeding by the Dutch metamorphosised flower into hyacinth we know today.

Description: Strap-like leaves and magnificent flowerheads carrying spikes of bell-shaped flowers on fleshy stems. Often sweetly scented. Good in beds, borders, tubs, pots and window boxes, especially close to the house because of the scent. Plant outside in groups. Flowers in blue, red, white, yellow, pink and mauve. Height 6-12"/15-30cm.

Flowers: April-May.

Site and soil: Deep well-drained soil, preferably light and rich, in sunny position. Feed with compost or leafmould.

Propagation: Plant September-October 5-6"/12-15cm deep and 5-6"/12-15cm apart. Never plant in wet ground. Do not increase easily.

Care and cultivation: Dead head, but allow foliage to die back. If left in ground mulch with compost or well-rotted manure in October or March. Bulbs degenerate easily if not fed. Many gardeners lift and store them instead.

IRIS

Iris   *N temperate regions*

Origins and history: Name from Latin 'iris'—eye. Among oldest of garden plants. 'Orris root' base of most perfumes. Many references to both white and blue irises through the Middle Ages. Developed later by the Dutch.

Description: 2 main groups:
Rhizomes: Good in borders. 3 types:
BEARDED IRIS: Several orchid-like flowers erect among dark green sword-like leaves.
BEARDLESS IRIS: Large handsome blooms.
CUSHION IRIS: Single flower of great size and beauty.
Bulbous: Good for cut flowers. Do very well in polluted areas.
DUTCH IRIS: Longest cultivated group—largest flowers and biggest colour variety. 3 basic groups:
I. reticulata: Dwarf, height 4-6"/10-15cm. Winter or early spring flowering.
I. xiphium: Summer flowering, including Dutch hybrids. Flowers June-July; height 12-24"/30-60cm.
I. juno: Distinctive bulbs, flowers April. Height 12-18"/30-45cm.
All types in very rich colours—yellow, purple, blue and white.

Flowers: May-July. Dwarf species flower earlier for spring colour.

Site and soil: Deeply-worked well-drained soil with some lime, particularly well-drained in winter. Needs sun in summer to ripen rhizomes if to bloom well. Bulbous types can be in partial shade.

Propagation: Plant rhizomes shallowly in early autumn so can get sunlight. Plant bulbous types early autumn 3-4"/75-100mm deep and 4"/100mm apart. Divide every 4 years as irises exhaust the soil very quickly. Divide in July after flowering. *Or*, cut roots to propagate—each cut section must have an 'eye'.

Care and cultivation: Keep soil bare around rhizome irises. Keep moist while growing; protect with cloches in winter.

IXIA

Corn Lily   *South Africa*

Origins and history: Name from Latin 'ixia'—birdlime, referring to sticky juice in stems.

Description: 5 or 6 sword-like leaves with star-shaped flowers in spirals on loose spike in yellow, orange, pink, red, blue, green or purple. Good for cut flowers. Hardy only in mild areas. Height 12-18"/30-45cm.

Flowers: May-July.

Site and soil: Sandy limey soil in sunny position, with peat and leafmould added (and additional sand if necessary). Choose warm, sheltered spot.

Propagation: Plant October-November in very mild districts, March in cooler areas, 4"/100mm deep and 6"/15cm apart. Will die if left out in winter in cold districts. Lift in summer when foliage dies down.

Care and cultivation: If left out for winter cover with mulch to guard against frost. Remove mulch in spring.

LILIUM

Lily   *N hemisphere*

Origins and history: Name from the Celtic 'li'—white. Probably derived from white madonna lily. Among oldest cultivated plants—depicted in Minoan art 2000BC. Have always had a religious, medicinal and mythological significance.

Description: Host of flower forms, either reflexed, funnel or bell-shaped, drooping or horizontal, often fragrant. Lance-shaped leaves. Both tall and dwarf varieties, suitable for every place in the garden—any soil, shade or sun, tender or hardy, from border plants to naturalized areas. Good for cutting. Very versatile genus, but choose the right variety. Numerous cultivated varieties. This is another area for the specialist, though most hardy varieties are suitable for any garden. The Royal Horticultural Society has divided lilies into 9 recognized groups:

Asiatic hybrids: Upright flowers, borne singly.
Dutch hybrids: Woodland lilies liking acid soil. Flower in June.
L. candidum hybrids: The classic madonna lily—oldest known hybrids in this division. Lime-loving. Flower June-July.
American hybrids: From North America. Flower July.
Longiflorum hybrids: Greenhouse varieties—rare.
Trumpet hybrids: From Asiatic species. Flower June-August.
Oriental hybrids: From Japan. Flower August. Need open situation.
Other hybrids
Wild species: Great variation in cultural requirements and flowering times.

Flowers: May-September.

Site and soil: Well-drained but moisture-retentive soil, rich in humus. Lilies die in waterlogged soil, but must not be allowed to dry out. Some like lime, most do not. Need well-dug soil. If too wet, make raised beds, or plant on a layer of sand to assist drainage.

Propagation: Plant early summer varieties in autumn, July-September flowering varieties in spring. In heavy soil plant all lilies in spring. Bulbs are very distinctive with overlapping scales and no protective cover—they are easily damaged and need handling with care. Plant small bulbs 12"/30cm apart, large varieties 18"/45cm apart, in groups of 3 or more. Planting depth depends on variety—some are stem-rooting, but in general plant about 4"/100mm deep. Mulch stem-rooting varieties directly after planting. May not flower first season. Divide every few years. If necessary, store bulbs in peat—do not let them dry out or rot.

Care and cultivation: Feed with bone-

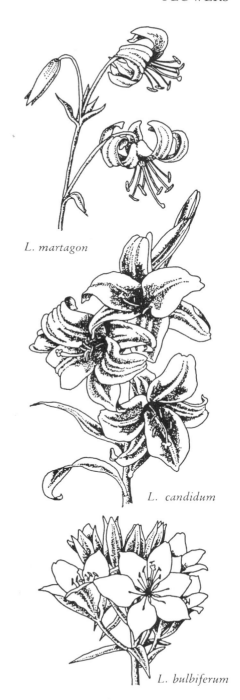

L. martagon

L. candidum

L. bulbiferum

meal. Water regularly. Mulch in summer to retain moisture. Dead head after flowering, cut back stem in autumn. Shelter from wind. Mulch in autumn with compost or leafmould, especially stem-rooting varieties. Stake tall varieties.

MUSCARI

Grape Hyacinth
S and E Europe, Central Asia

Origins and history: Name from the Greek 'moschos'—musk, referring to the scent. *M. comosum* from Mediterranean was cottage garden variety until gardeners turned to *M. botryoides*, the grape hyacinth we know today.

Description: Small free-flowering plants of blue, purple, white or bi-coloured bells in dense spikes, with grass-like leaves. Very good for naturalization, or beds and borders, though multiplies rapidly and can be invasive. Height 3-15"/7-37cm, depending upon variety.

Flowers: February-June, depending upon variety.

Site and soil: Any well-drained garden soil, preferably gritty. Add peat, leafmould, or well-rotted manure. Full sun.

Propagation: Plant in masses September-October, 3-4"/75-100mm deep and 2-3"/50-75mm apart. Divide every 3-4 years, when leaves turn yellow.

Care and cultivation: Dead head. Foliage takes a long time to die back—be patient.

Pests and diseases: Smut.

NARCISSUS

Narcissus, Lent Lily, Jonquil, Daffodil
Europe, Mediterranean, W Asia

Origins and history: Named after Narcissus in Greek mythology: whole family given that name by Linnaeus. The name 'daffodil' given to all trumpet-flowered varieties—traditional cottage garden flower; most popular spring flower for centuries. Most widespread native species *N. pseudonarcissus*—Lent Lily—used to be common. Cultivated narcissus grown in gardens since ancient Egypt.

Description: Distinction between daffodil and narcissus vague, especially with modern varieties. Roughly speaking, 'daffodil' refers to trumpet-shaped flowers; 'narcissus' to small-cupped forms; 'jonquil' to sweetly-scented rich yellow narcissus.

All have yellow, white, pink or orange flowers and strap-like leaves. Perfect for naturalizing—have grown wild in Britain since Roman times. Being hardy, they are good anywhere—beds, borders, boxes. Spread easily. Good for cutting. Miniatures good in rock gardens. Modern varieties bred from mid-nineteenth century, though in sixteenth century at least 24 species and cultivated varieties were being grown. Over 10,000 varieties available today—worldwide interest in breeding them, and the subject of much botanical debate. The Royal Horticultural Society divides the species into 12 groups:
Trumpet: 1 flower per stem, trumpet as long as or longer than the length of the other petals.
Large-cupped: 1 flower per stem, cup shorter than length of other petals, but more than ⅓ as long.
Small-cupped: 1 flower per stem, cup shorter than ⅓ length of other petals.
Double: Double flowers.
Triandrus: 1-6 flowers per stem, usually white, bowl-shaped cup.
Cyclamineus: 1 flower per stem, drooping thin trumpet with wavy edge, reflexed petals.
Jonquilla: 2-6 scented flowers per stem, usually white with short yellow cup.
Tazetta: 4-8 scented flowers per stem, usually white with short yellow cup.
Poeticus: 1 scented flower per stem, usually white, short yellow cup with red border, late-flowering.
Species, wild forms and wild hybrids
Split-corona hybrids: Cup split for ⅓ of its length.
Miscellaneous: Everything else.

Flowers: February-May, depending upon variety.

Site and soil: Very tolerant—will grow anywhere except deep shade or waterlogged soil, in any soil containing some humus. dig in compost, leafmould or peat. Ideally, use well-drained deeply dug garden soil in dappled shade, such as woodland.

Propagation: Bulbs of different species vary greatly in size and shape. Plant in late August or September, 5-6"/12-15cm deep, so tip of bulb is twice height of bulb below surface, and 6"/15cm apart (3-4"/75-100mm deep and 4"/100mm apart for miniatures). Scatter at random in naturalized drifts. Lift and divide every 5 or 6 years.

Care and cultivation: Require almost no attention once planted. Dead head, and leave foliage until it has died back in July. Water as necessary.

Pests and diseases: Eelworm, Narcissus Fly; Narcissus Fire.

ORNITHOGALUM

Star of Bethlehem   *Europe, Africa, Asia*

Origins and history: Brought to Britain by Crusaders. Naturalized in eastern England, though now rare. *O. umbellatum* cottage garden favourite since sixteenth century.

Description: Star or cup-shaped flowers borne in clusters, yellow or white, fragrant. Strap-like leaves. Some species very hardy —good naturalized in grass in large groups, especially in woodland. Others better in beds, borders and rock gardens. Height 6-18"/15-45cm depending upon variety.

Flowers: April-July, depending upon variety.

Site and soil: Well-drained soil, fairly rich in humus. Do well in lime. Sun or partial shade.

Propagation: Plant bulbs in October, 3"/75mm deep and 4"/100mm apart. Lift and divide every few years when leaves die back; replant immediately.

Care and cultivation: Leave foliage until it dies back in July. Dead head regularly.

POLYGONATUM

Solomon's Seal, Ladder to Heaven
N hemisphere

Origins and history: Name from the Greek 'poly'—many, and 'gonu'—knees, referring to the many stem joints. Used to make scent in sixteenth and seventeenth centuries. Native varieties. Cultivated in gardens since Middle Ages.

Description: Greenish-white bell-shaped flowers on short stalks borne from leaf axils. Lance-shaped leaves on long stems arranged in ladder-like fashion, hence 'ladder to heaven'. Plant of deciduous woodland. Height 12-50"/30-125cm.

Flowers: May-June.

Site and soil: Moisture-retentive well-drained soil, with leafmould, in partial shade. *P.×hybridum* likes sun, as long as bulb is shaded.

Propagation: Plant rhizomes Oct or March just below soil surface, 12"/30cm apart.

Lift and divide every few years in November. Cut rhizomes, making sure each portion has an 'eye', and replant.

Care and cultivation: Mulch in March. Cut down in November (not *P. hookeri*).

SCILLA

Squill, Bluebell, Wood Hyacinth
Europe, Asia, Africa

Origins and history: Named after the mythological nymph Scilla—'squill' is the anglicization. Native bluebell grown in cottage gardens since fifteenth century. More varieties in sixteenth century gardens than there are today. Bluebell has now been reclassified by botanists as *Endymion*, and may be under that name in catalogues.

Description: 2 groups:
Siberian Scilla (*S. siberica*) Early flowering (March-April): intense blue bell-like flowers. Height 3-6"/7-15cm.
Bluebell (*S. nutans*) Late spring flowering (May): tall blue, white or pink bell-like flowers on spikes with lush clumps of leaves. Height 10-12"/20-25cm. Spanish Bluebells (*S. campanulata*) used similarly in gardens and woods.
All types good in beds and naturalized. Can be very invasive.

Site and soil: Any well-drained soil in sun or partial shade.

Propagation: Plant in October for spring and early summer species, in March for late summer and autumn flowering species. Plant in drifts 3"/75mm deep and 4"/100mm apart. Small bulbs may not bloom first year. Lift and divide every 4-5 years after foliage has died back.

Care and cultivation: Dead head *S. nutans*, as it is a prolific self-seeder.

Pests and diseases: Eelworm; smut.

TULIPA

Tulip   *Europe, Near East*

Origins and history: Name from the Turkish 'tulbend'—turban, referring to shape of flower. British tulip is yellow, probably naturalized since sixteenth century. First species brought to Western Europe in 1559—became almost a cult flower. By 1629 there were 140 varieties. Has been cottage garden flower ever since.

Description: Bell-shaped or flat open flower, almost always single, in dramatic display of colours—white, yellow, red, purple, bi-coloured, and many other variants, even black. Broad leaves at or near ground level. Outstanding for spring and early summer bedding. Miniatures for rock gardens. Good for cutting. Height 3-36"/7-90cm, depending upon variety. Classification under constant revision—now about 4,000 names in 15 divisions! Main divisions are:

Single early tulips: Mid-April. Height 6-15"/15-37cm.

Double early tulips: Late April. Height 10-15"/25-37cm.

Mendel tulips: April-May. Height 16-24"/40-60cm.

Triumph tulips: April-May. Height 16-24"/40-60cm. (Superseding Mendel tulips.)

Darwin hybrid tulips: Newest division. Late April. Height 22-28"/55-70cm.

Darwin tulips: Best-known. Early May. Height 26-32"/65-80cm.

Lily-flowered tulips: April-May. Height 20-26"/50-65cm.

Cottage tulips: Vary a lot. Sometimes multi-flowered. Old cottage garden varieties. May. Height 9-36"/22-90cm.

Rembrandt tulips: 'Broken', i.e. striped colours, as painted by Rembrandt at the height of tulipomania. Early May. Height 16-30"/40-75cm.

Parrot tulips: Exceptionally large flowers with frilly edges, developed in the seventeenth century. Early May. Height 18-26"/45-65cm.

Double late tulips: Fat double flowers, sometimes 2 colours. From mid-May. Height 16-24"/16-30cm.

Species tulips and their hybrids: Most well known are *kaufmanniana* hybrids, from a wild Turkestan species discovered in the late nineteenth century—good for naturalizing. Other species are *fosteriana* and *greigii*—many new varieties from both in recent years.

Wild tulips are surprisingly easily available. Flower February-May. Mostly dwarf. Will naturalize well.

Flowers: March-June.

Site and soil: Sunny or partially shaded position, sheltered from strong wind. Well-drained, never waterlogged, preferably heavy soil. Do not grow tulips in the same place for too long.

Propagation: Plant end October to mid-December, depending upon variety, 5-6"/12-15cm deep, so tip of bulb is twice the height of the bulb below surface, and 6"/15cm apart. Water soil after planting. Often a good idea to lift tulips after flowering and store for winter—bulbs can deteriorate when left in soil. In a well-drained soil will manage for a few years, but flowers will be smaller each year.

Care and cultivation: Dead head; leave the leaves to feed the bulb. Mulch with compost or leafmould. Keep weed-free.

Pests and diseases: Mice, slugs, eelworm. Tulip fire—a fungus that stunts infected shoots. Lift and burn affected plants, and do not plant tulips again in the same place for several years.

Shrubs and Trees

The way we stand, you can see we have grown up this
way together, out of the same soil, with the same
rains, leaning in the same way toward the sun. . . .
And we are various, and amazing in our variety, and
our differences multiply, so that edge after edge of the
endlessness of possibility is exposed. You know we
have grown this way for years. And to no purpose
you can understand. Yet what you fail to know we
know, and the knowing is in us, how we have grown
this way, why these years were not one of them
heedless, why we are shaped the way we are, not all
straight to your purpose, but to ours. And how we are
each purpose, how each cell, how light and soil are in
us, how we are in the soil, how we are in the air, how
we are both infinitesimal and great and how we are
infinitely without any purpose you can see, in the way
we stand, each alone, yet none of us separable, . . . all
exquisite as we stand, each moment heeded in this
cycle, no detail unlovely.

Susan Griffin
'Forest', from *Woman and Nature*

Shrubs and Trees

Shrubs and trees are the skeleton of the garden, the permanent features around which the more ephemeral flowers are planted.

Think carefully before you plant a tree. It may be there for much longer than you are. Trees and shrubs can be moved when young, but they much prefer not to be. One of the commonest mistakes in planting trees and shrubs is to put the young plants too close together. I have worked in a garden where spreading shrubs and forest trees had been planted within a foot or two of each other, and we inherited the heartbreaking task of selecting the survivors and thinning out the rest. Even a giant redwood grows from seed, so never take any woody plant into your garden unless you know its final height and spread, and have worked out whether your land can ultimately accommodate it.

When a tree outgrows the human interest that put it there, it is the tree that goes. Your response to our loss of deciduous forest may well be that you want to plant an oak, ash or beech tree, but if your garden is only twenty feet square, there are alternatives. There are many beautiful small trees, both separate species and dwarf varieties of the forest trees, that fit small gardens, and can have a safe home there until they die. It is surely better to live with a weeping birch or flowering cherry than to cut down a chestnut in its prime.

Trees and shrubs change the habitat for everything else in the garden. If your garden is thick with trees, you will have a shady woodland environment, ideal for some plants, hopeless

for others. A thick hedge may protect your garden from prevailing winds and create a sheltered suntrap for tender plants that could never manage out in the open. Crabapple and cherry trees will bring the birds, buddleia the butterflies. Shrubs and trees are much better windbreaks than solid walls, and when used as a visual barrier can also create the illusion of a forest between your garden and the adjacent industrial estate.

Many trees and shrubs are very hardy and will get on by themselves, but with all woody plants it is worth spending time and trouble establishing them well, pruning and training them early in their life to prevent later problems, watching carefully for pests and diseases. These are plants that are going to be in your life for a long time, so love them well at the beginning and there will be ample rewards.

There are trees and shrubs for almost every situation. Some are exceptionally hardy, some resist pollution well, some positively enjoy chalk or heavy clay. Some of our loveliest garden shrubs are only partially hardy in cold areas, but may delight in sea breezes. Look at the following lists, which will tell you what should do well where, ask your neighbours, and choose carefully—there is no joy in watching a plant struggling for survival over the years.

After the initial planning and attention, trees and shrubs are the easiest plants to live with. They require a minimum of care—perhaps an annual mulch and pruning, perhaps not even that. As long as they are planted in well-weeded, nourishing soil you need not worry too much about creating special beds for them; they keep down weeds by themselves; you can run your lawn right up to them; and they are relatively child-resistant, surviving den-building and footballs much better than softer plants. If you want a beautiful garden you hardly have to touch, go for the tough, common shrubs and trees.

Cuttings can be taken from most shrubs and trees (the lists give details), inserted into cutting compost, left to root, potted on, and then planted out. Layering and the separation of suckers (if own roots) are even easier. As with flowers, many varieties will not breed true from seed, so the tree and shrub lists only mention seeds when for some reason this is the preferable method.

One of the most obvious divisions of woody plants is between deciduous and evergreen. Evergreens have the advantage of providing your garden with a touch of green in winter. However, many garden evergreens tend to be less hardy than deciduous trees and shrubs, often coming from warmer climates. Deciduous trees and shrubs are perfectly adapted to temperate climates, whereas most garden evergreens evolved in places where the climate is less sharply differentiated than ours. For this reason, evergreens are usually planted in spring, not autumn, and may need a little more shelter and cosseting in their early years. They dislike being replanted, having no season when they are dormant. For this reason it is a good idea to buy evergreens, and particularly conifers, in containers. They are susceptible to drought and should be watered well until they are established, and mulched so that the soil retains its moisture.

Another important distinction to make is that between conifers, and flowering trees and shrubs, both deciduous and evergreen. Botanically, conifers are much older, and spread their multitudinous seed by wind, so their inconspicuous flowers have not evolved to attract insects. Most of them are evergreen—with exceptions like larch—and their leaves are very acidic, so little will grow happily under them. They come in numerous species and varieties, from miniatures suitable for rockeries, to towering trees, providing a foil of muted shades of green, grey or even gold to the surrounding garden —in winter they will look quite magical in the snow when there is nothing else flourishing. If you have the space and the interest you can create a collection of conifers, using the enormous scope of colour, shape and habit to grow a shrubbery which is subtle, if slightly sombre.

The distinction between trees and shrubs is one of convenience. A shrub used to be defined as a many-stemmed woody plant less than 15'/5m high, and a tree as a plant with one main trunk which is more than 15'/5m high. Habit is now the main defining feature. I once had a garden in Shetland, the greatest asset of which was a tree—a sycamore all of five feet high. It had grown to the height of the wall behind it and then stopped, but it was the only tree in my life for several years, and it definitely counted.

The lists indicate whether a plant is deciduous (D), semi-evergreen (SE) or evergreen (E); many families have species in all these categories. The conifers are listed separately; otherwise shrubs and trees are differentiated, because this is probably the main distinction you will need to make when planning your garden. Remember that the varieties of one family can differ dramatically. You may go out to buy yourself a *Viburnum*, and end up with anything from a native Guelder Rose to a rare winter-flowering species from China that will need all your care and attention, and fill up only half the space you intended it to. You may buy an attractive little conifer from the garden centre and find it is a species that can grow to 150 feet high—do choose very carefully. The best book to turn to is the latest edition of *Hillier's Manual of Trees and Shrubs*, which is clear, comprehensive, and up-to-date, being reprinted every three or four years. Hilliers' nurseries are a familiar resource to many gardeners, and the *Manual* originally arose from their excellent catalogues. It gives a detailed description of each variety, plus site and soil requirements, country of origin, and date of introduction or breeding. It has the added advantage of being in the reference section of most public libraries.

The plants described in the lists are hardy in Britain, and on the whole pests and diseases will not be too much of a problem. In the lists we have only described the ailments to which a species is particularly susceptible.

Shrubs

The Victorians went in for shrubberies in a big way. Like conservatories, they were a response to the vast influx of plants introduced by the nineteenth century plant collectors. Many shrubs thrive in dappled shade, and formal shrubberies were often planted under a canopy of forest trees, in beds interspersed by winding walks, and rustic seats for proposing on.

The development of shrubberies and shrub gardens was a gradual process. Ever since the Tradescants had brought back new flowering shrubs from Virginia in the seventeenth century, foreign shrubs had been grown and enjoyed. Before that, a small number of shrubs had been used, more often for hedging and topiary than as free-standing specimen plants.

In the last three centuries, shrubs have gradually infiltrated further and further into the garden. Today the approach is usually to let them alone as much as possible, using pruning only for early training and to cut out dead or diseased wood and to improve the quality and quantity of flowers, fruits or bark colour, rather than to impose artificial shapes. We allow shrubs where formal gardeners of earlier years would have been scandalized to see them—the mixed border is a twentieth century response to less space, less available labour, and a desire to make use of the many different kinds of plants available to us. Many common shrubs are spring-flowering, so the mixed border often starts its annual display with shrubs and bulbs, giving way to herbaceous perennials and perhaps some summer-flowering shrubs. After the first frosts of autumn, when the annuals and perennials have gone, the shrubs come back into their own, and a few evergreens will keep us company through the winter.

Given more space, a shrub bed becomes a possibility. Ideally, a shrub bed will be an island bed in a lawn, so you can take advantage of all its aspects. The hardier shrubs can shelter the less hardy, and you can plan carefully to provide the right conditions for each species. In a large shrub bed, just as with perennials, it is better to group two or three smaller species together and to repeat the groupings, rather than having a hotchpotch of every plant you can lay your hands on.

Another way of using shrubs is as part of a semi-wild area, informal and low in maintenance. Areas of woodland lend themselves to this kind of treatment—rhododendrons and azaleas prefer an acid woodland soil with trees overhead, and many other shrubs are at home naturalized in woodland. Once established, shrubs can also keep down long rough grass, and will provide their own weed-inhibiting cover, although care has to be taken not to damage shrubs when cutting the grass.

There are shrubs for the most awkward places—climbers that can cope with blank north-facing walls, berberis or hawthorn to provide an impenetrable hedge, and aucuba and privet to hide the dustbins and keep the traffic fumes out of your front yard. For more favourable sites there is an enormous variety of beautiful and exotic shrubs to choose from. The lists concentrate on common shrubs which do well in most habitats, but if you want something rarer, more demanding, and perhaps more rewarding, the scope is infinite.

Hedges

Hedges are, of course, shrubs planted in rows, either informally or clipped to shape. One might think this was obvious, but it contradicts the idea that some plants come as hedges—like privet and box—and others just don't —like fuchsia or rose. This is a pity, because there is often much more scope in selecting a hedge than people think.

Hedges provide shelter from wind and frost and traffic pollution, privacy from passing eyes and ears, and a sheltered space of your own enclosed in walls of living green. A thick hedge is tougher than a paling fence, and keeps sound out better. It keeps the weather out better than a solid wall, and everything out better than a wire fence. A disadvantage is that it takes up space. I have an ancient beech hedge twelve feet high which keeps out the north wind and is beautiful all year round, but it is four feet thick, and takes up goodness from the soil a good deal further afield than that. In the only place where a

vegetable bed comes near it, the lettuces gradually shrink in size as they approach it. Next to the lawn, however, it creates a windless suntrap that could not be bettered.

If you want a hedge to bound your garden, consider what it has to protect you from. The hedge is going to take the brunt of what you want to shut out, and it must be tough enough to do it. It may be exposed to the teeth of the east wind or herds of cows, in which case you will want a hardy agricultural-type hedge of hawthorn or beech. It may have to soak up the fumes of a hundred buses a day, in which case privet or aucuba might be sensible choices. It may have to repel human invaders—try gorse or berberis or holly. Holly is also good if you need frost protection. If you want complete privacy, make sure your choice of hedging grows tall enough without becoming gappy at its base, and remember that only evergreens will provide a year-round screen. Think too about the time scale—chamaecyparis will give you a reasonable hedge within a few years; if you are planning for your grandchildren, plant yew and they will have a hedge to be proud of. If on the other hand you face south across the Channel, fuchsia may revel in the sun and sea air.

Hedges often have to grow where you would not expect any other plant to tolerate the conditions. The space between houses, particularly, is often deeply shaded, full of draughts, and traps the frosts weeks after everywhere else. Holly, hawthorn and privet are all tough enough for such conditions. You may need to give the young plants shelter while they become established, such as a temporary fence, but make sure you are not just funnelling the wind straight on to your young plants.

In places where your hedge is not

required to protect you from such adverse conditions, you have more scope to use less hardy plants which give a greater display of flowers or foliage. If the prospect from your front garden is sheltered and pleasant, you may want to delineate your boundary with a low aromatic hedge of lavender or box, or an informal hedge of flowering shrubs which are not trimmed tightly to shape—the choice is plentiful. You may want to separate one part of the garden from another. A hedge like this doesn't even need to be free-standing. Given a trellis or some preliminary fencing, you can have hedges of climbing rose, jasmine or forsythia. Hedges can be low or high—anything from a box hedge a few inches high to a beech hedge of sixty feet. (If you don't believe me, take the road from Perth into the Cairngorms by way of the Devil's Elbow and look out to your left.)

The ground where you are planning to put your hedge may need attention, especially if it has not been cultivated before. Double dig a strip 6'/2m wide if you possibly can—a narrow trench won't give the organisms in the soil a chance to do their work properly. Dig in compost or well-rotted manure. Leave the dug soil to settle, preferably over winter. In spring, dig a trench 2'/60cm wide and deep. If the ground is waterlogged you may have to provide drainage—a layer of brick or rubble—at the bottom of the trench, or raise a strip 24"/60cm wide and 12"/30cm high. Buy plants about 1-2'/30-60cm high, depending upon the species. It may be tempting to buy bigger plants and create an instant barrier, but it is not usually worth it, as your hedge will never become as well-established as one grown from younger plants. Make quite sure you plant far enough apart. The temptation is to plant too close together so you have your hedge quicker. Eventually the plants will struggle for soil and light, and some will be choked to death. Fill in the trench when the plants are in place, and tread them in firmly and water them as you would with any shrub.

Hedges usually require more pruning than free-standing shrubs. Most deciduous hedges profit from being cut back the spring after they are planted (but not beech, which should be left for one to two years). Once hedges are established, they will need trimming annually, or even bi-annually for strongly-growing species. The times to do this are given in the lists under individual plants. Shears are the usual tool, with electric hedge trimmers coming into their own if you have enormous lengths of hedging.

Hedges left unpruned will send strong shoots upwards—after all, many of them are really trees. You may have to lop these off at a suitable place just below the height of the hedge. A long-neglected hedge may require more drastic treatment. You can cut some species back hard to a basic framework: it will be worth a season's exposure to restore its shape. If you have an agricultural-type hedge abutting on to pasture, you might think about the old country method of laying a hedge. It consists of severing chosen shoots across half their width, then bending them all at the same angle, interlacing them with upright stakes or shoots. The unwanted shoots are cut back to ground level. This will keep the cows out of your garden: but if you can, find someone to show you how to do it.

Ground cover

Ground cover is a carpet of plants of which miracles are expected. If you have areas of your garden that are not suitable for beds or borders, being too shady, or too rough, too interspersed with tree roots, couch grass or old bricks, you are likely to think 'ground cover' to yourself, and expect some long-suffering low-growing shrub to take it from there.

In fact, low-growing spreading shrubs, once established, can make an excellent job of covering the ground in awkward conditions, but they need as much help to get established as you can give them. Ground cover cannot be expected to fight all your perennial weeds for you. Most are ideal for shade, which fewer flowers will enjoy. The fact that they spread themselves will mean that you don't have to delve among matted tree roots to get them planted. Once established, they keep the weeds down by leaving them no space at all. It is vital that they succeed in this, and that they require little composting or feeding, because once they have covered the ground there is not much you can do to help them. There is no more dispiriting task than trying to weed among the ground cover that has not been able to withstand the competition. It is anything but labour-saving.

The answer is, as with all shrubs, to make as thorough a job of preparing and planting as you are able. The soil should be dug as well as it can be, and cleaned of weeds, especially perennials. Add compost or well-rotted manure before planting, or peat if suitable. Plant each shrub with space around it in which to spread, and during the first year or two keep the site weeded, and water if necessary. Watering is particularly important on steep slopes. These are often ideal sites for ground cover, which will hold the soil in place and spread over awkward banks. Don't expect the ground cover to hold its own until it is well established. Then it will

reward you and take over the problem of a difficult site for years, often with no further attention at all.

For difficult sites, use tougher ground cover. Some are native plants and will thrive in wild or semi-wild conditions. Periwinkle (*Vinca*) is excellent, with the added advantage, as well as glossy evergreen leaves, of delicate flowers in season. Ivy, often despised by gardeners, will grow where nothing else will, and there are more garden varieties than most people are aware of. *Lamium* is another tough character, and *Hypericum* species can also do well under competition. Prostrate conifers are another good option, though they require a little lateral thinking to choose them as ground cover.

If you have acid soil and open ground, you can go for heather—both *Erica* and *Calluna*. Heather does not require a rich soil, and there are now so many cultivated varieties that you can create a garden with a wide spectrum of flower colour, foliage, habit and flowering time, which with planning can be blended together to give you a combination of shade and colour, and continuous flowering from one year's end to the other. In a small area, plan for a shorter flowering time—spring and winter, for example—to avoid a patchy effect. Once established, heather will keep the weeds down, and requires little maintenance, though it likes to be mulched with peat or compost to keep it moist, and should be trimmed after flowering. It tolerates semi-wild conditions, though it does require sunlight and adequate moisture.

As with hedges, when conditions are less exacting the scope is wider. Ground cover can be useful in shrubberies, shrub beds and borders, and in the shade of trees. Many shrub families have ground cover species or varieties, which are indicated in the lists. If you have large areas of bare soil, some form of ground cover is well worth considering. Nature abhors a vacuum, and will otherwise keep you busy all summer in the useless occupation of keeping land empty.

Climbers and wall plants

A climber is a plant whose stem cannot support it to grow vertically, so it has adapted either to climb up other plants or to creep along the ground. 'Wall plants' are shrubs which, with the right pruning, can be trained to climb up walls and fences. Many wall plants prefer the microclimate of a wall to that of open ground. Both types of plant can be highly ornamental in the garden. They can be used to enhance house walls and fences, stone walls and tree stumps. The advantages are obvious— for the use of very little ground space a dramatic feature can be added to a garden. A wisteria may take up two square feet of flower bed, yet cover a house. However small your garden, you still have the option of expanding upwards. Climbers are useful for screening, too. With the help of a fence or trellis you can convert the view of the oil tank from your kitchen window into a cheering display of rose or clematis.

If you are planning to have climbers growing up your walls, there are certain points to consider. First, aspect is important. North and east walls can only take the toughest—many ivies, for example, will survive anything. The more tender climbers ideally require a south-facing aspect and a sheltered site. If you have a sheltered angle which catches the sun and shuts out wind and frost, then you have a home for wisteria or clematis, and with fragrant plants you have the bonus that the two walls will trap the scent. Secondly, think of the materials your house is built of. If it needs repainting or harling every few years, then most climbers are out unless you can devise support systems that can be gently lowered while the job is done. A lime-washed wall will change the pH of the soil surrounding it, a point to consider for all plants adjoining the house. I grow cowslips at the foot of my house wall, where my normally peaty soil gets a generous dose of lime.

Thirdly, you have to think about how the plant is going to stay up. Climbers are adapted to make their own way vertically, but they have different systems for doing so. There are a few self-clingers like ivy: they send out small sensitive rootlets which find their way into any tiny crack in a wall and cling on. Virginia Creeper has little adhesive pads that will clamp on to any surface. For a large expanse of bare wall, you are thus saved the headache of providing support, but you can never move the plant, so house-painting is out. Self-clingers may also damage walls by loosening plaster and mortar.

Some climbers cling on by tendrils. The pea family is probably the most familiar example, and clematis does the same. Some of the leaf stalks have evolved a new function, and reach out, searching for any small support to which they can then cling. They do need such support, which can be provided with green garden wire, or plastic or wooden trellis. Other climbers climb by twining, either around other plants or around themselves—these are the stranglers like honeysuckle and bindweed. Flanders and Swan were right— one twines one way and one the other, and nothing can make them change it. Wisteria is another twiner. Twiners need strong support, but after the early years the old wood will become rigid and hold itself up. The last category is the scramblers—roses and briars—which use their back-curving thorns to provide purchase on other hapless shrubs and trees, thus shoving their way upwards. Again they must be given strong support.

It is important to have the support ready before it is needed. It is much easier to undertake building operations when the site is still empty of plants, so the plant will not be left literally hanging around while you provide something for it to climb up. Make supports strong, and provide for the ultimate spread of the plant. You will have to tie wall plants to the supports, as they have no natural means of clinging.

As always, give plenty of attention to planting. Bear in mind that the root system is going to support a large area, and dig in plenty of compost or well-rotted manure. Sites close to houses may be poor in nutrients, consisting of builder's rubble and very dry soil. You may have to dig out a large hole and fill it with good humus. Plant a little way away from the house wall to avoid the foundations and the water that may wash down the wall. Remember that building regulations prohibit the blocking of ventilators, or the piling of soil above a damp course. Add bonemeal before planting. Plant and water in the usual way, and cosset the young plant until it is established. With climbers, you may need to guide the young plant to the wall by means of a cane. Set the cane in the hole when you plant, and fix it to the wall or support. Container-grown plants will arrive with the stake already in position.

Climbing plants may need some initial pruning to train them to the area they are to climb. Wall plants almost certainly will. Vigorous climbers may need cutting back. Care must be taken to keep them from blocking gutters or pulling slates off roofs. Some climbers may profit from cutting back the shoots that have just flowered if they flower on new wood. More detailed pruning advice is given in the lists.

Trees

We now know more clearly than ever before that trees matter: reafforestation is a vital concern to anyone who cares more about life on Earth than about making money. In our own gardens we may have space for only one or two small trees, but they are a potent symbol of our concern for the whole.

Making a desert is easy. Human beings contributed to the creation of the Sahara and Gobi deserts. They were responsible for the dustbowl in North America, and are now creating a new desert in Brazil. In a desert the ecology is simple: most of the land is sterile, the topsoil having been lost to the wind long ago, and where there is no soil or water, there is little life.

The forest is the antithesis of the desert. The primeval forests of our planet developed over thousands of years to reach a climax ecology, an intricate and infinitely varied pattern of life, interdependent, precarious when disturbed, and irreplaceable when lost.

We need trees in order to live on this planet. They hold down the soil with their roots, protecting it from erosion. They give shelter to multitudinous forms of life—plant, insect, bird and animal. They transpire vast amounts of water into the atmosphere, a protection against drought and subsequent famine. They transform carbon dioxide into oxygen, which is what we breathe. Like all green plants, they supply the rest of life with energy from the sun. The tree of life is a symbol common to many religions, and in some cultures the cutting down of a living tree is prohibited. If we allow ourselves to realise it, trees are vital for our physical survival and for the nourishment of our souls.

We live in a world where the interests of short-term profit override concern for the survival of the trees. The primeval forests are vanishing at the rate of hundreds of acres every day. It is thought that the destruction of the Brazilian rain forests may bring about a planetary climatic disaster, and upset the balance of chemicals which constitutes our air. While the felling of the northern coniferous forest, mostly to make paper, is not potentially so disastrous, being to a certain extent balanced by replanting of fast-growing species, it adds to the overall reduction of the world's forest area. The destruction continues regardless of the peril.

Coming closer to our own gardens, we live in a country that was once mainly covered by broad-leaved deciduous forest, as in most temperate regions. Our land belonged to the trees long before it belonged to us. The primeval forest would have been impassable, full of decaying vegetation and rotting trees, marshy in places, overrun by scrub and creepers wherever the light could penetrate. It would have been no place for us, and because primeval woodland and settled human habitation cannot co-exist, it was the woodland which went.

Our forests were destroyed long ago, by slash-and-burn agriculture, the need for firewood, and later for timber. The last oak forests of England supplied the British navy with ships, and the early foundries with fuel for smelting. What we now think of as forest is almost entirely plantation, carefully forested and cleared of undergrowth, the trees spaced out to avoid undue competition, planted for timber, as game coverts, or simply to look at and walk in. Yet they still provide a complicated ecosystem, refuge for our diminishing wildlife, and a source of non-human solace to us.

But our planted woodlands are also under threat. They are vanishing under the demands of agriculture and urban spread. The loss of trees to the landscape is irreparable, but it is not only the trees we are destroying—as the trees disappear, the habitats of birds and animals vanish, threatening the future of our native songbirds, small animals, and insects.

Our heritage of trees has been much abused, but much has also been given us. Not only do we live in a temperate region which abounded in beautiful native trees, but the plant collectors have brought us many new species to enrich our landscape. The Romans brought trees with them—including the sweet chestnut and the walnut. From the sixteenth century onwards, trees were imported not only for the fruits they bore, but for their interest and beauty. The Tradescants were the first to bring back North American species, among them the red maple and the witch hazel. Most introductions for the next two centuries came from the forests of North America. In 1824 Douglas started collecting in Canada, and found many new conifers. Trees from China and Japan came steadily from the eighteenth century onwards. The southern hemisphere followed, and recent introductions like the Australian eucalyptus are now commonplace in British gardens. Some trees still stand to mark a particular era, like the monkey puzzle, first brought from Chile in 1797, which became a Victorian craze. A monkey puzzle in a Victorian suburban garden is as much of a cliché as a mulberry tree (planted by Queen Elizabeth) in a sixteenth century garden.

As gardeners and potential planters

of trees, we are faced on the one hand with planetary catastrophe and on the other with a wealth of diverse and fascinating material from all over the world. The most important thing is not to get carried away. Unless you have a lot of space you cannot give home to a full-grown forest tree. While single trees do not grow as tall as those making their way skyward in a forest surrounded by other tall trees, a full-sized oak, beech or lime, let alone a redwood or cedar of Lebanon, is going to make any suburban patch look pretty silly. This need not mean forgoing your chosen species—most of the great trees now have smaller garden varieties which will fit into a smaller landscape, but you will still need to think carefully about light and space. Plant well away from buildings, drains, rockeries and vegetable plots, and one day you can underplant it with woodland shrubs or flowers. If you inherit mature trees you are lucky indeed—they take a long time to grow.

The advantages to you of having trees in your garden are not quantifiable—their presence will make a difference to your life. In practical terms, they will completely change your garden. The dimension of height will alter both the perspective and the ecology. Just as in a rain forest there is a whole strata of life that is lived in the canopy of trees, just one or two trees in your garden will provide a new habitat, most particularly for birds. You will be providing a different ecology again under the trees, which you can use to create a shrubbery or woodland garden. Trees will cast welcome shade in summer, and give added shelter in winter. An evergreen tree is a particular focal point in winter and a dark foil to new growth in summer, while a deciduous tree will provide you with a panorama of the changing seasons that cannot be surpassed.

Trees and their influence do not stay within human boundaries. The tree next door will give you as much as it gives its owner. Trees as part of a landscape are common to everybody, and people can care passionately about trees that are not strictly part of their own patch. In the landscaping of human habitats, trees are of paramount importance. In the south, plane trees have been the saving of many city streets—they are very resistant to pollution as their bark renews itself every year, and so are ideal trees for the inner city. In the north their rôle is often taken over by the sycamore. In rural areas, the loss of the elm trees from Dutch elm disease has denuded many villages of most of their trees, to the detriment of the whole.

Planting trees is a job worth doing well. Care in the early years will be amply repaid later. Choose young trees if you can—not more than three or four years old. Larger trees are awkward to move, and will never settle as well. Water young trees regularly, and feed them with compost, well-rotted manure, or the leafmould that would naturally be found in a forest. You can also give bonemeal. Prune trees carefully in the first years if necessary to get the basic shape you want.

If you plant a tree, you are in a small way helping to reverse a planetary process of destruction. You are changing the environment for many creatures that are not human, and probably quite a few that are, not only the people who live on your road today, but those who will live there in fifty or a hundred years' time. It makes a difference.

Shrubs

AUCUBA

Spotted Laurel   *Japan*

Origins and history: First referred to by Kaempfer, a Dutchman who visited Japan in 1692. Not brought to West until the nineteenth century, when it caused a sensation and was soon ubiquitous. Less popular now: probably a reaction. The first male plant was brought to the West by Robert Fortune—before that there were no red berries!

Description: E Tough shrub with shiny dark green or variegated leaves, very like laurel. Unisexual—need male and female plants to produce red berries on female bushes. To ensure cross-pollination plant 1 male to every 3 female plants. Height 6-12'/2-4m; spread 5-7'/1.6-2.2m; shape round, bushy and dense.

Uses: Will thrive in any conditions—very useful in gardens where pollution is bad, where the soil is poor, or there is no sun. Will even do well in tubs in the back yard, and brings year-round green into the most wretched environments.

Site and soil: Does best in ordinary garden soil in sun or partial shade.

Propagation: Take cuttings 4-6"/10-15cm long, with a heel, of lateral shoots in September. Insert in cutting compost in a cold frame. Plant in nursery rows following April. Grow on for 2 years, then plant in final position.

Care and cultivation: No pruning necessary. If you need to cut plant back, cut back older wood in April.

BERBERIS

Barberry
N & S America, Europe, N Africa, Asia

Origins and history: Kerr sent the earliest varieties from the Far East in the early nineteenth century. *B. darwinii* found by Darwin in Chile in 1884. Hooker found *B. hookerii* in Tibet in 1924. Has very varied history—species discovered in many locations over a 150-year period.

Description: D and E Large genus (450 species), offering many garden species and varieties. All have yellow wood and small

Berberis gagnepainii

yellow cup-shaped flowers growing in clusters, sharp spines, and dense growth. Evergreen varieties have glossy foliage; deciduous varieties have bright autumn colours and bright berries that last into winter. Height 2-10'/0.7-3m (depending on variety); spread similar; shape dense. Bewildering choice—be sure to check height and spread when you buy, they can vary greatly. Evergreen varieties from *B. darwinii* and *B. stenophylla*. Most deciduous varieties from *B. thunbergii*.

Flowers: April-July.

Uses: Good in shrub beds and borders—useful as hardy in exposed positions. Hedges 2-12'/0.6-3.6m high are decorative and excellent for repelling intruders. Some species good in tubs.

Site and soil: Any ordinary garden soil in sun or partial shade. Will produce more flowers and berries in good light.

Propagation: Take 3-4″/75-100mm long lateral shoots with heel in September. Insert in cutting compost in a cold frame. Plant in nursery rows in April, grow on for 1-2 years, then plant in permanent position. Can divide and replant suckers October-March. For hedges, plant 9-24″/22-60cm apart (according to variety) from October to April.

Care and cultivation: Pruning not necessary. Can cut back deciduous species in February; evergreens after flowering. Thin out old or damaged wood. Trim deciduous hedges in September, evergreens after flowering.

Pests and diseases: Honey fungus.

BUDDLEIA

Butterfly Bush   *America, Africa, Asia*

Origins and history: Named after Adam Buddle, botanist and clergyman in Essex in the seventeenth and eighteenth centuries. *B. davidii* brought from China by Abbé David in 1866. Other species came from different parts of the world during the nineteenth century.

Description: D or E Profuse, sweet-scented tubular flowers in clusters on long arching branches. Very attractive to insects, especially bees and butterflies. Height 4-20′/1.2-6m depending on variety; spread similar; shape wide-spreading, long branches—must be pruned for tidy shape. *B. davidii* by far the commonest: has naturalized widely, especially in cities. Seeds easily in crannies of walls, rocks, buildings etc. Many garden varieties. *B. alternifolia* larger and less common. *B. crispa* and *B. globosa* have also produced common garden varieties. Many tender varieties too.

Flowers: June-October, depending on variety.

Uses: Very easy and quick to grow. Does well in shrub beds and borders, and in less favourable spots.

Site and soil: Any well-drained garden soil in full sun. *B. davidii* does well on chalk or lime. Grow tender varieties in shelter of wall or house.

Propagation: Take cuttings 4-5″/10-12cm long of lateral shoots, with a heel, in July or August. Insert in cutting compost in a cold frame. Plant out in nursery rows in

May, and plant in final position in October or the following March.

Care and cultivation: *B. davidii* flowers on new growth—cut back in March to within 2-3″/50-75mm of old wood. *B. globosa* and *B. alternifolia* flower on previous year's growth—prune back shoots after flowering. With *B. alternifolia* can remove as much as ⅔ of all stems after flowering.

BUXUS

Box   *Europe, W Asia, N Africa*

Origins and history: Traditional cottage garden plant; used for hedging, and in knot gardens and topiary.

Description: E Small glossy dark green leaves growing on dense bushes. Inconspicuous pale green scented flowers in April. Leaves smell of cat's piss. Untrimmed species box hedges can reach 10′/3m high, though most edging species 6-24″/15-60cm high. Can be trimmed to whatever shape you like. *B. sempervirens* native plant—Common Box. Has numerous varieties, some more compact, several with variegated leaves.

Uses: Excellent for clipped hedges because of its dense growth. Traditionally used for formal hedges and topiary. Good as dense and impenetrable evergreen barrier, or tiny hedge to formal borders.

Site and soil: Any well-drained garden soil in sun or partial shade. Can tolerate exposed sites and shade of overhanging trees.

Propagation: Take cuttings 3-4″/75-100mm long August-September and insert in cutting compost in a cold frame. Plant in nursery rows in April or May. Grow on 1-2 years, then plant in permanent positions March-October.

Care and cultivation: Trim formal hedges in August. If box has become overgrown, cut back hard in April. Give hedges an occasional mulch of compost or well-rotted manure.

Pests and diseases: Rust.

CALLUNA

Heather, Ling   *N W Europe*

Origins and history: Native British heath. Became popular garden plant in nineteenth century.

Description: E Scale-like leaves in varying colours according to variety—green, gold,

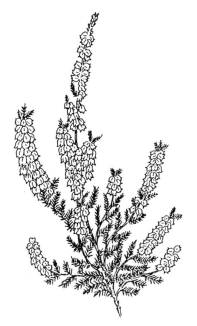

Calluna vulgaris

silver, bronze and red, with single or double small flowers in white, pink, red or purple, in long spikes. Height 9-24"/22-60cm according to species; spread 12-18"/30-45cm. Varieties from *C. vulgaris*—hundreds of named varieties. Breeding heathers has become a specialized hobby. Choose carefully from catalogues to get a balance of colour, foliage, flowers, flowering times and heights.

Flowers: July-November depending on variety.

Uses: Can be used in all kinds of gardens on peaty soil. Can make heather beds or whole heather gardens using *Calluna*, *Erica*, and acid-loving shrubs like rhododendrons. Naturalizes well. Good in rock gardens. As ground cover it will naturalize and hold its own on an acid soil in full sun. Some varieties make good low hedges, planted 12-18"/30-45cm apart.

Site and soil: Well-drained acid soil in full sun. Must not dry out. Peat soil is good.

Propagation: Take cuttings 1-2"/25-50mm long with heel August-October from lateral shoots. Insert into cutting compost in a cold frame. Plant in nursery bed when rooted, and grow on till around 3"/75mm high, then plant in permanent position. Or, layer healthy stems in March; sever a year later and plant out.

Care and cultivation: Leave dead flowers—will remain decorative until pruning time. In spring, clip dead flower stems back to foliage to keep neat. Prune back long and straggly shoots. Water in drought until established. Add peat when planting, and add mulch with peat and bonemeal at intervals.

Pests and diseases: Honey fungus.

CAMELLIA

India, China, Japan

Origins and history: Named after George Kamel, a Jesuit botanist, by Linnaeus. In fact camellias were first described by Kaempfer during a long trip to Japan in 1692. He found many varieties. The camellia is an important plant in Japan: it is related to the tea plant, and has been cultivated over many centuries. *C. japonica* first brought to Britain in the early eighteenth century by Lord Petrie—plants died from being kept in a hothouse, but cuttings survived, and by 1745 camellias were on sale in Britain. No new camellias were imported until the 1820s, when the Chandler and Low nursery began to sell camellias.

Description: E Glossy dark green leaves, and striking cup- or bowl-shaped flowers in white, pinks and reds. Single, semi-double and double varieties available. Height 6-12'/1.8-3.6m; spread 6-15'/1.8-4.5m. *C. japonica* is commonest species, producing numerous varieties. Hybrid *C. williamsii* (a cross between *C. japonica* and *C. saluenensis*) has given many hardy varieties —flowers November-April.

Flowers: February-May.

Uses: Used to be thought of as very tender, because frost can easily damage flower buds. As long as given a sheltered situation away from morning sunlight this is not a problem, and camellias can be used like rhododendrons and azaleas. Evergreen leaves provide year-round dense attractive bush, and when in flower camellias can be spectacular features on their own, especially next to the house or in tubs.

Camellia williamsii 'Mary Christian'

Site and soil: Any good lime-free soil in sheltered position, preferably facing west, in light shade or sun. Must have cool root run. Does not like wind or water-logged soil. Good against walls or in thin woodland. Does best in western districts.

Propagation: Take cuttings 3-4"/75-100mm long of lateral shoots June-August. Insert in cutting compost in cold frame. Plant out in nursery rows in spring. *Or*, layer large plants in September, and sever from parent plant after 18 months.

Care and cultivation: Pruning not necessary. Can cut back straggling branches in April, may get branches reverting to different flower colour (sports)—trace to source and remove. May need staking until established. Mulch with peat or leafmould. Dead head.

Pests and diseases: Frost damage to flowers. Birds (flowers); aphids. Honey fungus.

CHAENOMELES

Japonica, Japanese Quince *China, Japan*

Origins and history: Discovered in China

Description: Small round toothed deciduous leaves and red, pink or orange flowers, similar to apple blossom, in spring, followed by yellow apple-shaped fruits. Height 2-6'/60-180cm depending on species; spread 5-7'/1.5-2.1m; shape tangled, wide spreading bushes on woody stems unless pruned. *C. japonica* is original species. Several named varieties, growing up to 6'/1.8m high. *C. speciosa* has many garden varieties, flowering January-April. *C. superba* hybrid between the two species.

Uses: Very hardy. Does well anywhere with enough soil and plenty of sun, preferably against a wall. A tough reliable shrub, with colour in early spring.

Flowers: March-May.

Site and soil: Any ordinary garden soil in full sun, preferably trained against a wall or fence.

Propagation: Take cuttings 4"/100mm long of lateral shoots with a heel July or August. Insert in cutting compost in cold frame, and plant in nursery rows in spring. *Or*, layer long shoots in September. *Or*, dig up suckers with roots in autumn and replant.

Care and cultivation: Thin after flowering if necessary, selecting best leaders and removing surplus. If trained fanwise against a wall, cut back previous year's growth to 2-3 buds after flowering.

Pests and diseases: Fireblight; birds attack flowers.

CISTUS

Rock Rose   *Mediterranean*

Origins and history: 24 varieties described by Gerard as already in cultivation in Britain. Traditional cottage garden plant, brought back to popularity at the end of the nineteenth century by Gertrude Jekyll.

Description: E Single papery rose-like flowers in white, pink, purple or red, which bloom and die in a day, but are profuse during the flowering season, with spiky leaves on small bushes. Height 1-4'/30cm-1.2m depending on variety; shape low spreading bushes.

Flowers: April-May.

Uses: Good in hot dry places, especially in rock gardens. Useful for chalk or seaside gardens, where it does well.

Site and soil: Well-drained soil, which can be poor, in full sun, but sheltered from cold wind and frost.

Propagation: Not too slow to grow from seed—sow in seed compost in March and put in cold frame. Prick out into pots, pot on as necessary. Overwinter in cold frame, preferably for 2 years, and plant out where they are to stay in April or May. *Or*, Take cuttings 3-4"/74-100mm long of non-flowering shoots with a heel July or August, insert in cutting compost in cold frame, pot on and overwinter. Plant out April or May.

Care and cultivation: Pruning not necessary. May die if cut back severely. Can trim new shoots in March for more compact growth. Do not transplant, and always plant container-grown specimens.

Pests and diseases: Frost damage may make shoots die back.

CLEMATIS

Europe, Asia, N America

Origins and history: Native *C. vitalba* mentioned as cultivated plant by Gerard. Other species brought from China by David in nineteenth century, and from North America by Douglas. These discoveries have been followed up by other species throughout the last hundred years.

Description: D SE E Popular climbing shrub, clinging to support by twining leaf stalks, with cup- or bell-shaped flowers in pink, red, white, purple, or even yellow. Huge variety in habit and growth. One or two non-climbing species. Our native species is *C. vitalba* —Traveller's Joy— very good in wild gardens. Large-flowered hybrids usually from *C. jackmanii* (from Jackmans of Woking c.1860)—grow up to 12'/3.6m high and are spectacular, but smaller-flowered varieties are easier to cultivate, and come mostly from *C. montana*. There is a huge choice. Study catalogues carefully and work out exactly what you want.

Flowers: January-October according to variety.

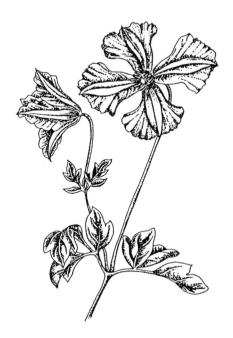

Clematis viticella

Uses: To climb anywhere—trellises, tree stumps, walls, houses. Must have support for leaf stems to twine round. Spectacular colour, and sometimes sweet scent.

Site and soil: Fertile, well-drained but moist soil, preferably alkaline. Stems need full sun, but roots should be shaded. Shelter from strong winds.

Propagation: Take stem cuttings 4-5"/10-12cm long of new wood with 2 buds at base in July. Insert in cutting compost at 60-64°F/16-18°C. Pot on rooted cuttings. Overwinter indoors in a frost-free place, and pot on. Plunge outdoors in April. Transplant to permanent site in October-November. *Or*, layer in March and transplant rooted cuttings in 1 year.

Care and cultivation: *C. montana* and its hybrids flower on short stalks off last year's growth. Need no pruning, but if need to cut back, do so after flowering. *C. jackmanii* and others flower on current season's growth. Cut back to within a few inches of previous year's growth in February. It is very important to know which kind you have! Mulch each spring with compost or well-rotted manure. Clematis can be temperamental—watch for hunger or thirst.

Pests and diseases: Slugs, Aphids. Powdery mildew. Clematis wilt—if shoots wilt and die quickly, cut them out at once.

CORNUS

Dogwood   *N hemisphere*

Origins and history: C. *alba* sent to Britain in eighteenth century from botanic gardens in St Petersburg. Popularized by Douglas, who rediscovered it in North America.

Description: D 2 main groups: some cultivated for bright red or yellow bark colour of young stems, giving colour in winter; others for coloured, sometimes variegated, leaves in summer and often brilliant autumn colours, with small star-shaped white or yellow flowers. Great variation in size and habit. C. *alba* is red-barked species, height 8-10'/2.4-3m, spread similar, small yellow-white flowers May-June. C. *stolonifera* for yellow-barked 'Flaviramea' and red-barked varieties. C. *kousa* and C. *florida* species for brighter flowering varieties in summer (C. *kousa* smaller; C. *florida* can spread up to 20'/6m).

Uses: Red-, yellow- and green-barked varieties provide unusual feature in winter; others often have bright autumn colours to fill gaps in the shrub border.

Site and soil: Any good garden soil. Some varieties don't like chalk. Full sun or partial shade.

Propagation: Take 3-4"/75-100mm cuttings with heel in July-August and insert in cutting compost in cold frame. Pot on rooted cuttings and overwinter in cold frame. Plant out in nursery rows in May. Grow on 2-3 years, then plant out in final position. Or, with some varieties, transplant rooted suckers in November.

Care and cultivation: Pruning not necessary with flowering varieties. For coloured bark in winter, cut back to within a few inches of the ground in early April, as the coloured bark comes on the new growth.

COTONEASTER

E Asia

Origins and history: 1 species plus garden varieties, brought from China in the late nineteenth century.

Description: D SE E Great variety; can range from prostrate to large bushes and trees. All have small 5-petalled white or pink flowers, usually followed by bright berries in autumn. Leaves vary in size— deciduous varieties usually have rich autumn colours. All very hardy. Take care to choose one of the right habit for your purpose. C. *horizontalis* most common species, used prostrate and against walls —called 'fishbone' or 'herringbone' because of the distinctive pattern of branches.

Uses: Ground cover—prostrate varieties, mostly from C. *dammeri*. Makes good hedges, especially C. *salicifolius*, C. *simonsii* and several others. Otherwise good shrub to grow anywhere. Does well in difficult places. Good against walls. 1 or 2 varieties small enough for rock gardens. Good in tubs. Attracts birds.

Site and soil: Any ordinary garden soil, preferably in full sun.

Propagation: Can grow easily from seed. Take seeds out of ripe berries in October, and sow in seed compost in cold frame. May take 18 months to germinate. Prick out into boxes and grow on, then plant out in nursery rows 2-3 years before planting in position. Self-seeds easily—just keep seedlings. Or, take heel cuttings 3-4"/75-100mm long. E—use ripe shoots in late August or September; D—ripening shoots in July or August. Insert in cutting compost in cold frame. Plant in nursery rows next April or May, grow on 2 years, then plant in permanent position. Or, layer in October or November and leave for 1 year.

Care and cultivation: Pruning not necessary. Cut back if grows too large, D in February, E in April. If training C. *horizontalis* against a wall, remove the branches coming away from and going into the wall.

Pests and diseases: Birds may eat berries. Fireblight—branches may die back and leaves shrivel. Silver leaf.

CYTISUS

Broom   *Europe, Asia Minor, N Africa*

Origins and history: British native and traditional cottage garden plant.

Description: D SE E Profusion of peaflower-shaped flowers in spring which cover stems and branches. Small leaves and thin branches, sometimes bare of leaves for several months of the year. Flowers usually yellow, but can be orange, red, purple, white or bi-coloured. If prostrate, can spread up to 10'/3m. *C. scoparius* is native plant—several hybrids from this. *C.xkewensis* is good for rock gardens—18"/45cm high. *C. albus* white species—very pretty.

Flowers: April-July.

Uses: Will cope with any soil except when waterlogged. Blaze of colour in spring. Good with heathers in acid soils. Naturalizes well. Prostrate and dwarf varieties good for rock gardens.

Site and soil: Any well-drained garden soil, preferably poor and sandy, in full sun. A few species dislike lime.

Propagation: Sow seeds in trays during April in cold frame. Prick out into pots and plunge outdoors. Transplant to permanent sites in September. *Or*, take cuttings 3-4"/75-100mm long of lateral shoots with a heel in August or September. Insert in cutting compost in cold frame. Pot on rooted cuttings, plunge outdoors, and plant out in final position in August or September.

Care and cultivation: Pruning is not often necessary. Can cut back new growth straight after flowering to about ⅓ new growth, to keep shrub trim. Never prune back to old wood, or plant will die. Dislikes being moved.

DAPHNE

Europe, Asia

Origins and history: Possibly a British native, only recorded as naturalized in 1759. Traditional cottage garden plant. Some new species introduced since. Can still be found wild.

Description: D SE E Sweetly-scented purplish-pink flowers in spring, on stiff upright stems. Dwarf or medium-sized shrubs. Hardy and relatively easy to grow. *D. mezereum* commonest; *D. blagayana* prostrate variety with white flowers. Height 1-5'/30cm-1.5m; spread 2-4'/60cm-1.2m; erect rounded habit.

Flowers: February-June.

Uses: Good in borders and rock gardens for spring colour and scent—plant near house or terrace. *D. mezereum* useful on chalk soils. *D. blagayana* good ground

Daphne burkwoodii

cover.

Site and soil: Any ordinary well-drained garden soil, including chalk, in sun or partial shade.

Propagation: Sow ripe seeds September-October in pots in cold frame. Pot on and grow on as for cuttings. *Or*, take cuttings 2-4"/50-100mm long of lateral non-flowering shoots with a heel July-September. Insert in cutting compost in cold frame. Pot on rooted cuttings next spring in potting compost and plunge outdoors. Pot on as necessary, and grow on 1-2 years. Plant out in permanent position.

Care and cultivation: Do not prune, except to remove damaged wood after flowering, and straggly growth in March. If *D. blagayana* has long bare prostrate stems, peg them down and cover with earth, and they will root into dense clumps. Need plenty of humus: mulch with leafmould or peat. Dislikes being moved. Buy container-grown plants.

Pests and diseases: Aphids.

DEUTZIA

E Asia

Origins and history: *D. scabra* discovered by Fortune in China in 1848. He also found *D. gracilis* in Japan. David found more in the 1870s.

Description: D Profuse white, pink or purple flowers, single or double. Very decorative in early summer, but untidy in habit. Very hardy. Height 3-10′/90cm-3m depending on variety; spread 3-8′/90cm-2.4m—needs controlling. *D. scabra* most common species. Several garden hybrids more compact than this—*D.×rosea* (3′/90cm) and *D.×hybrida* (4-6′/1.2-1.8m); several varieties of the latter.

Flowers: May-July.

Uses: Benefits from exposed sites, but not east-facing, as in sheltered places it can bloom too early, and the flowers can be damaged by frost. Easy to grow. Bright colour in early summer.

Site and soil: Any well-drained garden soil in sun or light shade. Good in woodland. Avoid too much exposure to frost.

Deutzia scabra plena

Propagation: Take cuttings 3-4″/75-100mm long of half-ripe lateral shoots July-August. Insert in cutting compost in cold frame. In April-May plant out rooted cuttings in nursery rows and grow on till autumn, then plant out in final position. Or, take 10-12″/25-30cm hardwood cuttings in October, insert in nursery bed, grow on 1 year, then plant out.

Care and cultivation: Prune after flowering. Remove flowering shoots at ground level, and thin out other crowded shoots at base. Cut out old wood.

ERICA

Heather, Heath   *Europe, Africa*

Origins and history: Native species, and others introduced early on. One of the first plants to be used extensively for hybridizing. In the early nineteeenth century William Herbert wrote a book about the varieties of *Erica*; hence great diversity today.

Description: E Over 500 species; huge variety of height and habit. Varieties hardy in Britain vary from 2″-20′/50mm-6m high. All have bell-shaped white, pink, purple or bi-coloured flowers, and needle-like leaves, which vary in colour, usually green, but can be orange, red or yellow. Choose with care, as the choice is so great. *E. arborea* (Tree Heath) can grow into a tree in favourable conditions in the south. Can get shrub-size varieties, dwarf and prostrate, with different colours of leaf and flower, and flowering times. Hybrids *E.×darleyensis* include many popular varieties. *E. cinerea* is our native bell heather, with many garden varieties. *E. ciliaris* (Dorset Heath) and *E. vagans* (Cornish Heath) are also native. There are vast numbers of hybrids and garden varieties from all these species.

Flowers: Can have ericas in bloom all year round with careful choice of varieties.

Uses: Particularly useful on acid soils. Can get ericas suitable for ground cover, border shrubs, naturalizing, specimen plants or even hedging. The heather garden is another area with full scope for the specialist—a good option for an easily maintained garden on acid soil.

Site and soil: Well-drained, preferably acid, soil. Keep moist, by adding peat if necessary. A few ericas also tolerate lime —*E. carnea, E. mediterranea* and

E.× darleyensis. Open position in full sun.

Propagation: Take cuttings July-October of sideshoots 1-2"/25-50mm long. Insert into cutting compost in cold frame. Plant rooted cuttings in nursery bed and grow on till 3"/75mm high, then plant out. *Or,* layer large stems from outside of plants. Should root after 1 year. Sever and plant out.

Care and cultivation: Trim back flower stems after flowering to keep compact. Never cut back to old wood. Mulch annually with peat. Likes bonemeal. Water in dry spells, especially during the first year.

ESCALLONIA
S America

Origins and history: *E. rubra* first to be discovered, brought from South America by Cruikshank in the 1820s. Others followed during the nineteenth century.

Description: E Dark green curiously-scented glossy leaves and short tubular flowers in white, red and pink, growing in clusters through the summer. Round leafy bush, height 6-10'/1.8-3m, spread 6'/1.8m. *E. macrantha* most common, especially for hedging. Several garden varieties and hybrids of varying height and hardiness. *E. rubra pygmaea* dwarf variety, good for rock gardens.

Flowers: June-September.

Uses: Does best on milder west coast. Good for borders and windbreaks from sea breezes. Good for hedges, especially in coastal areas.

Site and soil: Any well-drained garden soil, including lime, in sun or partial shade. In colder areas give shelter from north and east—a south-facing wall is ideal.

Propagation: Take cuttings 3-4"/75-100mm long of non-flowering shoots with heel in August and September. Insert in cutting compost in cold frame. Pot on rooted cuttings and overwinter in cold frame. Plunge outdoors in May and pot on. Plant out 1 year later. For hedging plant 18"/45cm apart in autumn or spring. Remove top of all shoots to promote bushy growth.

Care and cultivation: Cut back flower shoots after flowering. Trim hedges at same time. If pruned severely will have fewer flowers next year, but can be done to bring plant or hedge back into shape.

Escallonia macrantha

EUONYMUS
Spindle Tree, Spindleberry
Europe, Asia

Origins and history: Native shrub. First foreign species *E. fortunei*—sent from Japan by Robert Fortune in the 1860s. Others followed.

Description: D E Best known for autumn colours—lobed brightly-coloured fruits and autumn foliage in deciduous varieties; evergreens often variegated and grown for foliage. Flowers are inconspicuous. E less hardy than D—best in mild areas. *E. europaeus* D is native spindle tree: height 6-10'/1.8-3m, spread 4-10'/1.2-3m—some named varieties. *E. fortunei* and *E. japonica* both E Japanese varieties—upright and prostrate, plain and variegated varieties. Remember *Euonymus* is a second host for blackfly if you grow broad beans.

Flowers: May-June.

Uses: D brilliant autumn colour when much else in the border is fading. E makes good ground cover and hedging in mild areas, especially in coastal districts.

Site and soil: Any ordinary garden soil in sun or partial shade. Good on chalk soils. E varieties more shade-tolerant, but must be sheltered. Variegated varieties usually the most tender.

Propagation: Take cuttings 3-4"/75-100mm long with heel in August or September, insert in cutting compost in cold frame. Plant out rooted cuttings in April or May in nursery rows. Grow on 2 years and plant out. *Or*, layer shoots and leave for 1 year, then sever rooted layers and plant out. For hedges plant 15-18"/37-45cm apart, and pinch out growing points to encourage bushy growth.

Care and cultivation: D—pruning not usually necessary. Can be trimmed in February to keep shape. Clip evergreen hedges in April.

Pests and diseases: Powdery Mildew, Honey Fungus.

FORSYTHIA

E Asia, S E Europe

Origins and history: Collected by Robert Fortune in China in the 1840s.

Description: D Well-known early flowering shrub with yellow flowers which appear in spring before the leaves. Height 4-10'/1.2-3m; spread similar. Untidy habit. Few cultivated species, but with several hybrids and garden varieties. *F.*x *intermedia* most common garden variety. *F. suspensa* most common species.

Flowers: February-April, depending on variety.

Uses: Excellent for early spring colour. Hardy, and good for almost any soil or situation; good in cities and polluted areas. Will create hedge with some sort of support. Good against walls.

Site and soil: Any ordinary garden soil, preferably in sun or partial shade.

Propagation: Take cuttings 10-12"/25-30cm long of current season's growth in October. Insert in nursery bed outdoors. Plant in permanent position 1 year later. *Or*, layer in October and sever 1 year later (will sometimes layer naturally). For hedging, plant 18-24"/45-60cm apart, October to March.

Care and cultivation: Do not prune too hard, or you will get growth at the expense of flowers. Remove crowded shoots from centre of bush at base, and cut out oldest wood. If drastic pruning is necessary, spread it over 2-3 years. For training against walls, select shoots for fan-shaped frame and cut out others in early years until the shape is established. Shorten shoots after flowering to keep shrubs more compact. Clip hedges in April after flowering.

Pests and diseases: Birds attack flowers.

FUCHSIA

C & S America, New Zealand

Origins and history: Discovered by Plumier in sixteenth century, then lost again, and rediscovered in the seventeenth century.

Description: D Bell-like flowers in white, pink, red and purple, often bi-coloured. Very ornamental. Spectacular when in flower. Not fully hardy in cold areas. Varying habits and heights, according to variety. *F. magellanica* hardiest for outdoor cultivation in Britain—many good garden varieties from it. Few species of fuchsia used in gardens now—have been superseded by hybrids and garden varieties. Ancestry of these very often now lost.

Fuchsias are another highly complex area for the specialist, but they are also a delight to grow for the amateur.

Flowers: June-October.

Uses: Upright varieties can be used as specimen shrubs or against walls. Half hardy trailing varieties good for walls, tubs and hanging baskets, or used as bedding out plants; dwarfs for rock gardens. *F. magellanica* good for hedges in western coastal areas.

Site and soil: Any fertile well-drained garden soil in sun or partial shade. Must retain moisture.

Propagation: Take stem cuttings 2-3"/50-75mm long in July. Insert in cutting compost in cold frame. Pot on, overwinter and set out the following May, after the last frost.

Care and cultivation: In mild coastal areas little pruning is necessary except to cut out dead wood in spring. In colder areas, cut back almost to ground level in November like herbaceous plants. In very cold areas mulch crowns with straw, bracken or peat, weighed down to protect from frost. Add peat or leafmould mulch annually, and a little bonemeal. Water in dry periods.

GENISTA

Broom   *Europe, Asia*

Origins and history: 'Planta Genista' was the emblem of the Plantagenet kings of England. Native species.

Description: D Profuse peaflower-shaped flowers in gold or yellow on long, almost leafless, stems. Habit very diverse according to variety. Height anything from 6"-15'/15cm-4.5m. Difference between *Genista* and *Cytisus* controversial—to gardeners they are all broom!

Flowers: May-July.

Uses: Low-growing varieties—*G. lydia* and *G. hispanica*—make good ground cover, or good for rock gardens. Others make good hardy shrubs. Useful for poor soil, where they thrive.

Site and soil: Any well-drained, preferably light, garden soil. Too rich soil will produce fewer flowers. Sandy soil is best, in full sun.

Propagation: Seed is easier than cuttings, which can be difficult. Sow seeds in March and place in cold frame. Prick out into pots and plunge outdoors. Plant out between

October and April. Or, take cuttings 2-4"/50-100mm long of lateral shoots with heel in August. Insert in cutting compost in cold frame. Pot on in spring and plunge outdoors. Plant out between October and April.

Care and cultivation: Prune as little as possible; trim flower shoots lightly after flowering if necessary. Never cut back to old wood, or the plant will die. Dislikes being moved.

HAMAMELIS
Witch Hazel   *Asia, N America*

Origins and history: Siebold brought first example of *H. japonica* from Japan to the West in 1820s. *H. mollis* first collected for Vietch's Nurseries from China in 1877. Source of soothing lotion for skin.

Description: D Yellow or red spider-like flowers, sometimes sweet-scented, in winter or early spring, bright red and orange foliage in autumn. Hazel-like leaves. *H. mollis* (China) and *H. japonica* (Japan) most common species. *H.xintermedia* is garden hybrid between the two. *H. mollis* best for scent. Height 4-10'/1.2-3m; spread similar. Requires plenty of space for spread.

Flowers: January-March, depending on variety.

Uses: Very good for early scent and colour, and late colour in autumn. Very hardy—the early flowers are frost-resistant.

Site and soil: Well-drained, moist, preferably acid, garden soil in sun or partial shade. Shelter from cold winds. Dislikes lime.

Propagation: Take 4"/10cm cuttings of lateral shoots with heel in September, and insert them in cutting compost in cold frame. Pot on and plunge outside in May. Plant in nursery rows in autumn, grow on for 2 years, then plant in permanent position (cuttings can be quite difficult). Or (preferably), layer long shoots in September, sever and replant after 2 years.

Care and cultivation: Pruning unnecessary. Remove any suckers. Can cut back straggling shoots on old plants after flowering. Mulch with peat, well-rotted manure, leafmould or compost.

HEBE

Veronica *New Zealand*

Origins and history: First species brought by Richard Cunningham from explorations in New Zealand in 1834.

Description: E Large family of evergreen shrubs, grown for decorative foliage and flowers. Smaller-leaved varieties are generally hardier than large-leaved. Spikes of blue or white flowers. Height 6-60"/15-150cm, depending on variety; spread similar; neat and compact plants. Dozens—choose carefully to be sure you have correct hardiness, height and habit for your purpose. *H. armstrongii* (dwarf) and *H. cupressoides* among hardiest, with many hybrids from these and others.

Flowers: May-September, depending on variety.

Uses: Very useful shrubs which fit into almost any scheme. Prostrate variety *H. pinguifolia pagei* makes very decorative ground cover. Smaller varieties for rockeries. For hedges use *H. cupressoides* ('cypress-like')—hardier than most, makes small compact evergreen hedge. *Hebe* often used in coastal areas as salt-resistant. Only semi-hardy in colder districts, so use with care in north and east.

Site and soil: Any well-drained garden soil, including chalk, in partial shade or, preferably, full sun. Give adequate shelter. Do well in pots or tubs. Hebes will not thrive in cold or exposed places.

Propagation: Take cuttings 2-4"/50-100mm long of non-flowering shoots in July or August. Insert in cutting compost in cold frame. Pot on in April and plunge outdoors. Plant in permanent position in September.

Care and cultivation: Pruning unnecessary. Can cut back straggly shoots after flowering (or in spring for autumn-flowering varieties).

Pests and diseases: Honey fungus.

HEDERA

Ivy *Europe, Asia, N Africa*

Origins and history: Native plant. First became popular climber with the romantic movement in the eighteenth century, after which new varieties were bred.

Description: E If the right variety is chosen, ivy can be a useful and permanently decorative climber for walls, houses etc., with bright, dark green or variegated shiny leaves. Do not allow to become invasive. *H. helix* is native ivy—very tough, can climb 100'/30m. Some named varieties from this, often variegated. Leaves of *H. canariensis* turn bronze-green in winter—climbs 15-20'/4.5-6m. *H. colchica* 20-30'/6-9m. Many named varieties from these.

Uses: Will climb where nothing else will—self-clinging and some very hardy. Usually fast-growing. You can use it to hide almost anything. If given nothing to climb, ivy will happily cover difficult pieces of ground as ground cover.

Site and soil: Any garden soil in sun or shade. Variegated types prefer some sun.

Propagation: Take 3-5"/7-12cm cuttings of shoot tip in July or August from new runners. Insert in cutting compost in cold frame. Pot on and grow on until spring, then plant in permanent position

Care and cultivation: Cut back in February or March each year. Make sure it is doing no damage—clip away from roofs and gutters, and don't let it strangle trees.

Hebe 'Great Orme'

HYDRANGEA

Asia, Americas

Origins and history: Some varieties brought back from Japan by Fortune in 1860. Wilson discovered climbing hydrangea in China in 1899.

Description: D and E *H. macrophylla* commonest species; mop-head group: small star-shaped flowers in impressive clumps, in blue, purple, white, red or pink. Interesting in that ranges from blue through to pink according to acidity of soil; the more acid the soil the bluer the hydrangeas (in some species). Profusion of flowers in late summer; big light green leaves. Height 4-6'/1.2-1.8m; rounded shrub—can spread to some extent in mild areas. *H. macrophylla*; lace-cap group: has more delicate lacy flowers. Other species: *H. paniculata* has white cone-shaped flowers in August-September. *H. m. serrata* dwarf species, up to 36"/90cm.

Flowers: June-September depending on variety.

Uses: Flowers in late summer when there are often gaps in borders. Climbing variety good on north or east walls; self-clinging so very useful on houses.

Site and soil: Any fertile, moist, well-drained soil in sun or partial shade, preferably in sheltered position, as can be damaged by late frosts—don't face east (except climbers).

Propagation: Take cuttings 3"/75mm long from young sideshoots in June or July. Insert in cutting compost in cold frame. Pot on and plunge outdoors. Plant out in October. *H. petiolaris*—layer in summer. Sever and replant 1-2 years later.

Care and cultivation: Dead head when new buds form the following April—dead heads protect young growth (can use dead heads for dried flowers). Can thin out old shoots at ground level in March. Mulch in spring with well-rotted manure and peat. If you want to stop pink flowers turning purple on acid soil, add ground limestone. To stop blue flowers turning pink on alkaline soil, mulch with peat. *H. petiolaris* should be given support for first few years—may take time to establish itself. Then it will become self-clinging.

HYPERICUM

Rose of Sharon   *Europe, Asia*

Origins and history: St Johns Wort is our native species (*H. androsaemum*)—was used to cure melancholy and to avert evil. *H. calycinum* shrub species brought from Middle East in 1675 by George Whiler.

Description: E and D Big family. Shrub species have golden-yellow flowers with conspicuous stamens, bright red berries often turning black later, and colourful foliage in autumn. Height 1-6'/30-180cm, depending on variety; spreads widely. *H. calycinum* (12-18"/30-45cm) most common variety. Can get dwarf varieties suitable for rock gardens, e.g. *H. coris*, *H. olympicum*.

Flowers: June-October.

Uses: Good in sites that nothing else likes, particularly in shade. Reliable. *H.×moserianum* makes very attractive ground cover.

Site and soil: Any well-drained garden soil, preferably in sun, but tolerates shade. Dwarf varieties do best in mild areas.

Propagation: Take 2"/50mm cuttings of basal shoots in May or June. Insert in cutting compost in cold frame. Pot on and

Hydrangea macrophylla 'Hamburg'

overwinter in cold frame. Plant out in April. *H. calycinum* can be divided like a herbaceous perennial between October and March.

Care and cultivation: *H. calycinum* can be cut back to ground level in March; otherwise let it grow and cut it back to ground level every few years to keep it compact. For other varieties, cut out old or weak stems at base in April or May.

JASMINUM
Jasmine   *Asia, Europe*

Origins and history: *J. officinale* traditional cottage garden plant, originally from Persia: listed as growing in Britain on Syon estate in mid-sixteenth century. Gerard names *J. fruticans*—yellow-flowering in July. *J. nudiflorum* not brought to Britain until Fortune discovered it in 1840s—already an ancient and important cultivated plant in China, used to extract jasmine oil.

Description: D Winter Jasmine (*J. nudiflorum*) has bright yellow flowers November-April, and smooth, small dark green leaves—needs support against wall or fence; height up to 10'/3.6m. Other species are summer-flowering with white, yellow or pink flowers April-September—some climbers. *J. fruticans* dwarf variety, good on chalk. Various species and varieties of summer flowers, differing in height, colour and habit, so choose carefully. White Jasmine (*J. officinale*) is a climber, with white flowers July-September—twines itself around fences or trellises.

Uses: Winter jasmine provides colour when almost no other flowers are blooming. Scentless; will thrive anywhere, in shade or on north-facing walls, though flowers are susceptible to cold wind. Summer jasmines often sweet-scented and excellent in the shrub border; often tender and best grown in mild areas. Rapid growth.

Site and soil: Winter jasmine: any garden soil with any aspect but east. Needs wall or fence for support. Summer jasmines: any well-drained garden soil in sheltered position and sun. Not completely hardy in cold areas.

Propagation: Take cuttings 3-4"/75-100mm long of ripening wood in August or September. Insert in cutting compost in cold frame. Pot on and grow on, plant out following spring. *Or*, layer longer shoots in September/October. Sever after 1 year and plant out.

Care and cultivation: *J. nudiflorum*: cut back shoots that have flowered in March. Thin out old wood. Other species: thin out old shoots if necessary. Can cut back in spring if needed.

LAURUS
Bay, Bay Laurel   *Mediterranean*

Origins and history: The plant that Daphne turned into when pursued by Apollo (though no relation to *Daphne*). Traditional cottage garden plant in mild areas; grown for ornament and as culinary herb.

Description: E Aromatic shiny evergreen leaves. Inconspicuous yellow flowers in April. Male and female plants—females have purple berries if pollinated. Height 10-18'/3-5.4m; full tree shape if left unpruned. Only 2 species: *L. nobilis* usually grown.

Uses: Like box, clips very well. Often used for topiary, especially grown in tubs in formal gardens. Best grown in tubs in colder areas—can then be moved to shelter in winter. Makes an excellent hedge in mild areas. Bay leaves are used as a culinary herb.

Laurus nobilis

Site and soil: Any ordinary garden soil in sunny sheltered position. Is not fully hardy in frost or cold wind. Does best in mild and coastal areas.

Propagation: Take 4″/100mm cuttings of lateral shoots with heel in August or September. Insert in cutting compost in cold frame. Pot on and plant out in nursery bed following October. Grow on 1-2 years and plant out in spring.

Care and cultivation: Pruning not necessary. If you want to keep trimmed shrubs clip in May. To encourage young trees to develop central stem, cut back lateral shoots to 2-3 leaves. When central stem reaches right height, cut back tip to encourage bushiness. Thereafter trim tree to desired shape. Remove suckers.

Pests and diseases: If plants become sticky, may have scale insects.

LAVANDULA
Lavender   *Europe*

Origins and history: Name from Latin 'lavendus'—to be washed—used as toilet water since Roman times. Traditional cottage garden favourite. Mentioned frequently from thirteenth century onwards for its aromatic qualities.

Description: E Grey-leaved sweet-scented shrub, traditionally grown for grey-blue spiked flowers, which can be dried and used for their sweet scent. Compact habit makes it ideal for small formal hedges—much used in knot gardens. Short-lived. Height 18-42″/45-105cm, depending on variety. Old English Lavender is *L. spica* (36- 48″/ 90-120cm)—'Hidcote' the most popular variety, most compact. Can get white and pink flowered varieties as well as blue. Also French Lavender (*L. stochas*) and Dutch Lavender (*L. vera*).

Flowers: May-September.

Uses: Highly decorative, and flowers harvestable for sachets, pot-pourris etc. Harvest when flowering—hang upside down in cool place to dry. Good for edging paths or formal beds.

Site and soil: Any well-drained garden soil in sunny position. Likes lime best.

Propagation: Take 3-4″/75-100mm cuttings of non-flowering shoots in August and insert in cutting compost in cold frame. Pot on, overwinter, and plant out in spring. Lavender may self-seed. For hedges plant 9-12″/22-30cm apart.

Care and cultivation: Trim after flowering, removing all flower stems. If necessary, cut back hard in March or April. Old lavender plants can become straggly. Don't cut old wood. Mulch annually with compost or well-rotted manure.

Pests and diseases: Frost damage, Scab.

LIGUSTRUM
Privet   *Asia, Europe*

Origins and history: Native species *L. vulgare*. Berries traditionally used for green dye. Used in cottage gardens, both as shrubs and as hedging. Foreign species imported later.

Description: E D Oval shiny leaves, often variegated, varying from deep green to yellow, with sweet-smelling white flowers in June-July, and black berries in autumn. Natural habit either shrub or small tree if not pruned. When clipped makes dense hedge. *L. vulgare* has several garden varieties with variegated and coloured leaves. Other species from East Asia—*L. japonicum* and *L. lucidum* most common.

Uses: Probably most common hedging plant all over Britain—its ubiquity has earned it contempt, but it is exceedingly useful. Thrives in any soil, and is very tolerant of polluted atmosphere—a good plant in cities, where its thick screening is often most necessary.

Site and soil: Any garden soil in sun or shade.

Propagation: Take 4-6″/10-15cm hardwood cuttings in October, and insert out of doors in sheltered position. Grow on for 1 year and plant out. *Or,* insert in cold frame in August-September in cutting compost and plant out in nursery beds in April. For hedges plant 12-18″/30-45cm apart. On poor soil dig in compost or manure first.

Care and cultivation: Clip hedges in May and September. To establish new hedges, cut back all shoots to half length April after planting. Keep cutting back new growth by half its length each autumn to promote bushiness, until required height is reached. Privet grown on its own as shrub needn't be pruned. Cut out dead wood in spring if necessary.

Pests and diseases: Honey fungus. Leaf miners.

LONICERA

Honeysuckle, Woodbine   *N hemisphere*

Origins and history: Native plant, almost compulsory in cottage gardens. Reference to it in Earl of Lincoln's garden (now Lincolns Inn) before 1286. Honeysuckle arbours popular in Tudor gardens. *L. nitida* came from China in early nineteenth century, but only became popular a century later. Douglas brought new species from North America in the early nineteenth, and Wilson from China in the late nineteenth century.

Description: D SE E A large family of woodland plants, including shrubs and climbers. Tubular sweet-scented flowers with diverging lips in yellow, pink, cream, red or white. Diversity in leaf, flower, habit and flowering time. Most varieties flower for much of the summer. *L. periclymenum* is native honeysuckle or woodbine—many garden varieties. Other species from China and Japan—*L. nitida* most common for hedging. Lots of hybrids and varieties—choose carefully, considering habit, flowering time, E or D, flower shape and colour.

Uses: As climbers, will twine up fences, trellises and walls without requiring sunshine. Sweet-scented flowers for most of the summer. Lots of varieties. *L. nitida* makes dense evergreen hedge, given adequate support—tends to split lengthwise with age, and becomes gappy at base. *L. pileata* spreads rapidly, even in heavy shade, to provide ground cover—yellow-green flowers April-May. Border shrubs with more striking flowers also available.

Site and soil: Any well-drained fairly moist garden soil. Dig in peat or compost for climbers. Sun or partial shade. Keep base of climbers in shade. Shrub varieties need sheltered position. *L. nitida* does best in mild areas.

Propagation: Take 4"/100mm stem cuttings July or August and insert in cutting compost in cold frame. Pot on and plunge outside in April or May. Grow on till autumn and plant in final position. *Or*, take 8-12"/20-30cm hardwood cuttings September-October and insert in sheltered nursery bed. Plant out in final site 1 year later. *Or*, layer branches in autumn and sever one year later. Plant hedges at 9"/22cm apart.

Care and cultivation: Trim hedges in summer after flowering. Can cut straggly hedges back hard in April if necessary. Some honeysuckles flower on last year's wood—these can be cut back after flowering. Others flower on new wood—prune in winter if necessary. Don't prune climbers too often unless pushed for space. Mulch annually with peat, compost or well-rotted manure.

MAHONIA

Asia, N America

Origins and history: First species brought from North America early in the eighteenth century by John Bartram. Re-introduced by Douglas early nineteenth century. *M. bealii* brought from China by Fortune in the 1840s.

Description: E Sweet-smelling yellow globular flowers in clusters or spikes; purple berries in autumn. Large shiny evergreen holly-like leaves. Now very common in gardens. Height 3-10'/1-3m, depending on variety. *M. japonica* most common species, drooping sweet-scented flowers January-March. *M. bealii* (China) similar—

Mahonia aquifolium

flowers (erect spikes) December-February. *M. aquifolium* low-growing variety. Several garden varieties from these species.

Flowers: December-April, depending on variety.

Uses: Most species hardy. Year-round attraction with early flowers, attractive leaves and autumn berries. *M. aquifolium* good for ground cover. Also good as a low hedge.

Site and soil: Any well-drained garden soil in sun or partial shade. Likes chalk. Grows well under trees.

Propagation: Take tip cuttings 3-4"/75-100mm long in July, or take leaf cuttings October-November. Insert in cutting compost indoors. Pot on and keep sheltered from frost over winter. Plant out after 1 year. *Or*, layer in spring, and sever after 1 year. Ground cover species: dig up rooted suckers and replant.

Care and cultivation: Pruning not necessary. Can trim hedges or ground cover in April. Water and watch after planting—once settled will look after themselves.

PARTHENOCISSUS

Virginia Creeper, Boston Ivy
Asia, N America

Origins and history: First brought from Virginia by John Tradescant in 1650s. Veitch brought *P. tricuspidata* from Japan in 1860s, which quickly became most popular species.

Description: D Thin-stemmed vigorous climbers, attaching themselves to walls with tendrils or adhesive discs. Leaves vary in shape according to variety, with stunning autumn colours. Make sure you get the one you want. Very small flowers May-July. *P. tricuspidata* (Japan and China) most popular. *P. thomsonii* similar with decorative foliage. Also *P. quinquefolia* from North America—can be invasive on houses. Height 20-70'/6-21m.

Uses: Excellent for sides of houses, as one of few self-clinging climbers that tolerates either sun or shade.

Site and soil: Fertile well-drained garden soil in sun or partial shade. Dig in compost or well-rotted manure before planting.

Propagation: Take hardwood cuttings 10-12"/25-30cm long in autumn and insert at half length in sheltered nursery bed. Grow on for 1 year and plant out. *Or*, layer

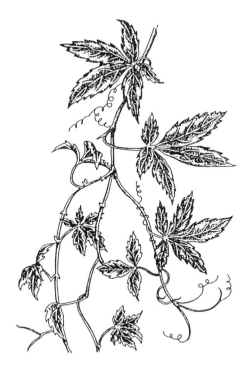

Parthenocissus henryana

stems in October-November and sever after 1 year. Supply young plants with cane to grow up.

Care and cultivation: Cut back excess growth in summer if necessary. Make sure roofs, gutters and windows are kept clear. Provide young plants with support until they become self-clinging.

Pests and diseases: Aphids, Scale Insects; Honey Fungus.

PERNETTYA

Prickly Heath   *S America*

Origins and history: Found near Magellan Straits by Joseph Banks on Cook's voyage round the world in 1769.

Description: E Chief attraction are the brightly-coloured pink fruits (disliked by birds) which last through the winter. Dark green shiny leaves and white heather-like flowers. Some plants unisexual—need male and female to set fruit on females. Height 24-36"/60-90cm; shape dense, and can become straggly. *P. mucronata* only garden species—several varieties, some with different coloured berries—white or red as well as pink.

Flowers: May-June.

Uses: Winter berries add colour at time when needed. Can form dense thicket if you have anything to hide. Good ground cover.

Site and soil: Any well-drained acid soil—hates lime—in sun or partial shade. Add peat when planting.

Propagation: Take cuttings 2"/50mm long September-October. Insert in cutting compost in cold frame. Plant out in nursery rows in spring and grow on 1-2 years, then plant in final position. Will self-seed freely.

Care and cultivation: Pruning not necessary. Can trim in summer. Cut back leggy plants to old wood late winter.

PHILADELPHUS

Mock Orange   *N hemisphere*

Origins and history: Often called 'Syringa', which causes confusion, as *Syringa* is the botanical name for Lilac. Traditional cottage garden flower, listed by Gerard in 1597. Introduced from Turkey in 1562, along with Lilac—hence the semantic confusion.

Description: D Usually white cup-shaped sweetly-scented flowers and mid-green strongly-veined leaves. In the evenings a scent of orange blossom will pervade the garden. Very hardy and long-lived. Height 3-10'/1-3m, depending on variety. Can get overcrowded and out of hand if left too long unpruned. Several hybrid and garden varieties. *P.* 'Belle Etoile' and *P.* 'Virginal' perhaps most common. Can get dwarf varieties, and a golden-leafed variety 'Aureus' from species *P. coronarius*, which is the original of most garden varieties.

Flowers: June-July.

Uses: Found in most shrubberies and shrub beds. Will grow in almost any soil and environment, indifferent to sea, wind or heavy pollution.

Site and soil: Any well-drained garden soil. Tolerates lime or acid. Full sun or partial shade.

Propagation: Take 4"/100mm cuttings of lateral shoots July or August and insert in cutting compost in cold frame. Plant out

Philadelphus 'Belle Etoile'

in nursery bed in spring, and transplant to permanent positions in October. *Or*, take 12"/30cm hardwood cuttings in October-November, and insert in nursery bed. Plant out 1 year later.

Care and cultivation: Thin out old flowering stems after flowering (usually in July), and give new wood space to grow and flower. May need to cut out old branches from centre.

PIERIS

Andromeda   *Asia, America*

Origins and history: *P. japonica* brought from Japan early nineteenth century by William Kerr. Other species followed.

Description: E Foliage startling copper or red colour in spring, fading to cream, and turning green later. Clusters of small white flowers resembling lily of the valley, on compact shrubs. Named varieties of *P. formosa* give best combinations of flowers and leaf colour. *P. japonica* also gives good flower display. Height 4-12'/1.2-3.6m, depending on variety.

Flowers: April-May.

Pieris forrestii

Uses: Very good addition to any peat-based garden—goes well with rhododendrons and azaleas. Red foliage good foil to dark green evergreen leaves in spring.

Site and soil: Any moist lime-free loam. Add more peat at planting. Sun or partial shade. Protect from eastern sun—danger of frost catching flowers.

Propagation: Take 3-4"/75-100mm cuttings of shoots in August. Insert in cutting compost in cold frame. Pot on and grow on for 2 years, then plant in final positions. Or (*P. formosa*), layer in September. Sever after 2 years and replant.

Care and cultivation: Pruning unnecessary. Dead head flowers in May. Can thin a little if overcrowded, but pruning will mean fewer flowers next year. Mulch every spring with peat or leafmould.

POTENTILLA
N hemisphere

Origins and history: *P. fruticosa* is the species from which nearly all shrub varieties are descended. Widely distributed through northern hemisphere—some native, some modern hybrids, mostly from Himalayan species. Some not discovered until the twentieth century.

Description: D Shrub species have white, yellow, red or orange flowers and deeply-cut leaves. Height 1-5'/30-150cm; compact shape. 2 garden species—*P. fruticosa* has produced numerous named varieties, with red as well as yellow flowers. *P. arbuscula* has some garden varieties, some of which are very similar to *P. fruticosa*.

Flowers: May-October.

Uses: Very hardy; will grow almost anywhere, requiring very little attention. Good in tubs, and as hedges.

Site and soil: Any well-drained garden soil in sun or partial shade. The more sun, the more flowers.

Propagation: Take 3"/75mm cuttings of lateral shoots with heel in September or October. Insert in cutting compost in cold frame. Plant out in nursery bed in May. Grow on, and plant in permanent site in October. Self-seeds.

Care and cultivation: Prune in March. Cut out weak or old stems at ground level. Shorten young stems if growing straggly.

PRUNUS
Cherry Laurel   *E Europe, Middle East*

Origins and history: Cultivated since sixteenth century as medicinal herb. Traditional cottage garden shrub.

Description: E Mostly trees in the genus, but the shrubs have a function of their own. Evergreen laurels most often used as hedges. Oblong shiny pointed leaves, dark green on top, pale green underneath. White flowers in April, followed by small black fruits. *P. laurocerasus* is cherry laurel or common laurel—several named varieties. *P. lusitanica* (Spain and Portugal) similar—variegated varieties—have red leaf stalks. Height 15-20'/4.5-6m; spread (unpruned) 20-30'/6-9m.

Flowers: April.

Uses: Very good for hedges, screens and windbreaks. Tolerant of shade and pollution. Can be used in shrubberies, especially under trees where shade is excessive for other shrubs. Tends to be associated with gloomy institutional gardens, but this isn't altogether fair. *P. lusitanica* used to be used for topiary.

Site and soil: Any normal garden soil. Preferably partial shade.

Propagation: Take cuttings 3-4"/75-100mm long of new shoots with heel in August. Insert in cutting compost in cold frame. Pot on and plant out in nursery rows in spring. Grow on 1-2 years, then plant out in final position.

Care and cultivation: Trim hedges in April-May. Will tolerate heavy pruning if necessary.

Pests and diseases: Mildew.

RHODODENDRON
Rhododendron, Azalea

Origins and history: 10 European species, around 25 in North America, and 31 in the Far East. 200 in Malaysia, and 400 in the region famed for rhododendrons—the Himalayas. A huge and complicated family. The first rhododendrons to come to Britain came from North America, brought by John Tradescant jr. *R. hirsutum* appears in his garden catalogue for 1656. The European rhododendrons did not appear until the 1760s, when *R. ponticum* was introduced from Spain. Late eighteenth century saw the introduction of other American species. The great moment came in 1820, when the seeds of *R. arboreum* arrived from the Himalayas, sent by Nathaniel Wallich. *R. arboreum* is tender, but has become the parent of hundreds of hardy varieties—most modern varieties are descended from it in some way. Hooker's expedition to the Himalayas in 1847-50 produced 43 more species. Later in the nineteenth century other collectors in the Himalayas added to the number. Rhododendrons became a craze, and because they adapted so well to the British—particularly the Scottish—climate, Britain became the centre of rhododendron breeding. This started at Kew in 1817 with *R.×hybridum* from North American parents. Breeding went on in the late nineteenth and twentieth centuries after the Himalayan species were established, and many more hardy varieties were introduced. During the twentieth century the breeding of rhododendrons has become vastly diverse and complicated—in 1980 alone 190 new names were added to the International Rhododendron Register. Most hybrids and varieties are unavailable commercially because they are too expensive to produce, but the choice is still bewildering. Anyone who applies their mind to the rhododendron family will soon realise that the classification of species and

Rhododendron 'Blue Diamond'
(dwarf hybrid)

varieties has been the subject of botanical research for over a century, and is by no means definitive yet. For a long time rhododendrons and azaleas were thought to be separate families. They are now officially classified together, but for practical purposes gardeners still make the distinction. Do not worry too much about classifications, but consider the available varieties and be quite sure you choose the plant you want.

Description: For convenience, rhododendrons and azaleas are described separately.

RHODODENDRONS
E Vary in size from prostrate to trees 30'/9m tall. Evergreen lance-shaped leaves vary in size and details from one variety to another, and are often very decorative. Flowers appear any time between February and August, but most varieties are spring-flowering—May and June are the months to visit rhododendron gardens. Flowers usually bell-shaped, sometimes fragrant, most often in clusters —white, pink, mauve, purple, yellow, red and orange. *R. ponticum* is the commonest tree rhododendron in Britain, naturalized in many areas, especially in Scotland. Spreading tree up to 20'/6m high; pinkish-purple flowers in June; hardy, good for windbreaks. Many other tree varieties available—don't necessarily take *ponticum*;

varieties of R. arboreum give a wide range of colours. The average garden, however, will need something smaller. Look for hardy hybrids—hundreds available at 3-6'/1-2m, and usually hardier than tree species. Consider colour, flowering time, leaf shape and ultimate height. If you are planting a rhododendron bed or shrubbery, you can either stagger flowering times (though this is only really effective on a large scale) or have a show in May and June. For dwarf varieties, there are modern compact rhododendrons, hybrids derived partly from Japanese species. These are hardy and flower mid-late May; height 3-4'/9C 120cm. Many other smaller hybrids witn different flowering times, less than 3'/1m high. R. repens is prostrate species.

AZALEAS
D or E Deciduous azaleas up to 10'/3m. Most likely to come across 'Mollis' hybrids (4-5'/1.2-1.5m); scentless flowers, brilliant autumn foliage colours. For scented azaleas, pick 'Ghent' hybrids (5-6'/1.5-2m); flower late May-June, mostly orange or yellow flowers. 'Knap Hill' and 'Exbury' hybrids 3-6'/1-2m; bred since 1945; flower late, usually in June, so a good bet in areas troubled by late frosts. Not many evergreen azalea species, but numerous hybrids from them. Evergreen azaleas are low spreading shrubs, flowering profusely in May. 'Kurume' (Japan) best-known hybrid strain; also 'Vuyk' (Holland), with small glossy leaves. Evergreen azaleas are more tender than deciduous ones.

Site and soil: Cannot grow rhododendrons on lime or chalk. Plant in acid soil, and add peat when planting. If leaves turn yellow may need more acid. Need partial shade and plenty of moisture. Most prefer sheltered position. Avoid exposure to east as early flowers may be damaged by frost. Preferably plant in shade of deep-rooting trees—trees with shallow roots will take too much moisture from the surface. Rhododendrons all have shallow roots.

Propagation: Easiest to layer branches in summer. Sever and replant after 2 years. Hybrids are usually grafted. Species can be grown from seed.

Care and cultivation: Dead head flowers of truss-flowered varieties by hand (unless you have an estate full, then don't bother). Mulch with peat, leaf mould or well-rotted manure. Keep young plants moist and free from weeds. Because of the acid soil

required, it is often difficult to grow other plants near established rhododendrons.

Pests and Diseases: Rhododendron leaf hopper (bright green with red stripes) lives on leaves from July onwards, and females lay eggs in bud scales. Rhododendron bug lives on leaf sap and causes mottling on leaf surface. Whitefly (especially azalea whitefly). Azalea gall—small swellings in young leaves and buds, which eventually shrivel up and turn brown: pick off infected areas. Rhododendron bud blast—buds turn brown or black and die. Rust; Silver Leaf.

RHUS
Sumach   *N America, Asia*

Origins and history: S. typhina brought by Tradescant from North America—cultivated since 1629.

Description: D Main feature is bright autumn foliage—large pinnate leaves which turn orange, red or purple, and colourful fruit clusters. Its suckers can make it invasive. Some species can cause skin rashes. R. typhina (Stag's Horn Sumach) from eastern North America the most common. R. glabra is smaller and more compact and controllable. Height 5-15'/1.5-4.5m, depending on variety.

Flowers: June-July. Red flowers more or less significant according to variety.

Uses: Autumn colour. Also very easy to grow, and adaptable to almost any environment.

Site and soil: Any ordinary garden soil in sunny position.

Propagation: Easy: remove suckers from October on, and plant in permanent positions. Or, layer shoots in March. Sever after 1-2 years.

Care and cultivation: Thin crowded shoots in March. Alternatively, for lots of autumn foliage, prune back to ground level between February and April.

RIBES
Flowering Currant   *N hemisphere*

Origins and history: R. sanguineum from western North America, discovered by botanist Menzies in 1793. RHS began to cultivate it in England from 1826—now very common. R. aureum also introduced early nineteenth century.

Description: D SE Same family as edible

Ribes sanguineum 'Pulborough Scarlet'

currants. Several ornamental species. Abundant white, yellow, pink or red flowers in March and April, and rounded pale green leaves. Very fast growing. Curranty smell. *R. sanguineum* most common—several named varieties. *R. aureum* has yellow flowers; *R. speciosum* fuchsia-like red flowers in May. Height 3-10'/1-3m, depending on variety.

Flowers: March-April.

Uses: Very quick to grow—instant shrub border. Bright spring colour. Hardy and easy to cultivate. Can be used for hedging.

Site and soil: Any well-drained garden soil in sun or light shade.

Propagation: Take 10-12"/25-30cm hardwood cuttings in autumn and insert in sheltered nursery bed. Plant out after 1 year.

Care and cultivation: Flowers on year-old wood, so cut back old wood after flowering in May.

SANTOLINA

Cotton Lavender   *Europe*

Origins and history: Traditional cottage garden plant; used as hedging in knot gardens.

Description: E Small round yellow flowers

on compact bushes with silver-grey finely-cut foliage. Sweet-scented. *S. chamaecyparissus* most common species. *S. virens* has green, not grey, leaves. *S. neapolitana* taller —up to 36"/90cm. Height 12-24"/30-60cm, depending on variety.

Flowers: June-August.

Uses: Can be used singly at front of border, or as low hedge. Pleasant to have by house or border because of its scent.

Site and soil: Any well-drained garden soil in sunny position.

Propagation: Take cuttings 2-3"/50-75mm long of new shoots in July-August. Insert in cutting compost in cold frame. Pot on and plunge outdoors in spring. Plant out in final position in September.

Care and cultivation: Dead head. Cut back hard after flowering, or will become straggly.

SENECIO

New Zealand

Origins and history: From Latin 'senex'—old man, referring to grey seed

Senecio laxifolius

cones. Largest family in plant world. Shrub species nearly all from New Zealand, brought to Britain during nineteenth century.

Description: E Related to our native groundsel and ragwort. Yellow daisy-like flowers and silver-grey foliage—oval leaves are down-covered. Best grown in coastal areas—not entirely hardy in cold districts. *S. greyi* and *S. laxifolius* most commonly-named species, but in fact a hybrid of these, *S.xsunshine* is even more likely to be found. Hybrids also related to *S. compactus*—a dwarf species which gives a more compact plant. Height 2-6'/60-180cm; shape wide-spreading.

Flowers: June-July.

Uses: Attractive foliage all year round. Resistant to salt spray. Can use for low hedges in sheltered areas.

Site and soil: Any well-drained garden soil, including chalk, in full sun. Needs shelter from cold wind or frost. Good by sea.

Propagation: Take 3-4"/75-100mm cuttings of new lateral shoots in August, and insert in cutting compost in cold frame. Plant out in nursery bed April-May and grow on. Plant in final position in October.

Care and cultivation: Cut out any frost-damaged shoots in spring, and thin if necessary.

SKIMMIA

E Asia

Origins and history: In 1820s Dutch botanist Kaempfer discovered first species in Japan. Fortune brought *S. japonica* to Britain in 1847, and *S. reevesiana* on a later trip.

Description: E Oval shiny leaves, small star-shaped cream-coloured flowers in spring, followed by poisonous red berries on female plants which remain through autumn and winter. Single sex plants; need at least 1 male to get berries on females. *S. japonica* most common species—many garden varieties from this. If you only want one plant make sure it is *S. reevesiana*—these are bisexual. Height 18-60"/45-150cm.

Flowers: March-April.

Uses: Year-round colour—flowers in spring, berries in autumn and winter. Compact and dense habit—easy to care for.

Skimmia japonica

Site and soil: Any well-drained, preferably acid, garden soil in sun or partial shade. *S. reevesiana* must be in lime-free soil.

Propagation: Take 3"/75mm cuttings with heel of lateral shoots in July-August. Insert in cutting compost in cold frame. Plant out in nursery bed following spring and grow on 2-3 years. Plant out in final position autumn or spring.

Care and cultivation: Pruning unnecessary.

SYRINGA

Lilac   Europe, Asia

Origins and history: Very familiar cottage garden shrub. *S. persica* brought from Mediterranean by Tradescant in mid-sixteenth century, whence it had come from Turkey, introduced along with *Philadelphus* in 1562. Related to the olive. By 1597 there were several species in British gardens listed by Gerard. Other varieties came from Far East in nineteenth century.

Description: D Very fragrant purple, pink, red or white flowers massed on heavy heads. Short but beautiful flowering season. *S. vulgaris* is common lilac, originally with lilac-coloured flowers, now numerous varieties in various colours. Other species

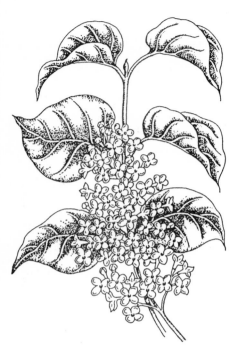

Syringa vulgaris

and varieties from them, though less common, are available. Height 6-12'/1.8-3.6m.

Flowers: May-June.

Uses: Beautiful spring display. Butterflies like it.

Site and soil: Any ordinary garden soil, in sun or partial shade. Likes chalk. Prefers milder areas or sheltered situation.

Propagation: Take 3-4"/75-100mm long cuttings of new shoots with heel in July-August. Insert in cutting compost in cold frame. Pot on and plant out in sheltered nursery bed in March. Grow on 1-2 years and plant out in final position.

Care and cultivation: Dead head if you can reach. Restrict suckers. Thin new shoots after flowering, and cut out weak branches.

Pests and diseases: Leaf Miner; Honey Fungus, Lilac Blight, Silver Leaf.

VIBURNUM

Guelder Rose, Wayfaring Tree
N hemisphere

Origins and history: Guelder Rose (*V. opulus*) and Wayfaring Tree (*V. lantana*) native shrubs and traditional in cottage gardens. Other species imported in last 2 centuries. Seeds of *V. farreri* brought to Europe by Jesuit d'Incarville from Far East in early eighteenth century, but not cultivated till 1909, when rediscovered by Farrer and Purdam. Other species discovered by Fortune in Far East.

Description: D E Very varied. Some flower in winter before leaves grow. Others flower in summer along with leaves. Others grown for bright berries and autumn colour. All have clusters of sweet-scented flowers, usually white or pink. *V. farreri* most popular of winter flowerers—very fragrant. *V. tinus* another, with several varieties. *V. opulus* is our native Guelder Rose—several garden varieties. Other summer flowerers are *V. davidii* (dramatic blue berries) and *V. plicatum* (Japanese Snowball). Many other species and varieties. Height and habit very variable, from ground cover to shrubs 12'/3.6m high. Remember *Viburnum* is a second host for blackfly if you grow broad beans.

Viburnum tinus

Flowers: December-June, depending on species.

Uses: A basic choice for the shrub bed—reliable, beautiful and fragrant. Winter flowerers particularly welcome in dark months. Can use for hedging. Copes well with pollution.

Site and soil: Any good garden soil, rich in humus, in sunny position. Do not expose winter flowerers to excessive frost or wind.

Propagation: Take cuttings of lateral shoots, with heel, 3-4"/75-100mm long in August-September. Insert in cutting compost in cold frame. Plant out in sheltered nursery bed in May and grow on 2-3 years. Plant in final position in October or March. *Or,* layer in September and sever after 1 year.

Care and cultivation: Pruning unnecessary. Can cut out old or damaged wood of winter flowerers in April or May; summer flowerers in June.

VINCA

Periwinkle   *Europe*

Origins and history: *V. minor* possibly a native plant, and traditional cottage garden flower. Used by Romans for making garlands. Grown in medieval monastery gardens. Medicinal plant—supposedly cures painful periods.

Description: E Mat-forming shrub that spreads by sending out runners. Glossy evergreen leaves, sometimes variegated. Blue, purple, red or white, flat-faced delicate flowers. 2 species: *V. major* (Greater Periwinkle) and *V. minor.* Several garden varieties, including ones with variegated leaves and pink or white flowers. Height 2-9"/5-22cm; spreads indefinitely.

Flowers: May-September, depending on variety.

Uses: Ideal ground cover plant in sun or shade—evergreen, dense, and requires very little attention. Good on rough banks, and will compete well with weeds if necessary, though can be invaded by grasses.

Site and soil: Any ordinary well-drained garden soil in sun or shade.

Propagation: Easy: divide between September and April and replant. Cut off a stem and insert it in soil—it will root very quickly.

Care and cultivation: May need to be cut back to stop spreading, and new runners may have to be dug up.

WEIGELA

E Asia

Origins and history: Named after von Weigel, German professor of botany, and sent to Britain by Fortune in 1845.

Description: D Pink, red or white (one species yellow) foxglove-like flowers in early summer on dense slow-growing bushes, attractive even when not in flower. *W. florida* (China) most common species —several garden varieties. Height 5-8'/1.5-2.4m, depending on variety.

Flowers: May-June.

Uses: Good in all kinds of garden. Very resistant to pollution and needs little attention. Good on banks.

Site and soil: Any well-drained, fairly moist soil in sun or partial shade.

Propagation: Take 10-12"/25-30cm long cuttings of current year's growth in October. Insert in sheltered nursery bed. Grow on for 1 year and plant out in final position in autumn.

Weigela florida variegata

Care and cultivation: Prune after flowering. Flowers come on new wood each year, so cut back some old stems when flowering is finished.

WISTERIA

E Asia, N America

Origins and history: Named after Wistar, American professor of botany. American species *W. frutescans* introduced to Britain in 1724 by Catesbury. *W. sinensis* imported from Canton by Benjamin Tain in 1816—created a sensation.

Description: D Spectacular climbers—peaflower-like purple or white flowers in drooping clusters. Sweet-scented. Strong twining stems can become rampant. *W. sinensis* most popular, though does best in milder areas. Several varieties of this. Take care—can become invasive on houses. *W. floribunda* less vigorous—some varieties of this. *W. sinensis* can climb 100'/30m; others 30'/9m or so.

Flowers: May-June.

Uses: Will climb walls, fences, arches, houses, anything—given something to twine up.

Site and soil: Any reasonable garden soil, enriched with compost or well-rotted manure. Best aspect south or west, to protect flowers from frost.

Propagation: Layer *W. sinensis*. Sever and replant after 1 year. Otherwise propagated by grafting—easiest to buy new plants.

Care and cultivation: Cut back stems by half each spring until good shape trained against wall. Keep cutting back to within 5 or 6 buds of old wood after flowering, as far as you can reach. Take care to keep wisteria off roofs and gutters.

Wisteria sinensis

Roses

Origins and history: Wild roses originated in central Asia, spread westwards to colonize Europe, and eastwards to North America. They are now native to all temperate climates. We have several native species, including *R. canina*, Dog Rose (which is used as the root stock for many of our cultivated roses), and *R. rubiginosa*, Sweet Briar (which is used as a rootstock for many climbers and ramblers).

In every culture that has known roses, they have been given a symbolic or mythological significance—we can see this clearly in our language, poetry, art and heraldry—and we find roses used similarly in other cultures, both ancient and modern.

Roses were first cultivated on a large scale in ancient Persia, where whole gardens were devoted to them. Roses grew in the hanging gardens of Babylon, and the first identifiable picture of roses comes from Crete. Sappho called the rose 'the queen of flowers'. The Romans probably introduced the Red Rose (*R. gallica*) and the White Rose (*R. alba*) to Britain. After the fall of Rome, England and France became the centres of rose cultivation.

By the end of the sixteenth century, five species were being used for the creation of garden varieties in Britain: *R. alba*, *R. gallica*, *R. centifolia* (Cabbage Rose), *R. moschata* (Musk Rose) and *R. damascena* (Damask Rose). This last was reputedly introduced by returning Crusaders, but in fact arrived via Italy in the sixteenth century. Gerard mentions all these species in his garden inventory. With the exception of Musk Roses (modern Musk Roses have a different descent) you will not need to look far to find descendants of all these roses.

Though some varieties are quite new, they are all referred to as Old-Fashioned Roses. In the early eighteenth century, either in Holland or France, *R. centifolia* produced a sport in which the seedcases and flower stalks were covered with a mossy growth. These first appeared in an English catalogue in 1724 as Moss Roses, and they too are still with us.

1800 is a convenient dividing line in rose history, as the nineteenth century saw the rapid development of Modern Roses. The first China Rose reached Britain at the very end of the eighteenth century, opening up a whole new avenue of possibilities. By 1815 a China Rose, *R. chinensis* had been crossed with an Autumn Damask Rose, and the first Bourbon hybrid was produced. Many more hybrids followed, first the Portland hybrids, then a group named the Hybrid Perpetuals, which extended their flowering season by flowering repeatedly, but not for nearly as long as we are used to today. The first China Roses were scentless, but in 1809 a scented China Rose was introduced, called 'Hume's Blush', and as its fragrance was likened to fresh tea, it was known as a Tea-Scented China Rose. Tea Roses were not very hardy, but when crossed with the Hybrid Perpetuals they produced the much tougher Hybrid Tea Roses, whose descendants are still with us in bewildering abundance. In 1885 a yellow Hybrid Tea Rose appeared, and its descendants extended the colour range from whites, pinks and reds to yellows, oranges and browns.

In 1875 a new strain appeared, the result of a cross between *R. chinensis* and the Japanese *R. multiflora*, a recurrent-flowering cluster-headed rose named the 'Polyantha Pompon'. In 1924 Polyantha Pompons and Hybrid Tea Roses were crossed to produce the Hybrid Polyanthas. After years of development the Hybrid Polyanthas were renamed 'Floribunda'.

In modern catalogues the largest groups will be the Hybrid Teas (Large-Flowered Roses) and the Floribundas (Cluster-Flowered Roses), and this is the first choice you will have to make. The precise dividing line between the two has been lost—they are often cross-bred, producing the Floribunda/Hybrid Tea group.

About 20 species have contributed to our modern rose hybrids, of which there are now over 25,000 varieties, and more are being added every year. The breeding of roses has become a vast and complex world into which nearly all gardeners have strayed a little way—around 80% of British gardens contain roses. Nearly all of these are Modern Roses, though the species and Old-Fashioned Roses have made a gradual comeback since the Second World War, and several firms now specialize in selling them. When you buy roses, go to a nursery or catalogue that offers a good selection of the vast range available—the possibilities are too great to be ignored.

Description: There is no space in this book to touch upon the infinite varieties of the rose. Instead I have indicated the main groups you will encounter, so you can select particular varieties within that framework. There are numerous books devoted to roses that will describe the long lists of varieties for you. Do study one before buying, and don't limit yourself.

SPECIES AND SHRUB ROSES

A shrub rose is one which flowers on the previous season's wood. Unlike a bush rose, therefore, it retains permanent branches which are left unpruned.

Species and Old-Fashioned Roses

All original species are shrubs. Our native rose species have 5-petalled pink flowers appearing on single stems May-June, followed by red hips, used for medicinal syrups and jellies. Hardy and very pest and disease resistant. It is possible to get the original species of some of our long-cultivated roses, but after so many years of breeding the distinction between true species and varieties is often not clear.

Old-Fashioned Roses, like species roses, grow on large bushes. Small flowers, often fragrant. Flowers come at same time, but often last many weeks, followed by ornamental hips. Shrubs are large, prickly, often straggly, requiring plenty of space but little maintenance.

Gallica Roses (descended from *R. gallica*) are the commonest Old-Fashioned Roses. Fairly compact (height and spread up to 48"/120cm); crimson, purple or even striped richly-scented flowers in June. Send out quantities of suckers which, being more vigorous, can crowd out varieties if unchecked—will create a thick hedge, easily taking over an area. 'Rosa Mundi' is most famous variety.

White Roses (descended from *R. alba*) reach 6'/2m height and spread; sweet-scented white or pink flowers in clusters May-June. Very hardy. Few prickles.

Cabbage or Provence Roses (descended from *R. centifolia*) mostly grow to 5'/150cm height and spread, though dwarf varieties available. Compact habit, but lax branches may require staking. Big double fragrant flowers June-July on thin stalks, so tend to hang down.

Moss Roses (*R. centifolia* 'Muscosa') distinguished by green or reddish silky resin-scented 'moss' on stems and sepals. Heavily-scented double or semi-double white to red flowers, June-July. Height 2-6'/60-180cm. Susceptible to mildew, especially white varieties.

Damask Roses (descended from *R. damascena*) are less straggly than other shrub roses; can reach 6'/2m in height. Scent is stunning, even for roses. 2 groups, Summer Damask and Autumn Damask. Summer Damask flowers June-July; large pink or white flowers and grey-green leaves. Autumn Damask (*R. damascena* 'Semperflorens') is descended from a sport of Summer Damask which flowers again in autumn. Short-lived; flowers pink; leaves dull green; hips long, slim and heavy.

You may come across shrub species of the nineteenth century roses. The China Rose itself is a shrub that flowers repeatedly June-September, but it is not very hardy. *R. c. minima*—a dwarf China Rose—has recently produced new hybrids.

Three species became very popular in the nineteenth century. *R. rugosa* and its descendants have fared best in our gardens, because it is very hardy, coming from northern Asia. Deep pink, strongly-scented single flowers recurring through summer into autumn; deep red hips; dense prickly branches which make a good hedge. Numerous varieties. *R. spinosissima* (Scotch Rose) is a small prickly shrub not more than 4'/1.2m with small sweet-scented white, pink or yellow flowers May-June. Suckers freely, and will form a dense thicket, excellent for a low hedge. *R. rubiginosa* (Sweet Briar) has been cultivated extensively in the past century, and has produced many garden hybrids.

Modern Shrub Roses

A response to increasing demand for shrub roses as a low-maintenance plant suitable for the mixed border. Hardy hybrids developed from rose species and the Old-Fashioned Roses. Height and spread usually about 6'/2m, usually with large single or semi-double flowers. Seldom fragrant, but flower repeatedly June-September, either singly or in clusters. Some varieties good for hedging, notably 'Nevada' (white, tinted pink). A few Hybrid Teas or Floribundas are strong enough, if left unpruned, to develop into shrubs, notably 'Peace' and 'Eden Rose' (HT) and 'Iceberg' (F).

BUSH ROSES

Some catalogues offer collections they have selected to go well together, at a cheaper rate. These will tend to be the most popular varieties. Consider height and vigour; you want roses of similar height in the same bed.

Hybrid Tea/Large-Flowered Roses

Flowers usually double (sometimes single), with reflexed petals that open from beautiful oval buds. Flowers can be 6"/15cm across. Flower continuously June-October. Oldest and newest varieties often very fragrant—scent is coming back into fashion. Flowers often grow singly, sometimes in clusters of 2 or 3, and can be all shades of white, pink, purple, red, yellow, orange, flame and brown, bi-coloured or shaded (there are even blue roses now). They grow on strong woody stems with prickles. Leaves divided into 7 oval leaflets, sometimes tinged with red. Shape of plant determined by the heavy pruning necessary. Height normally 24-48"/60-120cm after cutting back each year. Robust varieties like 'Peace' can reach 6'/2m if lightly pruned.

Floribunda/Cluster-Flowered Roses

Flowers grow in large clusters, flowering freely June-July, and again September-October. Flowers single, semi-double or double, 3-4"/75-100mm across; same colour range as Hybrid Teas. There are a few fragrant varieties. Stems are usually more branched than Hybrid Teas, as are not normally so heavily pruned. Height 18-36"/45-90cm, though some varieties reach 6'/2m.

Hybrid Tea and Floribunda Standard Roses

Standard roses are Hybrid Teas and Floribundas identical to the bush roses of the same names—the difference is solely in habit, standards being grafted on to 3'/90cm stems of *R. rugosa*, producing a tree-like head. A half-standard is budded at 2'/60cm. Not all varieties will produce the tree-like heads necessary for growing in this way. Standards are good as specimen trees in circular beds, for avenues or screening when planted in a row, or to give height among lower-growing plants. Weeping standards are ramblers budded on *R. rugosa.*

CLIMBERS AND RAMBLERS
Climbers have long flexible stems with clusters of small flowers borne on the lateral shoots. There is a vast range available, usually placed in 3 categories:

Species Climbers
Climbing roses descended from true climbing species. Tend to be very vigorous, and capable of spreading over a house wall or climbing a tree. White or yellow single fragrant flowers; often short flowering season June-July, occasionally repeating in August. There are Old-Fashioned varieties from climbing species.

Hybrid Tea/Floribunda Climbers
Often reclassified as Large-Flowered and Cluster-Flowered climbers. Descended from bush roses, single, semi-double or double. Flower repeatedly, usually June-July, but can be recurrent. Grow less vigorously than natural climbers. Climbers whose maximum height is 10'/3m are sometimes called Pillar Roses: being easier to maintain, they are more suitable for small gardens.

Modern Climbers
New hybrids which flower more profusely than older varieties. Reach about 10'/3m.

Ramblers
Ramblers are technically another form of climber, but form a distinct group. Mostly hybrids of *R. wichuriana*, a prostrate species from Japan, or *R. luciae*, with small glossy leaves. Reach 10-12'/3-4m long. Single, semi-double or double flowers June-July, a short but spectacular flowering time. Tendency to mildew, so best on trellises and arches where there is free air circulation.

MINIATURE ROSES
Mainly descended from *R. chinensis minima* crossed with Hybrid Teas or Floribundas. Long flowering season of China Rose June-October, and flower characteristics of Hybrid Tea or Floribunda. Dwarf forms took many years to create—colour range now covers all rose colour groups. Usually grow about 9"/22cm high, and should not exceed 15"/37cm. Unlike bush roses, best propagated from cuttings—they keep their dwarf habit. Best in groups, tubs or window boxes. Some varieties good for low hedges.

Site and soil: Open site in full sun, sheltered from cold wind and frost. Pollution

Rosa mundi

Floribunda 'Anna Wheatcroft'

Hybrid Tea 'Mme Louise Laperriere'

from sulphur is advantageous—it kills the commonest rose viruses, black spot and rust. Soil needs to be heavy, moist, rich and well-drained. If you want a formal rosebed in a wet garden, you will have to build a drainage system. Prefer a slightly acid soil (pH 6-6.5), but will cope with anything except too much sand, chalk or clay. A site which has held roses for many years can become 'rose-sick' and the roses cease to flourish—if this happens, grow roses in a different place when replanning the garden.

Prepare rosebeds thoroughly before planting. Must be at least 12"/30cm of dug topsoil. Add plenty of well-rotted manure or compost, preferably before September for planting in October or November. If using bare root or rootball roses in the north, plant in April. A few climbing varieties can cope with north-facing walls.

Traditionally, bush roses are grown in a formal bed with no underplanting. This is practical for dealing with the heavy feeding, constant pruning and dead heading necessary. However, if you hate bare soil, there is a tradition of underplanting roses with violas, and no one said you weren't allowed to use bedding plants or ground cover, but remember roses are hungry, so don't expect them to fight it out with the Michaelmas Daisies. You will also have a problem adding manure when the ground cover is mature.

The bare rosebed is the residual inheritance of the formal rose garden with symmetrical geometrically-shaped beds, enclosed by a stone wall or yew hedge. The beds were often edged wih box—a welcome touch of green in winter. These rose gardens were Victorian, a response to the creation of the bush roses themselves. In the modern garden, formality often lingers in the one bed sacred to roses. If you have such a bed, think about the long months of emptiness. Conifers may make a good background that will come into its own in winter.

Old-Fashioned shrub roses are usually far hardier, and do not require such a rich soil. Some are suitable for semi-wild settings.

Care and cultivation: Roses need nitrogen for leaf growth, phosphate for root, flower and seed development, and potassium for the flowers and general good health. Mulch every spring with compost, well-rotted manure, leafmould or peat, adding bonemeal or hoof and horn. Lawn-mowings are good to keep soil moist in summer. Give seaweed solution through the summer. A little dry wood ash added to a dry soil helps. Keep rose beds free of weeds.

Planting
Soak bare root roses for several hours before planting. Dig a hole at least 4-6"/10-15cm more than the root spread across, and 9"/22cm deep. Add a bucket of peat mixed with two handfuls of bonemeal to the hole. Look for the graft mark at the base of the plant—it should be about 1"/25mm below the soil surface for bush roses—otherwise plant at the original soil mark. You will find that the roots all grow in the same direction, so place the crown at one end of the hole and firm the soil beneath it. Spread the roots fanwise, cover and firm. If necessary, shorten the roots slightly with sharp secateurs.

Plant standard roses in the centre of a round hole. Plant shallowly, as there will be plenty of *rugosa* suckers to be cut back, and stake firmly, putting the stake in the hole first.

If you cannot plant your roses in autumn, they can be planted in March.

Water roses in dry conditions, especially when young.

Pruning
Shrub roses: Dead head recurrent flowerers. Old-Fashioned and species roses should be left to make hips. In winter, remove dead and diseased branches. Can thin out some stems to a few inches above ground level if necessary. Avoid cutting back stems more than a year old. The spring after planting, cut the soft tips back to firm wood on all main stems. This will give fewer flowers that year, but a stronger shrub.

Bush roses: Formal pruning of rose bushes is a nineteenth century phenomenon, necessary for Hybrid Teas and Floribundas. Roses planted in autumn should be pruned hard the following spring, but make sure you do it while the plant is still dormant. Remove dead wood, and cut Hybrid Teas back to 2 or 3 buds from the base, Floribundas to 4 or 5 buds. Each following spring, remove dead and damaged wood, then choose the strongest remaining shoots and cut them back to 4-6 buds from the base for Hybrid Teas, 6-7 for Floribundas. You can prune more lightly than this, cutting the shoots to half their length, but every few years you will need to prune back hard to retain the shape. Dead head during

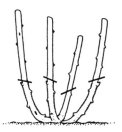

Newly-planted

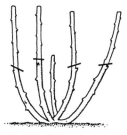

Established
HYBRID TEA

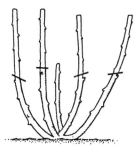

Newly-planted

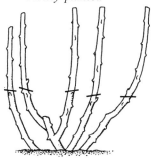

Established
FLORIBUNDA

How to prune your roses

flowering period.

Standard roses: Prune standard roses in exactly the same way as bush roses, treating the top of the trunk as the base of the plant.

Climbers: The spring after planting climbers, cut back main stems to 12-18"/30-45cm in the strong stems, just above the base in the weak ones. Each following spring, cut back the lateral branches to 2-3 buds. Do not cut back the new stems, but train them up the support where you want them.

Ramblers: Ramblers flower on the previous year's growth, like raspberries. Cut out the shoots that have just flowered back to ground level and tie the new shoots to supports to replace them. If you are short of new shoots, take some old ones back to 2-3 buds from the base, and they will send out new growth. Weeping standards should be pruned like ramblers, treating the top of the trunk as the base.

Miniature roses: Trim them if they become straggly, and thin the stems if they become overcrowded.

With all roses, remove suckers, except on ungrafted shrub roses if you want them to spread. Remove suckers by pulling them or cutting them at the roots.

Pruning is not as difficult as you might think, though in the hands of an expert it can become an art. The important thing about pruning is to do it, otherwise your Hybrid Teas and Floribundas will become too weak to flower well, and your climbers and ramblers will become a collapsed mess.

Prune in fairly cold weather so the sap is not rising, but not in severe frost. Cut cleanly, just above an outward-pointing eye. Do not leave prunings lying about—they may be diseased. Mulch as soon as possible after pruning—the harder you have pruned, the hungrier your roses will be.

Propagation: Nearly always by budding or grafting. Some species can be grown from seed. Miniatures are usually propagated by cuttings. An amateur would do best to choose a variety and buy it.

Pests and diseases: Species and shrub roses are usually very resistant. On other varieties: Aphids, Caterpillars, Leafhoppers, Sawflies, Chafer Beetles, Ants, Capsid Bugs; Die Back, Grey Mould, Mildew, Rust. Black spot: black or brown spots up to ½"/12mm across on leaves, followed by yellowing and dropping. The disease overwinters on fallen leaves—keep bed scrupulously clean.

Trees

ACER

Maple, Sycamore   *N hemisphere*

Origins and history: *A. campestre* (Field Maple) is native to Britain and Europe and common in hedgerows; used since Roman times for furniture. Sycamore native of southern Europe, introduced by the Romans and now ubiquitous. Norway Maple introduced by the seventeenth century. Sycamore and Norway Maple fast-growing and very hardy. American maples first introduced by Tradescant in the seventeenth century. *A. rubrum* (Japan) came in the early nineteenth century, though it had long been cultivated in the East. New varieties followed until well into the twentieth century.

Description: D Maples have clusters of small yellowish flowers and winged seeds for wind dispersal; many species have spectacular autumn foliage in yellow, orange or red. The Common Sycamore (*A. pseudoplatanus*) is a large tree, unsuitable for small gardens, as are many species of maple. There are now many small ornamental varieties, often with striking autumn foliage. Maples are a large family of about 200 species. *A. campestre* reaches about 20'/6m. *A. palmatum* (Japanese Maple) reaches 15'/5m, widely used for coloured foliage; many small and very beautiful varieties, the result of years of cultivation in Eastern gardens. *A. nikoense*, 15'/5m, deep red autumn foliage. *A. japonicum*, 20'/6m, bright red autumn foliage—also several Chinese species, usually 15-20'/5-6m, all with outstanding autumn colours. *A. platanoides* (Norway Maple) has many cultivated varieties: 'globosum' is an excellent compact variety. Height of Norway Maple varies according to variety—the forest tree can be 100'/30m high. Box Elder or Ash-leaved Maple (*A. negundo*) very fast-growing: 'variegatum' has variegated leaves and grows to 25'/8m. *A. griseum* (Paperbark Maple) has flaky light brown bark that peels off to expose inner orange bark; gives striking winter colour; slow-growing; reaches 15-20'/5-6m. *A. davidii*, 20'/6m, from China also has ornamental bark, in green and white.

Acer palmatum
Japanese Maple

Site and soil: Any moist, well-drained garden soil in sun or light shade. Sycamore and Norway Maple good in exposed conditions, and Sycamore copes well with pollution.

Propagation: Named varieties are usually grafted. Cuttings depend on species—*A. pseudoplatanus* and *A. negundo* will take easily from cuttings; Japanese Maples will not.

Care and cultivation: Pruning unnecessary. Norway Maples may need thinning. Cut out diseased or dead wood in autumn, never in spring as maples 'bleed' excessively.

Pests and Diseases: Aphids and Tar Spot on Sycamore. Coral Spot.

AESCULUS

Horse Chestnut   *N hemisphere*

Origins and history: Horse Chestnut is a native of the Balkans, brought to Europe from Istanbul by Clusius in the late sixteenth century, and naturalized in Britain since the seventeenth century.

Description: D An old favourite. Familiar palmate leaves with 5-7 leaflets come out in early spring. Upright red or white flower spikes open in May, with up to 100 flowers on each spike. Conkers in autumn in prickly cases. Dark bark and impressive oval silhouette in winter, but unsuitable where space is restricted. Can grow to 100'/30m; red varieties reach 50'/15m. *A. hippocastanum* is Horse Chestnut; *A.×carnea* is red-flowering hybrid, a cross between Horse Chestnut and *A. pavia*, the American Red Buckeye, used widely in parks and cities. Buckeyes from North America are also part of the *Aesculus* family—*A. parviflora* is a white-flowered shrub growing to 10'/3m which flowers in August, sometimes called Bottlebrush Buckeye.

Aesculus hippocastanum
Horse Chestnut

Site and soil: Any ordinary garden soil, preferably moist, in sun or partial shade. Copes well with pollution.

Propagation: Plant conkers—an excellent ploy for children—in nursery bed in September or October. Grow on for 3 years and plant out somewhere suitable.

Care and cultivation: Cut out diseased or dead wood in spring.

Pests and diseases: Aphids on *A. hippocastanum.*

ALNUS

Alder

Origins and history: Common Alder (*A. glutinosa*) is a British native, found in marshy ground and by water. Still sometimes grown for timber, though much less than formerly. Used to be used for making clogs. Green Alder (*A. viridis*, Europe) cultivated since 1820, but rare.

Description: D Oval dark green leaves come out early in spring, preceded by catkins—male ones in yellowish-green tassels, female in dark red clusters that ripen into distinctive woody cones. Trees often have multiple trunks if not pruned, otherwise they have a narrow silhouette. Grows rapidly. *Alnus* is closely related to the *Betula* family. *A. glutinosa* grows up to 80'/25m; seldom used as an ornamental tree, though a possibility for wet ground, and there are a few garden varieties, including a golden-leafed variety. Grey Alder (*A. incana*, Europe) also grows to 80'/25m, and is useful on dry ground as well. Italian Alder (*A. cordata*) is a striking species with shiny leaves and large cones, up to 50'/15m tall, not often seen in British gardens.

Site and soil: Moist or wet soil in sun or partial shade. Dislikes lime. Very good for conserving river banks. Sometimes used as a temporary expedient while waiting for slower trees to grow on the same site.

Propagation: Insert 9"/22cm stem cuttings in autumn in nursery bed. Grow on 2 years and plant out.

Care and cultivation: Pruning unnecessary. Cut out dead or diseased wood in spring.

BETULA

Birch
Northern hemisphere

Origins and history: *B. pendula* (Silver Birch) is native to Britain. Birch is a very useful tree—native Americans use it for canoes, Lapps for clothing, Scandinavians for roofing material. American and Asian species introduced into cultivation in Britain from the seventeenth century onwards.

Description: D Most species have distinctive white peeling bark; some yellow or orange. Male and female flowers come before leaves—drooping catkins are the male flowers, shorter catkins or clusters the female, both yellow-green. Triangular toothed leaves. Very hardy trees, adapted to harsh conditions and marginal land. Grows fast. *B. pendula* is the native Silver Birch, found wild throughout Europe and Asia with its distinctive black and white bark; grows up to 35′/11m; several garden varieties—'Youngii' is a compact weeping variety, excellent in a small garden; 'Purpurea' has purple leaves and branches; numerous other species. *B. albo-sinensis* (China)

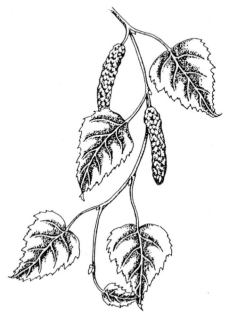

Betula pendula
Silver Birch

has orange bark. *B. humilis* is a shrubby variety from the tundra—very hardy. *B. papyrifera* is the Paper-Bark or Canoe Birch from North America—has whitest bark of all, which peels off in thin layers.

Site and soil: Any ordinary garden soil, preferably moist and acid (a shallow-rooted tree), in sun or partial shade. Keep away from beds and borders because of the wide-spreading root system.

Propagation: Sow seeds in nursery bed in March. Thin to 18″/45cm and grow on for 3 years. Plant out. Named varieties are usually grafted.

Care and cultivation: Remove dead or diseased wood in early spring.

Pests and diseases: Caterpillars; Rust, Bracket Fungus, Witch's Broom.

CRATAEGUS

Hawthorn, May, Quickthorn
Northern hemisphere

Origins and history: Originally 'hedge-thorn', used as agricultural hedging, usually by laying, for centuries. Called 'May' because it traditionally flowered in time for Mayday celebrations in southern Britain, though in 1752 the calendar was altered by eleven days, and the hawthorn has since often refused to comply! English hawthorn (*C. monogyna*) is legendarily descended from the tree grown from the staff of Joseph of Arimathea at Glastonbury (*C. monogyna* 'Praecox'), which flowers at Christmastime.

Description: D *C. monogyna* is the basis of most of our hedgerows. White saucer-shaped strong-scented flower clusters in May, a spectacular sight throughout the countryside, followed by familiar red 'haws' in autumn. All species bear hard sharp thorns, combined with a dense branching habit and a tendency to form multiple trunks. Excellent for impenetrable hedging or as a specimen tree. Many garden varieties available, descended from both native hawthorn and North American and Chinese species. Can have red, pink or white flowers, and red or orange berries, often with striking autumn foliage. *C. monogyna* can grow up to 25′/8m, but less in exposed places. Check the height of other varieties when you buy.

Site and soil: Any well-drained soil, preferably in full sun or partial shade. Tolerant of wind and pollution. Very hardy.

Propagation: Sow seeds in a nursery bed. Seeds take 18 months to germinate, so wait. When they appear, grow on for 3 years, and plant out. Named varieties bred by budding or grafting—buy them.

Care and cultivation: Prune in winter or early spring. For specimen trees you can thin the branches to let more light penetrate. Cut suckers from roots. Hedges: clip in summer after flowering. Hawthorn responds well to heavy pruning in July or August if necessary.

Pests and diseases: Caterpillars; Rust, Fireblight (don't plant near fruit trees).

FAGUS

Beech
Northern hemisphere

Origins and history: Common Beech (*F. sylvatica*) is native tree. Beech was once the dominant tree of the climax deciduous forest which covered much of the temperate northern hemisphere in higher altitudes, where it took the place of the oak. Native only to southern Britain. Few foreign imports grown; our own beech by far the commonest in gardens and hedges.

Description: D Beech woods distinctive for lack of undergrowth—the shade of the canopy is too dense and feeding roots too close to the soil surface. Familiar smooth grey pillar-like trunks. Glossy oval leaves with wavy edges produce brilliant spring and autumn colour. Inconspicuous male and female flowers on the same tree, followed by beechnuts in autumn. Many varieties of *F. sylvatica*, some with leaves of unusual colours—purple, copper, or variegated with yellow or white; leaves may be deeply indented. All varieties retain autumn leaves throughout winter on their young wood—which is why hedges always retain their leaves. Can get weeping beeches and beeches with tortuous branches. Take careful note of the ultimate height and spread of any variety—the species is a huge tree, up to 100'/30m high. Named varieties will usually be smaller, but be sure to check. Dawyck Beech (from Dawyck in the Tweed Valley where one seedling developed this way in the 1860s) is a useful variety as it grows in a tall column, taking up much less room if you don't mind its un-beech-like habit. If you have space, any variety, shade or habit of beech will become a beautiful focal point in your garden. Beech hedges are also attractive, with a curtain of leaves in summer and autumn leaves right through the winter, a tough, easily-maintained option for a hedge.

Site and soil: Any well-drained soil in open sunny position. Avoid heavy wet soils.

Propagation: *F. sylvatica*—sow beechnuts in nursery bed in autumn. Grow on for 2-3 years, then plant in permanent position. Some coloured-leaved varieties are grafted.

Care and cultivation: Pruning not necessary. Trim hedges August-November.

Pests and diseases: Beech Aphids; Beech Scale, Coral Spot, Bracket Fungus (when old or damaged), Apple Canker.

FRAXINUS

Ash
Northern hemisphere

Origins and history: Ash is the legendary Yggdrasil of Norse myth—like oak and beech, a tree with a long history of symbolic significance. *F. excelsior* is our native ash, one of the primeval trees of Europe's deciduous forest. Leaves were once used as a laxative and diuretic.

Description: D Pale grey bark, compound leaves of 4-6 leaflets with one terminal leaflet. Small purplish, white or petal-less flowers which come before the leaves in April-May—male and female flowers usually, but not always, on separate trees. Seeds come in familiar keys, which remain on the tree after the leaves have fallen. Leaves don't change colour in autumn. Prominent black buds noticeable on trees in winter. Almost all ashes in Britain are *F. excelsior*—which has weeping variety 'pendula'. *F. ornus*, 10-20'/3-6m, is a species with more spectacular flowers, often called Flowering Ash—whitish sweet-scented flowers in many-flowered heads. Ash is one of the tallest of European forest trees, can be over 100'/30m; 'pendula' reaches about 25'/8m. Fast-growing.

Site and soil: Any reasonable soil in sun or partial shade. Common Ash not only very tall, but widespreading, both in canopy and shallow roots—will need a very large area, otherwise choose a smaller variety. Good in wind or pollution.

Propagation: Sow seeds in October in a nursery bed. Grow on 3-4 years and plant out in permanent position. Named varieties are grafted.

Care and cultivation: Pruning unnecessary.

Pests and Diseases: Ash canker: small warts on bark turn to large black cankers—cut out affected wood.

ILEX
Holly
Europe, N Africa, Asia

Origins and history: *I. aquifolium* is native holly. Traditional tree of midwinter in Britain. Has been cultivated for so long that varieties now outnumber the original species, some from English holly, some hybrids between English holly and the native holly of the Azores.

Description: E (a few D) Shrub or small tree with glossy dark green prickly leaves and red berries in winter. Small white flowers in May-June, male and female usually on separate trees. Fruits turn red in September if male and female trees are growing together, and remain well into January. Many garden varieties—can get variegated leaves with yellow edges or yellow centres, but these are often male, so they do not carry berries. Get a female variegated variety if you can, such as *I.xaltarclarensis* 'Golden King' (sic!). *I.xaltarclarensis* are hybrids between native *I. aquifolium* and *I. perado* (Azores)—all called Highclere hybrids. Variegated plants are more tender, and surprisingly all hollies are at risk in very cold winters. Holly makes excellent hedges.

Site and soil: Any ordinary garden soil, preferably moist loam, in sun or shade (in shade the leaves will be less bright and glossy). Does well in pollution, salt air and exposed situations.

Propagation: Take 2-3"/50-75mm cuttings of well-ripened shoots with heel in August. Insert in cutting compost in cold frame. Plant out in nursery rows April-May. Grow on for 2 years then plant out in permanent sites. *Or*, layer in October. Separate after 2 years and plant out.

Care and cultivation: Pruning unnecessary. Clip hedges in April. Can cut overgrown hedges hard back to old wood if necessary. If variegated hollies send out shoots that have reverted to green, cut these out as soon as they appear.

Pests and Diseases: Holly leaf miner.

LABURNUM
S Europe

Origins and history: Cultivated in southern Europe in the Middle Ages, and reached Britain by the end of the sixteenth century. Has naturalized in some places.

Description: D Bright yellow peaflower-like flowers growing in hanging clusters 4-12"/10-30cm long, spectacular for 2 weeks in late May and early June, followed by thin pods containing black seeds. Like every other part of the plant, the seeds are very poisonous. A spreading tree with up-growing branches, smooth greenish bark and compound leaves with 3 pointed leaflets. Height up to 25'/7m. *L. anagyroides* is Common Laburnum—can get weeping variety 'pendulum'. *L. alpinum* is Scotch Laburnum—hardier, and flowers for longer, than Common Laburnum, and also has a weeping variety. Slow-growing—becomes gnarled with age.

Site and soil: Keep right away from children if possible—flowers and particularly pods are tempting—a child can be fatally poisoned by eating only 2 seeds. Any well-drained garden soil in sun or partial shade, not too exposed to wind.

Propagation: Sow seeds in October in seed compost in cold frame. Prick out into boxes, and plant out into nursery beds in spring. Plant in permanent sites the following autumn.

Care and cultivation: Pruning unnecessary. Stake young trees until established, and protect from rabbits if necessary (the bark is attractive food to them).

MAGNOLIA
China, Japan, N America

Origins and history: Named after the seventeenth century French botanist Pierre Magnol. *M.x soulangiana* (the most common magnolia) was originally bred in France, where new varieties were developed from Asian species. The American magnolias developed later than the Asian varieties. *M. grandiflora* comes from Bull Bay in south-eastern USA.

Description: D E Magnolias are perhaps the most spectacular of trees and shrubs. Most are spring-flowering, the flowers coming before or along with the new leaves. Evergreen varieties flower in summer or autumn. Young trees have few flowers, but

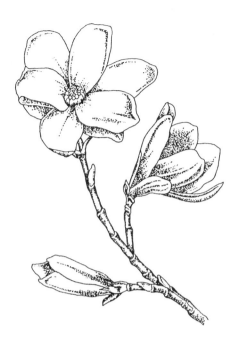

Magnolia × *soulangiana*

mature trees have spectacular and often fragrant blooms. *M. grandiflora* makes the most impressive tree, broad-spreading with a smooth grey bark, oval evergreen glossy leaves, and sweet-scented cup-shaped creamy-white flowers up to 10"/25cm across from July to October. *M.* × *soulangiana*, height 10-15'/3-5m, is a hybrid between 2 Chinese species, a spring-flowering deciduous magnolia with oblong leaves. The large tulip-shaped flowers are usually white tinged with pink, though there are pink and white varieties. *M. stellata* is a dwarf deciduous magnolia, height 8-10'/2.5-3m. *M. denudata* (Yulan or Lily Tree) is slow-growing with fragrant white cup-shaped flowers 5-6"/12-15cm across from March to May, height 10-15'/3-5m.

Site and soil: Any well-drained garden soil, enriched with compost or well-rotted manure, in full sun or light shade. Protect spring-flowering varieties from the north and east, or the flowers may be damaged by frost. *M. grandiflora* is best grown against a wall. *M.* × *soulangiana* good in pollution. Magnolias dislike chalk.

Propagation: Seeds *very* slow, and cuttings difficult. Best to layer shoots in March or April. Takes 2 years to root. Enrich site with leafmould and add sharp sand for drainage. Sever after 3 years and replant.

Care and cultivation: Pruning unnecessary. If training *M. grandiflora* against a wall, remove forward-facing shoots in April. Mulch in April.

Pests and Diseases: Frost damage.

MALUS

Crabapple   *Asia, Europe*

Origins and history: From the Middle Ages the juice of the native crabapple was important as a source of cider, wines, vinegar, and crabapple jelly. From the eighteenth century onward, when Siberian crabapples were introduced, many hybrids were developed. North American and Chinese species were introduced later, and much breeding followed from these—few original species are now used in gardens.

Description: D Ornamental crabapples are spectacular in spring, when smothered in sweet-scented pink flowers that gradually fade to white. Red and pink flowers are also available. Flowers either single, semi-double or double, with overlapping petals, followed by red, yellow or green fruit clustered along the branches. Can be harvested, or make a feast for birds. Small leaves with serrated edges. Hybrids bred for flower colour and abundance rather than harvest, because now mostly used as ornamentals—remember this if you want a good harvest. Japanese Crab (*M. floribunda*, 12-15'/3.5-4m) one of the earliest flowerers—small and reliable tree. *M. sargentii* (6-8'/1.8-2.4m) a good species, bush size and also Japanese. Other species from China, Japan and N America have produced numerous hybrids. *M.* 'John Downie' or 'Golden Hornet' (25-30'/8-9m) best if you want to harvest. *M.* × *purpurea* (20-25'/6-8m) has purple-tinged leaves and red or purple flowers—very ornamental. On the whole crabs are hardier than *Prunus* (Flowering Cherry).

Site and soil: Any well-drained garden soil, preferably in full sun. Enrich with compost or well-rotted manure.

Propagation: All hybrids and varieties are budded or grafted.

Care and cultivation: Stake standard trees for the first few years, and mulch them.

Remove dead or straggly branches in February.

Pests and diseases: See 'Apple' in the fruit section, though crabapples are tougher.

PLATANUS

Plane
N America, Asia

Origins and history: London Plane is a hybrid between *P. orientalis* (from Turkey and Greece) and *P. occidentalis* (from North America) cultivated since the 1640s, first recorded in 1663 in London. Introduced via Spain, hence sometimes called *P. hispanica*. By 1920s 60% of London trees were planes; widely used in cities in the last 200 years and often pollarded. It must have mitigated the effects of the Industrial Revolution for millions of people.

Description: D Huge fast-growing tree—can reach 120'/35m high. Smooth grey bark flakes off, revealing green, yellow or reddish patches. Five-lobed toothed leaves on reddish stalks. Male flowers yellow, female red, on the same tree, in clusters in April-May, followed by globular prickly seedheads in September and October.

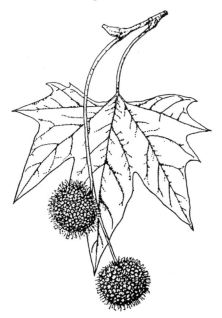

Platanus x *acerifolia*
London Plane

Leaves do not change colour in autumn. Grows rapidly, and will quickly overwhelm a small garden. Very resistant indeed to pollution and disease. *P.*x*hybrida* or *P.*x*acerifolia* is London Plane; can also get species *P. occidentalis* (Buttonwood, American Sycamore) not often found in Europe. *P. orientalis* has more deeply lobed leaves than London Plane, especially the variety 'digita'.

Site and soil: Any well-drained garden soil in sun or partial shade. Copes excellently with pollution.

Propagation: Take 8-10"/20-25cm cuttings of current season's wood in October and insert in sheltered nursery bed, grow on 3-4 years and plant out.

Care and cultivation: Pruning unnecessary, though planes are very tolerant of pruning, and branches can be thinned or even cut back hard.

POPULUS

Poplar   *Europe, Asia, N America*

Origins and history: Poplar has long been a commercially-grown tree. *P. alba* (White Poplar) native to Europe and Asia, long naturalised in Britain. Black Poplar (*P. nigra*) less common in Britain, largely replaced by Lombardy Poplar (*P. nigra* 'Italica'), introduced to Britain in 1750. Eastern Balsam Poplar cultivated in Britain since 1689, now rare. Western Balsam Poplar still widely used for shelter belts and roadsides.

Description: D Fast-growing trees with spreading roots that require plenty of space. Not long-lived, but can grow up to 100'/30m in 20 years. Male and female flowers in drooping catkins March-April, borne on separate trees. Female trees produce abundant fluffy white seeds, hence the name Cottonwood for some species. *P. alba* grows to 100'/30m; smooth grey bark, becoming blacker and rougher, large or small (depending on variety) 5-lobed oval leaves turn yellow in September. Balsam Poplars (*P. balsamifera*, N America) grow to 45'/14m—the leaves smell of balsam when unfolding. Black Poplar has triangular leaves, grey male catkins, greenish-white female. Commercially-grown poplars are mostly hybrids of American Cottonwoods and Black Poplar, and are familiar in the French landscape. Lombardy Poplar is one variety from this union—grows to

120'/36m. Interbreeding of different poplar species has produced many very useful fast-growing commercial species. *P. tremula* is Aspen; its grey-green leaves have long flattened stalks which tremble in the slightest breeze. Aspen crossed with White Poplar has produced the Grey Poplar (*P.×canescens*) which has a yellow-grey bark and grows to 100'/30m.

Site and soil: Any ordinary garden soil in sun or partial shade. Tolerates heavy clay. Good for windbreaks, planted 8-10'/2.4-3m apart. Keep at least 60'/20m from buildings or drains.

Propagation: Take 10-12"/25-30cm cuttings of leafless hardwood shoots and insert in nursery bed between October and December. Plant in permanent positions after 1 year. Or, remove suckers in winter and plant in permanent sites.

Care and cultivation: Pruning unnecessary. Remove any dead or unwanted branches in summer, not winter.

Pests and Diseases: Poplar beetle larvae. Bacterial canker of poplars: canker can develop on shoots and branches—cut out affected parts.

PRUNUS

Flowering Cherry, Almond, Plum, Peach

Origins and history: The first distinction to make is between the Gean (the native wild cherry) with all its varieties and descendants, and the Japanese Flowering Cherry. The former has been grown in Europe for centuries. The latter were cultivated to perfection for their beauty in Japanese gardens over a thousand years, but were not introduced to Europe until the twentieth century by Captain Collingwood Ingram. There were already many varieties in the Far East, and these have been dramatically increased since by breeders in the West. Plums, peaches and almonds have been similarly highly bred and hybridized. For orchard fruits see under 'Fruit', but many ornamental cherries are close relatives of our orchard trees, and every cherry tree is a thing of beauty in springtime.

Description: D Ornamental *Prunus* do not usually exceed 25'/8m high, and between March and May, depending upon their variety, are covered with long clusters of blossoms, pink or white cup-shaped 5-petalled flowers that often open out flat, either single or double. Leaves are oval or toothed on red stalks, turning gold in autumn. Now a very familiar springtime spectacle, particularly in town gardens. Multitude of species and varieties which can be quite bewildering, usually divided into 4 groups:

ORNAMENTAL CHERRIES
European Cherries
Most cultivated varieties are descendants of *P. avium* (Gean or Mazzard). Can grow to 40'/12m. White cup-shaped flowers in April in drooping clusters; leaves can turn crimson in autumn. *P. padus* (Bird Cherry) grows up to 50'/15m. Smooth dark brown strong-smelling bark, small white sweet-scented flowers in May. Ordinary cherries produce fruit in August. Many garden varieties.

Japanese Cherries
The choice is vast, and the trees can be very variable in shape. Flowers may be single, semi-double or double; white, pink or red. All have attractive autumn colours. Can get weeping forms, 'pendula', which were the first to reach Europe in the mid nineteenth century; double-flowered forms like *P.* 'Fukubana'; and winter-flowering forms, like *P.* 'Autumnalis'—in mild areas this will flower throughout winter, in colder areas both in autumn and spring.

When cherries were first used in British gardens, they were given Latin names which attempted to indicate their ancestry. This has become so complicated that now they are just catalogued as *Prunus* spp, followed by the Japanese name. Most popular is *P.* 'Kanzan'—this is the ubiquitous bright pink flowering cherry. If you look further you can find more subtle colours. Best to read the catalogues carefully and find the description that appeals to you most.

ORNAMENTAL ALMONDS
P. dulcis is the Common Almond, with nuts that can be harvested, with many varieties bred from it. Slender, long-pointed toothed leaves, and pink or white (*alba*) flowers growing in clusters March-April, usually single. *P.× amygdalo-persica* 'Pollardii' is a popular hybrid between a peach and an almond, with deep pink flowers in March and April. Almonds are even less hardy than ornamental peach.

ORNAMENTAL PLUM
P.× blireana has double pink flowers appearing with the slender purple leaves in April. 'Nigra', with dark purple leaves and

almost black ornamental plums, is an ancient hybrid between the native sloe or blackthorn (*P. spinosa*) and the Cherry Plum (*P. ceranifera*) from the Balkans. The latter has white flowers followed by small red or yellow cherry plums, and can be used as an ornamental hedge.

ORNAMENTAL PEACH

Short-lived trees which grow for 10-15 years. 10-25'/3-7.5m high. One of the first trees to flower in the spring; needs a sheltered position. Single pale pink, white or red flowers. *P. davidiana* (Chinese Peach) most common—can bloom as early as January. White-flowered variety *alba*. *P. persica* from China is Common Peach—not fully hardy in Britain. Grow in mild areas against a wall.

Site and soil: Any ordinary well-drained garden soil, preferably with some lime. Do not plant too deep or cultivate soil too deeply—*Prunus* are shallow-rooting. Plant in full sun. Tender species and varieties will need shelter.

Propagation: Varieties are budded or grafted. Plant in autumn while soil is still warm.

Care and cultivation: Pruning not necessary. Cut out damaged shoots and thin if required in late summer. Do not dig around the roots too often.

Pests and Diseases: Birds, especially bullfinches, eat young buds. Aphids. See under 'Cherry' and 'Plum' in the fruit section for diseases.

QUERCUS

Oak   *Temperate regions*

Origins and history: Much of Britain was once oakwood—even 500 years ago a third of the whole island was still covered by oak trees. Oak will quickly recolonize empty land, even now. Many of the forests were cut down for shipbuilding. Two oaks are native to Britain—*Q. robur* and *Q. petraea*. British oaks can be up to 500 years old. By the eighteenth century there were many cultivated varieties, and hybrids using some of the numerous foreign species.

Description: D and E *Q. robur* is the English Oak, a long-lived slow-growing tree, growing 15'/5m in 20 years. Can reach 150'/45m in height. Wide domed shape, with branches growing horizontally 50'/15m or more, defying gravity, and becoming huge and twisted. Oblong leaves

with rounded lobes turn to orange-brown in autumn. Male flowers in fluffy catkins, female green and small, followed by acorns in autumn, the nut in its cup-shaped husk. Canopy casts filtered shade, excellent for woodland shrubs. *Q. petraea* is the Sessile or Durmast Oak, best on light acid soils. Reaches 130'/40m. Grey bark, leaves darker green than English Oak, stalkless acorns—commoner in the West of Britain. *Q. cerris*—Turkey Oak (S Europe and the Middle East) reaches 140'/38m, and is one of the fastest-growing oaks, therefore widely planted. Acorns set in mossy cups; leaves vary in shape, shinier than the English Oak. *Q. ilex*—Holm Oak E (S Europe) is good in salt air and pollution, though dislikes extreme cold. Height up to 100'/30m. Leaves can be long and narrow or oval, with toothed or smooth margins. Acorns light green, not brown. Can be used for an evergreen hedge. *Q. rubra* (Red Oak, N America) is rare in Britain. Leaves turn from pale yellow in spring to green, then to bright red in autumn if the soil is acid enough. Height 110'/35m. Usual variety *Q. rubra maxima*. Can come across other less common imported varieties. Only plant an oak if you have room, but it will be worth it!

Site and soil: Any deep, well-drained garden soil in partial shade or, preferably, full sun.

Propagation: Sow acorns within 2 months of collecting, 3"/75mm apart in nursery rows. Thin to 18-22"/45-55cm after 1 year. Grow on 3-4 years and plant out in permanent site.

Care and cultivation: Mulch young trees annually with peat or leafmould. Remove dead or diseased branches in winter. Can remove some lateral branches of 2-3 year old trees in winter to get bare trunk.

Pests and diseases: Gall Wasps (oak apples), Caterpillars; Oak Phylloxera, Canker, Die Back, other fungal diseases.

SALIX

Willow   *N hemisphere*

Origins and history: Several species of willow are native to Britain. The bark was used medicinally to treat fevers and chills, and the stems for withies. Weeping Willow (*S. babylonica*) was introduced from China in the early eighteenth century—the story goes that it arrived as a withy used to tie a

Salix alba
White Willow

found in wet places. Weeping Willows are hybrids between native willows and *S. babylonica* from China—*S.×chrysocoma* most commonly planted; height 20-25'/6-8m; fast growing like most willows; slender leaves on yellow stems, long yellow male catkins March/April. For smaller gardens there are smaller varieties—*S. purpurea* 'Pendula' (America) or *S. capraea* 'Pendula'; or for non-weeping trees, *S. incana* and *S. elaeagnos* (Hoary Willow) or *S. daphnoides* (Violet Willow), both from southern Europe. *S. gracilistyla* (Japan) has red catkins.

Site and soil: Deep moist soil in full sun. Most enjoy damp conditions by water. Water encourages weeping things to grow towards it, probably because of the reflected light. Beware of planting willows near drains or septic tanks—their roots will make for the water and cause havoc. Large willow trees are *not* suitable for small gardens.

Propagation: Take 9-15"/22-37cm long hardwood cuttings in winter. Insert in moist soil in nursery bed. Plant out in permanent position 1 year later. *Or*, take a branch up to 10'/3m long in February and insert in permanent site up to half its length, and it will probably root. Only the Goat Willow is hard to propagate from cuttings.

Care and cultivation: Remove dead wood in winter. May need to trim back weeping branches. If growing willows for bark colour, cut back to 24-36"/30-60cm from ground in February.

Pests and diseases: Aphids, Scale insects, Sawfly, Larvae Galls; Anthracnose of willow — distorted leaves fall prematurely.

SAMBUCUS
Elder   *N hemisphere*

Origins and history: Closely related to viburnums. *S. nigra* native Elder. Elder was used for making whistles, and is still used for wines from both flowers and berries. Like Rowan in the north, Elder in the south had strong magical properties—was planted by house doors to keep evil away. Still commonly found where there has been human settlement. Almost all parts of the tree—leaves, flowers and berries—have medicinal uses. Smell of new wood repels flies—was used on horses to keep flies off.

parcel, and was subsequently planted by the poet Pope. The species is rare today, but numerous hybrids have been bred with hardy native willows, which are the weeping willows we see today.

Description: D Willows very variable in size and shape—often forgotten that there are many shrub forms suitable for smaller spaces (in fact most willow species are shrubs). Small native species can form thickets in damp places. *S. lanata* (Woolly Willow) grows from 2-4'/60-120cm; slow-growing with round felted leaves and big erect yellow catkins March-April. Our native trees are also graceful and attractive. *S. fragilis* (Crack Willow) is commonest tree, up to 50'/15m, with brittle branches arching from the stem or stems; grey scaly bark, narrow pointed leaves; male and female catkins on separate trees. *S. capraea* (Goat Willow, Pussy Willow) up to 52'/16m; greyish leaves and familiar male and female catkins which grow on separate trees; grey bark turns brown and cracked with age. *S. alba* (White Willow) up to 80'/25m; grey-green tapering leaves, catkins in May. *S. cinerea* (Grey Willow)

Description: D Small tree, 10-25'/3-8m high, with arching branches. Grey-brown bark; leaves divided into 5-7 sharply-toothed leaflets; creamy-white flattish sweet-scented flowers in July followed by shiny black berries in September. *S. nigra* common hedgerow tree. Some garden varieties: 'Aurea' has yellow-green leaves, 'Aurea-variegata' is variegated, 'Purpurea' has purple leaves.

Site and soil: Any garden soil in sun or shade. *S. nigra* useful as tolerates deep shade. Garden varieties require sun.

Propagation: Take 10-12"/25-30cm cuttings in October-November and insert in nursery bed. Grow on 1 year, then plant in permanent positions between October and March.

Care and cultivation: Can prune back hard in autumn or spring to encourage new growth, though will get fewer flowers and berries the following year.

SORBUS

Rowan, Mountain Ash, Whitebeam
Europe, Asia

Origins and history: In Scotland the Rowan (*S. aucuparia*) is a magical tree, like the Elder in the south, traditionally planted at the house door to keep away evil. Berries used medicinally, and to make wine and jelly. The Rowan is a symbolic tree in Celtic mythology as the ash is in Norse—the salmon pool of Grainne had a Rowan growing beside it. Whitebeams are close relations, *S. aria* being the native Whitebeam. The Wild Service Tree, *S. tominalis*, has been cultivated since 1750.

Description: D Rowan, *S. aucuparia*, is an upright tree, 15-25'/5-8m high, with smooth grey bark, compound leaves with 5-7 leaflets, often turning rich red in autumn. Creamy-white flowers growing in flat sweet-scented clusters in May and June, followed by large bunches of berries which ripen from yellow to orange to scarlet in August and September. Some garden varieties—'Asplenifolia' with lobed fern-like leaves; 'Beissneri' with orange bark; 'Fastigiata' with columnar growth. Whitebeam, *S. aria*, is a domed tree with smooth grey bark that becomes cracked with age. Oval toothed leaves with whitish hairs on lower surface that give the tree a glistening look—hence the name. Leaves turn yellow, then brown, then pale grey in autumn—

colours depend on variety. Creamy-white flowers in May and June in flattened clusters; fruits ripening from orange to dark red in September. Several garden varieties—'Lutescans' most spectacular foliage. Other related species from Asia and America, and some hybrids with native trees. *S. tominalis* (Wild Service Tree) is another native, but only of southern Britain, with maple-like leaves and small white flowers in May, followed by brown fruits. *S.xthuringiaca* (Bastard Service Tree) is not a relation, but a hybrid between Rowan and Whitebeam, much used in city planting—reaches 50'/15m high.

Site and soil: Any well-drained soil in sun or partial shade. Whitebeam does well in pollution or salt air. Likes chalk. Rowan likes acid soil; will not thrive on chalk. Very hardy.

Propagation: Take seeds from the berries in October and sow at once in boxes. Prick out and harden off. Plant out in nursery bed. Grow on 3-5 years, then plant in final position.

Care and cultivation: Pruning unnecessary.

Pests and Diseases: Fireblight, Apple canker.

TILIA

Lime, Linden   *Europe, W Asia*

Origins and history: Two native species—Broad-Leafed and Small-Leafed Lime. Leaves used as a cure for chills. Lime avenues became fashionable in the eighteenth century, partly because of an advertizing campaign on the part of the Dutch nursery growers because it was the easiest and most profitable tree to propagate. Tree native to most parts of Europe, but presents many problems to the gardener. Since the eighteenth century growers have worked towards producing a trouble-free lime, eliminating suckers and aphids, the two usual hazards.

Description: D Familiar fast-growing huge tree in large gardens and parks, and in avenues along streets. All species have small whitish sweet-smelling flowers in clusters which develop into nut-like fruits. Leaves may not change colour in autumn. *T. cordata* (Small-Leaved Lime) grows to 50'/15m; smooth grey bark, yellow-white flowers in July, dark green glossy rounded leaves from early spring. *T.*

platyphyllos (Large-Leaved Lime) up to 70'/21m; broad pale heart-shaped leaves, yellowish-white flowers June-July—several cultivated varieties. *T.×vulgaris* (Common Lime) is a hybrid of these two—most widely planted, reaches 130'/40m. Tall domed tree with dull grey bark, heart-shaped toothed leaves, yellowish-white flowers in July. *T. tomentosa* (Silver Lime) from SE Europe often planted—grows to 100'/30m, has whitish flowers, leaves silver on undersurface. *T. petiolaris* (Pendant Silver Lime) also from S Europe, 20-25'/6-8m; very fragrant flowers July-August. Limes have been much developed by breeders—numerous varieties. True species relatively rare.

Site and soil: Moist, well-drained garden soil in sun or partial shade.

Propagation: Easy—one of problems with lime trees is numerous suckers. Remove and replant. *Or,* layer shoots September or October. Sever after 2 years and replant.

Care and cultivation: Pruning unnecessary. Remove suckers as they appear at base. Can cut back lime trees hard if required—often pollarded in avenues.

Pests and Diseases: Aphids (excessively), galls, caterpillars; canker.

ULMUS

Elm   *Europe, Asia, N Africa*

Origins and history: The recent history of the elms is unhappy. Dutch Elm Disease has placed these trees under the threat of extinction. It is a fungus, transmitted by a beetle, that grows on the ring of new wood just inside the bark, blocking the sap vessels and so killing the tree. Until the advent of the disease, 70% of the hedgerow trees in the Midlands and East Anglia were elms—many have now gone. Elm has traditionally been regarded as unpredictable, both in its tendency to drop branches and its susceptibility to lightning. Wood used to make coffins. Basic component of English agricultural landscape until recently.

Description: D Fast-growing tall trees typical of rural landscape. *U. procera* (English Elm) grows to 120'/35m, with huge twisting branches growing upwards from tall trunk. Dark brown or grey deeply-scored bark, rounded oval leaves with toothed edges turn yellow in autumn, small dark reddish flowers followed by sterile seeds (tree propagates itself entirely by root

Ulmus procera
English Elm

suckers). Several garden varieties. Although other elm species may take the place of the English Elm, it is a unique tree, and they will never replace it. *U. glabra* (Wych or Scots Elm) grows to 130'/40m—doesn't get Dutch Elm Disease. Winged seeds ripen from light green to brown. Several varieties, including 'Pendula'—weeping variety. Does well in pollution and exposed situations. Seeds appear before leaves in spring. *U.× hollandica* (Dutch Elm)—a hybrid between Smooth-Leaved Elm and Wych Elm, grows to 120'/35m. *U. carpinifolia* (Smooth-Leaved Elm) grows to 100'/30m; numerous garden varieties. *U. laevis* (White Elm) rare in Britain but may increase in importance as is relatively resistant to Dutch Elm Disease. Most resistant of all is *U. parvifolia* (Chinese Elm); glossy green leaves stay on tree well into winter—almost an evergreen. All elms curious in that both flowers and seeds appear before the leaves, in a period of about 8 weeks. English Elm in particular retains its leaves well into the autumn, then they turn the light gold that is typical of the autumn landscape. It would be an immeasurable loss if the elms were to disappear.

Site and soil: Any deep well-drained garden soil in pen sunny position.

Propagation: Remove suckers in autumn. Grow on in nursery bed for 2 years. Plant out October or November. Varieties are budded or grafted.

Care and cultivation: Pruning unnecessary.

Pests and Diseases: Dutch Elm Disease, spread by elm bark beetle: it is important that English Elms are grown, as they are at risk of extinction. However, you will have to watch carefully for the first signs of the disease—brown leaves wither and hang on dead branches. The only hope if infection occurs is to inject the sap-stream of the tree with *Trichoderma viride*, a complicated procedure. It is of course a notifiable disease. If you plant an elm you are taking a risk, but possibly helping to save a species. Coral Spot, Canker, Honey Fungus.

Conifers

ABIES

Fir   *Northern hemisphere*

Origins and history: European Silver Fir (*A. alba*) originated in eastern Europe and spread widely through its use as a forestry tree—reaching Britain in 1603. Used to be among commonest trees, but has declined rapidly since 1950s. Some seventeenth century firs still survive in Scotland. Large number of firs introduced from eastern Europe and Asia in nineteenth century, and many hybrids and varieties produced. Two Japanese firs, notably Nikko Fir (*A. homolepis*), introduced 1861, and *A. veitchii*, introduced 1879. Silver firs of North America (called balsams in USA) also introduced during nineteenth century—Giant Fir (*A. grandis*) discovered by Douglas and introduced 1832, White Fir (*A. concolor*) 1872, Noble Fir (*A. procera*) 1825. All firs now declining in numbers—least familiar of our common conifers.

Description: E Very tall conical tree. Giant Fir can reach 330'/100m, but fir species are usually 100-150'/30-45m. Common Silver Fir up to 180'/55m. Needle-like foliage. Most species bear cones in Britain, but not until tree is quite an age, and then usually at top of tree out of sight. Cones disintegrate to produce winged seeds. Bark usually greyish, becoming scaly with age. Fir trees have distinctive smell, coming from the resin that often oozes from bark; crushed leaves give out strong scent. Fir trees naturally belong to cooler mountain ranges of the northern hemisphere. There are about 50 species and numerous varieties. Firs interbreed very easily. There are few dwarf varieties. There are some slow-growing varieties exist for the smaller garden and even the rock garden, which remain a manageable size for many years, e.g. *A. concolor* 'Glauca Compacta'. For average-sized gardens look for dwarf or slow-growing varieties. Can also get large variety of shades of needles and cones. Choose species or variety carefully.

Site and soil: Deep, slightly acid, moist, well-drained soil in light shade. *A. grandis* tolerates chalk if topsoil is kept acid. Firs are not suitable for polluted areas, or for very exposed places unless in groups.

Abies procera
Noble Fir

Propagation: Sow seeds in nursery bed in March. Grow on 2-4 years, and plant in permanent position.

Care and cultivation: Mulch young trees in May. Keep soil free of grass around tree until large enough to inhibit ground cover by itself. Do not allow main trunk to fork on young tree—cut out one leading shoot if it does.

Pests and Diseases: Die back. Adelgids suck sap and produce white tufts—the galls—on leaves and branches: pick off galls and burn them.

CEDRUS

Cedar   *S Europe, Asia*

Origins and history: *C. libani* (Cedar of Lebanon) are the oldest cedars in cultivation—some reckoned to be 2,500 years old. First cedar planted in Britain in 1646 by Dr Pocock in the rectory garden at Childrey (he had been embassy chaplain at Constantinople and had brought it back with him)—this cedar still flourishes. In 1670s cedars popularized by Evelyn, but not until these trees bore cones could they be planted on a large scale, which happened in the eighteenth century, when they became the rage. The only non-native tree used by Capability Brown. Planted less after Giant Firs and Redwoods arrived in nineteenth century. In 1839 the Atlantic Cedar (*C. atlantica*) arrived from Morocco—'Glauca' with blue foliage became most popular variety. Two other true cedars—*C. deodara* (Himalayas) and *C. brevifolia* (Cyprus), both smaller species and so became popular, though these are still too large for today's small garden.

Description: E Hardy, huge, long-lived trees suitable for parkland or big lawns. Rapid growth for the first few years, then gradually slowing down. Cedar of Lebanon distinctive spreading tree, up to 130'/40m high, with dark green needles and small barrel-shaped cones, producing winged seeds. Grey-brown deeply-scarred bark and resinous wood. *C. deodara* notable for drooping branches; blue-grey leaves turn dark green in mature trees. No cones until tree is about 40 years old. *C. atlantica* notable for variety 'Glauca' with blue foliage; can get weeping variety. Some compact varieties of cedar: try *C. libani* 'Nana' and 'Sargentii'.

Site and soil: Any ordinary well-drained garden soil in sunny position. Does well in coastal areas. Shelter young trees from early frosts. Do not plant in constricted area.

Propagation: Sow seeds in nursery bed in April. Grow on 3-4 years and plant out in permanent positions.

Care and cultivation: Stake young plants. Add peat and bonemeal when planting. Mulch in April for first few years. Pruning: maintain leader; cut out one leader if forking.

CHAMAECYPARIS

False Cypress   *N America, Japan*

Origins and history: False cypresses brought back from North America mid-nineteenth century. *C. nootkatensis* from NW America introduced mid-nineteenth century; its chief claim to fame is as the parent of the Leyland Cypress varieties. The ubiquitous *C. lawsoniana* (Lawson Cypress) arrived in Lawson's Nurseries in Edinburgh in 1845—since then over 200 varieties have been bred from it, and in the early twentieth century Lawson Cypress used to be the most widely-planted evergreen in British gardens.

Description: Original species of *C. lawsoniana* is a narrow conical tree 130-200'/40-60m high, with short spreading branches terminating in horizontal branchlets. Blue-green oval cones turn brown when ripe; winged seeds; grey-brown flaky bark. However, numerous varieties differ greatly from parent. Choose carefully. For larger garden varieties try 'Allumii' (final height 20'/6m); 'Columnaris Glauca' (20'/6m) with pale grey leaves; 'Fletcheri' (20'/6m) with dense blue-green leaves; or 'Lutea' (30'/ 9m), slightly pendulous with golden foliage.

Dwarf varieties: 'Ellwoodii' (10'/3m), grey-green, columnar in habit, slow-growing so can be used for several years as a miniature; 'Ellwood's Gold' (6'/1.8m), gold-yellow leaf tips in spring and early summer, slower growing than 'Ellwoodii'; 'Ellwood's White' has white leaf tips; 'Minima' (3'/90cm) is very slow-growing, round in habit, good in rockeries. 'Minima aurea' has gold foliage; 'Nana' (4'/1.2m) is conical in habit. Both 'Minima' and 'Nana' have blue-green varieties ('Glauca').

There are also varieties from Japanese species—*C. obtusa* has several varieties, most popular is 'Nana gracilis' (8'/2.5m), shiny green foliage, very slow growing so often used in rockeries. *C. pisifera* has several varieties—'Aurea' (up to 25'/8m) with gold leaves when new, and more popular 'Boulevard' (10'/3m) but used as a dwarf as very slow-growing, bluish leaves. *C. nootkatensis* rare, but variety 'Pendula' with long hanging branches is an interesting tree on exposed sites.

You will certainly find several varieties of *Chamaecyparis* in most nurseries. It has become ubiquitous in gardens. Do choose carefully. Height can vary from 3 to 30 feet (1-10m), and they can be any colour from gold to blue. Can be a miniature in a rockery, or a hedge. Be sure to get details before you buy.

Site and soil: Any ordinary well-drained garden soil in sun or partial shade. Grow gold varieties in full sun.

Propagation: Take 4"/100mm cuttings of new shoots with heel in May. Insert in cutting compost in cold frame. Pot on and plant out in nursery rows in autumn. Grow on for 3 years, then plant in permanent position.

Care and cultivation: Do not allow main shoot to fork on young trees. Cut out one leader if it does.

CRYPTOMERIA

Japanese Cedar　　*China, Japan*

Origins and history: Introduced from China in 1842, the Japanese form following in 1844. Used widely in Japan for forestry. Forest tree reaches 150'/45m. The variety used in Britain is *C. japonica* 'Elegans'.

Description: E *C. japonica* 'Elegans' is a very slow-growing tree, maximum height 15'/4.5m. Has permanent juvenile foliage, soft and feathery, growing on sweeping branches, green in summer, purple or reddish in winter. Several dwarf varieties, e.g. 'Compressa' (3'/90cm), oval in habit with rich red leaves in winter; and 'Vilmoriniana' (3'/90cm). 'Elegans nana' and 'Elegans compacta' are slower-growing and more compact forms of 'Elegans'.

Site and soil: Slightly acid, deep, damp, well-drained soil in sheltered sunny position.

Propagation: Take 3"/75mm long cuttings in September and insert in cutting compost in a cold frame. Pot on and plunge outdoors. Plant out in nursery rows the following autumn and grow on for 2 years,

then plant out in permanent position.

Care and cultivation: Do not allow main shoot to fork on young trees. Cut out one leader in spring if it does.

X CUPRESSOCYPARIS LEYLANDII

Leyland Cypress　　*N America*

Origins and history: Cross between *Cupressus macrocarpa* (Monterey Cypress) and *Chamaecyparis nootkatensis*, both from NW America. Leyland noticed the hybrid in 1888, and grew it on his estate in Northumberland—called the 'Haggerston Grey'. Crossed again in 1911, and these hybrids called 'Leighton Green'—rarer because harder to propagate. Has become very popular in last 15 years, ousting *C. lawsoniana* as the most widely-planted conifer in British gardens.

Description: E In British gardens *leylandii* are easily the fastest-growing conifer—can put on 4'/1.2m per year. This, plus their hardiness, accounts for their sudden popularity for instant hedging or screening. Can reach 50'/15m. Columnar tree with greygreen leaves on horizontal branchlets like *Chamaecyparis*; little round cones on 'Leighton Green', rarely get cones on 'Haggerston Grey'.

Site and soil: Any well-drained fairly deep garden soil in sun or partial shade. Remember that this is a tall, greedy, fast-growing conifer—don't use it if you haven't the space.

Propagation: Take 4"/100mm cuttings of side shoots in September or October. Insert in cutting compost in cold frame. Plant out rooted cuttings in nursery bed and grow on. Plant in permanent positions the following autumn.

Care and cultivation: Cut hedges in autumn, also in spring if necessary.

CUPRESSUS

Cypress　　*N America, Europe*

Origins and history: Italian Cypress (*C. sempervirens*) is the classic columnar tree of the Mediterranean. It only grows in the mildest parts of England, and is rarely seen. Monterey Cypress (*C. macrocarpa*) from California was introduced in the nineteenth century, and became a popular garden tree until replaced by x *Cupressocyparis leylandii*. Modern varieties of cypress are from *C. macrocarpa* or *C. arizonica.*

Description: E *C. macrocarpa* is a fast-growing tree, can reach 100'/30m. Starts off columnar, but becomes spreading and flat-topped with maturity. Twigs covered in scaly leaves that are lemon-scented when crushed; small green or purple cones; reddish-brown peeling bark. *C. arizonica* similar—leaves turn greyish with age; brown stringy bark. Juvenile trees are quite unlike mature trees, with pale green foliage. *C. macrocarpa* difficult in small gardens as hates pruning—choose one of its varieties instead: 'Donard Gold', 'Goldcrest' or 'Lutea' all with golden leaves, and all excellent for hedging.

Site and soil: Any well-drained garden soil in sunny position. Avoid exposed sites for less hardy varieties.

Propagation: Take 3-4"/75-100mm cuttings of side shoots with heel in September or October and insert in cutting compost in a cold frame. Pot on in spring and transfer to permanent positions the following autumn.

Care and cultivation: Don't allow main shoot to fork in young trees—cut one leader if it does.

Pests and diseases: Aphids, mites.

JUNIPERUS

Juniper   *N hemisphere*

Origins and history: *J. communis* is our native juniper, found as hillside scrub—the berries are used for gin and seasoning. Several garden varieties are descended from it. Chinese Juniper (*J. chinensis*) cultivated for centuries in East, and first brought to Kew in 1804. 60 or more varieties from it, now widely used in British gardens. Eastern Red Cedar (*J. virginiana*) from North America introduced to Britain in seventeenth century (used for making pencils) also has numerous varieties. Prostrate Juniper (*J. horizontalis*) also from North America—brought to England around 1830 and widely used since as ground cover.

Description: E Upright species spreading, conical, irregular or prostrate; slow-growing. Prickly cypress-like leaves; green, black or bluish berries; peeling bark. Numerous varieties from all cultivated species—enormous variety in habit, foliage colour and height, from 20'/6m tree to prostrate ground cover—make sure you are getting the one you want. *J. communis* grows to

Juniperus communis

10'/3m, but can get dwarf forms—'Compressa' (24"/60cm) best for rock gardens. *J. chinensis* grows to 20'/6m—dwarf forms 'Japonica' (6'/2m) or 'Stricta' (5'/1.5m). Family of spreading dwarf forms from hybrid *J.x media*—'Pfitzerana' (3'/90cm) most popular. 'Blaauw' has blue foliage, 'Plumosa Aurea' has golden. *J. horizontalis* (12"/30cm) spreads up to $18ft^2/1.5m^2$ and has blue-green leaves—'Douglasii' most common variety (turns more purple in winter), 'Glauca' a flatter form.

Site and soil: Any ordinary well-drained garden soil in sun or partial shade. Tolerates lime.

Propagation: Take 3"/75mm long cuttings September or October of side shoots with heel, and insert in cutting compost in a cold frame. Pot on in spring and plant out in nursery rows the following autumn. Grow on for 1 or 2 years, and plant out in permanent position.

Care and cultivation: Pruning unnecessary.

Pests and Diseases: Juniper scale—encrusts leaves and stems. Caterpillars of Juniper Webber Moth eat leaves.

LARIX

Larch   *N hemisphere*

Origins and history: European Larch (*L. decidua*) comes from the Alps, introduced to England in 1620. Very common in rural areas; used widely for forest planting. In 1861 Veitch's Nurseries introduced Japanese Larch (*L. kaempferi*). Hybrid from Japanese and European larches *L.×eurolepis* bred around 1900. Other species come from China. *L. occidentalis* (North America) has had varying success in Britain since the nineteenth century—grown in colder areas.

Description: D Narrow conical tree, becomes spreading with age. Lower branches turn upwards at ends. Soft deciduous needles, beautiful bright green in spring, turning darker, then golden in autumn. Small red cones with rounded scales. Very fast growing. *L. kaempferi* grows faster than *L. decidua*, and is more disease-resistant. *L. decidua* grows to 55'/16m, *L.×eurolepis* to 65'/20m, *L. kaempferi* to 60'/18m—*not* suitable for the average-sized garden.

Site and soil: Any moist garden soil in open sunny position.

Propagation: Cuttings difficult. Sow seeds in March in nursery bed. Transplant to permanent positions after 2 years.

Care and cultivation: Do not allow leading shoot to fork on young trees: cut out one leader if it does.

Pests and diseases: Adelgids (see 'Abies'), sawfly.

PICEA

Spruce   *N hemisphere*

Origins and history: *P. abies* (Norway Spruce) came to Britain by 1500 to be grown for timber—most widespread European timber tree. Popular since Victorian times as our familiar Christmas tree. *P. omorika* (Serbian Spruce) is the other European species, grown in Britain since late nineteenth century. Now used extensively in cities, because it can withstand pollution.

Some Asian species grown in England since nineteenth century; other commonly-grown species from North America. Most common in forestry plantation in Britain is Sitka Spruce (*P. sitchensis*), introduced 1830s. More ornamental is Brewer Spruce (*P. breweriana*) with weeping branches, introduced in 1897. Many other less common species; many varieties developed.

Description: E Tall conical trees, often with drooping branches. Hard needle-like prickly leaves attached to twigs by small pegs which remain when twigs drop, giving branches a knobbly look. Oval drooping cones with brown scales, ripen from first season. Smooth brown bark becomes flaky with age. *P. abies* grows to 130'/40m, *P. omorika* to 100-160'/ 30-50m. Species *not* suitable for average garden, but there are many dwarf forms: *P. abies* 'Clanbrassiliana' (36"/90cm) very slow-growing, bush-shaped, and round when young. *P. nidiformis* only 12"/30cm, flat-topped. *P. glauca* also has common dwarf form 'Albertiana Conica', 4'/1.2m. *P. pungens* good for blue-leaved varieties, 'Koster' (25'/8m) or 'Moerheim Blue' (25'/8m).

Site and soil: Any deep, moist, fairly acid garden soil in sun or partial shade. Shelter young trees from spring frosts.

Propagation: Sow seeds in a cold frame in March. Plant out in nursery rows 1 year later, and grow on 2-3 years, then plant out in permanent positions.

Care and cultivation: Do not allow leading shoot to fork on young trees. Cut out one leader if it does.

Pests and diseases: Adelgids (see 'Abies'), Spruce Aphid, Mites, Rust, Stem canker.

PINUS

Pine   *N hemisphere*

Origins and history: Scots Pine (*P. sylvestris*) is native British pine. A little of the original Scottish pine forest remains from the Ice Age near Loch Rannoch. Now used extensively for plantations. Other European pines imported for forestry, notably the Corsican Pine, a variety of *P. nigra*. Many of numerous pine species have been imported from Asia and North America, varying from shrubs to forest trees. Bhutan Pine (*P. wallichiana*) introduced from Himalayas in 1823. *P. parviflora* is Japanese White Pine, brought with other species in 1860s. North America has given us most species, beginning with Weymouth Pine (*P. strobus*) around 1705, at Longleat. *P. contorta* (Lodgepole Pine, NW America) is very adaptable, and much used in forestry.

Description: E Trees conical when young, becoming flat-topped, asymetrical or rounded with age. Tall—Scots Pine can reach 130'/40m and most other species reach 100-130'/30-40m. Long needle-like leaves and woody cones that vary in shape according to species. Scots Pine has round pink cones that turn green the following year, becoming grey-brown and pointed in the third year before producing winged seeds; also has distinctive scaly bark. Can get slow-growing or dwarf varieties of Scots Pine suitable for most gardens—'Aurea' reaches 20'/6m, with blue-green needles that turn yellow in summer and gold in winter; 'Beuvronensis' will grow only 2'/60cm in 10 years, low, broad and rounded in habit and suitable for rock gardens, grey leaves, red buds. *P. strobus* also has dwarf form 'Nana'—blue-green leaves, reaches about 6'/2m in height but very slow-growing. *P. mugo*, a mountain pine from southern Europe, is a shrub species, up to 10'/3m tall with several prostrate varieties. Apart from dwarf varieties, pines are not suitable for small gardens, but if you can find a small variety (they are hard to get) it will make a welcome change from the more common conifers.

Site and soil: Well-drained acid soil in full sun. Cannot tolerate pollution. *P. sylvestris* will tolerate lime. Hardy—flourishes on exposed sites. Tolerates drought when established.

Propagation: Sow seeds in seed compost in a cold frame in March. Plant out following spring in nursery bed and grow on 2-3 years, then plant in permanent position. Named varieties are grafted.

Care and cultivation: Pruning unnecessary.

Pests and diseases: Adelgids (see 'Abies').

PSEUDOTSUGA

Douglas Fir   *N America*

Origins and history: First discovered by Menzies in 1792—now called *P. menziesii*. Douglas sent home seeds in 1827, hence Douglas Fir. Some trees planted from seed in Britain in 1828 still stand today. Most important forestry tree in North America —very good timber.

Description: E Very tall fast-growing tree—in native country can reach 260'/80m; tallest in Britain is 175'/55m at Dunkeld. Pyramid shaped, becoming flat-topped with age. Long aromatic needles, dark green above with two silvery lines on undersides. Brown cylindrical cones hang downwards (unlike *Abies*). Reddish corky bark becomes deeply scored with age. *P. menziesii* only species cultivated in Britain; certainly not suitable for small gardens, though can get dwarf forms: 'Glauca' (35'/11m) slow-growing with bluish leaves; 'Fletcheri' (2'/60cm) flat-topped shrub in habit. May be hard to find dwarf forms, but like pine may make an interesting change from more common conifers. Species can be used for hedging; responds to clipping.

Site and soil: Moist, fertile, deep garden soil in full sun. Dislikes chalk. Likes high rainfall. An exposed site will cause the brittle crown to become thin.

Propagation: Sow seeds in March in a cold frame. Prick out and harden off. Plant out in nursery bed. Grow on for 2 years and plant in permanent positions.

Care and cultivation: Do not allow main trunk to fork on young trees—cut out one leader if it does.

TAXUS

Yew   *Europe, Asia, N Africa*

Origins and history: *T. baccata* (English Yew) is our native tree. A legendary tree, renowned for longevity—some in Britain said to be 1,500 years old, and oldest in world reputed to be 3,000 years old. Traditionally planted in churchyards, for which there are rational explanations: yew is poisonous and the wall round the churchyard kept cattle out; yew was also used to make longbows. In the Middle Ages yew was the only conifer in England besides shrub juniper. Holly and ivy were the only other evergreens, and like these two, yew was a symbol of renewal. Also used for mazes. Some varieties of yew: in 1777 a weeping yew was noticed in Shropshire and bred from, and in 1778 Irish Yew (an upright yew) was discovered, and has since been propagated widely entirely by cuttings. There are American and Japanese yews, but these have never been planted much here. English Yew is unrivalled.

Description: E Very slow-growing tree,

Taxus baccata
English Yew

reaching 80'/25m. Rounded tree with dense horizontal branches and sharp pointed needle-like leaves, dark green above and yellowish-green below, which remain on the tree about 8 years before they fall. Male and female flowers grow on separate trees, unlike other conifers. Male flowers are small, round and yellow. Female flowers are very small and green. The fruit is fleshy, bright red and berry-like. Reddish-brown flaking bark becomes deeply scarred with age. 'Fastigiata' is upright variety (Irish Yew). 'Dovastonii' (Westfelton Yew) has long branches with hanging twigs and foliage. Both these varieties have golden-leaved forms. Dwarf varieties: 'Repandens' is a low-growing yew, good for ground cover, and *T. horizontalis* 'Semperaurea' a golden dwarf form, growing 2'/60cm in 10 years.

All parts of yew—bark, leaves and seeds —are poisonous; a danger to animals and children.

Yew is excellent for hedging, very dense and even. Withstands clipping and topiary, and makes a perfect background to a garden, especially dark green forms—only replaced by cypress and *leylandii* because they are speedier.

Site and soil: Any moist, fertile garden soil, including chalk, lime or peat, in full sun or deep shade. Very hardy, can withstand exposed position, drought and pollution. As a hedge it will shelter your garden from anything, given time. Avoid marshy ground.

Propagation: Take 3"/75mm long cuttings of side shoots with heel in September or October. Plant rooted cuttings out in nursery rows and grow on for 2 years, then plant in permanent position.

Care and cultivation: Pruning unnecessary. Clip hedges at any time of year.

Pests and Diseases: Scale insects. Leaves will turn yellow if ground is too wet.

THUJA

Arbor-vitae   *N America, Asia*

Origins and history: *T. occidentalis* (White Cedar) was the first American tree to be grown in Europe, in Paris in 1553. Has since become ubiquitous. *T. plicata* (Red Cedar) introduced to Britain in 1853. Chinese Thuja (*T. orientalis*) seldom cultivated in Britain because it is less hardy, though introduced in the nineteenth century. *Thuja* has produced vastly differing varieties over the years of cultivation.

Thuja occidentalis
White Cedar

Description: E Forest trees—White Cedar reaches 65'/20m; Red Cedar 130'/40m. Narrow conical shape, becoming irregular with age. Scale-like leaves grow on flattened twigs (very like *Chamaecyparis*). Small round brown cones. White Cedar has orange-brown bark; Red Cedar reddish-brown. Aromatic leaves when crushed.

Numerous varieties of the two American species. *T. occidentalis*: 'Lutea' has gold-tipped leaves; many dwarf varieties, some gold-leaved, e.g. 'Rheingold' reaches 3'/90cm and turns russet in winter, and 'Hetz Midget', the smallest at 12"/30cm and widely used in rockeries. *T. plicata* has a golden form 'Zebrina' which is a full-sized tree, and 'Hillieri', a slow-growing variety.

Site and Soil: Any ordinary, deep, preferably moist, garden soil in sheltered position in full sun.

Propagation: Seeds are particularly variable with *Thuja*. Take 3"/75mm long tip cuttings in September or October, and insert in cutting compost in a cold frame. Plant out rooted cuttings in a nursery bed and grow on 1-2 years, then plant in permanent position.

Care and cultivation: Pruning unnecessary.

Pests and Diseases: Excessive cold may turn leaves brown.

About the Authors

Margaret Elphinstone grew up in England with various gardens. She read English at Durham University, and went on to Glasgow, where she began her career as a gardener by scattering a packet of mixed annuals around the green at the back of a tenement, after which she decided to be a writer. Gardens gradually infiltrated again, helped by eight years in Shetland, and most of all by the Findhorn garden in Morayshire, where she worked for four years. She is now working as a gardener and writer in Galloway, where she lives with her two daughters. She has also published stories and articles, and a novel, *The Incomer* (The Women's Press, 1987).

Julia Langley was born in Lincolnshire, and played in hedges and ditches for eight glorious years on the family farm. She grew sunflowers and marigolds as a child, enjoyed the parks and gardens of Sheffield where she took a degree in English and History, and then trained in gardening at the North Wales College of Horticulture. For three years she helped to establish the walled vegetable garden at Laurieston Hall in Galloway, and for the last ten years she has been a gardener in her own and other people's gardens. She has three sons, is a member of the Henry Doubleday Research Association and a committee member of the Dumfries and Galloway Soil Association, and a lay minister of the Order of Buddhist Contemplatives.

Further Reading

Banks, Roger (1983) *Old Cottage Garden Flowers* World's Work

Beckett, Kenneth A. (1981) *Growing Hardy Perennials* Croom Helm

Berrall, Julia S. (1966) *The Garden: An Illustrated History* Penguin

Berrisford, Judith (1966) *The Wild Garden* Faber and Faber

Bloom *et al* (1984) *Garden Plants for Everyone* Hamlyn

Brown, Jane (1982) *Gardens of a Golden Afternoon: The Story of a Partnership, Edwin Lutyens and Gertrude Jekyll* Allen Lane

Bruce, M.C. (1946) *Common Sense Compost Making* Faber and Faber

Bryan-John, E. (1977) *Small World Vegetable Gardening: Growing Your Own in Limited Spaces* Pitman

Chinery, Michael (1977) *The Natural History of the Garden* Collins

Chinery, Michael (1972) *A Field Guide to the Insects of Britain and Northern Europe* Collins

Creasy, Rosalind (1982) *Edible Landscaping* Sierra Books

Crockett, James Underwood (1978) *Trees* Time Life International

De Bray, Lys (1978) *The Wild Garden: An Illustrated Guide to Weeds* Weidenfeld and Nicholson

Doerflinger, Frederic (1973) *The Bulb Book* David and Charles

Easey, Ben (1976) Practical Organic Gardening Faber and Faber

Fish, Margery (1961) *Cottage Garden Flowers* Faber and Faber

Fish, Margery (1964) *Ground Cover Plants* Collingridge

Fisher, John (1982) *The Origins of Garden Plants* Constable

Fleming, Laurence and Alan Gore (1979) *The English Garden* Michael Joseph

Gault, S. Miller (1976) *The Dictionary of Shrubs in Colour* Ebury Press

Genders, Roy (1973) *Bulbs: A Complete Handbook* Robert Hale

'Golden Hands' (1975) *Favourite Perennial Flowers* Marshall Cavendish

Gorer, Richard (1980) *Illustrated Guide to Trees* Ward Lock

Gorer, Richard (1981) *Garden Flowers from Seed: An Illustrated Dictionary* Webb and Bower

Griffith, Anna N. (1980) *Collins Guide to Alpines and Rock Garden Plants* Collins

Grounds, Roger (1973) *The Complete Handbook of Pruning* Macmillan

Hadfield, Miles (1960) *A History of British Gardening* Murray

Hanssen, Maurice and Jill Marsden (1984) *E For Additives* Thorsons

Harris, Cyril C. (1974) *The Rose Garden: Old-Fashioned and Scented Roses* Ward Lock

Hatfield, Audrey Wynne (1969) *How to Enjoy your Weeds* Frederick Muller

Hay, Jim (1985) *Vegetables Naturally* Century

Hellyer, Arthur (1982) *Garden Shrubs* Dent

Henry Doubleday Research Association booklets:
Fruit Pest and Disease Control
Vegetable Pest and Disease Control
Raised Bed Gardening
Herb Growing the Organic Way
Feeding the Soil the Organic Way
Potato Growing for Gardeners
Save Your Own Seed

Her Majesty's Stationery Office (1972) *Home Preservation of Fruit and Vegetables*

Her Majesty's Stationery Office (1969) *Beneficial Insects and Mites*

BIBLIOGRAPHY

Hessayon, D.G. (1983) *The Tree and Shrub Expert* pbi

Hessayon, D.G. (1984) *The Flower Expert* pbi

Hessayon, D.G. (1985) *The Vegetable Expert* pbi

Hillier's Manual of Trees and Shrubs David and Charles (1984)

Hills, Lawrence (1977) *Organic Gardening* Penguin

Hills, Lawrence (1979) *Grow Your Own Fruit and Vegetables* Faber

Hills, Lawrence (1983) *A Month By Month Guide to Organic Gardening* Thorsons

Hinde, Thomas (1983) *Stately Gardens of Britain* Ebury Press

Hobhouse, Penelope (ed.) (1983) *Gertrude Jekyll on Gardening* Collins

Hollis, Leonard (1970) *Roses* Collingridge

Howes, F.N. (1974) *A Dictionary of Useful and Everyday Plants and Their Common Names* Cambridge University Press

Huxley, Anthony (1974) *Plant and Planet* Penguin

Huxley, Anthony (1984) *Green Inheritance* Collins/Harvill

Hyams, Edward (1952) *Soil and Civilization* John Murray

Hyams, Edward (1971) *A History of Gardens and Gardening* Dent

Hyams, Edward (1979) *The Story of England's Flora* Kestrel Books

Jeavons, John (1979) *How To Grow More Vegetables* Ten Speed Press

Kessell, Mervyn (1981) *Rhododendrons and Azaleas* Blandford Press

Kimberton Hills Agricultural Calendar; A Beginner's Guide for Understanding the Influence of Cosmic Rhythms in Farming and Gardening (1985) Kimberton Hills

King, Ronald (1979) *The Quest for Paradise: A History of the World's Gardens* Whittet Books

Kitto, Dick (1984) *Composting* Thorsons

Lawrence, Eleanor (ed.) (1985) *The Illustrated Book of Trees and Shrubs* Octopus

Loewenfeld, Claire and Philippa Back (1974) *The Complete Book of Herbs and Spices* David and Charles

Lucas Phillips, C.E. (1968) *The Modern Flower Garden* Heinemann

Lucas Phillips, C.E. (1976) *The Small Garden* Pan

MacFadyen, D. (1982) *A Cottage Flora* Webb and Bower

Masefield, G.B. *et al* (1975) *The Oxford Book of Food Plants* Oxford University Press

Mollison, Bill and David Holmgren (1978) *Permaculture One* Tagari

Mollison, Bill and David Holmgren (1979) *Permaculture Two* Tagari

Mooney, Pat Roy (1979) *Seeds of the Earth: A Private or Public Resource?* International Coalition for Development Action

Pearson, R. (ed.) (1981) *The Wisley Book of Gardening: A Guide for Enthusiasts* Collingridge

Pfeiffer, Ehrenfried (1983) *Soil Fertility, Renewal and Preservation* Lanthorn Press

Philbrick, Helen and Richard B. Gregg (1967) *Companion Plants* Stuart and Watkins

Reader's Digest (1978) *Encyclopaedia of Garden Plants and Flowers* Reader's Digest

Reader's Digest (1981) *New Illustrated Guide to Gardening* Reader's Digest

Reader's Digest (1984) *Guide to Creative Gardening* Reader's Digest

Robertson, Laurel *et al* (1979) *Laurel's Kitchen: A Handbook for Vegetarian Cookery and Nutrition* Routledge and Kegan Paul

Robinson, William (1983, first published 1881) *The Wild Garden* Century

Robinson, William (1985, first published 1883) *The English Flower Garden* Hamlyn

Rose, Peter Q. (1982) *Climbers and Wall Plants* Blandford Press

Royal Horticultural Society (1974) *The Fruit Garden Displayed* RHS

Royal Horticultural Society (1981) *The Vegetable Garden Displayed* RHS

St Barbe Baker, Richard (1970) *My Life My Trees* Findhorn

Salter, P.J. *et al* (1979) *Know and Grow Vegetables* Oxford University Press

Sandys-Winsh (1982) *Garden Law* Shaw and Sons

Scott-James, Anne (1975) *Sissinghurst: The Making of a Garden* Michael Joseph

Scott-James, Anne and Osbert Lancaster (1977) *The Pleasure Garden* John Murray

Scott-James, Anne (1981) *The Cottage Garden* Penguin

Scourse, Nicolette (1983) *The Victorians and Their Flowers* Croom Helm

Simmons, Alan F. (1978) *Simmons' Manual of Fruit* David and Charles

Smith, Geoffrey (1973) *Shrubs and Small Trees* Hamlyn

Stevenson, Violet (1985) *The Wild Garden* Windward

Stickland, Sue (1986) *Planning the Organic Herb Garden* Thorsons

Stuart, David C. (1984) *The Kitchen Garden: A Historical Guide to Traditional Crops* Robert Hale

Temple, Jack (1986) *Gardening Without Chemicals* Thorsons

Thun, Maria (1979) *Work on the Land and the Constellations* Lanthorn Press

Thun, Maria and Matthias (1985) *Working with the Stars* Lanthorn Press

Vaclav, Vetvicka (1985) *The Illustrated Book of Trees and Shrubs* Octopus

Venison, Tony (1968) *Starting With Rock Plants* Collingridge

Young, Norman (1971) *The Complete Rosarian: The Development, Cultivation and Reproduction of Roses* Hodder and Stoughton

Useful Addresses

Biodynamic Agricultural Association
Woodman Lane,
Stourbridge,
West Midlands
DY9 9PX
Magazine twice yearly; books and calendars available.

Henry Doubleday Research Association
National Centre for Organic Gardening,
Ryton-on-Dunsmore,
Coventry
CV8 3LG
Quarterly newsletter, free advice, catalogue of seeds and organic sundries, organic garden to visit, shop

W. Robinson and Sons Ltd.
Sunnybank,
Forton, Preston,
Lancashire
PR3 0BN
Suppliers of onion seed: 'Mammoth Improved' and 'Mammoth Red'.

Royal Horticultural Society
Wisley,
Woking,
Surrey
GU23 6QB
A large and learned organization; publishes numerous manuals and reference books (not organic). If you need to identify the variety of any tree fruit, send 3 good fruits, with leaves, and £1.00, to the RHS variety identification service.

Soil Association
86-88 Colston Street,
Bristol
BS1 5BB
Magazine, good booklist.

The Scottish Organic Gardener
Brigton Gardens Cottage,
Douglastown,
by Forfar,
Angus
DD8 1TL
A newsletter for organic gardeners living in Scotland.

Index

Certain page numbers are set off in **bold type** to indicate where the main information about the subject in question may be found.